Śrī Caitanya-caritāmṛta

BOOKS by
His Divine Grace A.C. Bhaktivedanta Swami Prabhupāda

Bhagavad-gītā As It Is
Śrīmad-Bhāgavatam, Cantos 1-5 (15 Vols.)
Śrī Caitanya-caritāmṛta (17 Vols.)
Teachings of Lord Caitanya
The Nectar of Devotion
Śrī Īśopaniṣad
Easy Journey to Other Planets
Kṛṣṇa Consciousness: The Topmost Yoga System
Kṛṣṇa, The Supreme Personality of Godhead (3 Vols.)
Transcendental Teachings of Prahlād Mahārāja
Kṛṣṇa, the Reservoir of Pleasure
The Perfection of Yoga
Beyond Birth and Death
On the Way to Kṛṣṇa
Rāja-vidyā: The King of Knowledge
Elevation to Kṛṣṇa Consciousness
Kṛṣṇa Consciousness: The Matchless Gift
Back to Godhead Magazine (Founder)

A complete catalogue is available upon request

International Society for Krishna Consciousness
3764 Watseka Avenue
Los Angeles, California 90034

All Glory to Śrī Guru and Gaurāṅga

ŚRĪ CAITANYA-CARITĀMṚTA

of Kṛṣṇadāsa Kavirāja Gosvāmī

Madhya-līlā
Volume Two

"The Narrations Concerning Mādhavendra Purī, Sākṣi Gopāla and Sārvabhauma Bhaṭṭācārya"

with the original Bengali text,
Roman transliterations, synonyms,
translation and elaborate purports

by

HIS DIVINE GRACE

A.C. Bhaktivedanta Swami Prabhupāda

Founder-Ācārya of the International Society for Krishna Consciousness

THE BHAKTIVEDANTA BOOK TRUST
New York · Los Angeles · London · Bombay

Readers interested in the subject matter of this book
are invited by the International Society for Krishna Consciousness
to correspond with its Secretary.

International Society for Krishna Consciousness
3764 Watseka Avenue
Los Angeles, California 90034

Library of Congress Catalogue Card Number: 73-93206
International Standard Book Number: 0-912776-64-1

Printed in the United States of America

Contents

Introduction

Śrī Caitanya-caritāmṛta is the principal work on the life and teachings of Śrī Kṛṣṇa Caitanya. Śrī Caitanya is the pioneer of a great social and religious movement which began in India a little less than five hundred years ago and which has directly and indirectly influenced the subsequent course of religious and philosophical thinking not only in India but in the recent West as well.

Caitanya Mahāprabhu is regarded as a figure of great historical significance. However, our conventional method of historical analysis—that of seeing a man as a product of his times—fails here. Śrī Caitanya is a personality who transcends the limited scope of historical settings.

At a time when, in the West, man was directing his explorative spirit toward studying the structure of the physical universe and circumnavigating the world in search of new oceans and continents, Śrī Kṛṣṇa Caitanya, in the East, was inaugurating and masterminding a revolution directed inward, toward a scientific understanding of the highest knowledge of man's spiritual nature.

The chief historical sources for the life of Śrī Kṛṣṇa Caitanya are the *kaḍacās* (diaries) kept by Murāri Gupta and Svarūpa Dāmodara Gosvāmī. Murāri Gupta, a physician and close associate of Śrī Caitanya's, recorded extensive notes on the first twenty-four years of Śrī Caitanya's life, culminating in his initiation into the renounced order, *sannyāsa*. The events of the rest of Caitanya Mahāprabhu's forty-eight years are recorded in the diary of Svarūpa Dāmodora Gosvāmī, another of Caitanya Mahāprabhu's intimate associates.

Śrī Caitanya-caritāmṛta is divided into three sections called *līlās,* which literally means "pastimes"—*Ādi-līlā* (the early period), *Madhya-līlā* (the middle period) and *Antya-līlā* (the final period). The notes of Murāri Gupta form the basis of the *Ādi-līlā,* and Svarūpa Dāmodara's diary provides the details for the *Madhya-* and *Antya-līlās.*

The first twelve of the seventeen chapters of *Ādi-līlā* constitute the preface for the entire work. By referring to Vedic scriptural evidence, this preface establishes Śrī Caitanya as the *avatāra* (incarnation) of Kṛṣṇa (God) for the age of Kali—the current epoch, beginning five thousand years ago and characterized by materialism, hypocrisy and dissension. In these descriptions, Caitanya Mahāprabhu, who is identical with Lord Kṛṣṇa, descends to liberally grant pure love of God to the fallen souls of this degraded age by propagating *saṅkīrtana*—literally, "congregational glorification of God"—especially by organizing massive public chanting of the *mahā-mantra* (Great Chant for Deliverance). The esoteric purpose of Lord Caitanya's appearance in the world is revealed, his co-*avatāras* and principal devotees are described and his teachings are summarized. The remaining portion of *Ādi-līlā,* chapters thirteen through seventeen, briefly recounts his divine birth and his life until he accepted the renounced order. This includes his childhood miracles, schooling, marriage and early philosophical confrontations, as well as his organization of a widespread *saṅkīrtana* movement and his civil disobedience against the repression of the Mohammedan government.

The subject of *Madhya-līlā,* the longest of the three divisions, is a detailed narration of Lord Caitanya's extensive and eventful travels throughout India as a renounced mendicant, teacher, philosopher, spiritual preceptor and mystic. During this period of six years, Śrī Caitanya transmits his teachings to his principal disciples. He debates and converts many of the most renowned philosophers and theologians of his time, including Śaṅkarites, Buddhists and Muslims, and incorporates their many thousands of followers and disciples into his own burgeoning numbers. A dramatic account of Caitanya Mahāprabhu's miraculous activities at the giant Jagannātha Cart Festival in Orissa is also included in this section.

Antya-līlā concerns the last eighteen years of Śrī Caitanya's manifest presence, spent in semiseclusion near the famous Jagannātha temple at Jagannātha Purī in Orissa. During these final years, Śrī Caitanya drifted deeper and deeper into trances of spiritual ecstasy unparalleled in all of religious and literary history, Eastern or Western. Śrī Caitanya's perpetual and ever-increasing religious beatitude, graphically described in the eyewitness accounts of Svarūpa Dāmodara Gosvāmī, his constant companion during this period, clearly defy the investigative and descriptive abilities of modern psychologists and phenomenologists of religious experience.

The author of this great classic, Kṛṣṇadāsa Kavirāja Gosvāmī, born in the year 1507, was a disciple of Raghunātha dāsa Gosvāmī, a confidential follower of Caitanya Mahāprabhu. Raghunātha dāsa, a renowned ascetic saint, heard and memorized all the activities of Caitanya Mahāprabhu told to him by Svarūpa Dāmodara. After the passing away of Śrī Caitanya and Svarūpa Dāmodara, Raghunātha dāsa, unable to bear the pain of separation from these objects of his complete devotion, traveled to Vṛndāvana, intending to commit suicide by jumping from Govardhana Hill. In Vṛndāvana, however, he encountered Rūpa Gosvāmī and Sanātana Gosvāmī, the most confidential disciples of Caitanya Mahāprabhu. They convinced him to give up his plan of suicide and impelled him to reveal to them the spiritually inspiring events of Lord Caitanya's later life. Kṛṣṇadāsa Kavirāja Gosvāmī was also residing in Vṛndāvana at this time, and Raghunātha dāsa Gosvāmī endowed him with a full comprehension of the transcendental life of Śrī Caitanya.

By this time, several biographical works had already been written on the life of Śrī Caitanya by contemporary and near-contemporary scholars and devotees. These included *Śrī Caitanya-carita* by Murāri Gupta, *Caitanya-maṅgala* by Locana dāsa Ṭhākura and *Caitanya-bhāgavata.* This latter text, a work by Vṛndāvana dāsa Ṭhākura, who was then considered the principal authority on Śrī Caitanya's life, was highly revered. While composing his important work, Vṛndāvana dāsa, fearing that it would become too voluminous, avoided elaborately describing many of the events of Śrī Caitanya's life, particulary the later ones. Anxious to hear of these later pastimes, the devotees of Vṛndāvana requested Kṛṣṇadāsa Kavirāja Gosvāmī, whom they respected as a great saint, to compose a book to narrate these episodes in detail. Upon this request, and with the permission and blessings of the Madana-mohana Deity of Vṛndāvana, he began compiling *Śrī Caitanya-caritāmṛta,* which, due to its biographical excellence and thorough exposition of Lord Caitanya's profound philosophy and teachings, is regarded as the most significant of biographical works on Śrī Caitanya.

He commenced work on the text while in his late nineties and in failing health, as he vividly describes in the text itself: "I have now become too old and disturbed in invalidity. While writing, my hands tremble. I cannot remember anything, nor can I see or hear properly. Still I write, and this is a great wonder." That he nevertheless completed, under such debilitating conditions, the greatest literary gem of medieval India is surely one of the wonders of literary history.

This English translation and commentary is the work of His Divine Grace A. C. Bhaktivedanta Swami Prabhupāda, the world's most distinguished teacher of Indian religious and philosophical thought. His commentary is based upon two Bengali commentaries, one by his teacher Śrīla Bhaktisiddhānta Sarasvatī Gosvāmī, the eminent Vedic scholar who predicted, "The time will come when the people of the world will learn Bengali to read *Śrī Caitanya-caritāmṛta,*" and the other by Śrīla Bhaktisiddhānta's father, Bhaktivinoda Ṭhākura.

His Divine Grace A. C. Bhaktivedanta Swami Prabhupāda is himself a disciplic descendant of Śrī Caitanya Mahāprabhu, and he is the first scholar to execute systematic English translations of the major works of Śrī Caitanya's followers. His consummate Bengali and Sanskrit scholarship and intimate familiarity with the precepts of Śrī Kṛṣṇa Caitanya are a fitting combination that eminently qualifies him to present this important classic to the English-speaking world. The ease and clarity with which he expounds upon difficult philosophical concepts lures even a reader totally unfamiliar with Indian religious tradition into a genuine understanding and appreciation of this profound and monumental work.

The entire text, with commentary, presented in seventeen lavishly illustrated volumes by the Bhaktivedanta Book Trust, represents a contribution of major importance to the intellectual, cultural and spiritual life of contemporary man.

His Divine Grace
A. C. Bhaktivedanta Swami Prabhupāda
Founder-Ācārya of the International Society for Krishna Consciousness

The temple of Gopīnāthajī in Remuna, India, where Śrī Caitanya Mahāprabhu fell unconscious aft
narrating the story of Mādhavendra Purī.

ṣīra-corā-gopīnātha, the Deity who stole a pot of condensed milk for His devotee, Mādhavendra urī.

The temple of Sākṣi-gopāla in Kaṭaka, where Śrī Caitanya Mahāprabhu heard the story of the Lord's acting as a witness for His devotee.

Sārvabhauma Bhaṭṭācārya's room at Purī, the site where Lord Caitanya exhibited many transcendental pastimes.

PLATE ONE

"After taking bath at Govinda-kuṇḍa, Mādhavendr Purī sat beneath a tree to take his evening rest. Whil he was sitting beneath the tree, an unknown cowher boy came with a pot of milk, placed it before Mādha vendra Purī, and, smiling, addressed him as follow 'Please drink the milk I have brought. Why don't yo beg some food to eat? What kind of meditation ar you undergoing?' When he saw the beauty of that boy Mādhavendra Purī became very satisfied. Hearing Hi sweet words, he forgot all hunger and thirst. (*pp.12-13*)

PLATE TWO

"As soon as the people of the village understood that the Deity was going to be installed, they brought their entire stocks of rice, dahl and wheat flour. They brought such large quantities that the entire surface of the top of the hill was filled. All the cooked rice was stacked on *palāśa* leaves, which were on new cloths spread over the ground. Around the stack of cooked rice were stacks of chappatis, and all the vegetables and liquid vegetable preparations were placed in different pots and put around them. Pots of yogurt, milk, buttermilk and *śikhariṇī,* sweet rice, cream and solid cream were placed alongside the vegetables. In this way the Annakūṭa ceremony was performed, and Mādhavendra Purī Gosvāmī personally offered everything to Gopāla." (*pp.31-34*)

PLATE THREE

"Finishing his daily duties, the priest went to tak rest. In a dream he saw the Gopīnātha Deity come t talk to him, and He spoke as follows. 'Please get up an open the door of the temple. I have kept one pot sweet rice for the *sannyāsī,* Mādhavendra Purī. This po of sweet rice is just behind My cloth curtain. You di not see it because of My tricks. A *sannyāsī* name Mādhavendra Purī is sitting in the vacant marketplac Please take this pot of sweet rice from behind Me an deliver it to him.' Awaking from the dream, the prie immediately rose from bed and thought it wise to tak a bath before entering the Deity's room. He the opened the temple door. According to the Deity directions, the priest found the pot of sweet ric behind the cloth curtain." (*pp.65-67*)

PLATE FOUR

"Mādhavendra Purī took rest that night in th temple, but toward the end of the night he ha another dream. He dreamed that Gopāla came befor him and said: 'O Mādhavendra Purī, I have alread received all the sandalwood and camphor. Now ju grind all the sandalwood together with the campho and then smear the pulp on the body of Gopīnāth daily until it is finished. There is no difference betwee My body and Gopīnātha's body. They are one and th same. Therefore if you smear the sandalwood pulp o the body of Gopīnātha, you will naturally also smear on My body. Thus the temperature of My body will b reduced. You should not hesitate to act according t My order. Believing in Me, just do what is needed.' (*pp.82-83*)

PLATE FIVE

"After saying this, Lord Caitanya Mahāprabhu read the famous verse of Mādhavendra Purī. That verse is just like the moon. It has spread illumination all over the world. Mādhavendra Purī recited this verse again and again at the end of his material existence. Thus uttering this verse, he attained the ultimate goal of life.

'O My Lord! O most merciful master! O master of Mathurā! When shall I see You again? Because of My not seeing You, My agitated heart has become unsteady. O most beloved one, what shall I do now?'

When Śrī Caitanya Mahāprabhu recited this verse, He immediately fell to the ground unconscious. He was overwhelmed and had no control over Himself. When Lord Śrī Caitanya Mahāprabhu fell to the ground in ecstatic love, Lord Nityānanda took Him on His lap. Crying, Caitanya Mahāprabhu then got up again." (*pp.98-102*)

PLATE SIX

"All the townspeople went to see the witness Gopāla, and when they saw the Lord actually standing there, they all offered their respectful obeisances. When the people arrived, they were very pleased to see the beauty of Gopāla, and when they heard that He had actually walked there, they were all surprised. Then the elderly *brāhmaṇa*, being very pleased, came forward and immediately fell like a stick in front of Gopāla. Thus in the presence of all the townspeople, Lord Gopāla bore witness that the elderly *brāhmaṇa* had offered his daughter in charity to the young *brāhmaṇa*." (*pp.164-165*)

MURLIDHAR DAS

PLATE SEVEN

"When Lord Caitanya Mahāprabhu went to th temple of Lord Śiva known as Kapoteśvara, Nityānand Prabhu, who was keeping His staff in custody, brok the staff in three parts and threw it into the Rive Bhārgīnadī. Later this river became known as Daṇḍa bhāṅgā-nadī." (*p.180*)

PLATE EIGHT

"For seven days continuously, Śrī Caitany Mahāprabhu listened to the Vedānta philosophy ex pounded by Sārvabhauma Bhaṭṭācārya. Howeve Caitanya Mahāprabhu did not say anything and did nc indicate whether it was right or wrong. He simply sa there and listened to the Bhaṭṭācārya. On the eight day, Sārvabhauma Bhaṭṭācārya said to Caitany Mahāprabhu: 'You have been listening to the Vedānt philosophy from me continuously for seven days. Yo have simply been listening, fixed in Your silence. Sinc You do not say whether You think it is right or wrong, cannot know whether You are actually understandin Vedānta philosophy or not." (*pp.258-259*)

PLATE NINE

"How greatly fortunate are Nanda Mahārāja, the cowherd men and all the inhabitants of Vrajabhūmi There is no limit to their fortune because the Absolute Truth, the source of transcendental bliss, the eternal Supreme Brahman, has become their friend." (*pp.277-278*)

CHAPTER 4

Śrī Mādhavendra Purī's Devotional Service

In his *Amṛta-pravāha-bhāṣya,* Śrīla Bhaktivinoda Ṭhākura gives the following summary of the Fourth Chapter. Passing along the path of Chatrabhoga and coming to Vṛddhamantreśvara, Śrī Caitanya Mahāprabhu reached the border of Orissa. On His way He enjoyed transcendental bliss by chanting and begging alms in different villages. In this way He reached the celebrated village of Remuṇā, where there is a Deity of Gopīnātha. There He narrated the story of Mādhavendra Purī, as He had heard it from His spiritual master, Īśvara Purī. The narration is as follows.

One night while in Govardhana, Mādhavendra Purī dreamed that the Gopāla Deity was within the forest. The next morning he invited his neighborhood friends to accompany him to excavate the Deity from the jungle. He then established the Deity of Śrī Gopālajī on top of Govardhana Hill with great pomp. Gopāla was worshiped, and the Annakūṭa festival was observed. This festival was known everywhere, and many people from the neighboring villages came to join. One night the Gopāla Deity again appeared to Mādhavendra Purī in a dream and asked him to go to Jagannātha Purī to collect some sandalwood pulp and smear it on the body of the Deity. Having received this order, Mādhavendra Purī immediately started for Orissa. Traveling through Bengal, he reached Remuṇā village and there received a pot of condensed milk (*kṣīra*) offered to the Deity of Gopīnāthajī. This pot of condensed milk was stolen by Gopīnātha and delivered to Mādhavendra Purī. Since then, the Gopīnātha Deity has been known as Kṣīra-corā-gopīnātha, the Deity who stole the pot of condensed milk. After reaching Jagannātha Purī, Mādhavendra Purī received permission from the King to take out one *maṇa* of sandalwood and eight ounces of camphor. Aided by two men, he brought these things to Remuṇā. Again He saw in a dream that Gopāla at Govardhana Hill desired that very sandalwood to be turned into pulp mixed with camphor and smeared over the body of Gopīnāthajī. Understanding that that would satisfy the Gopāla Deity at Govardhana, Mādhavendra Purī executed the order and returned to Jagannātha Purī.

Śrī Caitanya Mahāprabhu narrated this story for Lord Nityānanda Prabhu and other devotees and praised the pure devotional service of Mādhavendra Purī. When He recited some verses composed by Mādhavendra Purī, He went into an ecstatic mood. But when He saw that many people were assembled, He checked Himself and ate some sweet rice *prasāda.* Thus He passed that night, and the next morning He again started for Jagannātha Purī.

TEXT 1

যস্মৈ দাতুং চোরয়ন্ ক্ষীরভাণ্ডং
গোপীনাথঃ ক্ষীরচোরাভিধোঽভূৎ ।
শ্রীগোপালঃ প্রাদুরাসীদ্বশঃ সন্
যৎপ্রেম্ণা তং মাধবেন্দ্রং নতোঽস্মি ॥ ১ ॥

yasmai dātuṁ corayan kṣīra-bhāṇḍaṁ
gopīnāthaḥ kṣīra-corābhidho 'bhūt
śrī-gopālaḥ prādurāsīd vaśaḥ san
yat-premṇā taṁ mādhavendraṁ nato 'smi

SYNONYMS

yasmai—unto whom; *dātum*—to deliver; *corayan*—stealing; *kṣīra-bhāṇḍam*—the pot of sweet rice; *gopīnāthaḥ*—Gopīnātha; *kṣīra-corā*—stealer of a pot of sweet rice; *abhidhaḥ*—celebrated; *abhūt*—became; *śrī-gopālaḥ*—Śrī Gopāla Deity; *prādur-āsīt*—appeared; *vaśaḥ*—captivated; *san*—being; *yat-premṇā*—by his love; *tam*—unto him; *mādhavendram*—Mādhavendra Purī, who was in the Madhva-sampradāya; *nataḥ asmi*—I offer my respectful obeisances.

TRANSLATION

I offer my respectful obeisances unto Mādhavendra Purī, who was given a pot of sweet rice stolen by Śrī Gopīnātha, celebrated thereafter as kṣīra-corā. Being pleased by Mādhavendra Purī's love, Śrī Gopāla, the Deity at Govardhana, appeared to the public vision.

PURPORT

Bhaktivinoda Ṭhākura annotates that this Gopāla Deity was originally installed by Vajra, the grandson of Kṛṣṇa. Mādhavendra Purī rediscovered Gopāla and established Him on top of Govardhana Hill. This Gopāla Deity is still situated at Nāthadvāra and is under the management of descendants of Vallabhācārya. The worship of the Deity is very luxurious, and one who goes there can purchase varieties of *prasāda* by paying a small price.

TEXT 2

জয় জয় গৌরচন্দ্র জয় নিত্যানন্দ ।
জয়াদ্বৈতচন্দ্র জয় গৌরভক্তবৃন্দ ॥ ২ ॥

jaya jaya gauracandra jaya nityānanda
jayādvaitacandra jaya gaura-bhakta-vṛnda

SYNONYMS

jaya jaya gauracandra—all glories to Śrī Caitanya Mahāprabhu; *jaya nityānanda*—all glories to Lord Nityānanda; *jaya advaita-candra*—all glories to Advaita Prabhu; *jaya gaura-bhakta-vṛnda*—all glories to the devotees of the Lord.

TRANSLATION

All glories to Lord Caitanya Mahāprabhu! All glories to Nityānanda Prabhu! All glories to Advaita Prabhu! And all glories to all the devotees of Lord Caitanya!

TEXTS 3-4

নীলাদ্রিগমন, জগন্নাথ-দরশন ।
সার্বভৌম ভট্টাচার্য-প্রভুর মিলন ॥ ৩ ॥
এ সব লীলা প্রভুর দাস বৃন্দাবন ।
বিস্তারি' করিয়াছেন উত্তম বর্ণন ॥ ৪ ॥

nīlādri-gamana, jagannātha-daraśana
sārvabhauma bhaṭṭācārya-prabhura milana

e saba līlā prabhura dāsa vṛndāvana
vistāri' kariyāchena uttama varṇana

SYNONYMS

nīlādri-gamana—going to Jagannātha Purī; *jagannātha-daraśana*—visiting the temple of Lord Jagannātha; *sārvabhauma bhaṭṭācārya*—with Sārvabhauma Bhaṭṭācārya; *prabhura*—of the Lord; *milana*—meeting; *e saba*—all these; *līlā*—pastimes; *prabhura*—of the Lord; *dāsa vṛndāvana*—Vṛndāvana dāsa Ṭhākura; *vistāri'*—elaborating; *kariyāchena*—has done; *uttama*—very nice; *varṇana*—description.

TRANSLATION

The Lord went to Jagannātha Purī and visited Lord Jagannātha's temple. He also met with Sārvabhauma Bhaṭṭācārya. All these pastimes have been very elaborately explained by Vṛndāvana dāsa Ṭhākura in his book Caitanya-bhāgavata.

TEXT 5

সহজে বিচিত্র মধুর চৈতন্য-বিহার ।
বৃন্দাবনদাস-মুখে অমৃতের ধার ॥ ৫ ॥

sahaje vicitra madhura caitanya-vihāra
vṛndāvana-dāsa-mukhe amṛtera dhāra

SYNONYMS

sahaje—naturally; *vicitra*—wonderful; *madhura*—sweet; *caitanya*—of Lord Caitanya Mahāprabhu; *vihāra*—the activities; *vṛndāvana-dāsa*—of Vṛndāvana dāsa Ṭhākura; *mukhe*—from the mouth; *amṛtera*—of nectar; *dhāra*—shower.

TRANSLATION

By nature all the activities of Śrī Caitanya Mahāprabhu are very wonderful and sweet, and when they are described by Vṛndāvana dāsa Ṭhākura, they become like a shower of nectar.

TEXT 6

অতএব তাহা বর্ণিলে হয় পুনরুক্তি ।
দম্ভ করি' বর্ণি যদি তৈছে নাহি শক্তি ॥ ৬ ॥

ataeva tāhā varṇile haya punarukti
dambha kari' varṇi yadi taiche nāhi śakti

SYNONYMS

ataeva—therefore; *tāhā*—such activities; *varṇile*—if describing; *haya*—there is; *punarukti*—repetition; *dambha kari'*—being proud; *varṇi*—I describe; *yadi*—if; *taiche*—such; *nāhi*—there is not; *śakti*—power.

TRANSLATION

Therefore I very humbly submit that since these incidents have already been nicely described by Vṛndāvana dāsa Ṭhākura, I would be very proud to repeat the same thing, and this would not be very good. I do not have such powers.

TEXT 7

চৈতন্যমঙ্গলে যাহা করিল বর্ণন ।
সূত্ররূপে সেই লীলা করিয়ে সূচন ॥ ৭ ॥

caitanya-maṅgale yāhā karila varṇana
sūtra-rūpe sei līlā kariye sūcana

SYNONYMS

caitanya-maṅgale—in the book named *Caitanya-maṅgala; yāhā*—whatever; *karila varṇana*—has described; *sūtra-rūpe*—in the form of short codes; *sei līlā*—those pastimes; *kariye sūcana*—I shall present.

TRANSLATION

I am therefore presenting in short codes all those events already described in the Caitanaya-maṅgala [now known as Caitanya-bhāgavata] by Vṛndāvana dāsa Ṭhākura.

TEXT 8

তাঁর সূত্রে আছে, তেঁহ না কৈল বর্ণন ।
যথাকথঞ্চিৎ করি' সে লীলা কথন ॥ ৮ ॥

tāṅra sūtre āche, teṅha nā kaila varṇana
yathā-kathañcit kari' se līlā kathana

SYNONYMS

tāṅra—his; *sūtre*—in the codes; *āche*—there are; *teṅha*—he; *nā kaila varṇana*—did not describe; *yathā-kathañcit*—something of them; *kari'*—doing; *se*—these; *līlā*—of pastimes; *kathana*—narration.

TRANSLATION

Some of the incidents in his codes he did not describe elaborately, and so I shall try to describe them in this book.

TEXT 9

অতএব তাঁর পায়ে করি নমস্কার ।
তাঁর পায় অপরাধ না হউক্ আমার ॥ ৯ ॥

ataeva tāṅra pāye kari namaskāra
tāṅra pāya aparādha nā ha-uk āmāra

SYNONYMS

ataeva—therefore; *tāṅra pāye*—at his lotus feet; *kari*—I do; *namaskāra*—obeisances; *tāṅra pāya*—to the lotus feet of Vṛndāvana dāsa Ṭhākura; *aparādha*—offense; *nā*—not; *ha-uk*—let it happen; *āmāra*—my.

TRANSLATION

I thus offer my respectful obeisances unto the lotus feet of Vṛndāvana dāsa Ṭhākura. I hope that I will not offend his lotus feet by this action.

TEXT 10

এইমত মহাপ্রভু চলিলা নীলাচলে ।
চারি ভক্ত সঙ্গে কৃষ্ণকীর্তন-কুতূহলে ॥ ১০ ॥

ei-mata mahāprabhu calilā nīlācale
cāri bhakta saṅge kṛṣṇa-kīrtana-kutūhale

SYNONYMS

ei-mata—in this way; *mahāprabhu*—Lord Caitanya Mahāprabhu; *calilā*—proceeded; *nīlācale*—toward Jagannātha Purī; *cāri bhakta*—four devotees; *saṅge*—with; *kṛṣṇa-kīrtana*—for chanting of the holy name of Kṛṣṇa; *kutūhale*—in great eagerness.

TRANSLATION

Śrī Caitanya Mahāprabhu proceeded toward Jagannātha Purī with four of His devotees, and He chanted the holy name of the Lord, the Hare Kṛṣṇa mantra, with great eagerness.

TEXT 11

ভিক্ষা লাগি' একদিন এক গ্রাম গিয়া ।
আপনে বহুত অন্ন আনিল মাগিয়া ॥ ১১ ॥

bhikṣā lāgi' eka-dina eka grāma giyā
āpane bahuta anna ānila māgiyā

SYNONYMS

bhikṣā lāgi'—for *prasāda; eka-dina*—in one day; *eka grāma*—to one village; *giyā*—going; *āpane*—personally; *bahuta*—a great quantity; *anna*—of rice and other eatables; *ānila*—brought; *māgiyā*—begging.

TRANSLATION

Each day Śrī Caitanya Mahāprabhu personally went to a village and collected a great quantity of rice and other grains for the preparation of prasāda.

TEXT 12

পথে বড় বড় দানী বিঘ্ন নাহি করে ।
তা' সবারে কৃপা করি' আইলা রেমুণারে ॥ ১২ ॥

pathe baḍa baḍa dānī vighna nāhi kare
tā' sabāre kṛpā kari' āilā remuṇāre

SYNONYMS

pathe—on the way; *baḍa baḍa*—big, big; *dānī*—toll or tax collector; *vighna*—hindrances; *nāhi*—not; *kare*—make; *tā' sabāre*—to all of them; *kṛpā kari'*—showing mercy; *āilā*—reached; *remuṇāre*—the village known as Remuṇā.

TRANSLATION

There were many rivers on the way, and at each river there was a tax collector. They did not hinder the Lord, however, and He showed them mercy. Finally He reached the village of Remuṇā.

PURPORT

There is a railway station named Baleśvara, and five miles to the west is a village named Remuṇā. The temple of Kṣīra-corā-gopīnātha still exists in this village, and within the temple the *samādhi* tomb of Rasikānanda Prabhu, the chief disciple of Śyāmānanda Gosvāmī, can still be found.

TEXT 13

রেমুণাতে গোপীনাথ পরম-মোহন ।
ভক্তি করি' কৈল প্রভু তাঁর দরশন ॥ ১৩ ॥

remuṇāte gopīnātha parama-mohana
bhakti kari' kaila prabhu tāṅra daraśana

SYNONYMS

remuṇāte—in that village of Remuṇā; *gopīnātha*—the Deity of Gopīnātha; *parama-mohana*—very attractive; *bhakti kari'*—with great devotion; *kaila*—did; *prabhu*—the Lord; *tāṅra*—of Him; *daraśana*—visit.

TRANSLATION

The Deity of Gopīnātha in the temple at Remuṇā was very attractive. Lord Caitanya visited the temple and offered His obeisances with great devotion.

TEXT 14

তাঁর পাদপদ্ম নিকট প্রণাম করিতে।
তাঁর পুষ্প-চূড়া পড়িল প্রভুর মাথাতে ॥ ১৪ ॥

tāṅra pāda-padma nikaṭa praṇāma karite
tāṅra puṣpa-cūḍā paḍila prabhura māthāte

SYNONYMS

tāṅra pāda-padma—the lotus feet of Gopīnātha; *nikaṭa*—near; *praṇāma*—obeisances; *karite*—while offering; *tāṅra*—His; *puṣpa-cūḍā*—helmet of flowers; *paḍila*—fell down; *prabhura*—of the Lord; *māthāte*—on the head.

TRANSLATION

When Śrī Caitanya Mahāprabhu offered His obeisances at the lotus feet of the Gopīnātha Deity, the helmet of flowers on the head of Gopīnātha fell down and landed on the head of Caitanya Mahāprabhu.

TEXT 15

চূড়া পাঞা মহাপ্রভুর আনন্দিত মন।
বহু নৃত্যগীত কৈল লঞা ভক্তগণ ॥ ১৫ ॥

cūḍā pāñā mahāprabhura ānandita mana
bahu nṛtya-gīta kaila lañā bhakta-gaṇa

SYNONYMS

cūḍā pāñā—getting the helmet; *mahāprabhura*—of Lord Śrī Caitanya Mahāprabhu; *ānandita*—pleased; *mana*—the mind; *bahu*—various kinds; *nṛtya-gīta*—dancing and chanting; *kaila*—performed; *lañā*—with; *bhakta-gaṇa*—the devotees.

TRANSLATION

When the Deity's helmet fell upon His head, Śrī Caitanya Mahāprabhu became very pleased, and thus He chanted and danced in various ways with His devotees.

TEXT 16

প্রভুর প্রভাব দেখি' প্রেম-রূপ-গুণ।
বিস্মিত হইলা গোপীনাথের দাসগণ ॥ ১৬ ॥

prabhura prabhāva dekhi' prema-rūpa-guṇa
vismita ha-ilā gopīnāthera dāsa-gaṇa

SYNONYMS

prabhura—of the Lord; *prabhāva*—the influence; *dekhi'*—seeing; *prema-rūpa*—His beauty; *guṇa*—and His qualities; *vismita ha-ilā*—became struck with wonder; *gopīnāthera*—of the Gopīnātha Deity; *dāsa-gaṇa*—the servants.

TRANSLATION

All the servants of the Deity were struck with wonder due to Śrī Caitanya Mahāprabhu's intense love, His exquisite beauty and His transcendental qualities.

TEXT 17

নানারূপে প্রীত্যে কৈল প্রভুর সেবন ।
সেই রাত্রি তাহাঁ প্রভু করিলা বঞ্চন ॥ ১৭ ॥

nānā-rūpe prītye kaila prabhura sevana
sei rātri tāhāṅ prabhu karilā vañcana

SYNONYMS

nānā-rūpe—in various ways; *prītye*—on account of love; *kaila*—did; *prabhura*—of the Lord; *sevana*—service; *sei rātri*—that night; *tāhāṅ*—there; *prabhu*—Lord Caitanya Mahāprabhu; *karilā*—did; *vañcana*—passing.

TRANSLATION

Because of their love for Śrī Caitanya Mahāprabhu, they served Him in many ways, and that night the Lord stayed at the temple of Gopīnātha.

TEXT 18

মহাপ্রসাদ-ক্ষীর-লোভে রহিলা প্রভু তথা ।
পূর্বে ঈশ্বরপুরী তাঁরে কহিয়াছেন কথা ॥ ১৮ ॥

mahāprasāda-kṣīra-lobhe rahilā prabhu tathā
pūrve īśvara-purī tāṅre kahiyāchena kathā

SYNONYMS

mahā-prasāda—for the remnants of foodstuff; *kṣīra*—sweet rice; *lobhe*—in eagerness; *rahilā*—remained; *prabhu*—the Lord; *tathā*—there; *pūrve*—before that; *īśvara-purī*—Īśvara Purī, His spiritual master; *tāṅre*—unto Him; *kahiyāchena*—told; *kathā*—a narration.

TRANSLATION

The Lord remained there because He was very eager to receive the remnants of sweet rice offered to the Gopīnātha Deity, having heard a narration from His spiritual master, Īśvara Purī, of what had once happened there.

TEXT 19

'ক্ষীরচোরা গোপীনাথ' প্রসিদ্ধ তাঁর নাম ।
ভক্তগণে কহে প্রভু সেই ত' আখ্যান ॥ ১৯ ॥

'kṣīra-corā gopīnātha' prasiddha tāṅra nāma
bhakta-gaṇe kahe prabhu sei ta' ākhyāna

SYNONYMS

kṣīra-corā gopīnātha—the Gopīnātha who stole the pot of sweet rice; *prasiddha*—very famous; *tāṅra nāma*—His name; *bhakta-gaṇe*—to all the devotees; *kahe*—tells; *prabhu*—the Lord; *sei ta' ākhyāna*—that narration.

TRANSLATION

That Deity was known widely as Kṣīra-corā-gopīnātha, and Caitanya Mahāprabhu told His devotees the story of how the Deity became so famous.

TEXT 20

পূর্বে মাধবপুরীর লাগি' ক্ষীর কৈল চুরি ।
অতএব নাম হৈল 'ক্ষীরচোরা হরি' ॥ ২০ ॥

pūrve mādhava-purīra lāgi' kṣīra kaila curi
ataeva nāma haila 'kṣīra-corā hari'

SYNONYMS

pūrve—formerly; *mādhava-purīra lāgi'*—for Mādhavendra Purī; *kṣīra*—sweet rice; *kaila*—did; *curi*—steal; *ataeva*—therefore; *nāma*—the name; *haila*—became; *kṣīra-corā hari*—the Lord who stole a pot of sweet rice.

TRANSLATION

Formerly the Deity had stolen a pot of sweet rice for Mādhavendra Purī; therefore He became very famous as the Lord who stole the sweet rice.

TEXT 21

পূর্বে শ্রীমাধব-পুরী আইলা বৃন্দাবন ।
ভ্রমিতে, ভ্রমিতে গেলা গিরি গোবর্ধন ॥ ২১ ॥

pūrve śrī-mādhava-purī āilā vṛndāvana
bhramite, bhramite gelā giri govardhana

SYNONYMS

pūrve—formerly; *śrī-mādhava-purī*—Śrīla Mādhavendra Purī; *āilā*—came; *vṛndāvana*—to Vṛndāvana; *bhramite bhramite*—while traveling; *gelā*—went; *giri govardhana*—to the hill known as Govardhana.

TRANSLATION

Once, Śrī Mādhavendra Purī traveled to Vṛndāvana, where he came upon the hill known as Govardhana.

TEXT 22

প্রেমে মত্ত,—নাহি তাঁর রাত্রিদিন-জ্ঞান ।
ক্ষণে উঠে, ক্ষণে পড়ে, নাহি স্থানাস্থান ॥ ২২ ॥

preme matta,——nāhi tāṅra rātri-dina-jñāna
kṣaṇe uṭhe, kṣaṇe paḍe, nāhi sthānāsthāna

SYNONYMS

preme matta—maddened in the ecstasy of love of Kṛṣṇa; *nāhi*—there was not; *tāṅra*—of him; *rātri-dina-jñāna*—knowledge of day and night; *kṣaṇe*—sometimes; *uṭhe*—stands; *kṣaṇe paḍe*—sometimes falls; *nāhi*—there was no sense; *sthāna-asthāna*—a proper place or not.

TRANSLATION

Mādhavendra Purī was almost mad in his ecstasy of love of Godhead, and he did not know whether it was day or night. Sometimes he stood up, and sometimes he fell to the ground. He could not discriminate whether he was in a proper place or not.

TEXT 23

শৈল পরিক্রমা করি' গোবিন্দকুণ্ডে আসি' ।
স্নান করি, বৃক্ষতলে আছে সন্ধ্যায় বসি' ॥ ২৩ ॥

śaila parikramā kari' govinda-kuṇḍe āsi'
snāna kari, vṛkṣa-tale āche sandhyāya vasi'

SYNONYMS

śaila—the hill; *parikramā*—circumambulation; *kari'*—finishing; *govinda-kuṇḍe*—to the bank of the Govinda-kuṇḍa; *āsi'*—coming there; *snāna kari*—taking a bath; *vṛkṣa-tale*—under the shade of a tree; *āche*—is; *sandhyāya*—in the evening; *vasi'*—resting.

TRANSLATION

After circumambulating the hill, Mādhavendra Purī went to Govinda-kuṇḍa and took his bath. He then sat beneath a tree to take his evening rest.

TEXT 24

গোপাল-বালক এক দুগ্ধ-ভাণ্ড লঞা ।
আসি' আগে ধরি' কিছু বলিল হাসিয়া ॥ ২৪ ॥

gopāla-bālaka eka dugdha-bhāṇḍa lañā
āsi' āge dhari' kichu balila hāsiyā

SYNONYMS

gopāla-bālaka—cowherd boy; *eka*—one; *dugdha-bhāṇḍa lañā*—taking a pot of milk; *āsi'*—coming; *āge dhari'*—holding it in front; *kichu*—something; *balila*—said; *hāsiyā*—smiling.

TRANSLATION

While he was sitting beneath a tree, an unknown cowherd boy came with a pot of milk, placed it before Mādhavendra Purī, and, smiling, addressed Him as follows.

TEXT 25

পুরী, এই দুগ্ধ লঞা কর তুমি পান ।
মাগি' কেনে নাহি খাও, কিবা কর ধ্যান ॥ ২৫ ॥

purī, ei dugdha lañā kara tumi pāna
māgi' kene nāhi khāo, kibā kara dhyāna

SYNONYMS

purī—O Mādhavendra Purī; *ei dugdha lañā*—taking this milk; *kara tumi pāna*—drink it; *māgi'*—by begging; *kene*—why; *nāhi*—not; *khāo*—you eat; *kibā*—what; *kara*—do; *dhyāna*—meditation.

TRANSLATION

"Please drink the milk I have brought. Why don't you beg some food to eat? What kind of meditation are you undergoing?"

TEXT 26

বালকের সৌন্দর্যে পুরীর হইল সন্তোষ।
তাহার মধুর-বাক্যে গেল ভোক-শোষ ॥ ২৬ ॥

bālakera saundarye purīra ha-ila santoṣa
tāhāra madhura-vākye gela bhoka-śoṣa

SYNONYMS

bālakera—of the boy; *saundarye*—in the beauty; *purīra*—of Mādhavendra Purī; *ha-ila*—was; *santoṣa*—very much satisfaction; *tāhāra*—of Him; *madhura-vākye*—by the sweet words; *gela*—forgot; *bhoka-śoṣa*—all hunger and thirst.

TRANSLATION

When he saw the beauty of that boy, Mādhavendra Purī became very satisfied. Hearing His sweet words, he forgot all hunger and thirst.

TEXT 27

পুরী কহে,—কে তুমি, কাহাঁ তোমার বাস।
কেমতে জানিলে, আমি করি উপবাস ॥ ২৭ ॥

purī kahe,——ke tumi, kāhāṅ tomāra vāsa
ke-mate jānile, āmi kari upavāsa

SYNONYMS

purī kahe—Mādhavendra Purī inquired from the boy; *ke tumi*—who are You; *kāhāṅ tomāra vāsa*—where do You reside; *ke-mate*—how; *jānile*—You know; *āmi kari upavāsa*—I am fasting.

TRANSLATION

Mādhavendra Purī said: "Who are You? Where do You reside? And how did You know that I was fasting?"

TEXT 28

বালক কহে,—গোপ আমি, এই গ্রামে বসি।
আমার গ্রামেতে কেহ না রহে উপবাসী ॥ ২৮ ॥

bālaka kahe,——gopa āmi, ei grāme vasi
āmāra grāmete keha nā rahe upavāsī

SYNONYMS

bālaka kahe—the boy said; *gopa āmi*—I am a cowherd boy; *ei grāme vasi*—I reside in this village; *āmāra grāmete*—in My village; *keha*—anyone; *nā*—not; *rahe*—remains; *upavāsī*—without food.

TRANSLATION

The boy replied: "Sir, I am a cowherd boy, and I reside in this village. In My village, no one fasts.

TEXT 29

কেহ অন্ন মাগি' খায়, কেহ দুগ্ধাহার।
অযাচক-জনে আমি দিয়ে ত' আহার ॥ ২৯ ॥

keha anna māgi' khāya, keha dugdhāhāra
ayācaka-jane āmi diye ta' āhāra

SYNONYMS

keha—someone; *anna*—food; *māgi'*—begging; *khāya*—eats; *keha*—someone; *dugdha-āhāra*—drinks milk; *ayācaka-jane*—a person who does not beg; *āmi*—I; *diye*—supply; *ta'*—certainly; *āhāra*—eatables.

TRANSLATION

"In this village a person can beg food from others and thus eat. Some people drink only milk, but if a person does not ask anyone for food, I supply him all his eatables.

TEXT 30

জল নিতে স্ত্রীগণ তোমারে দেখি' গেল।
স্ত্রীসব দুগ্ধ দিয়া আমারে পাঠাইল ॥ ৩০ ॥

jala nite strī-gaṇa tomāre dekhi' gela
strī-saba dugdha diyā āmāre pāṭhāila

SYNONYMS

jala nite—for bringing water; *strī-gaṇa*—the women; *tomāre*—you; *dekhi' gela*—saw you and went; *strī-saba*—all the women; *dugdha*—milk; *diyā*—giving; *āmāre*—Me; *pāṭhāila*—have sent.

TRANSLATION

"The women who come here to take water saw you, and they supplied Me with this milk and sent Me to you."

TEXT 31

গোদোহন করিতে চাহি, শীঘ্র আমি যাব।
আরবার আসি আমি এই ভাণ্ড লইব ॥ ৩১ ॥

go-dohana karite cāhi, śīghra āmi yāba
āra-bāra āsi āmi ei bhāṇḍa la-iba

SYNONYMS

go-dohana karite cāhi—I want to milk the cows; *śīghra*—very soon; *āmi yāba*—I must go; *āra-bāra*—again; *āsi*—coming back; *āmi*—I; *ei*—this; *bhāṇḍa*—pot; *la-iba*—will take it back.

TRANSLATION

The boy continued: "I must go very soon to milk the cows, but I shall return and take back this milk pot from you."

TEXT 32

এত বলি' গেলা বালক না দেখিয়ে আর।
মাধব-পুরীর চিত্তে হইল চমৎকার ॥ ৩২ ॥

eta bali' gelā bālaka nā dekhiye āra
mādhava-purīra citte ha-ila camatkāra

SYNONYMS

eta bali'—saying this; *gelā*—went; *bālaka*—the boy; *nā*—not; *dekhiye*—could be seen; *āra*—any more; *mādhava-purīra*—of Mādhavendra Purī; *citte*—in the mind; *ha-ila*—there was; *camatkāra*—wonder.

TRANSLATION

Saying this, the boy left the place. Indeed, He suddenly could be seen no more, and Mādhavendra Purī's heart was filled with wonder.

TEXT 33

দুগ্ধ পান করি' ভাণ্ড ধুঞা রাখিল।
বাট দেখে, সে বালক পুনঃ না আইল ॥ ৩৩ ॥

dugdha pāna kari' bhāṇḍa dhuñā rākhila
bāṭa dekhe, se bālaka punaḥ nā āila

SYNONYMS

dugdha—milk; *pāna kari'*—drinking; *bhāṇḍa*—the pot; *dhuñā*—washing; *rākhila*—kept aside; *bāṭa dekhe*—looks at the path; *se bālaka*—the boy; *punaḥ*—again; *nā āila*—did not come back.

TRANSLATION

After drinking the milk, Mādhavendra Purī washed the pot and put it aside. He looked toward the path, but the boy never returned.

TEXT 34

বসি' নাম লয় পুরী, নিদ্রা নাহি হয় ।
শেষরাত্রে তন্দ্রা হৈল,—বাহ্যবৃত্তি-লয় ॥ ৩৪ ॥

vasi' nāma laya purī, nidrā nāhi haya
śeṣa-rātre tandrā haila,——bāhya-vṛtti-laya

SYNONYMS

vasi'—sitting there; *nāma laya*—chants the Hare Kṛṣṇa *mahā-mantra; purī*—Mādhavendra Purī; *nidrā*—sleep; *nāhi haya*—there was not; *śeṣa-rātre*—at the end of the night; *tandrā*—dozing; *haila*—there was; *bāhya-vṛtti*—of external activities; *laya*—stop.

TRANSLATION

Mādhavendra Purī could not sleep. He sat and chanted the Hare Kṛṣṇa mahā-mantra, and at the end of the night he dozed a little, and his external activities stopped.

TEXT 35

স্বপ্নে দেখে, সেই বালক সম্মুখে আসিঞা ।
এক কুঞ্জে লঞা গেল হাতেতে ধরিঞা ॥ ৩৫ ॥

svapne dekhe, sei bālaka sammukhe āsiñā
eka kuñje lañā gela hātete dhariñā

SYNONYMS

svapne—in a dream; *dekhe*—he saw; *sei bālaka*—the very same boy; *sammukhe*—in front; *āsiñā*—coming; *eka kuñje*—in one of the bushes; *lañā*—taking him; *gela*—went; *hātete dhariñā*—holding him by the hand.

TRANSLATION

In a dream Mādhavendra Purī saw the very same boy. The boy came before him and, holding his hand, took him to a bush in the jungle.

TEXT 36

কুঞ্জ দেখাঞা কহে,—আমি এই কুঞ্জে রই।
শীত-বৃষ্টি-বাতাগ্নিতে মহা-দুঃখ পাই ॥ ৩৬ ॥

kuñja dekhāñā kahe,——āmi ei kuñje ra-i
śīta-vṛṣṭi-vātāgnite mahā-duḥkha pāi

SYNONYMS

kuñja dekhāñā—while showing him the bush; *kahe*—He says; *āmi*—I; *ei*—this; *kuñje*—in the bush; *ra-i*—reside; *śīta-vṛṣṭi*—in chilly cold and in showering rain; *vāta*—in severe wind; *agnite*—and in scorching heat; *mahā-duḥkha pāi*—I am experiencing great pain.

TRANSLATION

The boy showed Mādhavendra Purī the bush and said: "I reside in this bush, and because of this I suffer very much from severe cold, rain showers, winds and scorching heat.

TEXT 37

গ্রামের লোক আনি' আমা কাঢ়' কুঞ্জ হৈতে।
পর্বত-উপরি লঞা রাখ ভালমতে ॥ ৩৭ ॥

grāmera loka āni' āmā kāḍha' kuñja haite
parvata-upari lañā rākha bhāla-mate

SYNONYMS

grāmera—of the village; *loka*—the people; *āni'*—bringing; *āmā*—Me; *kāḍha'*—take out; *kuñja haite*—from this bush; *parvata-upari*—on the top of the hill; *lañā*—taking Me; *rākha*—keep Me; *bhāla-mate*—very nicely.

TRANSLATION

"Please bring the people of the village and get them to take Me out of this bush. Then have them situate Me nicely on top of the hill.

TEXT 38

এক মঠ করি' তাহাঁ করহ স্থাপন।
বহু শীতল জলে কর শ্রীঅঙ্গ মার্জন ॥ ৩৮ ॥

eka maṭha kari' tāhāṅ karaha sthāpana
bahu śītala jale kara śrī-aṅga mārjana

SYNONYMS

eka—one; *maṭha*—temple; *kari'*—constructing; *tāhāṅ*—there; *karaha*—do; *sthāpana*—installment; *bahu*—much; *śītala*—cold; *jale*—in water; *kara*—do; *śrī-aṅga*—My transcendental body; *mārjana*—washing.

TRANSLATION

"Please construct a temple on top of that hill," the boy continued, "and install Me in that temple. After this, wash Me with large quantities of cold water so that My body may be cleansed.

TEXT 39

বহুদিন তোমার পথ করি নিরীক্ষণ।
কবে আসি' মাধব আমা করিবে সেবন॥ ৩৯॥

bahu-dina tomāra patha kari nirīkṣaṇa
kabe āsi' mādhava āmā karibe sevana

SYNONYMS

bahu-dina—many days; *tomāra*—of you; *patha*—the path; *kari*—I do; *nirīkṣaṇa*—observing; *kabe*—when; *āsi'*—coming; *mādhava*—Mādhavendra Purī; *āmā*—Me; *karibe*—he will do; *sevana*—serving.

TRANSLATION

"For many days I have been observing you, and I have been wondering, 'When will Mādhavendra Purī come here to serve Me?'

TEXT 40

তোমার প্রেমবশে করি' সেবা অঙ্গীকার।
দর্শন দিয়া নিস্তারিব সকল সংসার॥ ৪০॥

tomāra prema-vaśe kari' sevā aṅgīkāra
darśana diyā nistāriba sakala saṁsāra

SYNONYMS

tomāra—your; *prema-vaśe*—by being subjugated by the love; *kari'*—doing; *sevā*—of service; *aṅgīkāra*—acceptance; *darśana diyā*—giving audience; *nistāriba*—I shall deliver; *sakala*—all; *saṁsāra*—the material world.

TRANSLATION

"I have accepted your service due to your ecstatic love for Me. Thus I shall appear, and by My audience all fallen souls will be delivered.

TEXT 41

'শ্রীগোপাল' নাম মোর,—গোবর্ধনধারী ।
বজ্রের স্থাপিত, আমি ইহাঁ অধিকারী ॥ ৪১ ॥

'śrī-gopāla' nāma mora,——govardhana-dhārī
vajrera sthāpita, āmi ihāṅ adhikārī

SYNONYMS

śrī-gopāla nāma—the name Śrī Gopāla; *mora*—My; *govardhana-dhārī*—the lifter of Govardhana Hill; *vajrera*—by Vajra, the grandson of Kṛṣṇa; *sthāpita*—installed; *āmi*—I; *ihāṅ*—here; *adhikārī*—the authority.

TRANSLATION

"My name is Gopāla. I am the lifter of Govardhana Hill. I was installed by Vajra, and here I am the authority.

TEXT 42

শৈল-উপরি হৈতে আমা কুঞ্জে লুকাঞা ।
ম্লেচ্ছ-ভয়ে সেবক মোর গেল পলাঞা ॥ ৪২ ॥

śaila-upari haite āmā kuñje lukāñā
mleccha-bhaye sevaka mora gela palāñā

SYNONYMS

śaila-upari—the top of the hill; *haite*—from; *āmā*—Me; *kuñje*—in the bushes; *lukāñā*—concealing; *mleccha-bhaye*—from fear of the Mohammedans; *sevaka*—servant; *mora*—My; *gela*—went; *palāñā*—running away.

TRANSLATION

"When the Mohammedans attacked, the priest who was serving Me hid Me in this bush in the jungle. Then he ran away out of fear of the attack.

TEXT 43

সেই হৈতে রহি আমি এই কুঞ্জ-স্থানে ।
ভাল হৈল আইলা আমা কাঢ় সাবধানে ॥ ৪৩ ॥

sei haite rahi āmi ei kuñja-sthāne
bhāla haila āilā āmā kāḍha sāvadhāne

SYNONYMS

sei haite—from that time; *rahi*—reside; *āmi*—I; *ei*—this; *kuñja-sthāne*—in the bush; *bhāla haila*—it was very good; *āilā*—you have come; *āmā*—Me; *kāḍha*—take out; *sāvadhāne*—with care.

TRANSLATION

"Since the priest went away, I have been staying in this bush. It is very good that you have come here. Now just remove Me with care."

TEXT 44

এত বলি' সে-বালক অন্তর্ধান কৈল।
জাগিয়া মাধবপুরী বিচার করিল ॥ ৪৪ ॥

eta bali' se-bālaka antardhāna kaila
jāgiyā mādhava-purī vicāra karila

SYNONYMS

eta bali'—saying this; *se-bālaka*—that very boy; *antardhāna kaila*—disappeared; *jāgiyā*—awakening; *mādhava-purī*—Mādhavendra Purī; *vicāra*—consideration; *karila*—made.

TRANSLATION

After saying this, the boy disappeared. Then Mādhavendra Purī woke up and began to consider his dream.

TEXT 45

শ্রীকৃষ্ণকে দেখিনু মুঞি নারিনু চিনিতে।
এত বলি' প্রেমাবেশে পড়িলা ভূমিতে ॥ ৪৫ ॥

śrī-kṛṣṇake dekhinu muñi nārinu cinite
eta bali' premāveśe paḍilā bhūmite

SYNONYMS

śrī-kṛṣṇake dekhinu—saw Lord Kṛṣṇa personally; *muñi*—I; *nārinu*—was unable; *cinite*—to identify; *eta bali'*—saying this; *prema-āveśe*—in the ecstasy of love; *paḍilā*—fell down; *bhūmite*—on the ground.

TRANSLATION

Mādhavendra Purī began to lament: "I saw Lord Kṛṣṇa directly, but I could not recognize Him!" Thus he fell down on the ground in ecstatic love.

TEXT 46

ক্ষণেক রোদন করি, মন কৈল ধীর ।
আজ্ঞা-পালন লাগি' হইলা সুস্থির ॥ ৪৬ ॥

kṣaṇeka rodana kari, mana kaila dhīra
ājñā-pālana lāgi' ha-ilā susthira

SYNONYMS

kṣaṇeka—for some time; *rodana kari*—crying; *mana*—mind; *kaila*—made; *dhīra*—pacified; *ājñā*—the order; *pālana*—of executing; *lāgi'*—for the matter; *ha-ilā*—became; *su-sthira*—silent.

TRANSLATION

Mādhavendra Purī cried for some time, but then he fixed his mind on executing the order of Gopāla. Thus he became tranquil.

TEXT 47

প্রাতঃস্নান করি' পুরী গ্রামমধ্যে গেলা ।
সব লোক একত্র করি' কহিতে লাগিলা ॥ ৪৭ ॥

prātaḥ-snāna kari' purī grāma-madhye gelā
saba loka ekatra kari' kahite lāgilā

SYNONYMS

prātaḥ-snāna—morning bath; *kari'*—finishing; *purī*—Mādhavendra Purī; *grāma-madhye*—within the village; *gelā*—entered; *saba loka*—all the people; *ekatra kari'*—assembling; *kahite lāgilā*—began to speak.

TRANSLATION

After taking his morning bath, Mādhavendra Purī entered the village and assembled all the people. Then he spoke as follows.

TEXT 48

গ্রামের ঈশ্বর তোমার—গোবর্ধনধারী ।
কুঞ্জে আছে, চল, তাঁরে বাহির যে করি ॥ ৪৮ ॥

grāmera īśvara tomāra——govardhana-dhārī
kuñje āche, cala, tāṅre bāhira ye kari

SYNONYMS

grāmera—of the village; *īśvara*—the proprietor; *tomāra*—your; *govardhana-dhārī*—the lifter of Govardhana Hill; *kuñje āche*—in the bushes in the jungle; *cala*—let us go; *tāṅre*—Him; *bāhira ye kari*—take out.

TRANSLATION

"The proprietor of this village, Govardhana-dhārī, is lying in the bushes. Let us go there and rescue Him from that place.

TEXT 49

অত্যন্ত নিবিড় কুঞ্জ,—নারি প্রবেশিতে।
কুঠারি কোদালি লহ দ্বার করিতে ॥ ৪৯ ॥

atyanta niviḍa kuñja,——nāri praveśite
kuṭhāri kodāli laha dvāra karite

SYNONYMS

atyanta—very much; *niviḍa*—dense; *kuñja*—bushes; *nāri*—we are not able; *praveśite*—to enter; *kuṭhāri*—chopper; *kodāli*—spade; *laha*—take; *dvāra karite*—to make a way.

TRANSLATION

"The bushes are very dense, and we will not be able to enter the jungle. Therefore take choppers and spades to clear the way."

TEXT 50

শুনি' লোক তাঁর সঙ্গে চলিলা হরিষে।
কুঞ্জ কাটি' দ্বার করি' করিলা প্রবেশে ॥ ৫০ ॥

śuni' loka tāṅra saṅge calilā hariṣe
kuñja kāṭi' dvāra kari' karilā praveśe

SYNONYMS

śuni'—hearing; *loka*—the people; *tāṅra*—him; *saṅge*—with; *calilā*—went; *hariṣe*—with great pleasure; *kuñja kāṭi'*—cutting the bushes; *dvāra*—a way; *kari'*—making; *karilā praveśe*—entered.

TRANSLATION

After hearing this, all the people accompanied Mādhavendra Purī with great pleasure. According to his directions, they cut down bushes, cleared a path and entered the jungle.

TEXT 51

ঠাকুর দেখিল মাটী-তৃণে আচ্ছাদিত।
দেখি' সব লোক হৈল আনন্দে বিস্মিত ॥ ৫১ ॥

ṭhākura dekhila māṭī-tṛṇe ācchādita
dekhi' saba loka haila ānande vismita

SYNONYMS

ṭhākura—the Deity; *dekhila*—they saw; *māṭī*—with dirt; *tṛṇe*—and grass; *ācchādita*—covered; *dekhi'*—seeing; *saba loka*—all the people; *haila*—became; *ānande*—with pleasure; *vismita*—amazed.

TRANSLATION

When they saw the Deity covered with dirt and grass, they were all struck with wonder and pleasure.

TEXT 52

আবরণ দূর করি' করিল বিদিতে।
মহা-ভারী ঠাকুর– কেহ নারে চালাইতে ॥ ৫২ ॥

āvaraṇa dūra kari' karila vidite
mahā-bhārī ṭhākura——keha nāre cālāite

SYNONYMS

āvaraṇa—the covering; *dūra kari'*—clearing away; *karila vidite*—declared; *mahā-bhārī*—very heavy; *ṭhākura*—the Deity; *keha*—anyone; *nāre*—not able; *cālāite*—to cause to move.

TRANSLATION

After they cleansed the body of the Deity, some of them said: "The Deity is very heavy. No one person can move Him."

TEXT 53

মহা-মহা-বলিষ্ঠ লোক একত্র করিঞা।
পর্বত-উপরি গেল পুরী ঠাকুর লঞা ॥ ৫৩ ॥

mahā-mahā-baliṣṭha loka ekatra kariñā
parvata-upari gela purī ṭhākura lañā

SYNONYMS

mahā-mahā-baliṣṭha—who are very strong; *loka*—persons; *ekatra kariñā*—assembling; *parvata-upari*—to the top of the hill; *gela*—went; *purī*—Mādhavendra Purī; *ṭhākura lañā*—taking the Deity.

TRANSLATION

Since the Deity was very heavy, some of the stronger men assembled to carry Him to the top of the hill. Mādhavendra Purī also went there.

TEXT 54

পাথরের সিংহাসনে ঠাকুর বসাইল ।
বড় এক পাথর পৃষ্ঠে অবলম্ব দিল ॥ ৫৪ ॥

pātharera siṁhāsane ṭhākura vasāila
baḍa eka pāthara pṛṣṭhe avalamba dila

SYNONYMS

pātharera—of stone; *siṁha-āsane*—on a throne; *ṭhākura*—the Deity; *vasāila*—installed; *baḍa*—big; *eka*—one; *pāthara*—stone; *pṛṣṭhe*—at the back; *avalamba*—support; *dila*—gave.

TRANSLATION

A big stone was made into a throne, and the Deity was installed upon it. Another big stone was placed behind the Deity for support.

TEXT 55

গ্রামের ব্রাহ্মণ সব নব ঘট লঞা ।
গোবিন্দ-কুণ্ডের জল আনিল ছানিঞা ॥ ৫৫ ॥

grāmera brāhmaṇa saba nava ghaṭa lañā
govinda-kuṇḍera jala ānila chāniñā

SYNONYMS

grāmera—of the village; *brāhmaṇa*—*brāhmaṇa* priests; *saba*—all; *nava*—nine; *ghaṭa*—water pots; *lañā*—bringing; *govinda-kuṇḍera*—of the lake known as Govinda-kuṇḍa; *jala*—the water; *ānila*—brought; *chāniñā*—filtering.

TRANSLATION

All the brāhmaṇa priests of the village gathered together with nine water pots, and water from Govinda-kuṇḍa lake was brought there and filtered.

TEXT 56

নব শতঘট জল কৈল উপনীত ।
নানা বাদ্য-ভেরী বাজে, স্ত্রীগণ গায় গীত ॥ ৫৬ ॥

nava śata-ghaṭa jala kaila upanīta
nānā vādya-bherī bāje, strī-gaṇa gāya gīta

SYNONYMS

nava—nine; *śata-ghaṭa*—hundreds of water pots; *jala*—water; *kaila*—made; *upanīta*—brought; *nānā*—various; *vādya*—musical sounds; *bherī*—bugles; *bāje*—vibrate; *strī-gaṇa*—all the women; *gāya*—chant; *gīta*—various songs.

TRANSLATION

When the Deity was being installed, nine hundred pots of water were brought from Govinda-kuṇḍa. There were musical sounds of bugles and drums and the singing of women.

TEXT 57

কেহ গায়, কেহ নাচে, মহোৎসব হৈল ।
দধি, দুগ্ধ, ঘৃত আইল গ্রামে যত ছিল ॥ ৫৭ ॥

keha gāya, keha nāce, mahotsava haila
dadhi, dugdha, ghṛta āila grāme yata chila

SYNONYMS

keha gāya—some sing; *keha nāce*—some dance; *mahotsava haila*—there was a festival; *dadhi*—yogurt; *dugdha*—milk; *ghṛta*—clarified butter; *āila*—was brought; *grāme*—in the village; *yata*—as much; *chila*—as there was.

TRANSLATION

During the festival at the installation ceremony, some people sang and some danced. All the milk, yogurt and clarified butter in the village was brought to the festival.

TEXT 58

ভোগ-সামগ্রী আইল সন্দেশাদি যত ।
নানা উপহার, তাহা কহিতে পারি কত ॥ ৫৮ ॥

bhoga-sāmagrī āila sandeśādi yata
nānā upahāra, tāhā kahite pāri kata

SYNONYMS

bhoga-sāmagrī—ingredients for eatables to be offered; *āila*—brought in; *sandeśa-ādi*—sweetmeats; *yata*—all kinds of; *nānā*—various; *upahāra*—presentations; *tāhā*—that; *kahite*—to say; *pāri*—I am able; *kata*—how much.

TRANSLATION

Various foods and sweetmeats, as well as other kinds of presentations, were brought there. I am unable to describe all these.

TEXT 59

তুলসী আদি, পুষ্প, বস্ত্র আইল অনেক ।
আপনে মাধবপুরী কৈল অভিষেক ॥ ৫৯ ॥

tulasī ādi, puṣpa, vastra āila aneka
āpane mādhava-purī kaila abhiṣeka

SYNONYMS

tulasī—*tulasī* leaves; *ādi*—and others; *puṣpa*—flowers; *vastra*—garments; *āila*—arrived; *aneka*—in great quantity; *āpane*—personally; *mādhava-purī*—Śrī Mādhavendra Purī; *kaila*—executed; *abhiṣeka*—the bathing of the Deity at the beginning of the installation ceremony.

TRANSLATION

The villagers brought a large quantity of tulasī leaves, flowers, and various kinds of garments. Then Śrī Mādhavendra Purī personally began the abhiṣeka [bathing ceremony].

PURPORT

In the *Hari-bhakti-vilāsa* (6th *Vilāsa,* verse 30) it is stated that the Deity should be bathed in water mixed with yogurt and milk, accompanied by the sounds of conchshells, bells and other instruments and the chanting of the *mantra, oṁ bhagavate vāsudevāya namaḥ,* as well as the chanting of the *Brahma-saṁhitā* verses beginning *cintāmaṇi-prakara-sadmasu kalpa-vṛkṣa-lakṣāvṛteṣu surabhīr abhipālayantam.*

TEXT 60

অমঙ্গলা দূর করি' করাইল স্নান ।
বহু তৈল দিয়া কৈল শ্রীঅঙ্গ চিক্কণ ॥ ৬০ ॥

amaṅgalā dūra kari' karāila snāna
bahu taila diyā kaila śrī-aṅga cikkaṇa

SYNONYMS

amaṅgalā—all inauspiciousness; *dūra kari'*—driving away; *karāila*—caused; *snāna*—bathing; *bahu*—a great quantity; *taila*—oil; *diyā*—applying; *kaila*—made; *śrī-aṅga*—the body; *cikkaṇa*—glossy.

TRANSLATION

After all inauspicious things were driven away by the chanting of the mantra, the Deity's bathing ceremony started. First the Deity was massaged with a large quantity of oil, so that His body became very glossy.

TEXT 61

পঞ্চগব্য, পঞ্চামৃতে স্নান করাঞা ।
মহাস্নান করাইল শত ঘট দিঞা ॥ ৬১ ॥

pañca-gavya, pañcāmṛte snāna karāñā
mahā-snāna karāila śata ghaṭa diñā

SYNONYMS

pañca-gavya—in five kinds of products from the cow; *pañca-amṛte*—in a preparation made with five palatable foods; *snāna*—bath; *karāñā*—finishing; *mahā-snāna*—a vast bath with ghee and water; *karāila*—performed; *śata*—one hundred; *ghaṭa*—water pots; *diñā*—with.

TRANSLATION

After the first bathing, further bathings were conducted with pañca-gavya and then with pañcāmṛta. Then the mahā-snāna was performed with ghee and water, which had been brought in one hundred pots.

PURPORT

The ingredients of *pañca-gavya* are milk, yogurt, ghee (clarified butter), cow urine and cow dung. All these items come from the cow; therefore we can just imagine how important the cow is, since its urine and stool are required for bathing the Deity. The *pañcāmṛta* consists of five kinds of nectar—yogurt, milk, ghee, honey and sugar. The major portion of this preparation also comes from the cow. To make it more palatable, sugar and honey are added.

TEXT 62

পুনঃ তৈল দিয়া কৈল শ্রীঅঙ্গ চিক্কণ।
শঙ্খ-গন্ধোদকে কৈল স্নান সমাধান ॥ ৬২ ॥

punaḥ taila diyā kaila śrī-aṅga cikkaṇa
śaṅkha-gandhodake kaila snāna samādhāna

SYNONYMS

punaḥ—again; *taila diyā*—with oil; *kaila*—made; *śrī-aṅga*—the body of the Deity; *cikkaṇa*—shiny; *śaṅkha-gandha-udake*—in water scented with flowers and sandalwood pulp and kept within a conchshell; *kaila*—did; *snāna*—bath; *samādhāna*—execution.

TRANSLATION

After the mahā-snāna was finished, the Deity was again massaged with scented oil and His body made glossy. Then the last bathing ceremony was performed with scented water kept within a conchshell.

PURPORT

In his commentary on this occasion, Śrīla Bhaktisiddhānta Sarasvatī Ṭhākura quotes from the *Hari-bhakti-vilāsa.* Barley powder, wheat powder, vermillion powder, urad dahl powder and another powder preparation called *āvāṭā* (made by mixing banana powder and ground rice) are applied to the Deity's body with a brush made from the hair at the end of a cow's tail. This produces a nice finish. The oil smeared over the body of the Deity should be scented. To perform the *mahā-snāna,* at least two and a half mounds (about twenty-four gallons) of water are needed to pour over the body of the Deity.

TEXT 63

শ্রীঅঙ্গ মার্জন করি' বস্ত্র পরাইল।
চন্দন, তুলসী, পুষ্প-মালা অঙ্গে দিল ॥ ৬৩ ॥

śrī-aṅga mārjana kari' vastra parāila
candana, tulasī, puṣpa-mālā aṅge dila

SYNONYMS

śrī-aṅga—the transcendental body of the Deity; *mārjana kari'*—cleansing; *vastra*—garments; *parāila*—were put on; *candana*—sandalwood pulp; *tulasī*—*tulasī* leaves; *puṣpa-mālā*—garlands of flowers; *aṅge*—on the body; *dila*—were placed.

TRANSLATION

After the body of the Deity was cleansed, He was dressed very nicely with new garments. Then sandalwood pulp, tulasī garlands, and other fragrant flower garlands were placed upon the body of the Deity.

TEXT 64

ধূপ, দীপ, করি' নানা ভোগ লাগাইল ।
দধি-দুগ্ধ-সন্দেশাদি যত কিছু আইল ॥ ৬৪ ॥

dhūpa, dīpa, kari' nānā bhoga lāgāila
dadhi-dugdha-sandeśādi yata kichu āila

SYNONYMS

dhūpa—incense; *dīpa*—lamp; *kari'*—burning; *nānā*—various; *bhoga*—foodstuffs; *lāgāila*—were offered; *dadhi*—yogurt; *dugdha*—milk; *sandeśa*—sweetmeats; *ādi*—and others; *yata*—as much as; *kichu*—some; *āila*—received.

TRANSLATION

After the bathing ceremony was finished, incense and lamps were burned and all kinds of food offered before the Deity. These foods included yogurt, milk and as many sweetmeats as were received.

TEXT 65

সুবাসিত জল নবপাত্রে সমর্পিল ।
আচমন দিয়া সে তাম্বূল নিবেদিল ॥ ৬৫ ॥

suvāsita jala nava-pātre samarpila
ācamana diyā se tāmbūla nivedila

SYNONYMS

suvāsita jala—scented water; *nava-pātre*—in new pots; *samarpila*—were offered; *ācamana diyā*—when offering *ācamana* (water for washing the feet and mouth); *se*—he; *tāmbūla*—*pān* and spices; *nivedila*—offered.

TRANSLATION

The Deity was first offered many varieties of food, then scented drinking water in new pots, and then water for washing the mouth. Finally pān mixed with a variety of spices was offered.

TEXT 66

আরাত্রিক করি' কৈল বহুত স্তবন।
দণ্ডবৎ করি' কৈল আত্ম-সমর্পণ ॥ ৬৬ ॥

ārātrika kari' kaila bahuta stavana
daṇḍavat kari' kaila ātma-samarpaṇa

SYNONYMS

ārātrika—the performance of *ārātrika; kari'*—finishing; *kaila*—chanted; *bahuta*—varieties; *stavana*—of prayers; *daṇḍavat*—obeisances; *kari'*—offering; *kaila*—did; *ātma-samarpaṇa*—self-surrender.

TRANSLATION

After the last offering of tāmbūla and pān, bhoga-ārātrika was performed. Finally everyone offered various prayers and then obeisances, falling flat before the Deity in full surrender.

TEXT 67

গ্রামের যতেক তণ্ডুল, দালি, গোধূম-চূর্ণ।
সকল আনিয়া দিল পর্বত হৈল পূর্ণ ॥ ৬৭ ॥

grāmera yateka taṇḍula, dāli godhūma-cūrṇa
sakala āniyā dila parvata haila pūrṇa

SYNONYMS

grāmera—of the village; *yateka*—all; *taṇḍula*—the rice; *dāli*—dahl; *godhūma-cūrṇa*—wheat flour; *sakala*—all; *āniyā*—bringing; *dila*—offered; *parvata*—the top of the hill; *haila*—became; *pūrṇa*—filled.

TRANSLATION

As soon as the people of the village had understood that the Deity was going to be installed, they had brought their entire stocks of rice, dahl and wheat flour. They brought such large quantities that the entire surface of the top of the hill was filled.

TEXT 68

কুম্ভকার ঘরে ছিল যে মৃদ্ভাজন ।
সব আনাইল প্রাতে, চড়িল রন্ধন ॥ ৬৮ ॥

kumbhakāra ghare chila ye mṛd-bhājana
saba ānāila prāte, caḍila randhana

SYNONYMS

kumbhakāra—of the potters of the village; *ghare*—in the houses; *chila*—there was; *ye*—whatever; *mṛd-bhājana*—clay pots; *saba*—all; *ānāila*—brought; *prāte*—in the morning; *caḍila*—started; *randhana*—cooking.

TRANSLATION

When the villagers brought their stock of rice, dahl and flour, the potters of the village brought all kinds of cooking pots, and in the morning the cooking began.

TEXT 69

দশবিপ্র অন্ন রান্ধি' করে এক স্তূপ ।
জনা-পাঁচ রান্ধে ব্যঞ্জনাদি নানা সূপ ॥ ৬৯ ॥

daśa-vipra anna rāndhi' kare eka stūpa
janā-pāṅca rāndhe vyañjanādi nānā sūpa

SYNONYMS

daśa-vipra—ten *brāhmaṇas; anna*—food grains; *rāndhi'*—cooking; *kare*—do; *eka stūpa*—in one stack; *janā-pāṅca*—five *brāhmaṇas; rāndhe*—cook; *vyañjana-ādi*—vegetables; *nānā*—various; *sūpa*—liquid.

TRANSLATION

Ten brāhmaṇas cooked the food grains, and five brāhmaṇas cooked both dry and liquid vegetables.

TEXT 70

বন্য শাক-ফল-মূলে বিবিধ ব্যঞ্জন।
কেহ বড়া-বড়ি-কড়ি করে বিপ্রগণ ॥ ৭০ ॥

vanya śāka-phala-mūle vividha vyañjana
keha baḍā-baḍi-kaḍi kare vipra-gaṇa

SYNONYMS

vanya śāka—spinach of the forest; *phala*—fruits; *mūle*—with roots; *vividha*—varieties; *vyañjana*—vegetables; *keha*—someone; *baḍā-baḍi*—*baḍā* and *baḍi;* *kaḍi*—from the pulp of dahl; *kare*—made; *vipra-gaṇa*—all the *brāhmaṇas.*

TRANSLATION

The vegetable preparations were made from various kinds of spinach, roots and fruits collected from the forest, and someone had made baḍā and baḍi by mashing dahl. In this way the brāhmaṇas prepared all kinds of food.

TEXT 71

জনা পাঁচ-সাত রুটি করে রাশি-রাশি।
অন্ন-ব্যঞ্জন সব রহে ঘৃতে ভাসি' ॥ ৭১ ॥

janā pāṅca-sāta ruṭi kare rāśi-rāśi
anna-vyañjana saba rahe ghṛte bhāsi'

SYNONYMS

janā pāṅca-sāta—five to seven men; *ruṭi*—*chappatis;* *kare*—make; *rāśi-rāśi*—in great quantity; *anna-vyañjana*—food grains and vegetables; *saba*—all; *rahe*—remained; *ghṛte*—in ghee; *bhāsi'*—overflooding.

TRANSLATION

Five to seven men had prepared a huge quantity of chappatis, which were sufficiently covered with ghee [clarified butter], as were all the vegetables, rice and dahl.

TEXT 72

নববস্ত্র পাতি' তাহে পলাশের পাত।
রান্ধি' রান্ধি' তার উপর রাশি কৈল ভাত ॥ ৭২ ॥

nava-vastra pāti' tāhe palāśera pāta
rāndhi' rāndhi' tāra upara rāśi kaila bhāta

SYNONYMS

nava-vastra—new cloth; *pāti'*—spreading; *tāhe*—on that; *palāśera pāta*—the leaves of *palāśa; rāndhi' rāndhi'*—cooking and cooking; *tāra upara*—on that; *rāśi*—stacked; *kaila*—made; *bhāta*—rice.

TRANSLATION

All the cooked rice was stacked on palāśa leaves, which were on new cloths spread over the ground.

TEXT 73

তার পাশে রুটি-রাশির পর্বত হইল।
সূপ-আদি-ব্যঞ্জন-ভাণ্ড চৌদিকে ধরিল ॥ ৭৩ ॥

tāra pāśe ruṭi-rāśira parvata ha-ila
sūpa-ādi-vyañjana-bhāṇḍa caudike dharila

SYNONYMS

tāra pāśe—around the stack of rice; *ruṭi*—of *chappatis; rāśira*—of stacks; *parvata*—another small hill; *ha-ila*—became; *sūpa-ādi*—of all liquid vegetables; *vyañjana*—and of all other vegetables; *bhāṇḍa*—pots; *caudike*—all around; *dharila*—were placed.

TRANSLATION

Around the stack of cooked rice were stacks of chappatis, and all the vegetables and liquid vegetable preparations were placed in different pots and put around them.

TEXT 74

তার পাশে দধি, দুগ্ধ, মাঠা, শিখরিণী।
পায়স, মথনী, সর পাশে ধরি আনি' ॥ ৭৪ ॥

tāra pāśe dadhi, dugdha, māṭhā, śikhariṇī
pāyasa, mathanī, sara pāśe dhari āni'

SYNONYMS

tāra pāśe—by the side of the vegetables; *dadhi*—yogurt; *dugdha*—milk; *māṭhā*—buttermilk; *śikhariṇī*—a sweet preparation made with yogurt; *pāyasa*—

sweet rice; *mathanī*—cream; *sara*—solid cream collected over yogurt; *pāśe*—by the side; *dhari*—keeping; *āni'*—bringing.

TRANSLATION

Pots of yogurt, milk, buttermilk and śikhariṇī, sweet rice, cream and solid cream were placed alongside the vegetables.

PURPORT

In this kind of ceremony, which is called *annakūṭa,* cooked rice is stacked like a small mountain for *prasāda* distribution.

TEXT 75

হেনমতে অন্নকূট করিল সাজন ।
পুরী-গোসাঞি গোপালেরে কৈল সমর্পণ ॥ ৭৫ ॥

hena-mate anna-kūṭa karila sājana
purī-gosāñi gopālere kaila samarpaṇa

SYNONYMS

hena-mate—in this way; *anna-kūṭa*—of the Annakūṭa ceremony; *karila*—did; *sājana*—performance; *purī-gosāñi*—Mādhavendra Purī; *gopālere*—unto the Gopāla Deity; *kaila*—did; *samarpaṇa*—offering.

TRANSLATION

In this way the Annakūṭa ceremony was performed, and Mādhavendra Purī Gosvāmī personally offered everything to Gopāla.

TEXT 76

অনেক ঘট ভরি' দিল সুবাসিত জল ।
বহুদিনের ক্ষুধায় গোপাল খাইল সকল ॥ ৭৬ ॥

aneka ghaṭa bhari' dila suvāsita jala
bahu-dinera kṣudhāya gopāla khāila sakala

SYNONYMS

aneka ghaṭa—many water pots; *bhari'*—filled; *dila*—offered; *suvāsita*—scented; *jala*—water; *bahu-dinera*—of many days; *kṣudhāya*—by hunger; *gopāla*—Gopāla; *khāila*—ate; *sakala*— everything.

TRANSLATION

Many water pots were filled with scented water for drinking, and Lord Śrī Gopāla, who had been hungry for many days, ate everything offered to Him.

TEXT 77

যদ্যপি গোপাল সব অন্ন-ব্যঞ্জন খাইল ।
তাঁর হস্ত-স্পর্শে পুনঃ তেমনি হইল ॥ ৭৭ ॥

yadyapi gopāla saba anna-vyañjana khāila
tāṅra hasta-sparśe punaḥ temani ha-ila

SYNONYMS

yadyapi—although; *gopāla*—Lord Gopāla; *saba*—all; *anna-vyañjana*—dahl, rice and vegetables; *khāila*—ate; *tāṅra*—His; *hasta*—of the hands; *sparśe*—by the touch; *punaḥ*—again; *temani*—exactly as before; *ha-ila*—became.

TRANSLATION

Although Śrī Gopāla ate everything offered, still, by the touch of His transcendental hand, everything remained as before.

PURPORT

The atheists cannot understand how the Supreme Personality of Godhead, appearing in the form of the Deity, can eat all the food offered by His devotees. In *Bhagavad-gītā* Kṛṣṇa says:

patraṁ puṣpaṁ phalaṁ toyaṁ
yo me bhaktyā prayacchati
tad ahaṁ bhakty-upahṛtam
aśnāmi prayatātmanaḥ

"If one offers Me with love and devotion a leaf, a flower, fruit or water, I will accept it." (Bg. 9.26) The Lord is *pūrṇa,* complete, and therefore He eats everything offered by His devotees. However, by the touch of His transcendental hand, all the food remains exactly as before. It is the quality that is changed. Before the food was offered, it was something else, but after it is offered the food acquires a transcendental quality. Because the Lord is *pūrṇa,* He remains the same even after eating. *Pūrṇasya pūrṇam ādāya pūrṇam evāvaśiṣyate.* The food offered to Kṛṣṇa is qualitatively as good as Kṛṣṇa; just as Kṛṣṇa is *avyaya,* indestructible, the food eaten by Kṛṣṇa, being identical with Him, remains as before.

Apart from this, Kṛṣṇa can eat the food with any one of His transcendental senses. He can eat by seeing the food, or by touching it. Nor should one think that it is necessary for Kṛṣṇa to eat. He does not become hungry like an ordinary human being; nonetheless, He presents Himself as being hungry, and as such, He can eat everything and anything, regardless of quantity. The philosophy underlying Kṛṣṇa's eating is understandable by our transcendental senses. When our senses are purified by constantly being engaged in the devotional service of the Lord, we can understand Kṛṣṇa's activities, names, forms, qualities, pastimes, and entourage.

ataḥ śrī-kṛṣṇa-nāmādi
na bhaved grāhyam indriyaiḥ
sevonmukhe hi jihvādau
svayam eva sphuraty adaḥ

"No one can understand Kṛṣṇa by the blunt material senses. But He reveals Himself to the devotees, being pleased with them for their transcendental loving service unto Him." (*Bh.r.s.* 1.2.234) The devotees understand Kṛṣṇa through revelation. It is not possible for a mundane scholar to understand Kṛṣṇa and His pastimes through research work on the nondevotional platform.

TEXT 78

ইহা অনুভব কৈল মাধব গোসাঞি ।
তাঁর ঠাঞি গোপালের লুকান কিছু নাই ॥ ৭৮ ॥

ihā anubhava kaila mādhava gosāñi
tāṅra ṭhāñi gopālera lukāna kichu nāi

SYNONYMS

ihā—this; *anubhava kaila*—perceived; *mādhava gosāñi*—Mādhavendra Purī Gosvāmī; *tāṅra ṭhāñi*— before him; *gopālera*—of Lord Gopāla; *lukāna*—secret; *kichu*—anything; *nāi*—there is not.

TRANSLATION

How Gopāla ate everything while the food remained the same was transcendentally perceived by Mādhavendra Purī Gosvāmī; nothing remains a secret to the devotees of the Lord.

TEXT 79

একদিনের উদ্‌যোগে ঐছে মহোৎসব কৈল ।
গোপাল-প্রভাবে হয়, অন্যে না জানিল ॥ ৭৯ ॥

eka-dinera udyoge aiche mahotsava kaila
gopāla-prabhāve haya, anye nā jānila

SYNONYMS

eka-dinera udyoge—by one day's attempt; *aiche*—such; *mahotsava*—festival; *kaila*—performed; *gopāla*—of Gopāla; *prabhāve*—by the potency; *haya*—is possible; *anye*—others; *nā*—not; *jānila*—know.

TRANSLATION

The wonderful festival and installation of Śrī Gopālajī was arranged in one day. Certainly all this was accomplished by the potency of Gopāla. No one but a devotee can understand this.

PURPORT

The Kṛṣṇa consciousness movement has spread all over the world within a very short time (within five years), and mundane people are very astonished at this. However, by the grace of Lord Śrī Caitanya Mahāprabhu, we understand that everything is possible by the grace of Kṛṣṇa. Why does Kṛṣṇa have to take five years? In five days He can spread His name and fame all over the world like wildfire. Those who have faith and devotion to Kṛṣṇa can understand that these things happen so wonderfully by the grace of Śrī Caitanya Mahāprabhu. We are simply the instruments. In the fierce Battle of Kurukṣetra, Arjuna was victorious within eighteen days simply because Kṛṣṇa's grace was on his side.

yatra yogeśvaraḥ kṛṣṇo
yatra pārtho dhanur-dharaḥ
tatra śrīr vijayo bhūtir
dhruvā nītir matir mama

"Wherever there is Kṛṣṇa, the master of all mystics, and wherever there is Arjuna, the supreme archer, there will also certainly be opulence, victory, extraordinary power and morality. That is my opinion." (Bg. 18.78)

If the preachers in our Kṛṣṇa consciousness movement are sincere devotees of Kṛṣṇa, Kṛṣṇa will always be with them because He is very kind and favorable to all His devotees. Just as Arjuna and Kṛṣṇa were victorious in the Battle of Kurukṣetra, this Kṛṣṇa consciousness movement will surely emerge victorious if we but remain sincere devotees of the Lord and serve the Lord according to the advice of predecessors (the six Gosvāmīs and other devotees of the Lord). As Narottama dāsa Ṭhākura has stated: *tāṅdera caraṇa sevi bhakta-sane vāsa, janame janame haya ei abhilāṣa*. The Kṛṣṇa consciousness devotees must always desire to remain in the society of devotees. *Bhakta-sane vāsa:* they cannot go outside the Kṛṣṇa conscious society or the movement. Within the society we must try to serve the predecessors by preaching Caitanya Mahāprabhu's cult and spreading His name and fame all over the world. If we attempt this seriously within the society, it will be successfully done. There is no question of estimating how this will happen in the mundane sense. But without a doubt, it happens by the grace of Kṛṣṇa.

TEXT 80

আচমন দিয়া দিল বিড়ক-সঞ্চয় ।
আরতি করিল লোকে, করে জয় জয় ॥ ৮০ ॥

ācamana diyā dila viḍaka-sañcaya
ārati karila loke, kare jaya jaya

SYNONYMS

ācamana—washing water; *diyā*—offering; *dila*—gave; *viḍaka-sañcaya*—betel nuts; *ārati karila*—*ārati* was performed; *loke*—all the people; *kare*—chant; *jaya jaya*—the words *jaya jaya,* "all glories."

TRANSLATION

Mādhavendra Purī offered water to Gopāla for washing His mouth, and he gave Him betel nuts to chew. Then, while ārati was performed, all the people chanted, "Jaya jaya!" ["All glories to Gopāla"].

TEXT 81

শয্যা করাইল, নূতন খাট আনাঞা ।
নব বস্ত্র আনি' তার উপরে পাতিয়া ॥ ৮১ ॥

śayyā karāila, nūtana khāṭa ānāñā
nava vastra āni' tāra upare pātiyā

SYNONYMS

śayyā—a bedstead; *karāila*—made; *nūtana*—new; *khāṭa*—bedstead; *ānāñā*—bringing; *nava vastra*—new cloth; *āni'*—bringing; *tāra*—of the cot; *upare*—on the top; *pātiyā*—spreading.

TRANSLATION

Arranging for the Lord's rest, Śrī Mādhavendra Purī brought a new cot, and over this he spread a new bedspread and thus made the bed ready.

TEXT 82

তৃণ-টাটি দিয়া চারিদিক্ আবরিল ।
উপরেতে এক টাটি দিয়া আচ্ছাদিল ॥ ৮২ ॥

tṛṇa-ṭāṭi diyā cāri-dik āvarila
uparete eka ṭāṭi diyā ācchādila

SYNONYMS

tṛṇa-ṭāṭi—straw mattress; *diyā*—with; *cāri-dik*—all around; *āvarila*—covered; *uparete*—on top; *eka*—one; *ṭāṭi*—similar straw mattress; *diyā*—with; *ācchādila*—covered.

TRANSLATION

A temporary temple was constructed by covering the bed all around with a straw mattress. Thus there was a bed and a straw mattress to cover it.

TEXT 83

পুরী-গোসাঞি আজ্ঞা দিল সকল ব্রাহ্মণে ।
আ-বাল-বৃদ্ধ গ্রামের লোক করাহ ভোজনে ॥ ৮৩ ॥

purī-gosāñi ājñā dila sakala brāhmaṇe
ā-bāla-vṛddha grāmera loka karāha bhojane

SYNONYMS

purī-gosāñi—Mādhavendra Purī; *ājñā*—order; *dila*—gave; *sakala brāhmaṇe*—to all the *brāhmaṇas*; *ā-bāla-vṛddha*—beginning from the children up to the old persons; *grāmera*—of the village; *loka*—the people; *karāha*—make; *bhojane*—take *prasāda.*

TRANSLATION

After the Lord was laid down to rest on the bed, Mādhavendra Purī gathered all the brāhmaṇas who had prepared the prasāda and said to them: "Now feed everyone sumptuously, from the children on up to the aged!"

TEXT 84

সবে বসি' ক্রমে ক্রমে ভোজন করিল ।
ব্রাহ্মণ-ব্রাহ্মণীগণে আগে খাওয়াইল ॥ ৮৪ ॥

sabe vasi' krame krame bhojana karila
brāhmaṇa-brāhmaṇī-gaṇe āge khāoyāila

SYNONYMS

sabe—all; *vasi'*—sitting; *krame krame*—by and by; *bhojana karila*—honored *prasāda* and ate it; *brāhmaṇa-brāhmaṇī-gaṇe*—the *brāhmaṇas* and their wives; *āge*—first; *khāoyāila*—were fed.

TRANSLATION

All the people gathered there sat down to honor the prasāda, and by and by they took food. All the brāhmaṇas and their wives were fed first.

PURPORT

According to the *varṇāśrama* system, the *brāhmaṇas* are always honored first. Thus at the festival, the *brāhmaṇas* and their wives were first offered the remnants of food, and then the others (*kṣatriyas, vaiśyas* and *śūdras*). This has always been the system, and it is still prevalent in India, even though the caste *brāhmaṇas* are not qualified. The system is still current due to the *varṇāśrama* institutional rules and regulations.

TEXT 85

অন্য গ্রামের লোক যত দেখিতে আইল ।
গোপাল দেখিয়া সবে প্রসাদ খাইল ॥ ৮৫ ॥

anya grāmera loka yata dekhite āila
gopāla dekhiyā saba prasāda khāila

SYNONYMS

anya—other; *grāmera*—of the villages; *loka*—people; *yata*—all; *dekhite*—to see; *āila*—came; *gopāla*—the Lord Gopāla; *dekhiyā*—seeing; *saba*—all; *prasāda*—remnants of food; *khāila*—partook.

TRANSLATION

Not only did the people of Govardhana village take prasāda, but also those who came from other villages. They also saw the Deity of Gopāla and were offered prasāda to eat.

TEXT 86

দেখিয়া পুরীর প্রভাব লোকে চমৎকার ।
পূর্ব অন্নকূট যেন হৈল সাক্ষাৎকার ॥ ৮৬ ॥

dekhiyā purīra prabhāva loke camatkāra
pūrva annakūṭa yena haila sākṣātkāra

SYNONYMS

dekhiyā—by seeing; *purīra*—of Mādhavendra Purī; *prabhāva*—the influence; *loke*—all the people; *camatkāra*—struck with wonder; *pūrva*—formerly; *annakūṭa*—the Annakūṭa ceremony during the time of Kṛṣṇa; *yena*—as if; *haila*—became; *sākṣātkāra*—directly manifest.

TRANSLATION

Seeing the influence of Mādhavendra Purī, all the people gathered there were struck with wonder. They saw that the Annakūṭa ceremony, which had been performed before during the time of Kṛṣṇa, was now taking place again by the mercy of Śrī Mādhavendra Purī.

PURPORT

Formerly, at the end of Dvāpara-yuga, all the cowherd men of Vṛndāvana had arranged to worship King Indra, but they gave this worship up, following the advice of Kṛṣṇa. Instead, they performed a ceremony whereby they worshiped the cows, *brāhmaṇas* and Govardhana Hill. At that time Kṛṣṇa expanded Himself and declared, "I am Govardhana Hill." In this way He accepted all the paraphernalia and foodstuff offered to Govardhana Hill. It is stated in the *Śrīmad-Bhāgavatam* (10.24.26, 31-33):

pacyantāṁ vividhāḥ pākāḥ
sūpāntāḥ pāya-sādayaḥ
saṁyāvā-pūpaśaṣkulyaḥ
sarva-dohaś ca gṛhyatām

kālātmanā bhagavatā
śakra-darpaṁ jighāṁsatā
proktaṁ niśamya nandādyāḥ
sādhv agṛhṇanta tad vacaḥ

tathā ca vyadadhuḥ sarvaṁ
yathāha madhusūdanaḥ
vācayitvā svasty ayanaṁ
tad dravyeṇa giri-dvijān

upahṛtya balīn sarvān
ādṛtā yavasaṁ gavām
godhanāni puras-kṛtya
giriṁ cakruḥ pradakṣiṇam

" 'Prepare very nice foodstuffs of all descriptions from the grains and ghee collected for the *yajña*. Prepare rice, dahl, then halavah, *pākorā, purī* and all kinds of milk preparations like sweet rice, sweetballs, *sandeśa, rasagullā* and *lāḍḍu*.'

"The Supreme Personality of Godhead, Kṛṣṇa, therefore advised the cowherd men to stop the Indra-yajña and begin the Govardhana-pūjā to chastise Indra, who was very much puffed up at being the supreme controller of the heavenly planets. The honest and simple cowherd men, headed by Nanda Mahārāja, accepted Kṛṣṇa's proposal and executed in detail everything He advised. They performed Govardhana worship and circumambulation of the hill. According to the instruction of Lord Kṛṣṇa, Nanda Mahārāja and the cowherd men called in learned *brāhmaṇas* and began to worship Govardhana Hill by chanting Vedic hymns and offering *prasāda*. The inhabitants of Vṛndāvana assembled together, decorated their cows and gave them grass. Keeping the cows in front, they began to circumambulate Govardhana Hill."

TEXT 87

সকল ব্রাহ্মণে পুরী বৈষ্ণব করিল।
সেই সেই সেবা-মধ্যে সবা নিয়োজিল ॥ ৮৭ ॥

sakala brāhmaṇe purī vaiṣṇava karila
sei sei sevā-madhye sabā niyojila

SYNONYMS

sakala brāhmaṇe—all the *brāhmaṇas* who were present there; *purī*—Mādhavendra Purī Gosvāmī; *vaiṣṇava karila*—elevated to the position of Vaiṣṇavas; *sei sei*—under different divisions; *sevā-madhye*—in rendering service; *sabā*—all of them; *niyojila*—were engaged.

TRANSLATION

All the brāhmaṇas present on that occasion were initiated by Mādhavendra Purī into the Vaiṣṇava cult, and Mādhavendra Purī engaged them in different types of service.

PURPORT

In the scriptures it is stated: *ṣaṭ-karma-nipuṇo vipro mantra-tantra-viśāradaḥ avaiṣṇavaḥ*. Even though a caste *brāhmaṇa* or a qualified *brāhmaṇa* is expert in the occupational duties of a *brāhmaṇa*, he is not necessarily a Vaiṣṇava. His duties are mentioned as six brahminical engagements. *Paṭhana* means that a *brāhmaṇa* must be conversant with the Vedic scriptures. He must also be able to teach others to study Vedic literatures. This is *pāṭhana*. He must also be expert in worshiping different deities and in performing the Vedic rituals (*yajana*). On account of this *yajana*, the *brāhmaṇa*, being the head of society, performs all the Vedic rituals for *kṣatriyas, vaiśyas,* and *śūdras.* This is called *yājana,* assisting others in performing ceremonies. The remaining two items are *dāna* and *pratigraha.* The *brāhmaṇa* accepts all kinds of contributions (*pratigraha*) from his followers (mainly, the *kṣatriyas, vaiśyas* and *śūdras*). But he does not keep all the money. He keeps only as much as required and gives the balance to others in charity (*dāna*).

In order for such a qualified *brāhmaṇa* to worship the Deity, he must be a Vaiṣṇava. Thus the Vaiṣṇava's position is superior to that of the *brāhmaṇa.* This example given by Mādhavendra Purī confirms that even though a *brāhmaṇa* may be very expert, he cannot become a priest or servitor of the Viṣṇu *mūrti* unless he is initiated in *vaiṣṇava-mantra.* After installing the Deity of Gopāla, Mādhavendra Purī initiated all the *brāhmaṇas* into Vaiṣṇavism. He then allotted the *brāhmaṇas* different types of service to the Deity. From four in the morning until ten at night (from *maṅgala-ārātrika* to *śayana-ārātrika*), there must be at least five or six *brāhmaṇas* to take care of the Deity. Six *ārātrikas* are performed in the temple, and food is frequently offered to the Deity and the *prasāda* distributed. This is the method of worshiping the Deity according to the rules and regulations set by predecessors. Our *sampradāya* belongs to the disciplic succession of Mādhavendra Purī, who belonged to the Madhva-sampradāya. We are in the disciplic succession of Śrī Caitanya Mahāprabhu, who was initiated by Śrī Īśvara Purī, a disciple of Mādhavendra Purī's. Our *sampradāya* is therefore called the Madhva-Gauḍīya-sampradāya. As such, we must carefully follow in the footsteps of Śrī Mādhavendra Purī and observe how he installed the Gopāla Deity on top of Govardhana Hill, how he arranged and performed the Annakūṭa ceremony in only one day, and so forth. Our installation of Deities in America and in the wealthy countries of Europe should be carried out in terms of Śrī Mādhavendra Purī's activities. All the servitors of the Deity must be strictly qualified as *brāhmaṇas* and, specifically, must engage in the Vaiṣṇava custom of offering as much *prasāda* as possible and distributing it to the devotees who visit the temple to see the Lord.

TEXT 88

পুনঃ দিন-শেষে প্রভুর করাইল উত্থান ।
কিছু ভোগ লাগাইল করাইল জলপান ॥ ৮৮ ॥

punaḥ dina-śeṣe prabhura karāila utthāna
kichu bhoga lāgāila karāila jala-pāna

SYNONYMS

punaḥ—again; *dina-śeṣe*—at the end of the day; *prabhura*—of the Lord; *karāila*—caused to do; *utthāna*—rising; *kichu*—some; *bhoga*—food; *lāgāila*—offered; *karāila*—caused to do; *jala*—water; *pāna*—drinking.

TRANSLATION

After taking rest, the Deity must be awakened at the end of the day, and immediately some food and some water must be offered to Him.

PURPORT

This offering is called *vaikāli-bhoga,* food offered at the end of the day.

TEXT 89

গোপাল প্রকট হৈল,— দেশে শব্দ হৈল ।
আশ-পাশ গ্রামের লোক দেখিতে আইল ॥ ৮৯ ॥

gopāla prakaṭa haila,——deśe śabda haila
āśa-pāśa grāmera loka dekhite āila

SYNONYMS

gopāla—Lord Gopāla; *prakaṭa haila*—has appeared; *deśe*—throughout the country; *śabda haila*—the news spread; *āśa-pāśa*—neighboring; *grāmera*—of the villages; *loka*—the people; *dekhite āila*—came to see.

TRANSLATION

When it was advertised throughout the country that Lord Gopāla had appeared atop Govardhana Hill, all the people from neighboring villages came to see the Deity.

TEXT 90

একেক দিন একেক গ্রামে লইল মাগিঞা ।
অন্নকূট করে সবে হরষিত হঞা ॥ ৯০ ॥

ekeka dina ekeka grāme la-ila māgiñā
anna-kūṭa kare sabe haraṣita hañā

SYNONYMS

ekeka dina—one day after another; *ekeka grāme*—one village after another; *la-ila*—took permission; *māgiñā*—begging; *anna-kūṭa kare*—perform the Annakūṭa ceremony; *sabe*—all; *haraṣita*—pleased; *hañā*—becoming.

TRANSLATION

One village after another was pleased to beg Mādhavendra Purī to allot them one day to perform the Annakūṭa ceremony. Thus, day after day, the Annakūṭa ceremony was performed for some time.

TEXT 91

রাত্রিকালে ঠাকুরেরে করাইয়া শয়ন ।
পুরী-গোসাঞি কৈল কিছু গব্য ভোজন ॥ ৯১ ॥

rātri-kāle ṭhākurere karāiyā śayana
purī-gosāñi kaila kichu gavya bhojana

SYNONYMS

rātri-kāle—at night; *ṭhākurere*—the Deity; *karāiyā*—causing to do; *śayana*—lying down for rest; *purī-gosāñi*—Mādhavendra Purī; *kaila*—did; *kichu*—some; *gavya*—milk preparation; *bhojana*—eating.

TRANSLATION

Śrī Mādhavendra Purī did not eat anything throughout the day, but at night, after laying the Deity down to rest, he took a milk preparation.

TEXT 92

প্রাতঃকালে পুনঃ তৈছে করিল সেবন ।
অন্ন লঞা একগ্রামের আইল লোকগণ ॥ ৯২ ॥

prātaḥ-kāle punaḥ taiche karila sevana
anna lañā eka-grāmera āila loka-gaṇa

SYNONYMS

prātaḥ-kāle—in the morning; *punaḥ*—again; *taiche*—just as before; *karila*—rendered; *sevana*—service; *anna lañā*—with food grains; *eka-grāmera*—of one village; *āila*—came; *loka-gaṇa*—the people.

TRANSLATION

The next morning, the rendering of service to the Deity began again, and people from one village arrived with all kinds of food grains.

TEXT 93

অন্ন, ঘৃত, দধি, দুগ্ধ,—গ্রামে যত ছিল ।
গোপালের আগে লোক আনিয়া ধরিল ॥ ৯৩ ॥

anna, ghṛta, dadhi, dugdha,——grāme yata chila
gopālera āge loka āniyā dharila

SYNONYMS

anna—food grain; *ghṛta*—ghee, or clarified butter; *dadhi*—yogurt; *dugdha*—milk; *grāme*—in the village; *yata*—as much; *chila*—as there was; *gopālera āge*—before the Deity Gopāla; *loka*—all people; *āniyā*—bringing; *dharila*—placed.

TRANSLATION

The inhabitants of the village brought to the Deity of Gopāla as much food grains, ghee, yogurt and milk as they had in their village.

PURPORT

Anna, ghṛta, dadhi and *dugdha* are food grains, ghee, yogurt and milk. Actually these are the basis of all food. Vegetables and fruits are subsidiary. Hundreds and thousands of recipes can be made out of grains, vegetables, ghee, milk and yogurt. The food offered to Gopāla in the Annakūṭa ceremony contained only these five ingredients. Only demoniac people are attracted to other types of food, which we will not even mention in this connection. We should understand that in order to prepare nutritious food, we require only grains, ghee, yogurt and milk. We cannot offer anything else to the Deity. The Vaiṣṇava, the perfect human being, does not accept anything not offered to the Deity. People are often frustrated with national food policies, but from the Vedic scriptures we find that if there are sufficient cows and grains, the entire food problem is solved. The *vaiśyas* (people engaged in agriculture and commerce) are therefore recommended in *Bhagavad-gītā* to produce grains and give protection to cows. Cows are the most important animal because they produce the miracle food, milk, from which we can prepare ghee and yogurt.

The perfection of human civilization depends on Kṛṣṇa consciousness, which recommends Deity worship. Preparations made from vegetables, grains, milk, ghee and yogurt are offered to the Deity and then distributed. Here we can see the difference between the East and the West. The people who came to see the Deity of Gopāla brought all kinds of food to offer the Deity. They brought all the food they had in stock, and they came before the Deity not only to accept *prasāda* for themselves, but to distribute it to others. The Kṛṣṇa consciousness movement vigorously approves this practice of preparing food, offering it to the Deity, and distributing it to the general population. This activity should be extended universally to stop sinful eating habits as well as other behavior befitting only demons. A demoniac civilization will never bring peace within the world. Since eating is the first necessity in human society, those engaged in solving the problems of preparing and distributing food should take lessons from Mādhavendra Purī and execute the Annakūṭa ceremony. When the people take to eating only *prasāda* offered to the Deity, all the demons will be turned into Vaiṣṇavas. When the people are Kṛṣṇa conscious, naturally the government will be so also. A

Kṛṣṇa conscious man is always a very liberal well-wisher of everyone. When such men head the government, the people will certainly be sinless. They will no longer be disturbing demons. It is then and then only that a peaceful condition can prevail in society.

TEXT 94

পূর্বদিন-প্রায় বিপ্র করিল রন্ধন ।
তৈছে অন্নকূট গোপাল করিল ভোজন ॥ ৯৪ ॥

pūrva-dina-prāya vipra karila randhana
taiche anna-kūṭa gopāla karila bhojana

SYNONYMS

pūrva-dina-prāya—almost like the previous day; *vipra*—all the *brāhmaṇas; karila*—did; *randhana*—cooking; *taiche*—similarly; *anna-kūṭa*—heaps of food; *gopāla*—the Deity of Lord Gopāla; *karila*—did; *bhojana*—eating.

TRANSLATION

The next day, almost like before, there was an Annakūṭa ceremony. All the brāhmaṇas prepared foodstuffs and Gopāla accepted them.

TEXT 95

ব্রজবাসী লোকের কৃষ্ণে সহজ পিরীতি ।
গোপালের সহজ-প্রীতি ব্রজবাসি-প্রতি ॥ ৯৫ ॥

vraja-vāsī lokera kṛṣṇe sahaja pirīti
gopālera sahaja-prīti vraja-vāsi-prati

SYNONYMS

vraja-vāsī—the inhabitants of Vṛndāvana (Vrajabhūmi); *lokera*—of the people; *kṛṣṇe*—unto Lord Kṛṣṇa; *sahaja*—natural; *pirīti*—love; *gopālera*—of Lord Gopāla; *sahaja*—natural; *prīti*—love; *vraja-vāsi-prati*—toward the inhabitants of Vrajabhūmi.

TRANSLATION

The ideal place to execute Kṛṣṇa consciousness is Vrajabhūmi, or Vṛndāvana, where the people are naturally inclined to love Kṛṣṇa and Kṛṣṇa is naturally inclined to love them.

PURPORT

In *Bhagavad-gītā* it is said: *ye yathā māṁ prapadyante tāṁs tathaiva bhajāmy aham.* There is a responsive cooperation between the Supreme Lord Kṛṣṇa and His devotees. The more a devotee sincerely loves Kṛṣṇa, the more Kṛṣṇa reciprocates, so much so that a highly advanced devotee can talk with Kṛṣṇa face to face. Kṛṣṇa confirms this in *Bhagavad-gītā:*

teṣāṁ satata-yuktānāṁ
bhajatāṁ prīti-pūrvakam
dadāmi buddhi-yogaṁ taṁ
yena mām upayānti te

"To those who are constantly devoted and worship Me with love, I give the understanding by which they can come to Me." (Bg. 10.10) The actual mission of human life is to understand Kṛṣṇa and return home, back to Godhead. Therefore one who is sincerely engaged in the service of the Lord with love and faith can talk with Kṛṣṇa and receive instructions by which he can speedily return home, back to Godhead. Today many scholars defend the science of religion, and they have some conception of the Supreme Personality of Godhead, but religion without practical experience of the Supreme Personality of Godhead is no religion at all. *Śrīmad-Bhāgavatam* describes this as a form of cheating. Religion means abiding by the orders of Kṛṣṇa, the Supreme Personality of Godhead. If one is not qualified to talk with Him and take lessons from Him, how can one understand the principles of religion? Thus talks of religion or religious experience without Kṛṣṇa consciousness are a useless waste of time.

TEXT 96

মহাপ্রসাদ খাইল আসিয়া সব লোক ।
গোপাল দেখিয়া সবার খণ্ডে দুঃখ-শোক ॥ ৯৬ ॥

mahā-prasāda khāila āsiyā saba loka
gopāla dekhiyā sabāra khaṇḍe duḥkha-śoka

SYNONYMS

mahā-prasāda—spiritualized foods offered to Kṛṣṇa; *khāila*—ate; *āsiyā*—coming; *saba*—all; *loka*—people; *gopāla*—the Deity of Śrī Gopāla; *dekhiyā*—seeing; *sabāra*—of all of them; *khaṇḍe*—disappears; *duḥkha-śoka*—all lamentation and unhappiness.

TRANSLATION

Throngs of people came from different villages to see the Deity of Gopāla, and they took mahā-prasāda sumptuously. When they saw the superexcellent form of Lord Gopāla, all their lamentation and unhappiness disappeared.

TEXT 97

আশ-পাশ ব্রজভূমের যত গ্রাম সব ।
এক এক দিন সবে করে মহোৎসব ॥ ৯৭ ॥

āśa-pāśa vraja-bhūmera yata grāma saba
eka eka dina sabe kare mahotsava

SYNONYMS

āśa-pāśa—neighboring; *vraja-bhūmera*—of Vrajabhūmi; *yata*—all; *grāma*—villages; *saba*—all; *eka eka*—one after another; *dina*—days; *sabe*—all; *kare*—perform; *mahotsava*—festivals.

TRANSLATION

All the villages in neighboring Vrajabhūmi [Vṛndāvana] became aware of the appearance of Gopāla, and all the people from these villages came to see Him. Day after day they all performed the Annakūṭa ceremony.

TEXT 98

গোপাল-প্রকট শুনি' নানা দেশ হৈতে ।
নানা দ্রব্য লঞা লোক লাগিল আসিতে ॥ ৯৮ ॥

gopāla-prakaṭa śuni' nānā deśa haite
nānā dravya lañā loka lāgila āsite

SYNONYMS

gopāla—of the Deity of Gopāla; *prakaṭa*—appearance; *śuni'*—hearing; *nānā*—various; *deśa*—countries; *haite*—from; *nānā*—various; *dravya*—things; *lañā*—bringing; *loka*—people; *lāgila*—began; *āsite*—to come.

TRANSLATION

In this way not only the neighboring villages but all the other provinces came to know of Gopāla's appearance. Thus people came from all over, bringing a variety of presentations.

TEXT 99

মথুরার লোক সব বড় বড় ধনী ।
ভক্তি করি' নানা দ্রব্য ভেট দেয় আনি' ॥ ৯৯ ॥

mathurāra loka saba baḍa baḍa dhanī
bhakti kari' nānā dravya bheṭa deya āni'

SYNONYMS

mathurāra—of the city of Mathurā; *loka*—the people; *saba*—all; *baḍa baḍa*—very big; *dhanī*—capitalists; *bhakti kari'*—out of devotion; *nānā dravya*—various kinds of things; *bheṭa*—presents; *deya*—gave; *āni'*—bringing.

TRANSLATION

The people of Mathurā, who are very big capitalists, also brought various presentations and offered them before the Deity in devotional service.

TEXT 100

স্বর্ণ, রৌপ্য, বস্ত্র, গন্ধ, ভক্ষ্য-উপহার ।
অসংখ্য আইসে, নিত্য বাড়িল ভাণ্ডার ॥ ১০০ ॥

svarṇa, raupya, vastra, gandha, bhakṣya-upahāra
asaṅkhya āise, nitya bāḍila bhāṇḍāra

SYNONYMS

svarṇa—gold; *raupya*—silver; *vastra*—garments; *gandha*—scents; *bhakṣya-upahāra*—presentations for eating; *asaṅkhya*—countless; *āise*—came; *nitya*—daily; *bāḍila*—increased; *bhāṇḍāra*—the store.

TRANSLATION

Thus countless presentations of gold, silver, garments, scented articles and eatables arrived. The store of Gopāla increased daily.

TEXT 101

এক মহাধনী ক্ষত্রিয় করাইল মন্দির ।
কেহ পাক-ভাণ্ডার কৈল, কেহ ত' প্রাচীর ॥ ১০১ ॥

eka mahā-dhanī kṣatriya karāila mandira
keha pāka-bhāṇḍāra kaila, keha ta' prācīra

SYNONYMS

eka—one; *mahā-dhanī*—very rich man; *kṣatriya*—of the royal order; *karāila*—constructed; *mandira*—a temple; *keha*—someone; *pāka-bhāṇḍāra*—clay pots for cooking; *kaila*—made; *keha*—someone; *ta'*—certainly; *prācīra*—the boundary walls.

TRANSLATION

One very rich kṣatriya of the royal order constructed a temple, someone made cooking utensils, and someone constructed boundary walls.

TEXT 102

এক এক ব্রজবাসী এক এক গাভী দিল ।
সহস্র সহস্র গাভী গোপালের হৈল ॥ ১০২ ॥

eka eka vraja-vāsī eka eka gābhī dila
sahasra sahasra gābhī gopālera haila

SYNONYMS

eka eka—each and every; *vraja-vāsī*—resident of Vṛndāvana; *eka eka*—one; *gābhī*—cow; *dila*—contributed; *sahasra sahasra*—thousands and thousands; *gābhī*—cows; *gopālera*—of Gopāla; *haila*—there were.

TRANSLATION

Each and every family residing in the land of Vrajabhūmi contributed one cow. In this way, thousands of cows became the property of Gopāla.

PURPORT

This is the way to install the Deity, construct the temple and increase the property of the temple. Everyone should be enthusiastic to contribute to the construction of the temple for the Deity, and everyone should also contribute food for the distribution of *prasāda*. The devotees should preach the gospel of devotional service and thus engage people in practical service to the Deity. Wealthy people can also be attracted to take part in these activities. In this way everyone will become spiritually inclined, and the entire society will be converted to Kṛṣṇa consciousness. The desire to satisfy the material senses will automatically diminish, and the senses will become so purified that they will be able to engage in *bhakti* (devotional service to the Lord). *Hṛṣīkeṇa hṛṣīkeśa-sevanaṁ bhaktir ucyate.* By serving the Lord, one's senses are gradually purified. The engagement of one's purified senses in the service of Lord Hṛṣīkeśa is called *bhakti*. When the dormant propensity for *bhakti* is awakened, one can understand the Supreme Personality of Godhead as He is. *Bhaktyā mām abhijānāti yāvān yaś cāsmi tattvataḥ.* (Bg. 18.55) This is the process of giving humanity the chance to awaken Kṛṣṇa consciousness. Thus people can perfect their lives in all respects.

TEXT 103

গৌড় হইতে আইলা দুই বৈরাগী ব্রাহ্মণ।
পুরী-গোসাঞি রাখিল তারে করিয়া যতন ॥ ১০৩ ॥

gauḍa ha-ite āilā dui vairāgī brāhmaṇa
purī-gosāñi rākhila tāre kariyā yatana

SYNONYMS

gauḍa ha-ite—from Bengal; *āilā*—came; *dui*—two; *vairāgī*—of the renounced order; *brāhmaṇa*—persons born in *brāhmaṇa* families; *purī-gosāñi*—Mādhavendra Purī; *rākhila*—kept; *tāre*—them; *kariyā*—making; *yatana*—all efforts.

TRANSLATION

Eventually two brāhmaṇas in the renounced order arrived from Bengal, and Mādhavendra Purī, who liked them very much, kept them in Vṛndāvana and gave them all kinds of comforts.

TEXT 104

সেই দুই শিষ্য করি' সেবা সমর্পিল।
রাজ-সেবা হয়,—পুরীর আনন্দ বাড়িল ॥ ১০৪ ॥

sei dui śiṣya kari' sevā samarpila
rāja-sevā haya,——purīra ānanda bāḍila

SYNONYMS

sei dui—these two persons; *śiṣya kari'*—initiating; *sevā*—with the service; *samarpila*—entrusted; *rāja-sevā*—gorgeous performance of service; *haya*—is; *purīra*—of Mādhavendra Purī; *ānanda*—pleasure; *bāḍila*—increased.

TRANSLATION

These two were then initiated by Mādhavendra Purī, and he entrusted them with the daily service of the Lord. This service was performed continuously, and the worship of the Deity became very gorgeous. Thus Mādhavendra Purī was very pleased.

PURPORT

The Gosvāmīs started many temples, namely the Govinda temple, Gopīnātha, Madana-mohana, Rādhā-Dāmodara, Śyāmasundara, Rādhāramaṇa and Gokulānanda. The disciples of the Gosvāmīs were entrusted with the *sevā-pūjā* (Deity worship) of these temples. It was not that the disciples were family members of the original Gosvāmīs. Most of the Gosvāmīs were in the renounced order of life, and Jīva Gosvāmī in particular was a *brahmacārī*. At present, *sevāitas* assume the title of *gosvāmī* on the basis of their being engaged as *sevāitas* of the Deity. The *sevāitas* who have inherited their positions now assume proprietorship of the temples, and some of them are selling the Deities' property as if it were their own. However, the temples did not originally belong to these *sevāitas*.

TEXT 105

এইমত বৎসর দুই করিল সেবন ।
একদিন পুরী-গোসাঞি দেখিল স্বপন ॥ ১০৫ ॥

ei-mata vatsara dui karila sevana
eka-dina purī-gosāñi dekhila svapana

SYNONYMS

ei-mata—in this way; *vatsara*—years; *dui*—two; *karila*—performed; *sevana*—worship; *eka-dina*—one day; *purī-gosāñi*—Mādhavendra Purī; *dekhila*—saw; *svapana*—a dream.

TRANSLATION

In this way the Deity worship in the temple was very gorgeously performed for two years. Then one day Mādhavendra Purī had a dream.

TEXT 106

গোপাল কহে, পুরী আমার তাপ নাহি যায় ।
মলয়জ-চন্দন লেপ', তবে সে জুড়ায় ॥ ১০৬ ॥

gopāla kahe, purī āmāra tāpa nāhi yāya
malayaja-candana lepa', tabe se juḍāya

SYNONYMS

gopāla—the Deity of Gopāla; *kahe*—said; *purī*—My dear Mādhavendra Purī; *āmāra*—My; *tāpa*—body temperature; *nāhi*—does not; *yāya*—go away; *malaya-*

ja-candana—sandalwood produced in the Malaya Hills; *lepa'*—smear over the body; *tabe*—then; *se*—that; *juḍāya*—cools.

TRANSLATION

In his dream, Mādhavendra Purī saw Gopāla, who said: "My bodily temperature still has not decreased. Please bring sandalwood from the Malaya province and smear the pulp over My body to cool Me.

PURPORT

The Deity of Gopāla had been buried within the jungle for many years, and although He was installed and was offered thousands of pots of water, He still felt very hot. He therefore asked Mādhavendra Purī to bring sandalwood from the Malaya province. Sandalwood produced in Malaya is very popular. That province is situated on the western *ghāṭa,* and the hill Nīlagiri is sometimes known as Malaya Hill. The word *malaya-ja* is used to indicate the sandalwood produced in the Malaya Province. Sometimes the word Malaya refers to the modern country of Malaysia. Formerly this country also produced sandalwood, but now they have found it profitable to produce rubber trees. Although the Vedic culture was once prevalent in Malaysia, now all the inhabitants are Mohammedans. The Vedic culture is now lost in Malaysia, Java and Indonesia.

TEXT 107

মলয়জ আন, যাঞা নীলাচল হৈতে ।
অন্যে হৈতে নহে, তুমি চলহ ত্বরিতে ॥ ১০৭ ॥

malayaja āna, yāñā nīlācala haite
anye haite nahe, tumi calaha tvarite

SYNONYMS

malaya-ja—sandalwood; *āna*—bring; *yāñā*—coming; *nīlācala haite*—from Jagannātha Purī; *anye*—others; *haite*—from; *nahe*—not; *tumi*—you; *calaha*—go; *tvarite*—quickly.

TRANSLATION

"Bring sandalwood pulp from Jagannātha Purī. Kindly go quickly. Since no one else can do it, you must."

TEXT 108

স্বপ্ন দেখি' পুরী-গোসাঞির হৈল প্রেমাবেশ ।
প্রভু-আজ্ঞা পালিবারে গেলা পূর্বদেশ ॥ ১০৮ ॥

svapna dekhi' purī-gosāñira haila premāveśa
prabhu-ājñā pālibāre gelā pūrva-deśa

SYNONYMS

svapna dekhi'—after seeing the dream; *purī-gosāñira*—of Mādhavendra Purī; *haila*—there was; *prema-āveśa*—ecstasy on account of love of God; *prabhu-ājñā*—the order of the Lord; *pālibāre*—to execute; *gelā*—started; *pūrva-deśa*—for the eastern countries (Bengal).

TRANSLATION

After having this dream, Mādhavendra Purī Gosvāmī became very glad due to ecstasy of love of Godhead, and in order to execute the command of the Lord, he started east toward Bengal.

TEXT 109

সেবার নির্বন্ধ—লোক করিল স্থাপন ।
আজ্ঞা মাগি' গৌড়-দেশে করিল গমন ॥ ১০৯ ॥

sevāra nirbandha——loka karila sthāpana
ājñā māgi' gauḍa-deśe karila gamana

SYNONYMS

sevāra nirbandha—the arrangements for executing the daily routine of the worship of the Lord; *loka*—the people; *karila*—did; *sthāpana*—establish; *ājñā māgi'*—taking the order; *gauḍa-deśe*—toward Bengal; *karila*—did; *gamana*—going.

TRANSLATION

Before leaving, Mādhavendra Purī made all arrangements for regular Deity worship, and he engaged different people in various duties. Then, taking up the order of Gopāla, he started for Bengal.

TEXT 110

শান্তিপুর আইলা অদ্বৈতাচার্যের ঘরে ।
পুরীর প্রেম দেখি' আচার্য আনন্দ অন্তরে ॥ ১১০ ॥

śāntipura āilā advaitācāryera ghare
purīra prema dekhi' ācārya ānanda antare

SYNONYMS

śānti-pura—to the place known as Śāntipura; *āilā*—came; *advaita-ācāryera*—of Śrī Advaita Ācārya; *ghare*—to the home; *purīra prema*—the ecstatic love of Mādhavendra Purī; *dekhi'*—seeing; *ācārya*—Advaita Ācārya; *ānanda*—pleased; *antare*—within Himself.

TRANSLATION

When Mādhavendra Purī arrived at the house of Advaita Ācārya in Śāntipura, the Ācārya became very pleased upon seeing the ecstatic love of Godhead manifest in Mādhavendra Purī.

TEXT 111

তাঁর ঠাঞি মন্ত্র লৈল যতন করিঞা ।
চলিলা দক্ষিণে পুরী তাঁরে দীক্ষা দিঞা ॥ ১১১ ॥

tāṅra ṭhāñi mantra laila yatana kariñā
calilā dakṣiṇe purī tāṅre dīkṣā diñā

SYNONYMS

tāṅra ṭhāñi—from him; *mantra*—initiation; *laila*—accepted; *yatana*—efforts; *kariñā*—making; *calilā*—started; *dakṣiṇe*—toward the south; *purī*—Mādhavendra Purī; *tāṅre*—to Him (Advaita Ācārya); *dīkṣā*—initiation; *diñā*—giving.

TRANSLATION

Advaita Ācārya begged to be initiated by Mādhavendra Purī. After initiating Him, Mādhavendra Purī started for South India.

PURPORT

In this connection, Śrīla Bhaktisiddhānta Sarasvatī Ṭhākura comments that Advaita Ācārya took initiation from Mādhavendra Purī, who was a *sannyāsī* in the disciplic succession of the Madhva-sampradāya. According to Śrī Caitanya Mahāprabhu:

kibā vipra kibā nyāsī śūdra kene naya,
yei kṛṣṇa-tattva-vettā, sei 'guru' haya

"A person may be a *brāhmaṇa, sannyāsī,* a *śūdra* or whatever, but if he is well conversant in the science of Kṛṣṇa, he can become a *guru.*" (Cc. *Madhya* 8.128) This statement is supported by Śrī Mādhavendra Purī. According to the *pañcarātra* injunction, only a householder *brāhmaṇa* can initiate. Others cannot. When a person is initiated, it is assumed that he has become a *brāhmaṇa;* without being initiated by a proper *brāhmaṇa,* one cannot be converted into a *brāhmaṇa.* In other words, unless one is a *brāhmaṇa,* he cannot make another a *brāhmaṇa.* A *gṛhastha-brāhmaṇa* partaking of the *varṇāśrama-dharma* institution can secure various types of paraphernalia to worship Lord Viṣṇu through his honest labor. Actually, people beg to be initiated by these householder *brāhmaṇas* just to become successful in the *varṇāśrama* institution or to become free from material desires. It is therefore necessary for a spiritual master in the *gṛhastha-āśrama* to be a strict Vaiṣṇava. A spiritual master from the *sannyāsa* order has very little opportunity to perform *arcana,* Deity worship, but when one accepts a spiritual master from the transcendental *sannyāsīs,* the principle of Deity worship is not at all neglected. To implement this conclusion, Śrī Caitanya Mahāprabhu gave us His opinion in the verse *kibā vipra kibā nyāsī,* etc. This indicates that the Lord understood the weakness of society in its maintaining that only a *gṛhastha-brāhmaṇa* should be a spiritual master. Śrī Caitanya Mahāprabhu indicated that it does not matter whether the spiritual master is a *gṛhastha* (householder), a *sannyāsī* or even a *śūdra.* A spiritual master simply must be conversant in the essence of the *śāstra;* he must understand the Supreme Personality of Godhead. Only then can one become a spiritual master. *Dīkṣā* actually means initiating a disciple with transcendental knowledge by which he becomes freed from all material contamination.

TEXT 112

রেমুণাতে কৈল গোপীনাথ দরশন ।
তাঁর রূপ দেখিঞা হৈল বিহ্বল-মন ॥ ১১২ ॥

remuṇāte kaila gopīnātha daraśana
tāṅra rūpa dekhiñā haila vihvala-mana

SYNONYMS

remuṇāte—in the village of Remuṇā; *kaila*—did; *gopīnātha*—the Deity of Gopīnātha; *daraśana*—seeing; *tāṅra*—His; *rūpa*—beauty; *dekhiñā*—seeing; *haila*—became; *vihvala*—bewildered; *mana*—mind.

TRANSLATION

Going into South India, Śrī Mādhavendra Purī visited Remuṇā, where Gopīnātha is situated. Upon seeing the beauty of the Deity, Mādhavendra Purī was overwhelmed.

TEXT 113

'নৃত্যগীত করি' জগমোহনে বসিলা ।
'ক্যা ক্যা ভোগ লাগে ?' ব্রাহ্মণে পুছিলা ॥ ১১৩ ॥

nṛtya-gīta kari' jaga-mohane vasilā
'kyā kyā bhoga lāge?' brāhmaṇe puchilā

SYNONYMS

nṛtya-gīta kari'—after performing dancing and chanting; *jaga-mohane*—in the corridor of the temple; *vasilā*—he sat down; *kyā kyā*—what; *bhoga*—foods; *lāge*—they offer; *brāhmaṇe*—from the *brāhmaṇa* priest; *puchilā*—inquired.

TRANSLATION

In the corridor of the temple, from which people generally viewed the Deity, Mādhavendra Purī chanted and danced. Then he sat down there and asked a brāhmaṇa what kinds of foods they offered to the Deity.

TEXT 114

সেবার সৌষ্ঠব দেখি' আনন্দিত মনে ।
উত্তম ভোগ লাগে—এথা বুঝি অনুমানে ॥ ১১৪ ॥

sevāra sauṣṭhava dekhi' ānandita mane
uttama bhoga lāge——ethā bujhi anumāne

SYNONYMS

sevāra—of the worship; *sauṣṭhava*—excellence; *dekhi'*—seeing; *ānandita*—pleased; *mane*—in the mind; *uttama bhoga*—first-class foods; *lāge*—they offer; *ethā*—thus; *bujhi*—I understand; *anumāne*—by deduction.

TRANSLATION

From the excellence of the arrangements, Mādhavendra Purī understood by deduction that only the best food was offered.

TEXT 115

যৈছে ইহা ভোগ লাগে, সকলই পুছিব ।
তৈছে ভিয়ানে ভোগ গোপালে লাগাইব ॥ ১১৫ ॥

yaiche ihā bhoga lāge, sakala-i puchiba
taiche bhiyāne bhoga gopāle lāgāiba

SYNONYMS

yaiche—just like; *ihā*—here; *bhoga*—foods; *lāge*—they offer; *sakala-i*—all; *puchiba*—I shall inquire; *taiche*—similarly; *bhiyāne*—in the kitchen; *bhoga*—foods; *gopāle*—to Śrī Gopāla; *lāgāiba*—I shall arrange.

TRANSLATION

Mādhavendra Purī thought: "I shall inquire from the priest what foods are offered to Gopīnātha so that by making arrangements in our kitchen, we can offer similar foods to Śrī Gopāla."

TEXT 116

এই লাগি' পুছিলেন ব্রাহ্মণের স্থানে ।
ব্রাহ্মণ কহিল সব ভোগ-বিবরণে ॥ ১১৬ ॥

ei lāgi' puchilena brāhmaṇera sthāne
brāhmaṇa kahila saba bhoga-vivaraṇe

SYNONYMS

ei lāgi'—for this matter; *puchilena*—he inquired; *brāhmaṇera sthāne*—from the *brāhmaṇa; brāhmaṇa*—the priest; *kahila*—informed; *saba*—everything; *bhoga*—foods; *vivaraṇe*—in description.

TRANSLATION

When the brāhmaṇa priest was questioned in this matter, he explained in detail what kinds of foods were offered to the Deity of Gopīnātha.

TEXT 117

সন্ধ্যায় ভোগ লাগে ক্ষীর—'অমৃতকেলি'-নাম ।
দ্বাদশ মৃৎপাত্রে ভরি' অমৃত-সমান ॥ ১১৭ ॥

sandhyāya bhoga lāge kṣīra——'amṛta-keli'-nāma
dvādaśa mṛt-pātre bhari' amṛta-samāna

SYNONYMS

sandhyāya—in the evening; *bhoga*—foods; *lāge*—they offer; *kṣīra*—sweet rice; *amṛta-keli-nāma*—named *amṛta-keli; dvādaśa*—twelve; *mṛt-pātre*—earthen pots; *bhari'*—filling; *amṛta-samāna*—just like nectar.

TRANSLATION

The brāhmaṇa priest said: "In the evening the Deity is offered sweet rice in twelve earthen pots. Because the taste is as good as nectar [amṛta], it is named amṛta-keli.

TEXT 118

'গোপীনাথের ক্ষীর' বলি' প্রসিদ্ধ নাম যার ।
পৃথিবীতে ঐছে ভোগ কাহাঁ নাহি আর ॥ ১১৮ ॥

'gopīnāthera kṣīra' bali' prasiddha nāma yāra
pṛthivīte aiche bhoga kāhāṅ nāhi āra

SYNONYMS

gopīnāthera kṣīra—the sweet rice offered to Gopīnātha; *bali'*—as; *prasiddha*—celebrated; *nāma*—the name; *yāra*—of which; *pṛthivīte*—throughout the whole world; *aiche*—such; *bhoga*—food; *kāhāṅ*—anywhere; *nāhi*—not; *āra*—else.

TRANSLATION

"This sweet rice is celebrated throughout the world as gopīnātha-kṣīra. It is not offered anywhere else in the world."

TEXT 119

হেনকালে সেই ভোগ ঠাকুরে লাগিল ।
শুনি' পুরী-গোসাঞি কিছু মনে বিচারিল ॥ ১১৯ ॥

hena-kāle sei bhoga ṭhākure lāgila
śuni' purī-gosāñi kichu mane vicārila

SYNONYMS

hena-kāle—at this time; *sei bhoga*—that wonderful food; *ṭhākure*—in front of the Deity; *lāgila*—was placed; *śuni'*—hearing; *purī-gosāñi*—Mādhavendra Purī; *kichu*—something; *mane*—within the mind; *vicārila*—considered.

TRANSLATION

While Mādhavendra Purī was talking with the brāhmaṇa priest, the sweet rice was placed before the Deity as an offering. Hearing this, Mādhavendra Purī thought as follows.

TEXT 120

অযাচিত ক্ষীর প্রসাদ অল্প যদি পাই ।
স্বাদ জানি' তৈছে ক্ষীর গোপালে লাগাই ॥ ১২০ ॥

ayācita kṣīra prasāda alpa yadi pāi
svāda jāni' taiche kṣīra gopāle lāgāi

SYNONYMS

ayācita—without asking; *kṣīra*—sweet rice; *prasāda*—remnants of food; *alpa*—a little; *yadi*—if; *pāi*—I get; *svāda*—the taste; *jāni'*—knowing; *taiche*—similar; *kṣīra*—sweet rice; *gopāle*—to my Gopāla; *lāgāi*—I can offer.

TRANSLATION

"If, without my asking, a little sweet rice is given to me, I can then taste it and make a similar preparation to offer my Lord Gopāla."

TEXT 121

এই ইচ্ছায় লজ্জা পাঞা বিষ্ণুস্মরণ কৈল ।
হেনকালে ভোগ সরি' আরতি বাজিল ॥ ১২১ ॥

ei icchāya lajjā pāñā viṣṇu-smaraṇa kaila
hena-kāle bhoga sari' ārati bājila

SYNONYMS

ei icchāya—by this desire; *lajjā*—shame; *pāñā*—getting; *viṣṇu-smaraṇa*—remembrance of Lord Viṣṇu; *kaila*—did; *hena-kāle*—at that time; *bhoga*—the food; *sari'*—being finished; *ārati*—the *ārati* ceremony; *bājila*—was sounded.

TRANSLATION

Mādhavendra Purī became greatly ashamed when he desired to taste the sweet rice, and he immediately began to think of Lord Viṣṇu. While he was thus thinking of Lord Viṣṇu, the offering was completed, and the ārati ceremony began.

TEXT 122

আরতি দেখিয়া পুরী কৈল নমস্কার ।
বাহিরে আইলা, কারে কিছু না কহিল আর ॥ ১২২॥

ārati dekhiyā purī kaila namaskāra
bāhire āilā, kāre kichu nā kahila āra

SYNONYMS

ārati dekhiyā—after seeing the *ārati; purī*—Mādhavendra Purī; *kaila*—offered; *namaskāra*—obeisances; *bāhire āilā*—he went out; *kāre*—to anyone; *kichu*—anything; *nā*—not; *kahila*—say; *āra*—more.

TRANSLATION

After the ārati was finished, Mādhavendra Purī offered his obeisances to the Deity and then left the temple. He did not say anything more to anyone.

TEXT 123

অযাচিত-বৃত্তি পুরী—বিরক্ত, উদাস ।
অযাচিত পাইলে খা'ন, নহে উপবাস ॥ ১২৩ ॥

ayācita-vṛtti purī——virakta, udāsa
ayācita pāile khā'na, nahe upavāsa

SYNONYMS

ayācita-vṛtti—accustomed to avoid begging; *purī*—Mādhavendra Purī; *virakta*—unattached; *udāsa*—indifferent; *ayācita*—without begging; *pāile*—if getting; *khā'na*—he eats; *nahe*—if not; *upavāsa*—fasting.

TRANSLATION

Mādhavendra Purī avoided begging. He was completely unattached and indifferent to material things. He would not beg. If someone offered him some food, he would eat; otherwise he would fast.

PURPORT

This is the *paramahaṁsa* stage, the highest stage for a *sannyāsī.* A *sannyāsī* can beg from door to door just to collect food, but a *paramahaṁsa* who has taken *ayācita-vṛtti,* or *ajagara-vṛtti,* does not ask anyone for food. If someone offers him food voluntarily, he eats. *Ayācita-vṛtti* means being accustomed to refrain from begging, and *ajagara-vṛtti* indicates one who is compared to a python, the big snake that makes no effort to acquire food, but rather allows food to come automatically within its mouth. In other words, a *paramahaṁsa* simply engages exclusively in the service of the Lord, without caring even for eating or sleeping. It was stated about the six Gosvāmīs: *nidrāhāra-vihārakādi-vijitau.* In the *paramahaṁsa* stage one conquers the desire for sleep, food and sense gratification. One remains a humble, meek mendicant engaged in the service of the Lord day and night. Mādhavendra Purī had attained this *paramahaṁsa* stage.

TEXT 124

প্রেমামৃতে তৃপ্ত, ক্ষুধাতৃষ্ণা নাহি বাধে।
ক্ষীর-ইচ্ছা হৈল, তাহে মানে অপরাধে ॥ ১২৪ ॥

premāmṛte tṛpta, kṣudhā-tṛṣṇā nāhi bādhe
kṣīra-icchā haila, tāhe māne aparādhe

SYNONYMS

prema-amṛte tṛpta—being satisfied only in the loving service of the Lord; *kṣudhā-tṛṣṇā*—hunger and thirst; *nāhi*—not; *bādhe*—impede; *kṣīra*—for sweet rice; *icchā*—the desire; *haila*—became; *tāhe*—for that reason; *māne*—he considers; *aparādhe*—offense.

TRANSLATION

A paramahaṁsa like Mādhavendra Purī is always satisfied in the loving service of the Lord. Material hunger and thirst cannot impede his activities. When he desired to taste a little sweet rice offered to the Deity, he considered that he had committed an offense by desiring to eat what was being offered to the Deity.

PURPORT

It is advisable that food being offered to the Deity be covered when taken from the kitchen to the Deity room. In that way, others may not see it. Those who are not accustomed to following the advanced regulative devotional principles may desire to eat the food, and that is an offense. Therefore no one should be given a chance to even see it. However, when it is brought before the Deity, it must be uncovered. Seeing the food uncovered before the Deity, Mādhavendra Purī desired to taste a little of it so that he could prepare a similar sweet rice for his Gopāla. Mādhavendra Purī was so strict, however, that he considered this to be an offense. Consequently he left the temple without saying anything to anyone. The *paramahaṁsa* is therefore called *vijita-ṣaḍ-guṇa*. He must conquer the six material qualities—*kāma, krodha, lobha, moha, matsara,* and *kṣudhā-tṛṣṇā* (lust, anger, greed, illusion, enviousness, hunger and thirst.)

TEXT 125

গ্রামের শূন্যহাটে বসি' করেন কীর্তন।
এথা পূজারী করাইল ঠাকুরে শয়ন ॥ ১২৫ ॥

grāmera śūnya-hāṭe vasi' karena kīrtana
ethā pūjārī karāila ṭhākure śayana

SYNONYMS

grāmera—of the village; *śūnya-hāṭe*—in the vacant marketplace; *vasi'*—sitting down; *karena*—performs; *kīrtana*—chanting; *ethā*—in the temple; *pūjārī*—the priest; *karāila*—made; *ṭhākure*—the Deities; *śayana*—lying down.

TRANSLATION

Mādhavendra Purī left the temple and sat down in the village marketplace, which was vacant. Sitting there, he began to chant. In the meantime, the temple priest laid the Deity down to rest.

PURPORT

Although Mādhavendra Purī was not interested in eating and sleeping, his interest in chanting the *mahā-mantra* was as acute as if he were an aspiring transcendentalist rather than a *paramahaṁsa.* This means that even in the *paramahaṁsa* stage, one cannot give up chanting. Haridāsa Ṭhākura and the Gosvāmīs were all engaged in chanting a fixed number of rounds; therefore chanting on beads is very important for everyone, even though one may become a *paramahaṁsa.* This chanting can be executed anywhere, either inside or outside the temple. Mādhavendra Purī even sat down in a vacant marketplace to perform his chanting. As stated by Śrīnivāsa Ācārya in his prayers to the Gosvāmīs: *nāma-gāna-natibhiḥ.* A *paramahaṁsa* devotee is always engaged in chanting and rendering loving service to the Lord. Chanting the Lord's holy names and engaging in His service are identical. As stated in *Śrīmad-Bhāgavatam* (7.5.23), there are nine kinds of devotional service: hearing (*śravaṇam*), chanting (*kīrtanam*), remembering (*viṣṇoḥ smaraṇam*), serving (*pāda-sevanam*), worship of the Deity (*arcanam*), praying (*vandanam*), carrying out orders (*dāsyam*), serving Him as a friend (*sakhyam*), and sacrificing everything for the Lord (*ātma-nivedanam*). Although each process appears distinct, when one is situated on the absolute platform he can see that they are identical. For instance, hearing is as good as chanting, and remembering is as good as chanting or hearing. Similarly, engaging in Deity worship is as good as chanting, hearing or remembering. The devotee is expected to accept all nine processes of devotional service, but even if only one process is properly executed, he can still attain the highest position (*paramahaṁsa*) and go back home, back to Godhead.

TEXT 126

নিজ কৃত্য করি' পূজারী করিল শয়ন ।
স্বপনে ঠাকুর আসি' বলিলা বচন ॥ ১২৬ ॥

nija kṛtya kari' pūjārī karila śayana
svapane ṭhākura āsi' balilā vacana

SYNONYMS

nija kṛtya—his own duty; *kari'*—finishing; *pūjārī*—the *brāhmaṇa* priest in the temple; *karila*—took; *śayana*—rest; *svapane*—in a dream; *ṭhākura*—the Deity; *āsi'*—coming there; *balilā*—said; *vacana*—the words.

TRANSLATION

Finishing his daily duties, the priest went to take rest. In a dream he saw the Gopīnātha Deity come to talk to him, and He spoke as follows.

TEXT 127

উঠহ, পূজারী, কর দ্বার বিমোচন ।
ক্ষীর এক রাখিয়াছি সন্ন্যাসি-কারণ ॥ ১২৭ ॥

uṭhaha, pūjārī, kara dvāra vimocana
kṣīra eka rākhiyāchi sannyāsi-kāraṇa

SYNONYMS

uṭhaha—please get up; *pūjārī*—O priest; *kara*—just do; *dvāra*—the door; *vimocana*—opening; *kṣīra*—sweet rice; *eka*—one pot; *rākhiyāchi*—I have kept; *sannyāsi*—of the mendicant, Mādhavendra Purī; *kāraṇa*—for the reason.

TRANSLATION

"Please get up and open the door of the temple. I have kept one pot of sweet rice for the sannyāsī Mādhavendra Purī.

TEXT 128

ধড়ার অঞ্চলে ঢাকা এক ক্ষীর হয় ।
তোমরা না জানিলা তাহা আমার মায়ায় ॥ ১২৮ ॥

dhaḍāra añcale ḍhākā eka kṣīra haya
tomarā nā jānilā tāhā āmāra māyāya

SYNONYMS

dhaḍāra—of the cloth curtain; *añcale*—by the skirt; *ḍhākā*—covered; *eka*—one; *kṣīra*—pot of sweet rice; *haya*—there is; *tomarā*—you; *nā*—not; *jānilā*—knew; *tāhā*—that; *āmāra*—of Me; *māyāya*—by the trick.

TRANSLATION

"This pot of sweet rice is just behind My cloth curtain. You did not see it because of My tricks.

TEXT 129

মাধব-পুরী সন্ন্যাসী আছে হাটেতে বসিঞা ।
তাহাকে ত' এই ক্ষীর শীঘ্র দেহ লঞা ॥ ১২৯ ॥

mādhava-purī sannyāsī āche hāṭete vasiñā
tāhāke ta' ei kṣīra śīghra deha lañā

SYNONYMS

mādhava-purī—of the name Mādhavendra Purī; *sannyāsī*—a mendicant; *āche*—there is; *hāṭete*—in the marketplace; *vasiñā*—sitting; *tāhāke*—to him; *ta'*—certainly; *ei*—this; *kṣīra*—pot of sweet rice; *śīghra*—very quickly; *deha*—give; *lañā*—taking.

TRANSLATION

"A sannyāsī named Mādhavendra Purī is sitting in the vacant marketplace. Please take this pot of sweet rice from behind Me and deliver it to him."

TEXT 130

স্বপ্ন দেখি' পূজারী উঠি' করিলা বিচার ।
স্নান করি' কপাট খুলি, মুক্ত কৈল দ্বার ॥ ১৩০ ॥

svapna dekhi' pūjārī uṭhi' karilā vicāra
snāna kari' kapāṭa khuli, mukta kaila dvāra

SYNONYMS

svapna dekhi'—after seeing the dream; *pūjārī*—the priest; *uṭhi'*—getting up; *karilā*—made; *vicāra*—considerations; *snāna kari'*—taking his bath before entering the Deity room; *kapāṭa*—the door; *khuli*—opening; *mukta*—opened; *kaila*—made; *dvāra*—the doors.

TRANSLATION

Awaking from the dream, the priest immediately rose from bed and thought it wise to take a bath before entering the Deity's room. He then opened the temple door.

TEXT 131

**ধড়ার আঁচলতলে পাইল সেই ক্ষীর ।
স্থান লেপি' ক্ষীর লঞা হইল বাহির ॥ ১৩১ ॥**

*dhaḍāra āṅcala-tale pāila sei kṣīra
sthāna lepi' kṣīra lañā ha-ila bāhira*

SYNONYMS

dhaḍāra—of the mantle; *āṅcala-tale*—at the skirt; *pāila*—he got; *sei*—that; *kṣīra*—pot of sweet rice; *sthāna lepi'*—mopping that place; *kṣīra*—the pot of sweet rice; *lañā*—taking; *ha-ila*—he went; *bāhira*—out of the temple.

TRANSLATION

According to the Deity's directions, the priest found the pot of sweet rice behind the cloth curtain. He removed the pot and mopped up the place where it had been kept. He then went out of the temple.

TEXT 132

**দ্বার দিয়া গ্রামে গেলা সেই ক্ষীর লঞা ।
হাটে হাটে বুলে মাধবপুরীকে চাহিঞা ॥ ১৩২ ॥**

*dvāra diyā grāme gelā sei kṣīra lañā
hāṭe hāṭe bule mādhava-purīke cāhiñā*

SYNONYMS

dvāra diyā—closing the door; *grāme*—to the village; *gelā*—went; *sei*—that; *kṣīra*—pot of sweet rice; *lañā*—taking; *hāṭe hāṭe*—in every stall; *bule*— walks; *mādhava-purīke*—to Mādhavendra Purī; *cāhiñā*—calling.

TRANSLATION

Closing the door of the temple, he went to the village with the pot of sweet rice. He called out in every stall in search of Mādhavendra Purī.

TEXT 133

**ক্ষীর লহ এই, যার নাম 'মাধবপুরী' ।
তোমা লাগি' গোপীনাথ ক্ষীর কৈল চুরি ॥ ১৩৩ ॥**

kṣīra laha ei, yāra nāma 'mādhava-purī'
tomā lāgi' gopīnātha kṣīra kaila curi

SYNONYMS

kṣīra laha—take the pot of sweet rice; *ei*—this; *yāra*—whose; *nāma*— name; *mādhava-purī*—Mādhavendra Purī; *tomā lāgi'*—for you only; *gopīnātha*—the Deity of Lord Gopīnātha; *kṣīra*—the pot of sweet rice; *kaila*—did; *curi*—steal.

TRANSLATION

Holding the pot of sweet rice, the priest called: "Will he whose name is Mādhavendra Purī please come and take this pot! Gopīnātha has stolen this pot for you!"

PURPORT

The difference between the Absolute Truth and relative truth is explained here. Lord Gopīnātha has openly declared herein that He is a thief. He had stolen the pot of sweet rice, and this was not kept a secret because His act of stealing is a source of great transcendental bliss. In the material world, theft is criminal, but in the spiritual world the Lord's stealing is a source of transcendental bliss. Mundane rascals, who cannot understand the absolute nature of the Personality of Godhead, sometimes call Lord Śrī Kṛṣṇa immoral, but they do not know that His seemingly immoral activities, which are not kept secret, afford pleasure to the devotees. Not understanding the transcendental behavior of the Supreme Personality of Godhead, these rascals slur His character and immediately fall into the category of miscreants (rascals, lowest among men, demons and those whose knowledge is taken away by the illusory energy). Kṛṣṇa explains in *Bhagavad-gītā*:

na māṁ duṣkṛtino mūḍhāḥ
prapadyante narādhamāḥ
māyayāpahṛta-jñānā
āsuraṁ bhāvam āśritāḥ

"Those miscreants who are grossly foolish, lowest among mankind, whose knowledge is stolen by illusion, and who partake of the atheistic nature of demons, do not surrender unto Me." (Bg. 7.15)

Mundane rascals cannot understand that whatever Kṛṣṇa does, being absolute in nature, is all good. This quality of the Lord is explained in *Śrīmad-Bhāgavatam* (Tenth Canto). One may consider certain acts of a supremely powerful person to be immoral by mundane calculations, but this is not actually the case. For example, the sun absorbs water from the surface of the earth, but it does not absorb water only from the sea. It also absorbs water from filthy sewers and ditches containing urine and other impure substances. The sun is not polluted by absorbing such water. Rather, the sun makes the filthy place pure. If a devotee approaches the Supreme Personality of Godhead for an immoral or improper purpose, he nonetheless becomes purified; the Lord does not become infected. In *Śrīmad-Bhāgavatam* it is stated that if one approaches the Supreme Lord even out of lust, anger or fear (*kāmaṁ krodhaṁ bhayam*), he is purified. (*Bhāg.* 10.29.15) The *gopīs,* being young girls, approached Kṛṣṇa because He was a beautiful young boy. From the external point of view, they approached the Lord out of lust, and the Lord danced with them at midnight. From the mundane point of view, these activities may appear immoral because a married or unmarried young girl cannot leave home to mix with a young boy and dance with him. Although this is immoral from the mundane viewpoint, the activities of the *gopīs* are accepted as the highest form of worship because it was Lord Kṛṣṇa whom they approached with lusty desires in the dead of night.

But these things cannot be understood by nondevotees. One must understand Kṛṣṇa in *tattva* (truth). One should use his common sense and consider that if simply by chanting Kṛṣṇa's holy name one is purified, how then can the person Kṛṣṇa be immoral? Unfortunately, mundane fools are accepted as educational leaders and are offered exalted posts for teaching irreligious principles to the general populace. This is explained in *Śrīmad-Bhāgavatam* (7.5.31): *andhā yathāndhair upanīyamānāḥ.* Blind men are trying to lead other blind men. Due to the immature understanding of such rascals, common men should not discuss Kṛṣṇa's pastimes with the *gopīs.* A nondevotee should not even discuss His stealing sweet rice for His devotees. It is warned that one should not even think about these things. Although Kṛṣṇa is the purest of the pure, mundane people, thinking of Kṛṣṇa's pastimes that appear immoral, themselves become polluted. Śrī Caitanya Mahāprabhu therefore never publicly discussed Kṛṣṇa's dealings with the *gopīs.* He used to discuss these dealings only with three confidential friends. He never discussed *rāsa-līlā* publicly, as the professional reciters do, although they do not understand Kṛṣṇa or the nature of the audience. However, Śrī Caitanya Mahāprabhu encouraged the public chanting of the holy name on a huge scale for as many hours as possible.

TEXT 134

ক্ষীর লঞা সুখে তুমি করহ ভক্ষণে ।
তোমা-সম ভাগ্যবান্ নাহি ত্রিভুবনে ॥ ১৩৪ ॥

kṣīra lañā sukhe tumi karaha bhakṣaṇe
tomā-sama bhāgyavān nāhi tribhuvane

SYNONYMS

kṣīra lañā—taking the pot of sweet rice; *sukhe*—in happiness; *tumi*—you; *karaha*—do; *bhakṣaṇe*—eating; *tomā-sama*—like you; *bhāgyavān*—fortunate; *nāhi*—there is no one; *tri-bhuvane*—within the three worlds.

TRANSLATION

The priest continued: "Would the sannyāsī whose name is Mādhavendra Purī please come and take this pot of sweet rice and enjoy the prasāda with great happiness! You are the most fortunate person within these three worlds!"

PURPORT

Here is an example of a personal benediction by Kṛṣṇa's immoral activity. By Gopīnātha's stealing for His devotee, the devotee becomes the most fortunate person within the three worlds. Thus even the Lord's criminal activities make His devotee the most fortunate person. How can a mundane rascal understand the pastimes of Kṛṣṇa and judge whether He is moral or immoral? Since Kṛṣṇa is the Absolute Truth, there are no mundane distinctions such as moral and immoral. Whatever He does is good. This is the real meaning of "God is good." He is good in all circumstances because He is transcendental, outside the jurisdiction of this material world. Therefore, Kṛṣṇa can be understood only by those who are already living in the spiritual world. This is corroborated in *Bhagavad-gītā*:

māṁ ca yo 'vyabhicāreṇa
bhakti-yogena sevate
sa guṇān samatītyaitān
brahma-bhūyāya kalpate

"One who engages in full devotional service, who does not fall down in any circumstance, at once transcends the modes of material nature and thus comes to the level of Brahman." (Bg. 14.26)

One who is engaged in unalloyed devotional service to the Lord is already situated in the spiritual world (*brahma-bhūyāya kalpate*). In all circumstances, his activities and dealings with Kṛṣṇa are transcendental and thus not understandable by mundane moralists. It is therefore better not to discuss such activities among mundane people. It is better to give them the Hare Kṛṣṇa *mahā-mantra* so that they will be gradually purified and then come to understand the transcendental activities of Kṛṣṇa.

TEXT 135

এত শুনি' পুরী-গোসাঞি পরিচয় দিল ।
ক্ষীর দিয়া পূজারী তাঁরে দণ্ডবৎ হৈল ॥ ১৩৫ ॥

eta śuni' purī-gosāñi paricaya dila
kṣīra diyā pūjārī tāṅre daṇḍavat haila

SYNONYMS

eta śuni'—hearing this; *purī-gosāñi*—Mādhavendra Purī; *paricaya*—introduction; *dila*—gave; *kṣīra diyā*—delivering the pot of sweet rice; *pūjārī*— the priest; *tāṅre*—to him; *daṇḍavat haila*—offered obeisances.

TRANSLATION

Hearing this invitation, Mādhavendra Purī came out and identified himself. The priest then delivered the pot of sweet rice and offered his obeisances, falling flat before him.

PURPORT

A *brāhmaṇa* is not supposed to offer his obeisances by falling flat before anyone because a *brāhmaṇa* is considered to be in the highest caste. However, when a *brāhmaṇa* sees a devotee, he offers his *daṇḍavats.* This *brāhmaṇa* priest did not ask Mādhavendra Purī whether he was a *brāhmaṇa,* but when he saw that Mādhavendra Purī was such a bona fide devotee that Kṛṣṇa would even steal for him, he immediately understood the position of the saint. As stated by Śrī Caitanya Mahāprabhu: *kibā vipra, kibā nyāsī, śūdra kene naya / yei kṛṣṇa-tattva-vettā, sei 'guru' haya.* (Cc. *Madhya* 8.128) Had the *brāhmaṇa* priest been an ordinary *brāhmaṇa,* Gopīnātha would not have talked with him in a dream. Since the Deity spoke to both Mādhavendra Purī and the *brāhmaṇa* priest in dreams, practically speaking they were on the same platform. However, because Mādhavendra Purī was a senior *sannyāsī* Vaiṣṇava, a *paramahaṁsa,* the priest immediately fell flat before him and offered obeisances.

TEXT 136

ক্ষীরের বৃত্তান্ত তাঁরে কহিল পূজারী ।
শুনি' প্রেমাবিষ্ট হৈল শ্রীমাধবপুরী ॥ ১৩৬ ॥

kṣīrera vṛttānta tāṅre kahila pūjārī
śuni' premāviṣṭa haila śrī-mādhava-purī

SYNONYMS

kṣīrera vṛttānta—all the incidents that took place on account of the pot of sweet rice; *tāṅre*—to Mādhavendra Purī; *kahila*—explained; *pūjārī*—the priest; *śuni'*—hearing; *prema-āviṣṭa*—saturated with love of Godhead; *haila*—became; *śrī-mādhava-purī*—Śrīla Mādhavendra Purī.

TRANSLATION

When the story about the pot of sweet rice was explained to him in detail, Śrī Mādhavendra Purī at once became absorbed in ecstatic love of Kṛṣṇa.

TEXT 137

প্রেম দেখি' সেবক কহে হইয়া বিস্মিত।
কৃষ্ণ যে ইঁহার বশ,—হয় যথোচিত ॥ ১৩৭ ॥

prema dekhi' sevaka kahe ha-iyā vismita
kṛṣṇa ye iṅhāra vaśa,——haya yathocita

SYNONYMS

prema dekhi'—seeing the ecstatic position of Mādhavendra Purī; *sevaka*— the priest; *kahe*—said; *ha-iyā*—being; *vismita*—struck with wonder; *kṛṣṇa*— Lord Kṛṣṇa; *ye*—that; *iṅhāra*—by him; *vaśa*—obliged; *haya*—it is; *yathocita*—befitting.

TRANSLATION

Upon seeing the ecstatic loving symptoms manifest in Mādhavendra Purī, the priest was struck with wonder. He could understand why Kṛṣṇa had become so much obliged to him, and he saw that Kṛṣṇa's action was befitting.

PURPORT

A devotee can bring Kṛṣṇa perfectly under his control. This is explained in *Śrīmad-Bhāgavatam: ajita-jito 'py asi tais tri-lokyām.* (*Bhāg.* 10.14.3) Kṛṣṇa is never conquered by anyone, but a devotee can conquer Him through devotional service. As stated in *Brahma-saṁhita* (5.33): *vedeṣu durlabham adurlabham ātma-bhaktau.* One cannot understand Kṛṣṇa simply by reading Vedic literature. Although all Vedic literature is meant for understanding Kṛṣṇa, one cannot understand Kṛṣṇa without being a lover of Kṛṣṇa. Therefore along with the reading of Vedic literature (*svādhyāya*), one must engage in devotional worship of the Deity (*arcana-vidhi*). Together these will enhance the devotee's transcendental understanding of devotional service. *Śravaṇādi śuddha-citte karaye udaya* (Cc. *Madhya* 22.107). Love of Godhead is dormant within everyone's heart, and if one simply follows the standard process of devotional service, it is awakened. But foolish mundane people who simply read about Kṛṣṇa mistakenly think that He is immoral or criminal.

TEXT 138

এত বলি' নমস্করি' করিলা গমন।
আবেশে করিলা পুরী সে ক্ষীর ভক্ষণ ॥ ১৩৮ ॥

eta bali' namaskari' karilā gamana
āveśe karilā purī se kṣīra bhakṣaṇa

SYNONYMS

eta bali'—saying this; *namaskari'*—offering obeisances; *karilā gamana*—returned; *āveśe*—in ecstasy; *karilā*—did; *purī*—Purī Gosāñi; *se*—that; *kṣīra*—sweet rice; *bhakṣaṇa*—eating.

TRANSLATION

The priest offered his obeisances to Mādhavendra Purī and returned to the temple. Then, in ecstasy, Mādhavendra Purī ate the sweet rice offered to him by Kṛṣṇa.

TEXT 139

পাত্র প্রক্ষালন করি' খণ্ড খণ্ড কৈল ।
বহির্বাসে বান্ধি' সেই ঠিকারি রাখিল ॥ ১৩৯ ॥

pātra prakṣālana kari' khaṇḍa khaṇḍa kaila
bahir-vāse bāndhi' sei ṭhikāri rākhila

SYNONYMS

pātra—the pot; *prakṣālana kari'*—washing; *khaṇḍa khaṇḍa*—breaking into pieces; *kaila*—did; *bahir-vāse*—in his outer wrapper; *bāndhi'*—binding; *sei*—those; *ṭhikāri*—pieces of pot; *rākhila*—kept.

TRANSLATION

After this, Mādhavendra Purī washed the pot and broke it into pieces. He then bound all the pieces in his outer cloth and kept them nicely.

TEXT 140

প্রতিদিন একখানি করেন ভক্ষণ ।
খাইলে প্রেমাবেশ হয়,—অদ্ভুত কথন ॥ ১৪০ ॥

prati-dina eka-khāni karena bhakṣaṇa
khāile premāveśa haya,——adbhuta kathana

SYNONYMS

prati-dina—every day; *eka-khāni*—one piece; *karena*—does; *bhakṣaṇa*—eating; *khāile*—by eating; *prema-āveśa*—ecstasy; *haya*—there is; *adbhuta*—wonderful; *kathana*—narrations.

TRANSLATION

Each day, Mādhavendra Purī would eat one piece of that earthen pot, and after eating it he would immediately be overwhelmed with ecstasy. These are wonderful stories.

TEXT 141

'ঠাকুর মোরে ক্ষীর দিল—লোক সব শুনি' ।
দিনে লোক-ভিড় হবে মোর প্রতিষ্ঠা জানি' ॥ ১৪১ ॥

'ṭhākura more kṣīra dila——loka saba śuni'
dine loka-bhiḍa habe mora pratiṣṭhā jāni'

SYNONYMS

ṭhākura—the Lord; *more*—to me; *kṣīra*—sweet rice; *dila*—has given; *loka*—the people; *saba*—all; *śuni'*—after hearing; *dine*—at daytime; *loka*—of people; *bhiḍa*—crowd; *habe*—there will be; *mora*—my; *pratiṣṭhā*—fame; *jāni'*—knowing.

TRANSLATION

Having broken the pot and bound the pieces in his cloth Mādhavendra Purī began to think: "The Lord has given me a pot of sweet rice, and when the people hear of this tomorrow morning, there will be great crowds."

TEXT 142

সেই ভয়ে রাত্রি-শেষে চলিলা শ্রীপুরী ।
সেইখানে গোপীনাথে দণ্ডবৎ করি' ॥ ১৪২ ॥

sei bhaye rātri-śeṣe calilā śrī-purī
sei-khāne gopīnāthe daṇḍavat kari'

SYNONYMS

sei bhaye—fearing that; *rātri-śeṣe*—at the end of the night; *calilā*—left; *śrī-purī*—Śrī Mādhavendra Purī; *sei-khāne*—on that spot; *gopīnāthe*—to Lord Gopīnātha; *daṇḍavat*—obeisances; *kari'*—doing.

TRANSLATION

Thinking this, Śrī Mādhavendra Purī offered his obeisances to Gopīnātha on the spot and left Remuṇā before morning.

TEXT 143

চলি' চলি' আইলা পুরী শ্রীনীলাচল ।
জগন্নাথ দেখি' হৈলা প্রেমেতে বিহ্বল ॥ ১৪৩ ॥

cali' cali' āilā purī śrī-nīlācala
jagannātha dekhi' hailā premete vihvala

SYNONYMS

cali' cali'—walking and walking; *āilā*—he reached; *purī*—Jagannātha Purī; *śrī-nīlācala*—known as Nīlācala; *jagannātha dekhi'*—seeing Lord Jagannātha; *hailā*—became; *premete*—in love; *vihvala*—overwhelmed.

TRANSLATION

Walking and walking, Mādhavendra Purī finally reached Jagannātha Purī, which is also known as Nīlācala. There he saw Lord Jagannātha and was overwhelmed with loving ecstasy.

TEXT 144

প্রেমাবেশে উঠে, পড়ে, হাসে, নাচে, গায় ।
জগন্নাথ-দরশনে মহাসুখ পায় ॥ ১৪৪ ॥

premāveśe uṭhe, paḍe, hāse, nāce, gāya
jagannātha-daraśane mahā-sukha pāya

SYNONYMS

prema-āveśe—in loving ecstasy; *uṭhe*—sometimes stands; *paḍe*—sometimes falls; *hāse*—laughs; *nāce*—dances; *gāya*—sings; *jagannātha daraśane*—by seeing Lord Jagannātha in the temple; *mahā-sukha*—transcendental happiness; *pāya*—he felt.

TRANSLATION

When Mādhavendra Purī was overwhelmed in the ecstasy of love of Godhead, he sometimes stood up and sometimes fell to the ground. Sometimes he laughed, danced and sang. In this way he enjoyed transcendental bliss by seeing the Jagannātha Deity.

TEXT 145

'মাধবপুরী শ্রীপাদ আইল',—লোকে হৈল খ্যাতি ।
সব লোক আসি' তাঁরে করে বহু ভক্তি ॥ ১৪৫ ॥

'mādhava-purī śrīpāda āila',—loke haila khyāti
saba loka āsi' tāṅre kare bahu bhakti

SYNONYMS

mādhava-purī—Śrī Mādhavendra Purī; *śrīpāda*—*sannyāsī; āila*—has come; *loke*—among the people; *haila*—there was; *khyāti*—reputation; *saba loka*—all people; *āsi'*—coming; *tāṅre*—unto him; *kare*—do; *bahu*—much; *bhakti*—devotion.

TRANSLATION

When Mādhavendra Purī came to Jagannātha Purī, people were aware of his transcendental reputation. Therefore crowds of people came and offered him all sorts of respect in devotion.

TEXT 146

প্রতিষ্ঠার স্বভাব এই জগতে বিদিত ।
যে না বাঞ্ছে, তার হয় বিধাতা-নির্মিত ॥ ১৪৬ ॥

pratiṣṭhāra svabhāva ei jagate vidita
ye nā vāñche, tāra haya vidhātā-nirmita

SYNONYMS

pratiṣṭhāra—of reputation; *svabhāva*—the nature; *ei*—this; *jagate*—in the world; *vidita*—known; *ye*—the person who; *nā vāñche*—does not desire it; *tāra*—of him; *haya*—it is; *vidhātā-nirmita*—created by providence.

TRANSLATION

Even though one may not like it, reputation, as ordained by providence, comes to him. Indeed, one's transcendental reputation is known throughout the entire world.

TEXT 147

প্রতিষ্ঠার ভয়ে পুরী গেলা পলাঞা ।
কৃষ্ণ-প্রেমে প্রতিষ্ঠা চলে সঙ্গে গড়াঞা ॥ ১৪৭ ॥

pratiṣṭhāra bhaye purī gelā palāñā
kṛṣṇa-preme pratiṣṭhā cale saṅge gaḍāñā

SYNONYMS

pratiṣṭhāra bhaye—in fear of reputation; *purī*—Mādhavendra Purī; *gelā*—went away; *palāñā*—fleeing; *kṛṣṇa-preme*—in love of Kṛṣṇa; *pratiṣṭhā*—reputation; *cale*—goes; *saṅge*—simultaneously; *gaḍāñā*—gliding down.

TRANSLATION

Being afraid of his reputation [pratiṣṭhā], Mādhavendra Purī fled from Remuṇā. But the reputation brought by love of Godhead is so sublime that it goes along with the devotee, as if following him.

PURPORT

Almost all the conditioned souls within the material world are envious. Jealous people generally turn against one who automatically attains some reputation. This is natural for jealous people. Consequently, when a devotee is fit to receive worldly reputation, he is envied by many people. This is quite natural. When a person, out of humility, does not desire fame, people generally think him quite humble and consequently give him all kinds of fame. Actually a Vaiṣṇava does not hanker after fame or a great reputation. Mādhavendra Purī, the king of Vaiṣṇavas, bore his reputation, but he wanted to keep himself outside of the vision of the general populace. He wanted to cover his real identity as a great devotee of the Lord, but when people saw him overwhelmed in ecstasy in love of Godhead, they naturally gave credit to him. Actually a first-class reputation is due Mādhavendra Purī because he was a most confidential devotee of the Lord. Sometimes a *sahajiyā* presents himself as being void of desires for reputation (*pratiṣṭhā*) in order to become famous as a humble man. Such people cannot actually attain the platform of celebrated Vaiṣṇavas.

TEXT 148

যদ্যপি উদ্বেগ হৈল পলাইতে মন ।
ঠাকুরের চন্দন-সাধন হইল বন্ধন ॥ ১৪৮ ॥

yadyapi udvega haila palāite mana
ṭhākurera candana-sādhana ha-ila bandhana

SYNONYMS

yadyapi—although; *udvega*—anxiety; *haila*—there was; *palāite*—to go away; *mana*—the mind; *ṭhākurera*—of the Lord; *candana*—of the sandalwood; *sādhana*—the collecting; *ha-ila*—there was; *bandhana*—bondage.

TRANSLATION

Mādhavendra Purī wanted to leave Jagannātha Purī because the people were honoring him as a great devotee; however, this threatened to hinder his collecting sandalwood for the Gopāla Deity.

TEXT 149

জগন্নাথের সেবক যত, যতেক মহান্ত ।
সবাকে কহিল পুরী গোপাল-বৃত্তান্ত ॥ ১৪৯ ॥

jagannāthera sevaka yata, yateka mahānta
sabāke kahila purī gopāla-vṛttānta

SYNONYMS

jagannāthera sevaka—the servants of Lord Jagannātha; *yata*—all; *yateka mahānta*—all respectable devotees; *sabāke*—unto everyone; *kahila*—told; *purī*—Mādhavendra Purī; *gopāla-vṛttānta*—the narration of Gopāla.

TRANSLATION

Śrī Mādhavendra Purī told all the servants of Lord Jagannātha and all the great devotees there the story of the appearance of Śrī Gopāla.

TEXT 150

গোপাল চন্দন মাগে,—শুনি' ভক্তগণ ।
আনন্দে চন্দন লাগি' করিল যতন ॥ ১৫০ ॥

gopāla candana māge,——śuni' bhakta-gaṇa
ānande candana lāgi' karila yatana

SYNONYMS

gopāla—Lord Gopāla at Vṛndāvana; *candana*—sandalwood; *māge*—wants; *śuni'*—hearing; *bhakta-gaṇa*—all the devotees; *ānande*—in great pleasure; *candana lāgi'*—for sandalwood; *karila*—made; *yatana*—endeavor.

TRANSLATION

When all the devotees at Jagannātha Purī heard that the Gopāla Deity wanted sandalwood, in great pleasure they all endeavored to collect it.

TEXT 151

রাজপাত্র-সনে যার যার পরিচয় ।
তারে মাগি' কর্পূর-চন্দন করিলা সঞ্চয় ॥ ১৫১ ॥

rāja-pātra-sane yāra yāra paricaya
tāre māgi' karpūra-candana karilā sañcaya

SYNONYMS

rāja-pātra—government officers; *sane*—with; *yāra yāra*—whoever; *paricaya*—had acquaintance; *tāre māgi'*—begging them; *karpūra-candana*—camphor and sandalwood; *karilā*—made; *sañcaya*—collection.

TRANSLATION

Those who were acquainted with government officers met with them and begged for camphor and sandalwood, which they collected.

PURPORT

It appears that *malayaja-candana* (sandalwood) and camphor were used for the Jagannātha Deity. The camphor was used in His *ārātrika,* and the sandalwood was used to smear His body. Both these items were under government control; therefore the devotees had to meet with the government officials. Informing them of all the details, they attained permission to take the sandalwood and camphor outside Jagannātha Purī.

TEXT 152

এক বিপ্র, এক সেবক, চন্দন বহিতে ।
পুরী-গোসাঞির সঙ্গে দিল সম্বল-সহিতে ॥ ১৫২ ॥

eka vipra, eka sevaka, candana vahite
purī-gosāñira saṅge dila sambala-sahite

SYNONYMS

eka vipra—one *brāhmaṇa; eka sevaka*—one servant; *candana*—the sandalwood; *vahite*—to carry; *purī-gosāñira*—Mādhavendra Purī; *saṅge*—with; *dila*—gave; *sambala-sahite*—with the necessary expenditure.

TRANSLATION

One brāhmaṇa and one servant were given to Mādhavendra Purī just to carry the sandalwood. He was also given the necessary traveling expenses.

TEXT 153

ঘাটী-দানী ছাড়াইতে রাজপাত্র দ্বারে ।
রাজলেখা করি' দিল পুরী-গোসাঞির করে ॥১৫৩॥

ghāṭī-dānī chāḍāite rāja-pātra dvāre
rāja-lekhā kari' dila purī-gosāñira kare

SYNONYMS

ghāṭī-dānī—from the toll collectors; *chāḍāite*—to get release; *rāja-pātra*—papers showing governmental sanction; *dvāre*—at the gates; *rāja-lekhā*—governmental permission; *kari'*—showing; *dila*—delivered; *purī-gosāñira*—of Purī Gosāñi, Mādhavendra Purī; *kare*—into the hand.

TRANSLATION

To get past the toll collectors along the way, Mādhavendra Purī was supplied with the necessary release papers from government officers. The papers were placed in his hand.

TEXT 154

চলিল মাধবপুরী চন্দন লঞা ।
কতদিনে রেমুণাতে উত্তরিল গিয়া ॥ ১৫৪ ॥

calila mādhava-purī candana lañā
kata-dine remuṇāte uttarila giyā

SYNONYMS

calila—proceeded; *mādhava-purī*—Mādhavendra Purī; *candana lañā*—taking the sandalwood; *kata-dine*—after some days; *remuṇāte*—at the same temple of Remuṇā; *uttarila*—reached; *giyā*—going.

TRANSLATION

In this way Mādhavendra Purī started for Vṛndāvana with the burden of sandalwood, and after some days he again reached the village of Remuṇā and the Gopīnātha temple there.

TEXT 155

গোপীনাথ-চরণে কৈল বহু নমস্কার ।
প্রেমাবেশে নৃত্য-গীত করিলা অপার ॥ ১৫৫ ॥

gopīnātha-caraṇe kaila bahu namaskāra
premāveśe nṛtya-gīta karilā apāra

SYNONYMS

gopīnātha-caraṇe—at the lotus feet of Lord Gopīnātha; *kaila*—made; *bahu*—many; *namaskāra*—obeisances; *prema-āveśe*—in the ecstasy of love; *nṛtya-gīta*—dancing and chanting; *karilā*—performed; *apāra*—unlimitedly.

TRANSLATION

When Mādhavendra Purī reached the temple of Gopīnātha, he offered his respectful obeisances many times at the lotus feet of the Lord. In the ecstasy of love, he began to dance and sing without cessation.

TEXT 156

পুরী দেখি' সেবক সব সম্মান করিল।
ক্ষীরপ্রসাদ দিয়া তাঁরে ভিক্ষা করাইল ॥ ১৫৬ ॥

purī dekhi' sevaka saba sammāna karila
kṣīra-prasāda diyā tāṅre bhikṣā karāila

SYNONYMS

purī dekhi'—by seeing Mādhavendra Purī; *sevaka*—the priest or servant; *saba sammāna*—all respects; *karila*—offered; *kṣīra-prasāda*—sweet rice *prasāda*; *diyā*—offering; *tāṅre*—him; *bhikṣā karāila*—made to eat.

TRANSLATION

When the priest of Gopīnātha saw Mādhavendra Purī again, he offered all respects to him and, giving him the sweet rice prasāda, made him eat.

TEXT 157

সেই রাত্রে দেবালয়ে করিল শয়ন।
শেষরাত্রি হৈলে পুরী দেখিল স্বপন ॥ ১৫৭ ॥

sei rātre devālaye karila śayana
śeṣa-rātri haile purī dekhila svapana

SYNONYMS

sei rātre—on that night; *deva-ālaye*—in the temple; *karila*—did; *śayana*—sleeping; *śeṣa-rātri*—at the end of the night; *haile*—when it was; *purī*—Mādhavendra Purī; *dekhila*—saw; *svapana*—a dream.

TRANSLATION

Mādhavendra Purī took rest that night in the temple, but toward the end of the night he had another dream.

TEXT 158

গোপাল আসিয়া কহে,—শুন হে মাধব।
কর্পূর-চন্দন আমি পাইলাম সব ॥ ১৫৮ ॥

gopāla āsiyā kahe,——śuna he mādhava
karpūra-candana āmi pāilāma saba

SYNONYMS

gopāla—the Deity of Gopāla; *āsiyā*—coming; *kahe*—says; *śuna*—hear; *he*—O; *mādhava*—Mādhavendra Purī; *karpūra-candana*—the camphor and sandalwood; *āmi*—I; *pāilāma*—have received; *saba*—all.

TRANSLATION

Mādhavendra Purī dreamed that Gopāla came before him and said: "O Mādhavendra Purī, I have already received all the sandalwood and camphor.

TEXT 159

কর্পূর-সহিত ঘষি' এসব চন্দন।
গোপীনাথের অঙ্গে নিত্য করহ লেপন ॥ ১৫৯ ॥

karpūra-sahita ghaṣi' e-saba candana
gopīnāthera aṅge nitya karaha lepana

SYNONYMS

karpūra-sahita—with the camphor; *ghaṣi'*—grinding; *e-saba*—all this; *candana*—sandalwood; *gopīnāthera*—of Śrī Gopīnātha; *aṅge*—on the body; *nitya*—daily; *karaha*—do; *lepana*—smearing.

TRANSLATION

"Now just grind all the sandalwood together with the camphor and then smear the pulp on the body of Gopīnātha daily until it is finished.

TEXT 160

গোপীনাথ আমার সে একই অঙ্গ হয়।
ইঁহাকে চন্দন দিলে হবে মোর তাপ-ক্ষয় ॥ ১৬০ ॥

gopīnātha āmāra se eka-i aṅga haya
iṅhāke candana dile habe mora tāpa-kṣaya

SYNONYMS

gopīnātha—Lord Gopīnātha; *āmāra*—My; *se*—that; *eka-i*—one; *aṅga*—body; *haya*—is; *iṅhāke*—unto Him; *candana dile*—in offering this *candana*; *habe*—there will be; *mora*—My; *tāpa-kṣaya*—reduction of temperature.

TRANSLATION

"There is no difference between My body and Gopīnātha's body. They are one and the same. Therefore if you smear the sandalwood pulp on the body of Gopīnātha, you will naturally also smear it on My body. Thus the temperature of My body will be reduced.

PURPORT

Gopāla was situated in Vṛndāvana, which was far from Remuṇā. In those days, one had to pass through provinces governed by the Mohammedans, who sometimes hindered travelers. Considering the trouble of His devotee, Lord Gopāla, the greatest well-wisher of His devotees, ordered Mādhavendra Purī to smear the sandalwood pulp on the body of Gopīnātha, which was nondifferent from the body of Gopāla. In this way the Lord relieved Mādhavendra Purī from trouble and inconvenience.

TEXT 161

দ্বিধা না ভাবিহ, না করিহ কিছু মনে।
বিশ্বাস করি' চন্দন দেহ আমার বচনে॥ ১৬১॥

dvidhā nā bhāviha, nā kariha kichu mane
viśvāsa kari' candana deha āmāra vacane

SYNONYMS

dvidhā nā bhāviha—do not hesitate; *nā kariha*—do not do; *kichu*—anything; *mane*—in the mind; *viśvāsa kari'*—believing Me; *candana*—sandalwood; *deha*—offer; *āmāra vacane*—under My order.

TRANSLATION

"You should not hesitate to act according to My order. Believing in Me, just do what is needed."

TEXT 162

এত বলি' গোপাল গেল, গোসাঞি জাগিলা।
গোপীনাথের সেবকগণে ডাকিয়া আনিলা॥ ১৬২॥

eta bali' gopāla gela, gosāñi jāgilā
gopīnāthera sevaka-gaṇe ḍākiyā ānilā

SYNONYMS

eta bali'—saying this; *gopāla*—the Deity of Gopāla; *gela*—disappeared; *gosāñi jāgilā*—Mādhavendra Purī awoke; *gopīnāthera*—of Lord Gopīnātha; *sevaka-gaṇe*—to the servitors; *ḍākiyā*—calling; *ānilā*—brought them.

TRANSLATION

After giving these instructions, Gopāla disappeared, and Mādhavendra Purī awoke. He immediately called for all the servants of Gopīnātha, and they came before him.

TEXT 163

প্রভুর আজ্ঞা হৈল,—এই কর্পূর-চন্দন ।
গোপীনাথের অঙ্গে নিত্য করহ লেপন ॥ ১৬৩ ॥

prabhura ājñā haila,——ei karpūra-candana
gopīnāthera aṅge nitya karaha lepana

SYNONYMS

prabhura ājñā haila—there was an order of the Lord; *ei*—this; *karpūra*—camphor; *candana*—and sandalwood; *gopīnāthera aṅge*—on the body of Gopīnātha; *nitya*—daily; *karaha*—do; *lepana*—smearing.

TRANSLATION

Mādhavendra Purī said: "Smear the body of Gopīnātha with this camphor and sandalwood I have brought for Gopāla in Vṛndāvana. Do this regularly every day.

TEXT 164

ইঁহাকে চন্দন দিলে, গোপাল হইবে শীতল ।
স্বতন্ত্র ঈশ্বর—তাঁর আজ্ঞা সে প্রবল ॥ ১৬৪ ॥

iṅhāke candana dile, gopāla ha-ibe śītala
svatantra īśvara——tāṅra ājñā se prabala

SYNONYMS

iṅhāke—unto Gopīnātha; *candana dile*—when sandalwood will be given; *gopāla*—Lord Gopāla in Vṛndāvana; *ha-ibe*—will become; *śītala*—cool; *svatantra īśvara*—the most independent Supreme Personality of Godhead; *tāṅra*—His; *ājñā*—order; *se*—that; *prabala*—powerful.

TRANSLATION

"If the sandalwood pulp is smeared over the body of Gopīnātha, then Gopāla will be cooled. After all, the Supreme Personality of Godhead is completely independent; His order is all-powerful."

TEXT 165

গ্রীষ্মকালে গোপীনাথ পরিবে চন্দন ।
শুনি' আনন্দিত হৈল সেবকের মন ॥ ১৬৫ ॥

grīṣma-kāle gopīnātha paribe candana
śuni' ānandita haila sevakera mana

SYNONYMS

grīṣma-kāle—in the summer; *gopīnātha*—Lord Gopīnātha; *paribe*—will put on; *candana*—sandalwood pulp; *śuni'*—hearing; *ānandita*—pleased; *haila*—became; *sevakera*—of the servants; *mana*—the minds.

TRANSLATION

The servants of Gopīnātha became very pleased to hear that in the summer all the sandalwood pulp would be used to anoint the body of Gopīnātha.

TEXT 166

পুরী কহে,—এই দুই ঘষিবে চন্দন ।
আর জনা-দুই দেহ, দিব যে বেতন ॥ ১৬৬ ॥

purī kahe,——ei dui ghaṣibe candana
āra janā-dui deha, diba ye vetana

SYNONYMS

purī kahe—Mādhavendra Purī said; *ei dui*—these two assistants; *ghaṣibe*—will grind; *candana*—the sandalwood; *āra*—another; *janā-dui*—two men; *deha*—apply; *diba*—I shall pay; *ye*—that; *vetana*—salary.

TRANSLATION

Mādhavendra Purī said: "These two assistants will regularly grind the sandalwood, and you should also get two other people to help. I shall pay their salary."

TEXT 167

এই মত চন্দন দেয় প্রত্যহ ঘষিয়া ।
পরায় সেবক সব আনন্দ করিয়া ॥ ১৬৭ ॥

ei mata candana deya pratyaha ghaṣiyā
parāya sevaka saba ānanda kariyā

SYNONYMS

ei mata—in this way; *candana*—sandalwood; *deya*—gives; *pratyaha*—daily; *ghaṣiyā*—grinding; *parāya*—caused to put on; *sevaka*—servants; *saba*—all of it; *ānanda*—pleasure; *kariyā*—feeling.

TRANSLATION

In this way Gopīnāthajī was supplied ground sandalwood pulp daily. The servants of Gopīnātha were very pleased with this.

TEXT 168

প্রত্যহ চন্দন পরায়, যাবৎ হৈল অন্ত ।
তথায় রহিল পুরী তাবৎ পর্যন্ত ॥ ১৬৮ ॥

pratyaha candana parāya, yāvat haila anta
tathāya rahila purī tāvat paryanta

SYNONYMS

pratyaha—daily; *candana*—sandalwood pulp; *parāya*—smears over the body; *yāvat*—until; *haila*—there was; *anta*—an end; *tathāya*—there; *rahila*—remained; *purī*—Mādhavendra Purī; *tāvat*—that time; *paryanta*—until.

TRANSLATION

In this way the sandalwood pulp was smeared over the body of Gopīnātha until the whole stock was finished. Mādhavendra Purī stayed there until that time.

TEXT 169

গ্রীষ্মকাল-অন্তে পুনঃ নীলাচলে গেলা ।
নীলাচলে চাতুর্মাস্য আনন্দে রহিলা ॥ ১৬৯ ॥

grīṣma-kāla-ante punaḥ nīlācale gelā
nīlācale cāturmāsya ānande rahilā

SYNONYMS

grīṣma-kāla—of the summer season; *ante*—at the end; *punaḥ*—again; *nīlācale*—to Jagannātha Purī; *gelā*—went; *nīlācale*—in Jagannātha Purī; *cāturmāsya*—the four months for vows; *ānande*—in great pleasure; *rahilā*—remained.

TRANSLATION

At the end of summer, Mādhavendra Purī returned to Jagannātha Purī, where he remained with great pleasure during the whole period of Cāturmāsya.

PURPORT

The Cāturmāsya period begins in the month of Āṣāḍha (June-July) from the day of Ekādaśī called Śayanā-ekādaśī in the fortnight of the waxing moon. The period ends in the month of Kārtika (October-November) on the Ekādaśī day known as Utthāna-ekādaśī in the fortnight of the waxing moon. This four-month period is known as Cāturmāsya. Some Vaiṣṇavas also observe it from the full-moon day of Āṣāḍha until the full-moon day of Kārtika. That is also a period of four months. This period, calculated by the lunar months, is called Cāturmāsya, but others also observe Cāturmāsya according to the solar month from Śrāvaṇa to Kārtika. The whole period, either lunar or solar, takes place during the rainy season. Cāturmāsya should be observed by all sections of the population. It does not matter whether one is a *gṛhastha* or a *sannyāsī*. The observance is obligatory for all *āśramas*. The real purpose behind the vow taken during these four months is to minimize the quantity of sense gratification. This is not very difficult. In the month of Śrāvaṇa, one should not eat spinach. In the month of Bhādra, one should not eat yogurt, and in the month of Āśvina, one should not drink milk. One should not eat fish or other nonvegetarian food during the month of Kārtika. A nonvegetarian diet means fish and meat. Similarly, *masura* dahl and *urad* dahl are also considered nonvegetarian. These two dahls contain a great amount of protein, and food rich in protein is considered nonvegetarian. On the whole, during the four-month period of Cāturmāsya, one should practice giving up all food intended for sense enjoyment.

TEXT 170

শ্রীমুখে মাধব-পুরীর অমৃত-চরিত।
ভক্তগণে শুনাঞা প্রভু করে আস্বাদিত ॥ ১৭০ ॥

śrī-mukhe mādhava-purīra amṛta-carita
bhakta-gaṇe śunāñā prabhu kare āsvādita

SYNONYMS

śrī-mukhe—from the mouth of Śrī Caitanya Mahāprabhu; *mādhava-purīra*—of Mādhavendra Purī; *amṛta-carita*—nectarean characteristics; *bhakta-gaṇe*—the devotees; *śunāñā*—making hear; *prabhu*—the Lord; *kare*—does; *āsvādita*—relished.

TRANSLATION

Thus Śrī Caitanya Mahāprabhu personally praised the nectarean characteristics of Mādhavendra Purī, and while He related all this to the devotees, He personally relished it.

TEXT 171

প্রভু কহে,—নিত্যানন্দ, করহ বিচার।
পুরী-সম ভাগ্যবান্ জগতে নাহি আর ॥ ১৭১ ॥

prabhu kahe,——nityānanda, karaha vicāra
purī-sama bhāgyavān jagate nāhi āra

SYNONYMS

prabhu kahe—the Lord said; *nityānanda*—Nityānanda Prabhu; *karaha vicāra*—just consider; *purī-sama*—like Mādhavendra Purī; *bhāgyavān*—fortunate; *jagate*—in the world; *nāhi*— there is not; *āra*—anyone else.

TRANSLATION

Lord Śrī Caitanya Mahāprabhu asked Nityānanda Prabhu to judge whether there was anyone within the world as fortunate as Mādhavendra Purī.

TEXT 172

দুগ্ধদান-ছলে কৃষ্ণ যাঁরে দেখা দিল।
তিনবারে স্বপ্নে আসি' যাঁরে আজ্ঞা কৈল ॥ ১৭২ ॥

dugdha-dāna-chale kṛṣṇa yāṅre dekhā dila
tina-bāre svapne āsi' yāṅre ājñā kaila

SYNONYMS

dugdha-dāna-chale—on the plea of delivering milk; *kṛṣṇa*—Lord Kṛṣṇa; *yāṅre*—unto whom; *dekhā dila*—made His appearance; *tina-bāre*—three times; *svapne*—in dreams; *āsi'*—coming; *yāṅre*—unto whom; *ājñā*—order; *kaila*—gave.

TRANSLATION

Śrī Caitanya Mahāprabhu said: "Mādhavendra Purī was so fortunate that Kṛṣṇa personally appeared before him on the plea of delivering milk. Three times the Lord gave orders to Mādhavendra Purī in dreams.

TEXT 173

যাঁর প্রেমে বশ হঞা প্রকট হইলা ।
সেবা অঙ্গীকার করি' জগত তারিলা ॥ ১৭৩ ॥

yāṅra preme vaśa hañā prakaṭa ha-ilā
sevā aṅgīkāra kari' jagata tārilā

SYNONYMS

yāṅra—of whom; *preme*—by love of Godhead; *vaśa*—obliged; *hañā*—being; *prakaṭa*—manifest; *ha-ilā*—became; *sevā*—service; *aṅgīkāra*—acceptance; *kari'*—doing; *jagata*—the whole world; *tārilā*—delivered.

TRANSLATION

"Being obliged because of the loving affairs of Mādhavendra Purī, Lord Kṛṣṇa Himself appeared as the Gopāla Deity, and, accepting his service, He liberated the whole world.

TEXT 174

যাঁর লাগি' গোপীনাথ ক্ষীর কৈল চুরি ।
অতএব নাম হৈল 'ক্ষীরচোরা' করি' ॥ ১৭৪ ॥

yāṅra lāgi' gopīnātha kṣīra kaila curi
ataeva nāma haila 'kṣīra-corā' kari'

SYNONYMS

yāṅra—whom; *lāgi'*—on account of; *gopīnātha*—Lord Gopīnātha; *kṣīra*—sweet rice; *kaila*—did; *curi*—steal; *ataeva*—therefore; *nāma*—the name; *haila*—became; *kṣīra-corā*—the thief of sweet rice; *kari'*—making.

TRANSLATION

"On account of Mādhavendra Purī, Lord Gopīnātha stole the pot of sweet rice. Thus He became famous as Kṣīra-corā [the thief who stole the sweet rice].

TEXT 175

কর্পূর-চন্দন যাঁর অঙ্গে চড়াইল ।
আনন্দে পুরী-গোসাঞির প্রেম উথলিল ॥ ১৭৫ ॥

karpūra-candana yāṅra aṅge caḍāila
ānande purī-gosāñira prema uthalila

SYNONYMS

karpūra-candana—camphor and sandalwood; *yāṅra aṅge*—on whose body; *caḍāila*—put; *ānande*—in great pleasure; *purī-gosāñira*—of Mādhavendra Purī; *prema*—love of Godhead; *uthalila*—welled up.

TRANSLATION

"Mādhavendra Purī smeared the sandalwood pulp over the body of Gopīnātha, and in this way he was overpowered with love of Godhead.

TEXT 176

ম্লেচ্ছদেশে কর্পূর-চন্দন আনিতে জঞ্জাল ।
পুরী দুঃখ পাবে ইহা জানিয়া গোপাল ॥ ১৭৬ ॥

mleccha-deśe karpūra-candana ānite jañjāla
purī duḥkha pābe ihā jāniyā gopāla

SYNONYMS

mleccha-deśe—through the countries where Mohammedans ruled; *karpūra-candana*—camphor and sandalwood; *ānite*—to bring; *jañjāla*—inconvenience; *purī*—Mādhavendra Purī; *duḥkha*—unhappiness; *pābe*—will get; *ihā*—this; *jāniyā*—knowing; *gopāla*—Gopāla.

TRANSLATION

"In the provinces of India governed by the Mohammedans, there was much inconvenience in traveling with sandalwood and camphor. Because of this, Mādhavendra Purī might have gotten into trouble. This became known to the Gopāla Deity.

TEXT 177

মহা-দয়াময় প্রভু—ভকতবৎসল ।
চন্দন পরি' ভক্তশ্রম করিল সফল ॥ ১৭৭ ॥

mahā-dayā-maya prabhu——bhakata-vatsala
candana pari' bhakta-śrama karila saphala

SYNONYMS

mahā—very; *dayā-maya*—merciful; *prabhu*—the Lord; *bhakata-vatsala*—very attached to His devotees; *candana pari'*—putting on the sandalwood; *bhakta-śrama*—the trouble of the devotee; *karila*—made; *saphala*—successful.

TRANSLATION

"The Lord is very merciful and attached to His devotees, so when Gopīnātha was covered with sandalwood pulp, Mādhavendra Purī's labor became successful."

TEXT 178

পুরীর প্রেম-পরাকাষ্ঠা করহ বিচার ।
অলৌকিক প্রেম চিত্তে লাগে চমৎকার ॥ ১৭৮ ॥

purīra prema-parākāṣṭhā karaha vicāra
alaukika prema citte lāge camatkāra

SYNONYMS

purīra—of Mādhavendra Purī; *prema-parā-kāṣṭhā*—the standard of intense love of Godhead; *karaha*—just make; *vicāra*—judgment; *alaukika*—uncommon; *prema*—love of Godhead; *citte*—in the mind; *lāge*—strikes; *camatkāra*—wonder.

TRANSLATION

Caitanya Mahāprabhu placed the standard of Mādhavendra Purī's intense love before Nityānanda Prabhu for judgment. "All his loving activities are un-

common," Caitanya Mahāprabhu said. "Indeed, one is struck with wonder to hear of his activities."

PURPORT

When the living entity feels spiritual separation from Kṛṣṇa (*kṛṣṇa-viraha*), he has achieved the prime success of life. When one becomes disinterested in material things, he is simply experiencing the other side of attraction for material things. However, feeling separation from Kṛṣṇa and engaging in the service of the Lord to fulfill His mission constitute the best example of love of Kṛṣṇa. Śrī Caitanya Mahāprabhu wanted to point out this intense love of Kṛṣṇa exhibited by Mādhavendra Purī. All Caitanya Mahāprabhu's devotees later followed in the footsteps of Mādhavendra Purī, serving the Lord without personal considerations.

TEXT 179

পরম বিরক্ত, মৌনী, সর্বত্র উদাসীন ।
গ্রাম্যবার্তা-ভয়ে দ্বিতীয়-সঙ্গ-হীন ॥ ১৭৯ ॥

parama virakta, maunī, sarvatra udāsīna
grāmya-vārtā-bhaye dvitīya-saṅga-hīna

SYNONYMS

parama virakta—totally renounced or unattached; *maunī*—silent; *sarvatra*—everywhere; *udāsīna*—uninterested; *grāmya-vārtā*—of mundane topics; *bhaye*—in fear; *dvitīya*—second; *saṅga*—associate; *hīna*—without.

TRANSLATION

Caitanya Mahāprabhu continued: "Śrī Mādhavendra Purī used to remain alone. He was completely renounced and always very silent. He was uninterested in everything material, and for fear of talking about mundane things, he always lived without a companion.

TEXT 180

হেন-জন গোপালের আজ্ঞামৃত পাঞা ।
সহস্র ক্রোশ আসি' বুলে চন্দন মাগিঞা ॥ ১৮০ ॥

hena-jana gopālera ājñāmṛta pāñā
sahasra krośa āsi' bule candana māgiñā

SYNONYMS

hena-jana—such a personality; *gopālera*—of the Gopāla Deity; *ājñā-amṛta*—the nectarean order; *pāñā*—getting; *sahasra*—a thousand; *krośa*—a distance of two miles; *āsi'*—coming; *bule*—walks; *candana*—sandalwood; *māgiñā*—begging.

TRANSLATION

"After receiving the transcendental orders of Gopāla, this great personality traveled thousands of miles just to collect sandalwood by begging.

TEXT 181

ভোকে রহে, তবু অন্ন মাগিঞা না খায় ।
হেন-জন চন্দন-ভার বহি' লঞা যায় ॥ ১৮১ ॥

bhoke rahe, tabu anna māgiñā nā khāya
hena-jana candana-bhāra vahi' lañā yāya

SYNONYMS

bhoke—hungry; *rahe*—remains; *tabu*—still; *anna*—food; *māgiñā*—begging; *nā*—does not; *khāya*—eat; *hena-jana*—such a person; *candana-bhāra*—the load of sandalwood; *vahi'*—carrying; *lañā*—taking; *yāya*—goes.

TRANSLATION

"Although Mādhavendra Purī was hungry, he would not beg food to eat. This renounced person carried a load of sandalwood for the sake of Śrī Gopāla.

TEXT 182

'মণেক চন্দন, তোলা-বিশেক কর্পূর ।
গোপালে পরাইব'—এই আনন্দ প্রচুর ॥ ১৮২ ॥

'maṇeka candana, tolā-viśeka karpūra
gopāle parāiba'——ei ānanda pracura

SYNONYMS

maṇeka candana—one mound of sandalwood; *tolā*—a measurement of weight; *viśeka*—twenty; *karpūra*—camphor; *gopāle*—on Gopāla; *parāiba*—I shall smear; *ei*—this; *ānanda*—pleasure; *pracura*—sufficient.

TRANSLATION

"Without considering his personal comforts, Mādhavendra Purī carried one maund [about eighty-two pounds] of sandalwood and twenty tolās [about eight ounces] of camphor to smear over the body of Gopāla. This transcendental pleasure was sufficient for him.

TEXT 183

উৎকলের দানী রাখে চন্দন দেখিঞা ।
তাহাঁ এড়াইল রাজপত্র দেখাঞা ॥ ১৮৩ ॥

utkalera dānī rākhe candana dekhiñā
tāhāṅ eḍāila rāja-patra dekhāñā

SYNONYMS

utkalera—of Orissa; *dānī*—toll officer; *rākhe*—takes; *candana*—sandalwood; *dekhiñā*—seeing; *tāhāṅ*—there; *eḍāila*—escaped; *rāja-patra*—governmental release; *dekhāñā*—by showing.

TRANSLATION

"Since there were restrictions against taking the sandalwood out of the Orissa province, the toll official confiscated the stock, but Mādhavendra Purī showed him the release papers given by the government and consequently escaped difficulties.

TEXT 184

ম্লেচ্ছদেশ দূর পথ, জগাতি অপার ।
কেমতে চন্দন নিব—নাহি এ বিচার ॥ ১৮৪ ॥

mleccha-deśa dūra patha, jagāti apāra
ke-mate candana niba——nāhi e vicāra

SYNONYMS

mleccha-deśa—the countries governed by Mohammedans; *dūra patha*—long journey; *jagāti*—watchmen; *apāra*—unlimited; *ke-mate*—how; *candana*—the sandalwood; *niba*—I shall take; *nāhi*—there was not; *e*—this; *vicāra*—consideration.

TRANSLATION

"Mādhavendra Purī was not at all anxious during the long journey to Vṛndāvana through the provinces governed by the Mohammedans and filled with unlimited numbers of watchmen.

TEXT 185

সঙ্গে এক বট নাহি ঘাটীদান দিতে ।
তথাপি উৎসাহ বড় চন্দন লঞা যাইতে ॥ ১৮৫ ॥

saṅge eka vaṭa nāhi ghāṭī-dāna dite
tathāpi utsāha baḍa candana lañā yāite

SYNONYMS

saṅge—with him; *eka*—one; *vaṭa*—farthing; *nāhi*—there was not; *ghāṭī-dāna*—as a toll tax; *dite*—to give; *tathāpi*—still; *utsāha*—enthusiasm; *baḍa*—much; *candana*—sandalwood; *lañā*—taking; *yāite*—to go.

TRANSLATION

"Although Mādhavendra Purī did not have a farthing with him, he was not afraid to pass by the toll officers. His only enjoyment was in carrying the load of sandalwood to Vṛndāvana for Gopāla.

TEXT 186

প্রগাঢ়-প্রেমের এই স্বভাব-আচার ।
নিজ-দুঃখ-বিঘ্নাদির না করে বিচার ॥ ১৮৬ ॥

pragāḍha-premera ei svabhāva-ācāra
nija-duḥkha-vighnādira nā kare vicāra

SYNONYMS

pragāḍha—intense; *premera*—of love of Godhead; *ei*—this; *svabhāva*—natural; *ācāra*—behavior; *nija*—personal; *duḥkha*—inconvenience; *vighna*—impediments; *ādira*—and so on; *nā*—not; *kare*—does; *vicāra*—consideration.

TRANSLATION

"This is the natural result of intense love of Godhead. The devotee does not consider personal inconveniences or impediments. In all circumstances he wants to serve the Supreme Personality of Godhead.

PURPORT

It is natural for those who have developed intense love for Kṛṣṇa not to care for personal inconvenience and impediments. Such devotees are simply determined to execute the order of the Supreme Personality of Godhead or His representative, the spiritual master. In all circumstances, even amidst the greatest dangers, they undeviatingly carry on with the greatest determination. This definitely proves the intense love of the servitor. As stated in *Śrīmad-Bhāgavatam, tat te 'nukampāṁ susamīkṣyamāṇaḥ:* those who seriously desire to get free from the clutches of material existence, who have developed intense love for Kṛṣṇa, are worthy candidates for going back home, back to Godhead. An intense lover of Kṛṣṇa does not care for any number of material discomforts, scarcity, impediments or unhappiness. It is said that when one sees apparent unhappiness or distress in a perfect Vaiṣṇava, it is not at all unhappiness for him; rather, it is transcendental bliss. In the *Śikṣāṣṭaka,* Śrī Caitanya Mahāprabhu has also instructed: *āśliṣya vā pāda-ratām.* The intense lover of Kṛṣṇa is never deviated from his service, despite all difficulties and impediments brought before him.

TEXT 187

এই তার গাঢ় প্রেমা লোকে দেখাইতে।
গোপাল তাঁরে আজ্ঞা দিল চন্দন আনিতে॥ ১৮৭ ॥

ei tāra gāḍha premā loke dekhāite
gopāla tāṅre ājñā dila candana ānite

SYNONYMS

ei—this; *tāra*—of Mādhavendra Purī; *gāḍha*—intense; *premā*—love of Godhead; *loke*—unto the people; *dekhāite*—to show; *gopāla*—Lord Gopāla; *tāṅre*—to him; *ājñā*—order; *dila*—gave; *candana*—sandalwood; *ānite*—to bring.

TRANSLATION

"Śrī Gopāla wanted to show how intensely Mādhavendra Purī loved Kṛṣṇa; therefore He asked him to go to Nīlācala to fetch sandalwood and camphor.

TEXT 188

বহু পরিশ্রমে চন্দন রেমুণা আনিল।
আনন্দ বাড়িল মনে, দুঃখ না গণিল॥ ১৮৮ ॥

bahu pariśrame candana remuṇā ānila
ānanda bāḍila mane, duḥkha nā gaṇila

SYNONYMS

bahu—much; *pariśrame*—with labor; *candana*—sandalwood; *remuṇā*—to Remuṇā (the village of Gopīnātha); *ānila*—brought; *ānanda*—pleasure; *bāḍila*—increased; *mane*—in the mind; *duḥkha*—difficulties; *nā*—not; *gaṇila*—counted.

TRANSLATION

"With great trouble and after much labor, Mādhavendra Purī brought the load of sandalwood to Remuṇā. However, he was still very pleased; he discounted all the difficulties.

TEXT 189

পরীক্ষা করিতে গোপাল কৈল আজ্ঞা দান।
পরীক্ষা করিয়া শেষে হৈল দয়াবান্ ॥ ১৮৯ ॥

parīkṣā karite gopāla kaila ājñā dāna
parīkṣā kariyā śeṣe haila dayāvān

SYNONYMS

parīkṣā—test; *karite*—to make; *gopāla*—Lord Gopāla; *kaila*—did; *ājñā*—the order; *dāna*—giving; *parīkṣā*—the test; *kariyā*—making; *śeṣe*—at the end; *haila*—became; *dayā-vān*—merciful.

TRANSLATION

"To test the intense love of Mādhavendra Purī, Gopāla, the Supreme Personality of Godhead, ordered him to bring sandalwood from Nīlācala, and when Mādhavendra Purī passed this examination, the Lord became very merciful to him.

TEXT 190

এই ভক্তি, ভক্তপ্রিয়-কৃষ্ণ-ব্যবহার।
বুঝিতেও আমা-সবার নাহি অধিকার ॥ ১৯০ ॥

ei bhakti, bhakta-priya-kṛṣṇa-vyavahāra
bujhiteo āmā-sabāra nāhi adhikāra

SYNONYMS

ei bhakti—this type of devotion; *bhakta*—of the devotee; *priya*—and the most lovable object; *kṛṣṇa*—Lord Kṛṣṇa; *vyavahāra*—the behavior; *bujhiteo*—to understand; *āmā-sabāra*—of all of us; *nāhi*—there is not; *adhikāra*—the capacity.

TRANSLATION

"Such behavior exhibited in loving service between the devotee and the devotee's lovable object, Śrī Kṛṣṇa, is transcendental. It is not possible for a common man to understand. Common men do not even have the capacity."

TEXT 191

এত বলি' পড়ে প্রভু তাঁর কৃত শ্লোক ।
যেই শ্লোক-চন্দ্রে জগৎ কর্যাছে আলোক ॥ ১৯১ ॥

eta bali' paḍe prabhu tāṅra kṛta śloka
yei śloka-candre jagat karyāche āloka

SYNONYMS

eta bali'—saying this; *paḍe*—reads; *prabhu*—Lord Caitanya Mahāprabhu; *tāṅra*—by Mādhavendra Purī; *kṛta*—composed; *śloka*—verse; *yei*—that; *śloka-candre*—by the moonlike verse; *jagat*—all over the world; *karyāche*—produced; *āloka*—light.

TRANSLATION

After saying this, Lord Caitanya Mahāprabhu read the famous verse of Mādhavendra Purī. That verse is just like the moon. It has spread illumination all over the world.

TEXT 192

ঘষিতে ঘষিতে যৈছে মলয়জ-সার ।
গন্ধ বাড়ে, তৈছে এই শ্লোকের বিচার ॥ ১৯২ ॥

ghaṣite ghaṣite yaiche malayaja-sāra
gandha bāḍe, taiche ei ślokera vicāra

SYNONYMS

ghaṣite ghaṣite—rubbing and rubbing; *yaiche*—just as; *malaya-ja-sāra*—sandalwood; *gandha*—the flavor; *bāḍe*—increases; *taiche*—similarly; *ei*—this; *ślokera*—of the verse; *vicāra*—the consideration.

TRANSLATION

By continuous rubbing, the aroma of Malaya sandalwood increases. Similarly, by considering this verse, its importance increases.

TEXT 193

রত্নগণ-মধ্যে যৈছে কৌস্তুভমণি ।
রসকাব্য-মধ্যে তৈছে এই শ্লোক গণি ॥ ১৯৩ ॥

ratna-gaṇa-madhye yaiche kaustubha-maṇi
rasa-kāvya-madhye taiche ei śloka gaṇi

SYNONYMS

ratna-gaṇa—the valuable jewels; *madhye*—among; *yaiche*—just as; *kaustubha-maṇi*—the jewel known as Kaustubha-maṇi; *rasa-kāvya*—mellow poetry; *madhye*—among; *taiche*—similarly; *ei*—this; *śloka*—verse; *gaṇi*—I count.

TRANSLATION

As the kaustubha-maṇi is considered the most precious of valuable stones, this verse is similarly considered the best of mellow poems.

TEXT 194

এই শ্লোক কহিয়াছেন রাধা-ঠাকুরাণী ।
তাঁর কৃপায় স্ফুরিয়াছে মাধবেন্দ্র-বাণী ॥ ১৯৪ ॥

ei śloka kahiyāchena rādhā-ṭhākurāṇī
tāṅra kṛpāya sphuriyāche mādhavendra-vāṇī

SYNONYMS

ei—this; *śloka*—verse; *kahiyāchena*—has spoken; *rādhā-ṭhākurāṇī*—Śrīmatī Rādhārāṇī; *tāṅra*—Her; *kṛpāya*—by the mercy; *sphuriyāche*—has manifested; *mādhavendra*—of Mādhavendra Purī; *vāṇī*—the words.

TRANSLATION

Actually this verse was spoken by Śrīmatī Rādhārāṇī Herself, and by Her mercy only was it manifest in the words of Mādhavendra Purī.

TEXT 195

কিবা গৌরচন্দ্র ইহা করে আস্বাদন ।
ইহা আস্বাদিতে আর নাহি চৌঠজন ॥ ১৯৫ ॥

kibā gauracandra ihā kare āsvādana
ihā āsvādite āra nāhi cauṭha-jana

SYNONYMS

kibā—how excellent; *gaura-candra*—Lord Śrī Caitanya Mahāprabhu; *ihā*—this; *kare*—does; *āsvādana*—tasting; *ihā*—this verse; *āsvādite*—to taste; *āra*—another; *nāhi*—there is not; *cauṭha-jana*—a fourth man.

TRANSLATION

Only Śrī Caitanya Mahāprabhu has tasted the poetry of this verse. No fourth man is capable of understanding it.

PURPORT

This indicates that only Śrīmatī Rādhārāṇī, Mādhavendra Purī and Caitanya Mahāprabhu are capable of understanding the purport of this verse.

TEXT 196

শেষকালে এই শ্লোক পঠিতে পঠিতে।
সিদ্ধিপ্রাপ্তি হৈল পুরীর শ্লোকের সহিতে ॥ ১৯৬ ॥

śeṣa-kāle ei śloka paṭhite paṭhite
siddhi-prāpti haila purīra ślokera sahite

SYNONYMS

śeṣa-kāle—at the end; *ei śloka*—this verse; *paṭhite paṭhite*—by reciting repeatedly; *siddhi-prāpti*—attainment of perfection; *haila*—there was; *purīra*—of Mādhavendra Purī; *ślokera*—this verse; *sahite*—with.

TRANSLATION

Mādhavendra Purī recited this verse again and again at the end of his material existence. Thus uttering this verse, he attained the ultimate goal of life.

TEXT 197

অয়ি দীনদয়ার্দ্র নাথ হে মথুরানাথ কদাবলোক্যসে।
হৃদয়ং ত্বদলোককাতরং দয়িত ভ্রাম্যতি কিং করোম্যহম্॥১৯৭

ayi dīna-dayārdra nātha he
mathurā-nātha kadāvalokyase
hṛdayaṁ tvad-aloka-kātaraṁ
dayita bhrāmyati kiṁ karomy aham

SYNONYMS

ayi—O My Lord; *dīna*—on the poor; *dayā-ardra*—compassionate; *nātha*—O master; *he*—O; *mathurā-nātha*—the master of Mathurā; *kadā*—when; *avalokyase*—I shall see You; *hṛdayam*—My heart; *tvat*—of You; *aloka*—without seeing; *kātaram*—very much aggrieved; *dayita*—O most beloved; *bhrāmyati*—becomes overwhelmed; *kim*—what; *karomi*—shall do; *aham*—I.

TRANSLATION

"O My Lord! O most merciful master! O master of Mathurā! When shall I see You again? Because of My not seeing You, My agitated heart has become unsteady. O most beloved one, what shall I do now?"

PURPORT

The uncontaminated devotees who strictly depend on the Vedānta philosophy are divided into four *sampradāyas,* or transcendental parties. Out of the four *sampradāyas,* the Śrī Madhvācārya-sampradāya was accepted by Mādhavendra Purī. Thus he took *sannyāsa* according to *paramparā,* the disciplic succession. Beginning from Madhvācārya down to the spiritual master of Mādhavendra Purī, the *ācārya* named Lakṣmīpati, there was no realization of devotional service in conjugal love. Śrī Mādhavendra Purī introduced the conception of conjugal love for the first time in the Madhvācārya-sampradāya, and this conclusion of the Madhvācārya-sampradāya was revealed by Śrī Caitanya Mahāprabhu when He toured southern India and met the Tattvavādīs, who supposedly belonged to the Madhvācārya-sampradāya.

When Śrī Kṛṣṇa left Vṛndāvana and accepted the kingdom of Mathurā, Śrīmatī Rādhārāṇī, out of ecstatic feelings of separation, expressed how Kṛṣṇa can be loved in separation. Thus devotional service in separation is central to this verse. Worship in separation is considered by the Gauḍīya-Madhva-sampradāya to be the topmost level of devotional service. According to this conception, the devotee thinks of himself as very poor and neglected by the Lord. Thus he addresses the Lord as *dīna-dayārdra nātha,* as did Mādhavendra Purī. Such an ecstatic feeling is the highest form of devotional service. Because Kṛṣṇa had gone to Mathurā, Śrīmatī Rādhārāṇī was very much affected, and She expressed Herself thus: "My dear Lord, because of Your separation My mind has become overly agitated. Now tell Me, what can I do? I am very poor, and You are very merciful, so kindly have compassion upon Me and let Me know when I shall see You." Śrī Caitanya Mahāprabhu was always expressing the ecstatic emotions of Śrīmatī Rādhārāṇī that She exhibited when She saw Uddhava at Vṛndāvana. Similar feelings, experienced by Mādhavendra Purī, are expressed in this verse. Therefore, Vaiṣṇavas in the Gauḍīya-Madhva-sampradāya say that the ecstatic feelings experienced by Śrī Caitanya Mahāprabhu during His appearance came from Śrī Mādhavendra Purī through Īśvara Purī. All the devotees in the line of the Gauḍīya-Madhva-sampradāya accept these principles of devotional service.

TEXT 198

এই শ্লোক পড়িতে প্রভু হইলা মূর্চ্ছিতে ।
প্রেমেতে বিবশ হঞা পড়িল ভূমিতে ॥ ১৯৮ ॥

ei śloka paḍite prabhu ha-ilā mūrcchite
premete vivaśa hañā paḍila bhūmite

SYNONYMS

ei śloka—this verse; *paḍite*—reciting; *prabhu*—Lord Śrī Caitanya Mahāprabhu; *ha-ilā*—became; *mūrcchite*—unconscious; *premete*—in ecstatic love; *vivaśa*—uncontrolled; *hañā*—becoming; *paḍila*—fell down; *bhūmite*—on the ground.

TRANSLATION

When Śrī Caitanya Mahāprabhu recited this verse, He immediately fell to the ground unconscious. He was overwhelmed and had no control over Himself.

TEXT 199

আস্তে-ব্যস্তে কোলে করি' নিল নিত্যানন্দ ।
ক্রন্দন করিয়া তবে উঠে গৌরচন্দ্র ॥ ১৯৯ ॥

āste-vyaste kole kari' nila nityānanda
krandana kariyā tabe uṭhe gauracandra

SYNONYMS

āste-vyaste—in great dexterity; *kole*—on the lap; *kari'*—making; *nila*—took; *nityānanda*—Lord Nityānanda Prabhu; *krandana*—crying; *kariyā*—doing; *tabe*—at that time; *uṭhe*—got up; *gaura-candra*—Lord Śrī Caitanya Mahāprabhu.

TRANSLATION

When Lord Śrī Caitanya Mahāprabhu fell to the ground in ecstatic love, Lord Nityānanda took Him on His lap. Crying, Caitanya Mahāprabhu then got up again.

TEXT 200

প্রেমোন্মাদ হৈল, উঠি' ইতি-উতি ধায় ।
হুঙ্কার করয়ে, হাসে, কান্দে, নাচে, গায় ॥ ২০০ ॥

premonmāda haila, uṭhi' iti-uti dhāya
huṅkāra karaye, hāse, kānde, nāce, gāya

SYNONYMS

prema-unmāda—the madness of love; *haila*—there was; *uṭhi'*—getting up; *iti-uti dhāya*—runs here and there; *huṅkāra*—resounding; *karaye*—does; *hāse*—laughs; *kānde*—cries; *nāce*—dances; *gāya*—and sings.

TRANSLATION

Exhibiting ecstatic emotions, the Lord began to run here and there, making resounding noises. Sometimes He laughed, and sometimes cried, and sometimes danced and sang.

TEXT 201

'অয়ি দীন', 'অয়ি দীন' বলে বারবার ।
কণ্ঠে না নিঃসরে বাণী, নেত্রে অশ্রুধার ॥ ২০১ ॥

'ayi dīna', 'ayi dīna' bale bāra-bāra
kaṇṭhe nā niḥsare vāṇī, netre aśru-dhāra

SYNONYMS

ayi dīna—O my Lord, master of the poor; *ayi dīna*—O my Lord, master of the poor; *bale*—says; *bāra-bāra*—repeatedly; *kaṇṭhe*—in the throat; *nā*—not; *niḥsare*—comes out; *vāṇī*—the voice; *netre*—in the eyes; *aśru-dhāra*—torrents of tears.

TRANSLATION

Caitanya Mahāprabhu could not recite the whole verse. He simply said, "Ayi dīna, ayi dīna," repeatedly. Thus He could not speak, and profuse tears were in His eyes.

TEXT 202

কম্প, স্বেদ, পুলকাশ্রু, স্তম্ভ, বৈবর্ণ্য ।
নির্বেদ, বিষাদ, জাড্য, গর্ব, হর্ষ, দৈন্য ॥ ২০২ ॥

kampa, sveda, pulakāśru, stambha, vaivarṇya
nirveda, viṣāda, jāḍya, garva, harṣa, dainya

SYNONYMS

kampa—trembling; *sveda*—perspiration; *pulaka-aśru*—jubilation and tears; *stambha*—shock; *vaivarṇya*—loss of color; *nirveda*—disappointment; *viṣāda*—moroseness; *jāḍya*—loss of memory; *garva*—pride; *harṣa*—joy; *dainya*—humility.

TRANSLATION

Trembling, perspiration, jubilant tears, shock, fading of the bodily luster, disappointment, moroseness, loss of memory, pride, joy and humility were all visible in Śrī Caitanya Mahāprabhu's body.

PURPORT

In the *Bhakti-rasāmṛta-sindhu, jāḍya* is explained as loss of memory brought about by severe shock due to separation from the beloved. In that state of mind, one loses all concern for loss and gain, hearing and seeing, as well as all other considerations. This marks the preliminary appearance of illusion.

TEXT 203

এই শ্লোকে উঘাড়িলা প্রেমের কপাট ।
গোপীনাথ-সেবক দেখে প্রভুর প্রেমনাট ॥ ২০৩ ॥

ei śloke ughāḍilā premera kapāṭa
gopīnātha-sevaka dekhe prabhura prema-nāṭa

SYNONYMS

ei śloke—this verse; *ughāḍilā*—uncovered; *premera*—of conjugal love; *kapāṭa*—the door; *gopīnātha-sevaka*—the servants of the Gopīnātha Deity; *dekhe*—see; *prabhura*—of Lord Caitanya Mahāprabhu; *prema-nāṭa*—the dance in ecstatic love.

TRANSLATION

This verse uncovered the door of ecstatic love, and when it was exhibited, all the servants of Gopīnātha saw Caitanya Mahāprabhu dance in ecstasy.

TEXT 204

লোকের সংঘট্ট দেখি' প্রভুর বাহ্য হৈল ।
ঠাকুরের ভোগ সরি' আরতি বাজিল ॥ ২০৪ ॥

lokera saṅghaṭṭa dekhi' prabhura bāhya haila
ṭhākurera bhoga sari' ārati bājila

SYNONYMS

lokera—of people; *saṅghaṭṭa*—a crowd; *dekhi'*—seeing; *prabhura*—of Śrī Caitanya Mahāprabhu; *bāhya*—external consciousness; *haila*—appeared; *ṭhākurera*—of the Deity; *bhoga*—offering; *sari'*—finishing; *ārati*—performance of *ārati*; *bājila*—resounded.

TRANSLATION

When many people crowded around Śrī Caitanya Mahāprabhu, He regained His external senses. In the meantime, the offering to the Deity had been finished, and there was a resounding ārati performance.

TEXT 205

ঠাকুরে শয়ন করাঞা পূজারী হৈল বাহির ।
প্রভুর আগে আনি' দিল প্রসাদ বার ক্ষীর ॥ ২০৫ ॥

ṭhākure śayana karāñā pūjārī haila bāhira
prabhura āge āni' dila prasāda bāra kṣīra

SYNONYMS

ṭhākure—the Deity; *śayana*—lying down; *karāñā*—causing to do; *pūjārī*—the priest; *haila*—was; *bāhira*—out of the temple; *prabhura*—of Lord Śrī Caitanya Mahāprabhu; *āge*—in front; *āni'*—bringing; *dila*—offered; *prasāda*—the remnants of food; *bāra*—twelve; *kṣīra*—pots of sweet rice.

TRANSLATION

When the Deities were laid down to rest, the priest came out of the temple and offered all twelve pots of sweet rice to Lord Caitanya Mahāprabhu.

TEXT 206

ক্ষীর দেখি' মহাপ্রভুর আনন্দ বাড়িল ।
ভক্তগণে খাওয়াইতে পঞ্চ ক্ষীর লৈল ॥ ২০৬ ॥

kṣīra dekhi' mahāprabhura ānanda bāḍila
bhakta-gaṇe khāoyāite pañca kṣīra laila

SYNONYMS

kṣīra—the sweet rice; *dekhi'*—seeing; *mahāprabhura*—of Lord Śrī Caitanya Mahāprabhu; *ānanda*—the pleasure; *bāḍila*—increased; *bhakta-gaṇe*—the devotees; *khāoyāite*—to feed them; *pañca*—five pots; *kṣīra*—sweet rice; *laila*—accepted.

TRANSLATION

When all the pots of sweet rice, remnants left by Gopīnātha, were placed before Śrī Caitanya Mahāprabhu, He became very pleased. In order to feed the devotees, He accepted five of them.

TEXT 207

সাত ক্ষীর পূজারীকে বাহুড়িয়া দিল ।
পঞ্চক্ষীর পঞ্চজনে বাঁটিয়া খাইল ॥ ২০৭ ॥

sāta kṣīra pūjārīke bāhuḍiyā dila
pañca-kṣīra pañca-jane vāṅṭiyā khāila

SYNONYMS

sāta kṣīra—seven pots of sweet rice; *pūjārīke*—toward the *pūjārī*; *bāhuḍiyā*—pushing forward; *dila*—gave; *pañca-kṣīra*—five pots of sweet rice; *pañca-jane*—to five men; *vāṅṭiyā*—distributing; *khāila*—ate.

TRANSLATION

The seven remaining pots were pushed forward and delivered to the priest. Then the five pots of sweet rice the Lord had accepted were distributed among the five devotees, and they ate the prasāda.

TEXT 208

গোপীনাথ-রূপে যদি করিয়াছেন ভোজন।
ভক্তি দেখাইতে কৈল প্রসাদ ভক্ষণ ॥ ২০৮ ॥

gopīnātha-rūpe yadi kariyāchena bhojana
bhakti dekhāite kaila prasāda bhakṣaṇa

SYNONYMS

gopīnātha-rūpe—in His *arcā* incarnation as Gopīnātha; *yadi*—although; *kariyāchena*—has done; *bhojana*—eating; *bhakti*—devotional service; *dekhāite*—to exhibit; *kaila*—did; *prasāda bhakṣaṇa*—eating.

TRANSLATION

Being identical with the Gopīnātha Deity, Śrī Caitanya Mahāprabhu had already tasted and eaten the pots of sweet rice. Yet just to manifest devotional service, He again ate the pots of sweet rice as a devotee.

TEXT 209

নাম-সংকীর্তনে সেই রাত্রি গোঙাইলা।
মঙ্গল-আরতি দেখি' প্রভাতে চলিলা ॥ ২০৯ ॥

nāma-saṅkīrtane sei rātri goṅāilā
maṅgala-ārati dekhi' prabhāte calilā

SYNONYMS

nāma-saṅkīrtane—in congregational chanting; *sei*—that; *rātri*—night; *goṅāilā*—passed; *maṅgala-ārati*—the early *ārati*; *dekhi'*—after seeing; *prabhāte*—in the morning; *calilā*—departed.

TRANSLATION

Śrī Caitanya Mahāprabhu passed that night at the temple engaged in congregational chanting. In the morning, after seeing the maṅgala-ārati performance, He departed.

TEXT 210

গোপাল-গোপীনাথ-পুরীগোসাঞির গুণ ।
ভক্ত-সঙ্গে শ্রীমুখে প্রভু কৈলা আস্বাদন ॥ ২১০ ॥

gopāla-gopīnātha-purī-gosāñira guṇa
bhakta-saṅge śrī-mukhe prabhu kailā āsvādana

SYNONYMS

gopāla—of the Gopāla Deity; *gopīnātha*—of the Gopīnātha Deity; *purī-gosāñira*—of Mādhavendra Purī; *guṇa*—the qualities; *bhakta-saṅge*—with the devotees; *śrī-mukhe*—in His own mouth; *prabhu*—Śrī Caitanya Mahāprabhu; *kailā*—did; *āsvādana*—tasting.

TRANSLATION

In this way, Lord Śrī Caitanya Mahāprabhu personally tasted with His own mouth the transcendental qualities of Gopālajī, Gopīnātha and Śrī Mādhavendra Purī.

TEXT 211

এই ত' আখ্যানে কহিলা দোঁহার মহিমা ।
প্রভুর ভক্তবাৎসল্য, আর ভক্তপ্রেম-সীমা ॥ ২১১ ॥

ei ta' ākhyāne kahilā doṅhāra mahimā
prabhura bhakta-vātsalya, āra bhakta-prema-sīmā

SYNONYMS

ei ta'—thus; *ākhyāne*—in the narration; *kahilā*—described; *doṅhāra*—of the two; *mahimā*—the glories; *prabhura*—of Lord Śrī Caitanya Mahāprabhu; *bhakta-*

vātsalya—attachment for His devotees; *āra*—and; *bhakta-prema-sīmā*—the highest limit of ecstatic love by the devotee.

TRANSLATION

Thus I have described both the transcendental glories of Lord Caitanya Mahāprabhu's affection for His devotees and the highest limit of ecstatic love of God.

TEXT 212

শ্রদ্ধাযুক্ত হঞা ইহা শুনে যেই জন ।
শ্রীকৃষ্ণ-চরণে সেই পায় প্রেমধন ॥ ২১২ ॥

śraddhā-yukta hañā ihā śune yei jana
śrī-kṛṣṇa-caraṇe sei pāya prema-dhana

SYNONYMS

śraddhā-yukta—possessed of faith; *hañā*—being; *ihā*—this; *śune*—hears; *yei*—that; *jana*—person; *śrī-kṛṣṇa-caraṇe*—at the lotus feet of Lord Śrī Kṛṣṇa; *sei*—that person; *pāya*—gets; *prema-dhana*—the treasure of love of Godhead.

TRANSLATION

One who hears this narration with faith and devotion attains the treasure of love of Godhead at the lotus feet of Śrī Kṛṣṇa.

TEXT 213

শ্রীরূপ-রঘুনাথ-পদে যার আশ ।
চৈতন্যচরিতামৃত কহে কৃষ্ণদাস ॥ ২১৩ ॥

śrī-rūpa-raghunātha-pade yāra āśa
caitanya-caritāmṛta kahe kṛṣṇadāsa

SYNONYMS

śrī-rūpa—Śrīla Rūpa Gosvāmī; *raghunātha*—Śrīla Raghunātha dāsa Gosvāmī; *pade*—at the lotus feet; *yāra*—whose; *āśa*—expectation; *caitanya-caritāmṛta*—the book named *Caitanya-caritāmṛta*; *kahe*—describes; *kṛṣṇa-dāsa*—Śrīla Kṛṣṇadāsa Kavirāja Gosvāmī.

TRANSLATION

Praying at the lotus feet of Śrī Rūpa and Śrī Raghunātha, always desiring their mercy, I, Kṛṣṇadāsa, narrate Śrī Caitanya-caritāmṛta, following in their footsteps.

Thus end the Bhaktivedanta purports to the Śrī Caitanya-caritāmṛta, Madhya-līlā, *Fourth Chapter, describing Śrī Mādhavendra Purī's devotional service.*

CHAPTER 5

The Activities of Sākṣi-gopāla

Śrīla Bhaktivinoda Ṭhākura gives the following summary of the Fifth Chapter in his *Amṛta-pravāha-bhāṣya:* After passing through Yājapura, Śrī Caitanya Mahāprabhu reached the town of Kaṭaka (Cuttak) and there went to see the temple of Sākṣi-gopāla. While there, He heard the story of Sākṣi-gopāla from the mouth of Śrī Nityānanda Prabhu.

Once there were two *brāhmaṇas,* one elderly and the other young, who were inhabitants of a place known as Vidyānagara. After touring many places of pilgrimage, the two *brāhmaṇas* finally reached Vṛndāvana. The elderly *brāhmaṇa* was very satisfied with the service of the young *brāhmaṇa,* and he wanted to offer him his youngest daughter in marriage. The young *brāhmaṇa* received the promise of his elder before the Gopāla Deity of Vṛndāvana. Thus the Gopāla Deity acted as a witness. When both *brāhmaṇas* returned to Vidyānagara, the younger *brāhmaṇa* raised the question of this marriage, but the elderly *brāhmaṇa,* due to obligations to his friends and wife, answered that he could not remember his promise. Because of this, the younger *brāhmaṇa* returned to Vṛndāvana and narrated the whole story to Gopālajī. Thus Gopālajī, being obliged by the young man's devotional service, accompanied him to southern India. Gopālajī followed the younger *brāhmaṇa,* who could hear the tinkling sound of Gopālajī's ankle bells. When all the respectable gentlemen of Vidyānagara were assembled, Gopālajī testified to the promise of the elderly *brāhmaṇa.* Thus the marriage was performed. Later, the King of that country constructed a fine temple for Gopāla.

Afterwards, King Puruṣottama of Orissa was insulted by the King of Kaṭaka, who refused to give him his daughter in marriage and called him a sweeper of Lord Jagannātha. With the help of Lord Jagannātha, King Puruṣottama fought the King of Kaṭaka and defeated him. Thus he took charge of both the King's daughter and the state of Kaṭaka as well. At that time, Gopālajī, being very much obligated by the devotional service of King Puruṣottama, was brought to the town of Kaṭaka.

After hearing this narration, Śrī Caitanya Mahāprabhu visited the temple of Gopāla in great ecstasy of love of God. From Kaṭaka He went to Bhuvaneśvara and saw the temple of Lord Śiva. In this way, He gradually arrived at Kamalapura, and on the banks of the Bhārgī River He came to the temple of Lord Śiva, where He entrusted His *sannyāsa* staff to Nityānanda Prabhu. However, Nityānanda Prabhu broke the staff into three pieces and threw it into the Bhārgī River at a place known as Āṭhāranālā. Being angry at not getting His staff back, Śrī Caitanya

Mahāprabhu left the company of Nityānanda Prabhu and went alone to see the Jagannātha temple.

TEXT 1

পদ্ভ্যাং চলন্ যঃ প্রতিমা-স্বরূপো
ব্রহ্মণ্যদেবো হি শতাহগম্যম্ ।
দেশং যযৌ বিপ্রকৃতেঽদ্ভুতেহং
তং সাক্ষিগোপালমহং নতোঽস্মি ॥ ১ ॥

padbhyāṁ calan yaḥ pratimā-svarūpo
brahmaṇya-devo hi śatāha-gamyam
deśaṁ yayau vipra-kṛte 'dbhutehaṁ
taṁ sākṣi-gopālam ahaṁ nato 'smi

SYNONYMS

padbhyām—by the two legs; *calan*—walking; *yaḥ*—one who; *pratimā*—of the Deity; *svarūpaḥ*—in the form; *brahmaṇya-devaḥ*—the Supreme Lord of brahminical culture; *hi*—certainly; *śata-āha*—in one hundred days; *gamyam*—to be passed over; *deśam*—the country; *yayau*—went; *vipra-kṛte*—for the benefit of a *brāhmaṇa*; *adbhuta*—most wonderful; *īham*—activity; *tam*—unto that; *sākṣi-gopālam*—the Gopāla known as the witness Gopāla; *aham*—I; *nataḥ asmi*—offer respectful obeisances.

TRANSLATION

I offer my respectful obeisances unto the Supreme Personality of God [brahmaṇya-deva], who appeared as Sākṣi-gopāla to benefit a brāhmaṇa. For one hundred days He traveled through the country, walking on His own legs. Thus His activities are wonderful.

TEXT 2

জয় জয় শ্রীচৈতন্য জয় নিত্যানন্দ ।
জয়াদ্বৈতচন্দ্র জয় গৌরভক্তবৃন্দ ॥ ২ ॥

jaya jaya śrī-caitanya jaya nityānanda
jayādvaitacandra jaya gaura-bhakta-vṛnda

SYNONYMS

jaya—all glories; *jaya*—all glories; *śrī caitanya*—to Lord Śrī Caitanya Mahāprabhu; *jaya*—all glories; *śrī nityānanda*—to Lord Śrī Nityānanda Prabhu; *jaya*—all glories; *advaita-candra*—to Advaita Ācārya; *jaya*—all glories; *gaura-bhakta-vṛnda*—to the devotees of Lord Caitanya Mahāprabhu.

TRANSLATION

All glories to Lord Śrī Caitanya Mahāprabhu! All glories to Lord Nityānanda Prabhu! All glories to Śrī Advaita Prabhu! And all glories to the devotees of Śrī Caitanya Mahāprabhu!

TEXT 3

চলিতে চলিতে আইলা যাজপুর-গ্রাম ।
বরাহ-ঠাকুর দেখি' করিলা প্রণাম ॥ ৩ ॥

calite calite āilā yājapura-grāma
varāha-ṭhākura dekhi' karilā praṇāma

SYNONYMS

calite calite—walking on and on; *āilā*—reached; *yājapura-grāma*—the village of Yājapura-grāma; *varāha-ṭhākura*—the temple of Varāhadeva; *dekhi'*—seeing; *karilā*—offered; *praṇāma*—obeisances.

TRANSLATION

Walking and walking, Śrī Caitanya Mahāprabhu and His party finally arrived at Yājapura on the River Vaitaraṇī. There He saw the temple of Varāhadeva and offered His obeisances unto Him.

TEXT 4

নৃত্যগীত কৈল প্রেমে বহুত স্তবন ।
যাজপুরে সে রাত্রি করিলা যাপন ॥ ৪ ॥

nṛtya-gīta kaila preme bahuta stavana
yājapure se rātri karilā yāpana

SYNONYMS

nṛtya-gīta—dancing and chanting; *kaila*—executed; *preme*—in love of Godhead; *bahuta*—various; *stavana*—prayers; *yājapure*—in the village of Yājapura; *se rātri*—that night; *karilā*—did; *yāpana*—passing.

TRANSLATION

In the temple of Varāhadeva, Śrī Caitanya Mahāprabhu engaged in chanting and dancing and offered prayers. He passed that night in the temple.

TEXT 5

কটকে আইলা সাক্ষিগোপাল দেখিতে ।
গোপাল-সৌন্দর্য দেখি' হৈলা আনন্দিতে ॥ ৫ ॥

kaṭake āilā sākṣi-gopāla dekhite
gopāla-saundarya dekhi' hailā ānandite

SYNONYMS

kaṭake—in the town of Kaṭaka (Cuttak); *āilā*—arrived; *sākṣi-gopāla*—the witness Gopāla; *dekhite*—to see; *gopāla*—of the Deity of Gopāla; *saundarya*—the beauty; *dekhi'*—seeing; *hailā*—became; *ānandite*—very pleased.

TRANSLATION

Afterwards, Śrī Caitanya Mahāprabhu went to the town of Kaṭaka to see the temple of the witness Gopāla. When He saw the Deity of Gopāla, He was very much pleased with His beauty.

TEXT 6

প্রেমাবেশে নৃত্যগীত কৈল কতক্ষণ ।
আবিষ্ট হঞা কৈল গোপাল স্তবন ॥ ৬ ॥

premāveśe nṛtya-gīta kaila kata-kṣaṇa
āviṣṭa hañā kaila gopāla stavana

SYNONYMS

prema-āveśe—in the ecstasy of love of God; *nṛtya-gīta*—dancing and chanting; *kaila*—performed; *kata-kṣaṇa*—for some time; *āviṣṭa hañā*—being overwhelmed; *kaila*—offered; *gopāla stavana*—prayers to Gopāla.

TRANSLATION

While there, Śrī Caitanya Mahāprabhu engaged in chanting and dancing for some time, and being overwhelmed, He offered many prayers to Gopāla.

TEXT 7

সেই রাত্রি তাহাঁ রহি' ভক্তগণ-সঙ্গে ।
গোপালের পূর্বকথা শুনে বহু রঙ্গে ॥ ৭ ॥

sei rātri tāhāṅ rahi' bhakta-gaṇa-saṅge
gopālera pūrva-kathā śune bahu raṅge

SYNONYMS

sei rātri—that night; *tāhāṅ*—there; *rahi'*—remaining; *bhakta-gaṇa-saṅge*—with the other devotees; *gopālera*—of Lord Gopāla; *pūrva-kathā*—previous narration; *śune*—hears; *bahu*—much; *raṅge*—in pleasure.

TRANSLATION

That night Śrī Caitanya Mahāprabhu stayed in the temple of Gopāla, and along with all the devotees, He heard the narration of the witness Gopāla with great pleasure.

TEXT 8

নিত্যানন্দ-গোসাঞি যবে তীর্থ ভ্রমিলা ।
সাক্ষিগোপাল দেখিবারে কটক আইলা ॥ ৮ ॥

nityānanda-gosāñi yabe tīrtha bhramilā
sākṣi-gopāla dekhibāre kaṭaka āilā

SYNONYMS

nityānanda-gosāñi—Lord Nityānanda Prabhu; *yabe*—when; *tīrtha bhramilā*—traveled to the places of pilgrimage; *sākṣi-gopāla*—the witness Gopāla; *dekhibāre*—to see; *kaṭaka*—to the town of Kaṭaka; *āilā*—came.

TRANSLATION

Previously, when Nityānanda Prabhu had toured all over India to see different places of pilgrimage, He also had come to see Sākṣi-gopāla at Kaṭaka.

TEXT 9

সাক্ষিগোপালের কথা শুনি, লোকমুখে ।
সেই কথা কহেন, প্রভু শুনে মহাসুখে ॥ ৯ ॥

sākṣi-gopālera kathā śuni, loka-mukhe
sei kathā kahena, prabhu śune mahā-sukhe

SYNONYMS

sākṣi-gopālera—of the witness Gopāla; *kathā*—the narration; *śuni*—hearing; *loka-mukhe*—from the people; *sei kathā*—that narration; *kahena*—Nityānanda Prabhu narrates; *prabhu*—Lord Śrī Caitanya Mahāprabhu; *śune*—hears; *mahā-sukhe*—in great pleasure.

TRANSLATION

At that time, Nityānanda Prabhu had heard the story of Sākṣi-gopāla from the townspeople. He now recited this again, and Lord Caitanya Mahāprabhu heard the narration with great pleasure.

PURPORT

The Sākṣi-gopāla temple is situated between the Khurdā Road Junction railway station and the Jagannātha Purī station. The Deity is not presently situated in Kaṭaka, but when Nityānanda Prabhu traveled there, the Deity was present. Kaṭaka is a town in Orissa situated on the Mahānadī River. When Sākṣi-gopāla was brought from Vidyānagara in southern India, He stayed for some time at Kaṭaka. Thereafter, He was situated for some time in the Jagannātha temple. It seems that in the temple of Jagannātha, there was some disagreement between Jagannātha and Sākṣi-gopāla, a disagreement called *prema-kalaha,* a quarrel of love. In order to settle this love quarrel, the King of Orissa constructed a village about six miles from Jagannātha Purī. The village was called Satyavādī, and Gopāla was stationed there. Thereafter, a new temple was constructed. Now there is a Sākṣi-gopāla station, and people go there to see the witness Gopāla.

TEXT 10

পূর্বে বিদ্যানগরের দুই ত' ব্রাহ্মণ ।
তীর্থ করিবারে দুঁহে করিলা গমন ॥ ১০ ॥

pūrve vidyā-nagarera dui ta' brāhmaṇa
tīrtha karibāre duṅhe karilā gamana

SYNONYMS

pūrve—previously; *vidyā-nagarera*—of the town known as Vidyānagara; *dui*—two; *ta'*—certainly; *brāhmaṇa*—*brāhmaṇas; tīrtha karibāre*—to tour places of pilgrimage; *duṅhe*—both of them; *karilā*—began; *gamana*—journey.

TRANSLATION

Formerly at Vidyānagara in South India there were two brāhmaṇas who made a long tour to see different places of pilgrimage.

TEXT 11

গয়া, বারাণসী, প্রয়াগ—সকল করিয়া ।
মথুরাতে আইলা দুঁহে আনন্দিত হঞা ॥ ১১ ॥

gayā, vārāṇasī, prayāga——sakala kariyā
mathurāte āilā duṅhe ānandita hañā

SYNONYMS

gayā—the pilgrimage site of the name Gayā; *vārāṇasī*—Benares, or Kāśī; *prayāga*—Allahabad; *sakala*—all; *kariyā*—touring; *mathurāte*—Mathurā; *āilā*—they reached; *duṅhe*—both; *ānandita*—pleased; *hañā*—becoming.

TRANSLATION

First of all they visited Gayā, then Kāśī, then Prayāga. Finally, with great pleasure, they came to Mathurā.

TEXT 12

বনযাত্রায় বন দেখি' দেখে গোবর্ধন ।
দ্বাদশ-বন দেখি' শেষে গেলা বৃন্দাবন ॥ ১২ ॥

vana-yātrāya vana dekhi' dekhe govardhana
dvādaśa-vana dekhi' śeṣe gelā vṛndāvana

SYNONYMS

vana-yātrāya—in touring the different forests; *vana dekhi'*—while seeing the forests; *dekhe*—they see; *govardhana*—Govardhana Hill; *dvādaśa-vana dekhi'*—visiting the twelve forests in Vṛndāvana; *śeṣe*—at last; *gelā*—reached; *vṛndāvana*—Vṛndāvana.

TRANSLATION

After reaching Mathurā, they started visiting the different forests of Vṛndāvana and came to Govardhana Hill. They visited all twelve forests [vanas] and at last came to the town of Vṛndāvana.

PURPORT

The five forests situated on the eastern side of the River Yamunā are Bhadra, Bilva, Loha, Bhāṇḍīra and Mahāvana. The seven forests situated on the western side of the Yamunā are Madhu, Tāla, Kumuda, Bahulā, Kāmya, Khadira and Vṛndāvana. After visiting all these forests, these pilgrims went to a place known as Pañcakrośī Vṛndāvana. Out of the twelve forests, the Vṛndāvana forest extends from the town of Vṛndāvana up to Nanda-grāma and Varṣāna, a distance of thirty-two miles, within which the Pañcakrośī Vṛndāvana town is situated.

TEXT 13

বৃন্দাবনে গোবিন্দ-স্থানে মহাদেবালয় ।
সে মন্দিরে গোপালের মহাসেবা হয় ॥ ১৩ ॥

vṛndāvane govinda-sthāne mahā-devālaya
se mandire gopālera mahā-sevā haya

SYNONYMS

vṛndāvane—within Pañcakrośī Vṛndāvana; *govinda-sthāne*—at the place where the present Govinda temple is situated; *mahā-deva-ālaya*—a great temple; *se mandire*—in that temple; *gopālera*—of the Deity of Gopāla; *mahā-sevā*—gorgeous worship; *haya*—there is.

TRANSLATION

In the village of Pañcakrośī Vṛndāvana, at the site where the Govinda temple is now situated, there was a great temple where gorgeous worship of Gopāla was performed.

TEXT 14

কেশীতীর্থ, কালীয়-হ্রদাদিকে কৈল স্নান ।
শ্রীগোপাল দেখি' তাহাঁ করিলা বিশ্রাম ॥ ১৪ ॥

keśī-tīrtha, kālīya-hradādike kaila snāna
śrī-gopāla dekhi' tāhāṅ karilā viśrāma

SYNONYMS

keśī-tīrtha—the bathing place on the bank of the Yamunā known as Keśī-ghāṭa; *kālīya-hrada*—the bathing place on the bank of the Yamunā known as Kāliya-ghāṭa; *ādike*—in such different bathing places; *kaila*—did; *snāna*—bathing; *śrī-*

gopāla dekhi'—by visiting the temple of Gopāla; *tāhāṅ*—there; *karilā*—took; *viśrāma*—rest.

TRANSLATION

After taking baths at different bathing places along the River Yamunā, such as Keśī-ghāṭa and Kālīya-ghāṭa, the pilgrims visited the temple of Gopāla. Afterwards, they took rest in that temple.

TEXT 15

গোপাল-সৌন্দর্য দুঁহার মন নিল হরি'।
সুখ পাঞা রহে তাহাঁ দিন দুই-চারি ॥ ১৫॥

gopāla-saundarya duṅhāra mana nila hari'
sukha pāñā rahe tāhāṅ dina dui-cāri

SYNONYMS

gopāla-saundarya—the beauty of the Gopāla Deity; *duṅhāra*—of both of them; *mana*—the minds; *nila*—took away; *hari'*—carrying; *sukha pāñā*—feeling this transcendental happiness; *rahe*—remained; *tāhāṅ*—in that temple; *dina*—days; *dui-cāri*—two or four.

TRANSLATION

The beauty of the Gopāla Deity stole away their minds, and feeling great happiness, they remained there for two or four days.

TEXT 16

দুইবিপ্র-মধ্যে এক বিপ্র—বৃদ্ধপ্রায়।
আর বিপ্র—যুবা, তাঁর করেন সহায় ॥ ১৬ ॥

dui-vipra-madhye eka vipra——vṛddha-prāya
āra vipra——yuvā, tāṅra karena sahāya

SYNONYMS

dui-vipra-madhye—between the two *brāhmaṇas; eka vipra*—one *brāhmaṇa; vṛddha-prāya*—elderly man; *āra vipra*—the second *brāhmaṇa; yuvā*—young man; *tāṅra*—of the older *brāhmaṇa; karena*—does; *sahāya*—assistance.

TRANSLATION

One of the two brāhmaṇas was an old man, and the other was young. The young man was assisting the old one.

TEXT 17

ছোটবিপ্র করে সদা তাঁহার সেবন।
তাঁহার সেবায় বিপ্রের তুষ্ট হৈল মন ॥ ১৭ ॥

choṭa-vipra kare sadā tāṅhāra sevana
tāṅhāra sevāya viprera tuṣṭa haila mana

SYNONYMS

choṭa-vipra—the younger *brāhmaṇa; kare*—does; *sadā*—always; *tāṅhāra*—his (the old *brāhmaṇa's*); *sevana*—service; *tāṅhāra*—his; *sevāya*—by the service; *viprera*—of the old *brāhmaṇa; tuṣṭa*—pacified; *haila*—became; *mana*—the mind.

TRANSLATION

Indeed, the young brāhmaṇa always rendered service to the older one, and the old man, being very satisfied with his service, was pleased with him.

TEXT 18

বিপ্র বলে,—তুমি মোর বহু সেবা কৈলা।
সহায় হঞা মোরে তীর্থ করাইলা ॥ ১৮ ॥

vipra bale,——tumi mora bahu sevā kailā
sahāya hañā more tīrtha karāilā

SYNONYMS

vipra bale—the elderly *brāhmaṇa* says; *tumi*—you; *mora*—my; *bahu*—various; *sevā*—service; *kailā*—have rendered; *sahāya*—assistant; *hañā*—being; *more*—to me; *tīrtha*—pilgrimage; *karāilā*—helped to do.

TRANSLATION

The older man told the younger: "You have rendered various types of service to me. You have assisted me in traveling to all these places of pilgrimage.

TEXT 19

পুত্রেও পিতার ঐছে না করে সেবন।
তোমার প্রসাদে আমি না পাইলাম শ্রম ॥ ১৯ ॥

putreo pitāra aiche nā kare sevana
tomāra prasāde āmi nā pāilāma śrama

SYNONYMS

putreo—even my own son; *pitāra*—of the father; *aiche*—in this way; *nā*—not; *kare*—renders; *sevana*—service; *tomāra*—your; *prasāde*—by the mercy; *āmi*—I; *nā*—not; *pāilāma*—have gotten; *śrama*—fatigue.

TRANSLATION

"Even my own son does not render such service. By your mercy, I did not become fatigued while on this tour.

TEXT 20

কৃতঘ্নতা হয় তোমায় না কৈলে সম্মান।
অতএব তোমায় আমি দিব কন্যাদান ॥ ২০ ॥

kṛta-ghnatā haya tomāya nā kaile sammāna
ataeva tomāya āmi diba kanyā-dāna

SYNONYMS

kṛta-ghnatā—ungratefulness; *haya*—it is; *tomāya*—to you; *nā*—not; *kaile*—if doing; *sammāna*—respect; *ataeva*—therefore; *tomāya*—to you; *āmi*—I; *diba*—shall give; *kanyā-dāna*—my daughter as charity.

TRANSLATION

"If I do not show you any respect, I will be ungrateful. Therefore, I promise to give you my daughter in charity."

TEXT 21

ছোটবিপ্র কহে,—"শুন, বিপ্র-মহাশয়।
অসম্ভব কহ কেনে, যেই নাহি হয় ॥ ২১ ॥

choṭa-vipra kahe,—"śuna, vipra-mahāśaya
asambhava kaha kene, yei nāhi haya

SYNONYMS

choṭa-vipra—the younger *brāhmaṇa;* *kahe*—replies; *śuna*—hear; *vipra-mahāśaya*—my dear *brāhmaṇa;* *asambhava*—unlikely; *kaha*—you say; *kene*—why; *yei*—which; *nāhi*—not; *haya*—happens.

TRANSLATION

The younger brāhmaṇa replied: "My dear sir, please hear me. You are saying something very unusual. Such a thing never happens.

TEXT 22

মহাকুলীন তুমি—বিদ্যা-ধনাদি-প্রবীণ ।
আমি অকুলীন, আর ধন-বিদ্যা-হীন ॥ ২২ ॥

mahā-kulīna tumi——vidyā-dhanādi-pravīṇa
āmi akulīna, āra dhana-vidyā-hīna

SYNONYMS

mahā-kulīna—highly aristocratic; *tumi*—you; *vidyā*—education; *dhana-ādi*—riches; *pravīṇa*—enriched; *āmi*—I; *akulīna*—not aristocratic; *āra*—and; *dhana-vidyā-hīna*—without any wealth and education.

TRANSLATION

"You are a most aristocratic family man, well educated and very rich. I am not at all aristocratic, and I am without a decent education and have no wealth.

PURPORT

Due to pious activities, one can be enriched by four opulences: one may obtain birth in an aristocratic family, become highly educated, become very beautiful, or get a sufficient quantity of riches. These are symptoms of pious activities performed in one's past life. In India it is still current for an aristocratic family never to consider a marriage with a common family. Though the caste may be the same, to maintain the aristocracy such marriages are rejected. No poor man will dare marry the daughter of a rich man. Because of this, when the elderly *brāhmaṇa* offered the young *brāhmaṇa* his daughter, the young *brāhmaṇa* did not believe that it would be possible to marry her. Therefore he asked the elderly *brāhmaṇa* why he was proposing something unprecedented (*asambhava*). It was unheard of for an aristocratic person to offer his daughter to a person who was both uneducated and poor.

TEXT 23

কন্যাদান-পাত্র আমি না হই তোমার ।
কৃষ্ণপ্রীত্যে করি তোমার সেবা-ব্যবহার ॥ ২৩ ॥

kanyā-dāna-pātra āmi nā ha-i tomāra
kṛṣṇa-prītye kari tomāra sevā-vyavahāra

SYNONYMS

kanyā-dāna-pātra—a bridegroom suitable for one's daughter; *āmi*—I; *nā*—not; *ha-i*—am; *tomāra*—of you; *kṛṣṇa-prītye*—only for satisfaction of Kṛṣṇa; *kari*—I do; *tomāra*—of you; *sevā*—of service; *vyavahāra*—activities.

TRANSLATION

"Sir, I am not a suitable bridegroom for your daughter. I render service to you only for the satisfaction of Kṛṣṇa.

PURPORT

Both *brāhmaṇas* were pure Vaiṣṇavas. The younger man took special care of the older one simply to please Kṛṣṇa. In *Śrīmad-Bhāgavatam* Kṛṣṇa says, *mad-bhakta-pūjābhyadhikā:* "It is better to render service to My devotee." (*Bhāg.* 11.21.19) Thus, according to the Gauḍīya-Vaiṣṇava philosophy of Caitanya Mahāprabhu, it is better to be a servant of the servant of God. One should not try to serve Kṛṣṇa directly. A pure Vaiṣṇava serves a servant of Kṛṣṇa and identifies himself as a servant of a servant of Kṛṣṇa. This is pleasing to Lord Kṛṣṇa. Śrīla Narottama dāsa Ṭhākura confirms this philosophy: *chāḍiyā vaiṣṇava-sevā nistāra pāyeche kebā.* Unless one serves a liberated Vaiṣṇava, he cannot attain liberation by directly serving Kṛṣṇa. He must serve the servant of Kṛṣṇa.

TEXT 24

ব্রাহ্মণ-সেবায় কৃষ্ণের প্রীতি বড় হয়।
তাঁহার সন্তোষে ভক্তি-সম্পদ্ বাড়য়॥" ২৪ ॥

brāhmaṇa-sevāya kṛṣṇera prīti baḍa haya
tāṅhāra santoṣe bhakti-sampad bāḍaya"

SYNONYMS

brāhmaṇa-sevāya—by rendering service to a *brāhmaṇa; kṛṣṇera*—of Lord Kṛṣṇa; *prīti*—the satisfaction; *baḍa*—very great; *haya*—is; *tāṅhāra santoṣe*—by pleasing the Lord; *bhakti*—of devotional service; *sampad*—the opulence; *bāḍaya*—increases.

TRANSLATION

"Lord Kṛṣṇa is very pleased by service rendered to brāhmaṇas, and when the Lord is pleased, the opulence of one's devotional service increases."

PURPORT

In this regard, Śrīla Bhaktisiddhānta Sarasvatī Ṭhākura comments that the younger *brāhmaṇa* rendered service to the older one with the purpose of pleasing Kṛṣṇa. It was not a matter of ordinary worldly dealings. Kṛṣṇa is pleased when a Vaiṣṇava is rendered service. Because the younger *brāhmaṇa* served the older one, Lord Gopāla agreed to become a witness of the marriage negotiation in order to maintain the prestige of both devotees. Śrī Caitanya Mahāprabhu would certainly not have liked to hear about marital dealings unless such dealings were exchanged between two Vaiṣṇavas. Marriage arrangements and ceremonies belong to ordinary material *karma-kāṇḍa* sections of the scriptures. The Vaiṣṇavas, however, are not interested in any kind of *karma-kāṇḍa* dealings. Śrīla Narottama dāsa Ṭhākura says: *karma-kāṇḍa jñāna-kāṇḍa kevala viṣera bhāṇḍa.* For a Vaiṣṇava, the *karma-kāṇḍa* and *jñāna-kāṇḍa* sections of the *Vedas* are unnecessary. Indeed, a real Vaiṣṇava takes these sections as a poison pot (*viṣera bhāṇḍa*). Sometimes we take part in a marriage ceremony for our disciples, but this does not mean that we are interested in *karma-kāṇḍa* activities. Sometimes, not knowing the Vaiṣṇava philosophy, an outsider criticizes such activity, maintaining that a *sannyāsī* should not take part in a marriage ceremony between a young boy and girl. However, this is not a *karma-kāṇḍa* activity because our purpose is to spread the Kṛṣṇa consciousness movement. We are giving all facility to the general populace to take to Kṛṣṇa consciousness, and in order to fix the devotees in concentration on the service of the Lord, marriage is sometimes allowed. We have experienced that such married couples actually render very important service to the mission. Therefore, one should not misunderstand when a *sannyāsī* takes part in a marriage ceremony. Śrī Caitanya Mahāprabhu and Nityānanda Prabhu took great pleasure in hearing about the marriage ceremony between the young *brāhmaṇa* and the daughter of the elderly *brāhmaṇa.*

TEXT 25

বড়বিপ্র কহে,—"তুমি না কর সংশয় ।
তোমাকে কন্যা দিব আমি, করিল নিশ্চয় ॥" ২৫ ॥

baḍa-vipra kahe,—"tumi nā kara saṁśaya
tomāke kanyā diba āmi, karila niścaya"

SYNONYMS

baḍa-vipra—the older *brāhmaṇa; kahe*—replies; *tumi*—you; *nā*—not; *kara*—do; *saṁśaya*—doubt; *tomāke*—to you; *kanyā*—the daughter; *diba*—shall give; *āmi*—I; *karila*—made; *niścaya*—certainty.

TRANSLATION

The older brāhmaṇa replied: "My dear boy, do not doubt me. I will give you my daughter in charity. I have already decided this."

TEXT 26

ছোটবিপ্র বলে,—"তোমার স্ত্রীপুত্র সব।
বহু জ্ঞাতি-গোষ্ঠী তোমার বহুত বান্ধব ॥ ২৬ ॥

choṭa-vipra bale,——"tomāra strī-putra saba
bahu jñāti-goṣṭhī tomāra bahuta bāndhava

SYNONYMS

choṭa-vipra—the young *brāhmaṇa; bale*—says; *tomāra*—your; *strī-putra*—wife and sons; *saba*—all; *bahu*—many; *jñāti*—of family relations; *goṣṭhī*—group; *tomāra*—your; *bahuta*—many; *bāndhava*—friends.

TRANSLATION

The young brāhmaṇa said: "You have a wife and sons, and you have a large circle of relatives and friends.

TEXT 27

তা'-সবার সম্মতি বিনা নহে কন্যাদান।
রুক্মিণীর পিতা ভীষ্মক তাহাতে প্রমাণ ॥ ২৭ ॥

tā'-sabāra sammati vinā nahe kanyā-dāna
rukmiṇīra pitā bhīṣmaka tāhāte pramāṇa

SYNONYMS

tā'-sabāra—of all of them; *sammati*—consent; *vinā*—without; *nahe*—not; *kanyā-dāna*—giving the daughter in charity; *rukmiṇīra*—of Queen Rukmiṇī; *pitā*—father; *bhīṣmaka*—of the name Bhīṣmaka; *tāhāte*—of that; *pramāṇa*—evidence.

TRANSLATION

"Without the consent of all your friends and relatives, it is not possible to give me your daughter in charity. Just consider the story of Queen Rukmiṇī and her father, Bhīṣmaka.

TEXT 28

ভীষ্মকের ইচ্ছা,—কৃষ্ণে কন্যা সমর্পিতে।
পুত্রের বিরোধে কন্যা নারিল অর্পিতে॥" ২৮॥

bhīṣmakera icchā,——kṛṣṇe kanyā samarpite
putrera virodhe kanyā nārila arpite"

SYNONYMS

bhīṣmakera—of King Bhīṣmaka; *icchā*—the desire; *kṛṣṇe*—unto Kṛṣṇa; *kanyā*—daughter; *samarpite*—to give; *putrera*—of his son; *virodhe*—by the objection; *kanyā*—daughter; *nārila*—was unable; *arpite*—to offer.

TRANSLATION

"King Bhīṣmaka wanted to give his daughter, Rukmiṇī, in charity to Kṛṣṇa, but Rukmī, his eldest son, objected. Therefore he could not carry out his decision."

PURPORT

As stated in *Śrīmad-Bhāgavatam* (10.52.21):

rājāsīd bhīṣmako nāma
vidarbhādhipatir mahān
tasya pañcābhavan putrāḥ
kanyaikā ca varānanā

King Bhīṣmaka of Vidarbha wanted to offer Kṛṣṇa his daughter, Rukmiṇī, but Rukmī, the eldest of his five sons, objected. Therefore he withdrew his decision and decided to offer Rukmiṇī to the King of Cedi, Śiśupāla, who was a cousin of Kṛṣṇa's. However, Rukmiṇī conceived of a trick; she sent a letter to Kṛṣṇa asking Him to kidnap her. Thus in order to please Rukmiṇī, who was His great devotee, Kṛṣṇa kidnapped her. There ensued a great fight between Kṛṣṇa and the opposing party, headed by Rukmiṇī's brother Rukmī. Rukmī was defeated and, because of his harsh words against Kṛṣṇa, was about to be killed, but he was saved at the request of Rukmiṇī. However, Kṛṣṇa shaved off all of Rukmī's hair with His sword. Śrī Balarāma did not like this, and so to please Rukmiṇī, Balarāma rebuked Kṛṣṇa.

TEXT 29

বড়বিপ্র কহে,—"কন্যা মোর নিজ-ধন।
নিজ-ধন দিতে নিষেধিবে কোন্ জন॥ ২৯॥

baḍa-vipra kahe,——"kanyā mora nija-dhana
nija-dhana dite niṣedhibe kon jana

SYNONYMS

baḍa-vipra kahe—the elderly *brāhmaṇa* says; *kanyā*—the daughter; *mora*—my; *nija-dhana*—own property; *nija-dhana*—one's own property; *dite*—to give; *niṣedhibe*—will object; *kon*—what; *jana*—person.

TRANSLATION

The elderly brāhmaṇa said: "My daughter is my own property. If I choose to give my property to someone, who has the power to stop me?

TEXT 30

তোমাকে কন্যা দিব, সবাকে করি' তিরস্কার ।
সংশয় না কর তুমি, করহ স্বীকার ॥" ৩০ ॥

tomāke kanyā diba, sabāke kari' tiraskāra
saṁśaya nā kara tumi, karaha svīkāra"

SYNONYMS

tomāke—to you; *kanyā*—the daughter; *diba*—I shall offer; *sabāke*—all others; *kari'*—doing; *tiraskāra*—neglecting; *saṁśaya*—doubt; *nā*—not; *kara*—do; *tumi*—you; *karaha*—just do; *svīkāra*—acceptance.

TRANSLATION

"My dear boy, I will give my daughter to you in charity, and I will neglect the position of all others. Don't doubt me in this regard; just accept my proposal."

TEXT 31

ছোটবিপ্র কহে,—"যদি কন্যা দিতে মন ।
গোপালের আগে কহ এ সত্যবচন ॥" ৩১ ॥

choṭa-vipra kahe,——"yadi kanyā dite mana
gopālera āge kaha e satya-vacana"

SYNONYMS

choṭa-vipra kahe—the younger *brāhmaṇa* replies; *yadi*—if; *kanyā*—daughter; *dite*—to give in charity; *mana*—the mind; *gopālera*—of the Gopāla Deity; *āge*—in front; *kaha*—say; *e*—these; *satya-vacana*—words in truth.

TRANSLATION

The younger brāhmaṇa replied: "If you have decided to give your young daughter to me, then say so before the Gopāla Deity."

TEXT 32

গোপালের আগে বিপ্র কহিতে লাগিল।
'তুমি জান, নিজ-কন্যা ইহারে আমি দিল॥' ৩২॥

gopālera āge vipra kahite lāgila
'tumi jāna, nija-kanyā ihāre āmi dila'

SYNONYMS

gopālera āge—in front of the Gopāla Deity; *vipra*—the elderly *brāhmaṇa*; *kahite*—to speak; *lāgila*—began; *tumi jāna*—my Lord, please know; *nija-kanyā*—my own daughter; *ihāre*—to this boy; *āmi*—I; *dila*—have given in charity.

TRANSLATION

Coming before Gopāla, the elderly brāhmaṇa said: "My dear Lord, please witness that I have given my daughter to this boy."

PURPORT

In India it is still the custom for a daughter to be offered to someone simply by word. This is called *vāg-datta.* This means that the father, brother or guardian of a girl has given his word that she will be married to a certain man. Consequently, that daughter cannot be married to anyone else. She is reserved by virtue of the honest words of the father or guardian. There are many instances in which the parents of a female child have given someone a verbal promise that their daughter will be married to his son. Both parties agree to wait until the boy and girl are grown up, and then the marriage takes place. Following this custom, which is very old in India, the elderly *brāhmaṇa* promised to give his daughter to the younger *brāhmaṇa* in charity, and he promised this before the Gopāla Deity. In India the custom is to honor any promise made before the Deity. Such a promise cannot be canceled. In Indian villages, whenever there is a quarrel between two parties, they go to a temple to settle the quarrel. Whatever is spoken in front of the Deity is taken to be true, for no one would dare lie before the Deity. This same principle was followed in the Battle of Kurukṣetra. Therefore in the very beginning of *Bhagavad-gītā* it is stated: *dharma-kṣetre kuru-kṣetre.*

By not becoming God conscious, human society is deteriorating to the lowest standard of animal life. This Kṛṣṇa consciousness movement is very essential to reviving God consciousness among the general populace. If people actually become God conscious, all quarrels can be settled outside of court, as happened in the case of the two *brāhmaṇas* whose disagreement was settled by the witness Gopāla.

TEXT 33

ছোটবিপ্র বলে,—"ঠাকুর, তুমি মোর সাক্ষী ।
তোমা সাক্ষী বোলাইমু, যদি অন্যথা দেখি ॥" ৩৩ ॥

choṭa-vipra bale,——"ṭhākura, tumi mora sākṣī
tomā sākṣī bolāimu, yadi anyathā dekhi"

SYNONYMS

choṭa-vipra bale—the younger *brāhmaṇa* replied; *ṭhākura*—my dear Lord Gopāla; *tumi*—You; *mora*—my; *sākṣī*—witness; *tomā*—unto You; *sākṣī*—witness; *bolāimu*—I shall call as; *yadi*—if; *anyathā*—otherwise; *dekhi*—I see.

TRANSLATION

Then the younger brāhmaṇa addressed the Deity, saying, "My dear Lord, You are my witness. I shall call for You to testify if it is necessary later on."

TEXT 34

এত বলি' দুইজনে চলিলা দেশেরে ।
গুরুবুদ্ধ্যে ছোট-বিপ্র বহু সেবা করে ॥ ৩৪ ॥

eta bali' dui-jane calilā deśere
guru-buddhye choṭa-vipra bahu sevā kare

SYNONYMS

eta bali'—speaking this; *dui-jane*—both the *brāhmaṇas; calilā*—went; *deśere*—toward their own country; *guru-buddhye*—accepting the elderly *brāhmaṇa* as *guru*; *choṭa-vipra*—the young *brāhmaṇa*; *bahu*—various; *sevā*—services; *kare*—renders.

TRANSLATION

After these talks, the two brāhmaṇas started for home. As usual, the young brāhmaṇa accompanied the elderly brāhmaṇa as if the older brāhmaṇa were a guru [spiritual master] and rendered him service in various ways.

TEXT 35

দেশে আসি' দুইজনে গেলা নিজ-ঘরে ।
কত দিনে বড়-বিপ্র চিন্তিত অন্তরে ॥ ৩৫ ॥

deśe āsi' dui-jane gelā nija-ghare
kata dine baḍa-vipra cintita antare

SYNONYMS

deśe āsi'—after returning to their own country; *dui-jane*—both of them; *gelā*—went; *nija-ghare*—to their respective homes; *kata dine*—after some time; *baḍa-vipra*—the elderly *brāhmaṇa*; *cintita*—very anxious; *antare*—within.

TRANSLATION

After returning to Vidyānagara, each brāhmaṇa went to his respective home. After some time, the elderly brāhmaṇa became very anxious.

TEXT 36

তীর্থে বিপ্রে বাক্য দিলুঁ,—কেমতে সত্য হয় ।
স্ত্রী, পুত্র, জ্ঞাতি, বন্ধু জানিবে নিশ্চয় ॥ ৩৬ ॥

tīrthe vipre vākya diluṅ,——kemate satya haya
strī, putra, jñāti, bandhu jānibe niścaya

SYNONYMS

tīrthe—on pilgrimage; *vipre*—to a *brāhmaṇa*; *vākya*—word of honor; *diluṅ*—I have given; *kemate*—how; *satya*—true; *haya*—it is; *strī*—wife; *putra*—sons; *jñāti*—relatives; *bandhu*—friends; *jānibe*—will know; *niścaya*—certainly.

TRANSLATION

He began to think: "I have given my word to a brāhmaṇa in a holy place, and what I promised will certainly come to pass. I must now disclose this to my wife, sons, other relatives and friends."

TEXT 37

একদিন নিজ-লোক একত্র করিল ।
তা-সবার আগে সব বৃত্তান্ত কহিল ॥ ৩৭ ॥

eka-dina nija-loka ekatra karila
tā-sabāra āge saba vṛttānta kahila

SYNONYMS

eka-dina—one day; *nija-loka*—all his relatives; *ekatra*—in one place; *karila*—assembled; *tā-sabāra*—of all of them; *āge*—in front; *saba*—all; *vṛttānta*—narration; *kahila*—spoke.

TRANSLATION

Thus one day the elderly brāhmaṇa called for a meeting of all his relatives and friends, and before them all he narrated what had taken place in front of Gopāla.

TEXT 38

শুনি' সব গোষ্ঠী তার করে হাহাকার ।
'ঐছে বাত্ মুখে তুমি না আনিবে আর ॥ ৩৮ ॥

śuni' saba goṣṭhī tāra kare hāhā-kāra
'aiche vāt mukhe tumi nā ānibe āra

SYNONYMS

śuni'—hearing; *saba*—all; *goṣṭhī*—family members and friends; *tara*—of the elderly *brāhmaṇa*; *kare*—do; *hā-hā-kāra*—exclamation of disappointment; *aiche*—such; *vāt*—proposal; *mukhe*—in the mouth; *tumi*—you; *nā*—not; *ānibe*—should bring; *āra*—again.

TRANSLATION

When those who belonged to the family circle heard the narration of the old brāhmaṇa, they made exclamations showing their disappointment. They all requested that he not make such a proposal again.

TEXT 39

নীচে কন্যা দিলে কুল যাইবেক নাশ ।
শুনিঞা সকল লোক করিবে উপহাস ॥' ৩৯ ॥

nīce kanyā dile kula yāibeka nāśa
śuniñā sakala loka karibe upahāsa'

SYNONYMS

nīce—to a lower family; *kanyā*—daughter; *dile*—if offering; *kula*—family tradition; *yāibeka*—will go to; *nāśa*—destruction; *śuniñā*—hearing; *sakala*—all; *loka*—friends; *karibe*—will do; *upahāsa*—joking.

TRANSLATION

They unanimously agreed: "If you offer your daughter to a degraded family, your aristocracy will be lost. When people hear of this, they will make jokes and laugh at you."

TEXT 40

বিপ্র বলে,—"তীর্থ-বাক্য কেমনে করি আন।
যে হউক্, সে হউক, আমি দিব কন্যাদান॥" ৪০ ॥

vipra bale,——"tīrtha-vākya kemane kari āna
ye hauk, se hauka, āmi diba kanyā-dāna"

SYNONYMS

vipra bale—the *brāhmaṇa* says; *tīrtha-vākya*—the promise made on the pilgrimage; *kemane*—how; *kari*—I shall do; *āna*—otherwise; *ye hauk*—whatever may be; *se hauk*— let it take place; *āmi*—I; *diba*—shall give; *kanyā-dāna*—my daughter in charity.

TRANSLATION

The elderly brāhmaṇa said: "How can I undo the promise I made in a holy place while on pilgrimage? Whatever may happen, I must give him my daughter in charity."

TEXT 41

জ্ঞাতি লোক কহে,—'মোরা তোমাকে ছাড়িব'।
স্ত্রী-পুত্র কহে,—'বিষ খাইয়া মরিব' ॥ ৪১ ॥

jñāti loka kahe,——'morā tomāke chāḍiba'
strī-putra kahe,——'viṣa khāiyā mariba'

SYNONYMS

jñāti loka—the relatives; *kahe*—answer; *morā*—we all; *tomāke*—you; *chāḍiba*—will give up; *strī*—wife; *putra*—sons; *kahe*—say; *viṣa*—poison; *khāiyā*—drinking; *mariba*—we shall die.

TRANSLATION

The relatives unanimously said: "If you give your daughter to that boy, we shall give up all connection with you." Indeed, his wife and sons declared: "If such a thing happens, we shall take poison and die."

TEXT 42

বিপ্র বলে,—"সাক্ষী বোলাঞা করিবেক ন্যায়।
জিতি' কন্যা লবে, মোর ব্যর্থ ধর্ম হয়॥" ৪২॥

vipra bale,—"sākṣī bolāñā karibeka nyāya
jiti' kanyā labe, mora vyartha dharma haya'

SYNONYMS

vipra bale—the *brāhmaṇa* says; *sākṣī*—a witness; *bolāñā*—calling for; *karibeka*—there will be; *nyāya*—justice; *jiti'*—winning; *kanyā*—the daughter; *labe*—he will take; *mora*—my; *vyartha*—meaningless; *dharma*—religious principles; *haya*—will be.

TRANSLATION

The elderly brāhmaṇa said: "If I do not give my daughter to the young brāhmaṇa, he will call Śrī Gopālajī as a witness. Thus he will take my daughter by force, and in that case my religious principles will become meaningless."

TEXT 43

পুত্র বলে,—"প্রতিমা সাক্ষী, সেহ দূর দেশে।
কে তোমার সাক্ষী দিবে, চিন্তা কর কিসে॥ ৪৩॥

putra bale,—"pratimā sākṣī, seha dūra deśe
ke tomāra sākṣī dibe, cintā kara kise

SYNONYMS

putra bale—his son says; *pratimā*—the Deity; *sākṣī*—witness; *seha*—He also; *dūra*—distant; *deśe*—in country; *ke*—who; *tomāra*—of you; *sākṣī*—witness; *dibe*—will give; *cintā*—anxiety; *kara*—you do; *kise*—why.

TRANSLATION

His son replied: "The Deity may be a witness, but He is in a distant country. How can He come to bear witness against you? Why are you so anxious over this?

TEXT 44

নাহি কহি—না কহিও এ মিথ্যা-বচন।
সবে কহিবে—'মোর কিছু নাহিক স্মরণ॥' ৪৪॥

nāhi kahi——nā kahio e mithyā-vacana
sabe kahibe——'mora kichu nāhika smaraṇa'

SYNONYMS

nāhi kahi—I did not say; *nā kahio*—do not say; *e*—this; *mithyā-vacana*—false statement; *sabe*—only; *kahibe*—you shall say; *mora*—my; *kichu*—anything; *nāhika*—not; *smaraṇa*—remembrance.

TRANSLATION

"You do not have to flatly deny that you spoke such a thing. There is no need to make a false statement. Simply say that you do not remember what you said.

TEXT 45

তুমি যদি কহ,—'আমি কিছুই না জানি' ।
তবে আমি ন্যায় করি' ব্রাহ্মণেরে জিনি ॥" ৪৫ ॥

tumi yadi kaha,——'āmi kichui nā jāni'
tabe āmi nyāya kari' brāhmaṇere jini"

SYNONYMS

tumi—you; *yadi*—if; *kaha*—say; *āmi kichui nā jāni*—I do not remember anything; *tabe*—in that case; *āmi*—I; *nyāya kari'*—arguing; *brāhmaṇere*—the younger *brāhmaṇa*; *jini*—shall conquer.

TRANSLATION

"If you simply say, 'I do not remember,' I shall take care of the rest. By argument, I shall defeat the young brāhmaṇa."

PURPORT

The son of the elderly *brāhmaṇa* was an atheist and a follower of the Raghunātha-smṛti. He was very expert in dealing with pounds-shillings-pence, but he was fool number one. Consequently, he did not believe in the spiritual position of the Deity, nor did he have any faith in the Supreme Personality of Godhead. Therefore, as a typical idol worshiper, he considered the form of the Lord to be made of stone or wood. Thus he assured his father that the witness was only a stone Deity and was not capable of speaking. Besides that, he assured his father that the Deity was situated far away and consequently could not come to bear witness. In essence, he was saying: "Have no anxiety. You do not have to lie directly, but you should speak like a diplomat, like King Yudhiṣṭhira when he spoke to Droṇācārya—*aśvatthāmā hata iti gajaḥ*. Following this principle, simply say that you do not remember anything and are completely unaware of the statements given by the young *brāhmaṇa*. If you make the background like that, I shall know how to fill in the argument and defeat him by word jugglery. Thus I shall save you from having to give your daughter to him. In this way, our aristocracy will be saved. You have nothing to worry about."

TEXT 46

এত শুনি' বিপ্রের চিন্তিত হৈল মন ।
একান্ত-ভাবে চিন্তে বিপ্র গোপাল-চরণ ॥ ৪৬ ॥

eta śuni' viprera cintita haila mana
ekānta-bhāve cinte vipra gopāla-caraṇa

SYNONYMS

eta śuni'—hearing this; *viprera*—of the old *brāhmaṇa*; *cintita*—agitated; *haila*—became; *mana*—the mind; *ekānta-bhāve*—with single-minded attention; *cinte*—thinks; *vipra*—the *brāhmaṇa*; *gopāla-caraṇa*—of the lotus feet of Śrī Gopālajī.

TRANSLATION

Hearing this, the mind of the elderly brāhmaṇa became very agitated. Feeling helpless, he simply turned his attention to the lotus feet of Gopāla.

TEXT 47

'মোর ধর্ম রক্ষা পায়, না মরে নিজ-জন ।
দুই রক্ষা কর, গোপাল, লইনু শরণ ॥' ৪৭ ॥

'mora dharma rakṣā pāya, nā mare nija-jana
dui rakṣā kara, gopāla, lainu śaraṇa'

SYNONYMS

mora—my; *dharma*—religious principles; *rakṣā pāya*—spared; *nā*—not; *mare*—die; *nija-jana*—own kinsmen; *dui*—two; *rakṣā kara*—You kindly protect; *gopāla*—my Lord Gopāla; *lainu*—I have taken; *śaraṇa*—shelter under Your lotus feet.

TRANSLATION

The elderly brāhmaṇa prayed: "My dear Lord Gopāla, I have taken shelter of Your lotus feet, and therefore I request You to please protect my religious

principles from disturbance and at the same time save my kinsmen from dying."

TEXT 48

এইমত বিপ্র চিত্তে চিন্তিতে লাগিল ।
আর দিন লঘুবিপ্র তাঁর ঘরে আইল ॥ ৪৮ ॥

ei-mata vipra citte cintite lāgila
āra dina laghu-vipra tāṅra ghare āila

SYNONYMS

ei-mata—in this way; *vipra*—the elderly *brāhmaṇa;* *citte*—within the mind; *cintite*—to think; *lāgila*—began; *āra dina*—the next day; *laghu-vipra*—the young *brāhmaṇa;* *tāṅra*—his; *ghare*—to the home; *āila*—came.

TRANSLATION

The next day, the elderly brāhmaṇa was thinking deeply about this matter when the young brāhmaṇa came to his house.

TEXT 49

আসিঞা পরম-ভক্ত্যে নমস্কার করি' ।
বিনয় করিঞা কহে কর দুই যুড়ি' ॥ ৪৯ ॥

āsiñā parama-bhaktye namaskāra kari'
vinaya kariñā kahe kara dui yuḍi'

SYNONYMS

āsiñā—coming; *parama-bhaktye*—in great devotion; *namaskāra kari'*—offering obeisances; *vinaya kariñā*—with great humility; *kahe*—says; *kara*—hands; *dui*—two; *yuḍi'*—folding.

TRANSLATION

The young brāhmaṇa came to him and offered respectful obeisances. Then, very humbly folding his hands, he spoke as follows.

TEXT 50

'তুমি মোরে কন্যা দিতে কর্যাছ অঙ্গীকার ।
এবে কিছু নাহি কহ, কি তোমার বিচার ॥' ৫০ ॥

'tumi more kanyā dite karyācha aṅgīkāra
ebe kichu nāhi kaha, ki tomāra vicāra'

SYNONYMS

tumi—you; *more*—to me; *kanyā*—your daughter; *dite*—to give in charity; *karyācha*—have made; *aṅgīkāra*—a promise; *ebe*—now; *kichu*—something; *nāhi*—not; *kaha*—you say; *ki*—what; *tomāra*—your; *vicāra*—conclusion.

TRANSLATION

"You have promised to give your daughter in charity to me. Now you do not say anything. What is your conclusion?"

TEXT 51

এত শুনি' সেই বিপ্র রহে মৌন ধরি' ।
তাঁর পুত্র মারিতে আইল হাতে ঠেঙ্গা করি' ॥ ৫১ ॥

eta śuni' sei vipra rahe mauna dhari'
tāṅra putra mārite āila hāte ṭheṅgā kari'

SYNONYMS

eta śuni'—hearing this; *sei vipra*—the elderly *brāhmaṇa*; *rahe*—remains; *mauna dhari'*—holding silence; *tāṅra*—his; *putra*—son; *mārite*—to strike; *āila*—came out; *hāte*—in hand; *ṭheṅgā*—stick; *kari'*—taking.

TRANSLATION

After the young brāhmaṇa submitted this statement, the elderly brāhmaṇa remained silent. Taking this opportunity, his son immediately came out with a stick to strike the younger man.

TEXT 52

'আরে অধম ! মোর ভগ্নী চাহ বিবাহিতে ।
বামন হঞা চাঁদ যেন চাহ ত' ধরিতে ॥' ৫২ ॥

'āre adhama! mora bhagnī cāha vivāhite
vāmana hañā cāṅda yena cāha ta' dharite'

SYNONYMS

āre adhama—O most degraded one; *mora*—my; *bhagnī*—sister; *cāha*—you want; *vivāhite*—to marry; *vāmana*—a dwarf; *hañā*—being; *cāṅda*—the moon; *yena*—as if; *cāha*—you want; *ta'*—certainly; *dharite*—to capture.

TRANSLATION

The son said: "Oh, you are most degraded! You want to marry my sister, just like a dwarf who wants to catch the moon!"

TEXT 53

ঠেঞা দেখি' সেই বিপ্র পলাঞা গেল ।
আর দিন গ্রামের লোক একত্র করিল ॥ ৫৩ ॥

ṭheñā dekhi' sei vipra palāñā gela
āra dina grāmera loka ekatra karila

SYNONYMS

ṭheñā dekhi'—seeing the stick in his hand; *sei vipra*—the young *brāhmaṇa;* *palāñā gela*—fled from that place; *āra dina*—the next day; *grāmera loka*—the inhabitants of the village; *ekatra karila*—gathered in one place.

TRANSLATION

Seeing a stick in the hand of the son, the younger brāhmaṇa fled. The next day, however, he gathered together all the people of the village.

TEXT 54

সব লোক বড়বিপ্রে ডাকিয়া আনিল ।
তবে সেই লঘুবিপ্র কহিতে লাগিল ॥ ৫৪ ॥

saba loka baḍa-vipre ḍākiyā ānila
tabe sei laghu-vipra kahite lāgila

SYNONYMS

saba loka—all the village inhabitants; *baḍa-vipre*—to the senior *brāhmaṇa;* *ḍākiyā*—calling; *ānila*—brought; *tabe*—then; *sei laghu-vipra*—the junior *brāhmaṇa;* *kahite lāgila*—began to speak.

TRANSLATION

All the people of the village then called for the elderly brāhmaṇa and brought him to their meeting place. The young brāhmaṇa then began to speak before them as follows.

TEXT 55

'ইঁহ মোরে কন্যা দিতে করয়াছে অঙ্গীকার।
এবে যে না দেন, পুছ ইঁহার ব্যবহার॥' ৫৫॥

'iṅha more kanyā dite karyāche aṅgīkāra
ebe ye nā dena, pucha iṅhāra vyavahāra'

SYNONYMS

iṅha—this gentleman; *more*—to me; *kanyā*—his daughter; *dite*—to give in charity; *karyāche*—has made; *aṅgīkāra*—promise; *ebe*—now; *ye*—indeed; *nā*—not; *dena*—he gives; *pucha*—kindly ask; *iṅhāra*—of him; *vyavahāra*—the behavior.

TRANSLATION

"This gentleman has promised to hand over his daughter to me, yet now he does not follow his promise. Please ask him about his behavior."

TEXT 56

তবে সেই বিপ্রেরে পুছিল সর্বজন।
'কন্যা কেনে না দেহ, যদি দিয়াছ বচন॥' ৫৬॥

tabe sei viprere puchila sarva-jana
'kanyā kene nā deha, yadi diyācha vacana'

SYNONYMS

tabe—then; *sei*—that; *viprere*—*brāhmaṇa;* *puchila*—asked; *sarva-jana*—all the people; *kanyā*—daughter; *kene*—why; *nā deha*—you do not give in charity; *yadi*—if; *diyācha*—have given; *vacana*—word of honor.

TRANSLATION

All the people gathered there asked the elderly brāhmaṇa: "If you have already promised to give him your daughter in charity, why are you not fulfilling your promise? You have given your word of honor."

TEXT 57

বিপ্র কহে,—'শুন, লোক, মোর নিবেদন।
কবে কি বলিয়াছি, মোর নাহিক স্মরণ॥' ৫৭॥

vipra kahe,—'śuna, loka, mora nivedana
kabe ki baliyāchi, mora nāhika smaraṇa'

SYNONYMS

vipra kahe—the senior *brāhmaṇa* replied; *śuna*—please hear; *loka*—all people; *mora*—my; *nivedana*—submission; *kabe*—when; *ki*—what; *baliyāchi*—I have said; *mora*—my; *nāhika*—there is not; *smaraṇa*—remembrance.

TRANSLATION

The elderly brāhmaṇa said: "My dear friends, please hear what I have to submit. I do not exactly remember making a promise like that."

TEXT 58

এত শুনি' তাঁর পুত্র বাক্য-চ্ছল পাঞা ।
প্রগল্‌ভ হইয়া কহে সম্মুখে আসিঞা ॥ ৫৮ ॥

eta śuni' tāṅra putra vākya-cchala pāñā
pragalbha ha-iyā kahe sammukhe āsiñā

SYNONYMS

eta śuni'—hearing this; *tāṅra putra*—his son; *vākya-cchala*—for jugglery of words; *pāñā*—getting a chance; *pragalbha*—impudent; *ha-iyā*—becoming; *kahe*—says; *sammukhe*—in the front; *āsiñā*—coming.

TRANSLATION

When the elderly brāhmaṇa's son heard this, he took the opportunity to juggle some words. Becoming very impudent, he stood before the assembly and spoke as follows.

TEXT 59

'তীর্থযাত্রায় পিতার সঙ্গে ছিল বহু ধন ।
ধন দেখি এই দুষ্টের লৈতে হৈল মন ॥ ৫৯ ॥

'tīrtha-yātrāya pitāra saṅge chila bahu dhana
dhana dekhi ei duṣṭera laite haila mana

SYNONYMS

tīrtha-yātrāya—when touring the holy places; *pitāra*—my father; *saṅge*—with; *chila*—there was; *bahu*—much; *dhana*—money; *dhana*—money; *dekhi*—

seeing; *ei*—this; *duṣṭera*—of the rogue; *laite*—to take; *haila*—it was; *mana*—the intention.

TRANSLATION

"While touring various holy places of pilgrimage, my father carried much money. Seeing the money, this rogue decided to take it away.

TEXT 60

আর কেহ সঙ্গে নাহি, এই সঙ্গে একল।
ধুতুরা খাওয়াঞা বাপে করিল পাগল ॥ ৬০ ॥

āra keha saṅge nāhi, ei saṅge ekala
dhuturā khāoyāñā vāpe karila pāgala

SYNONYMS

āra—anyone; *keha*—else; *saṅge*—in company; *nāhi*—there was not; *ei*—this *brāhmaṇa; saṅge*—in company; *ekala*—alone; *dhuturā*—an intoxicant; *khāoyāñā*—making him eat; *vāpe*—my father; *karila*—made; *pāgala*—mad.

TRANSLATION

"There was no one besides this man with my father. Giving him an intoxicant known as dhuturā to eat, this rogue made my father mad.

TEXT 61

সব ধন লঞা কহে—'চোরে লইল ধন।'
'কন্যা দিতে চাহিয়াছে'—উঠাইল বচন ॥ ৬১ ॥

saba dhana lañā kahe——'core la-ila dhana'
'kanyā dite cāhiyāche'——uṭhāila vacana

SYNONYMS

saba—all; *dhana*—money; *lañā*—taking; *kahe*—says; *core*—a thief; *la-ila*—took; *dhana*—all the money; *kanyā*—the daughter; *dite*—to give in charity; *cāhiyāche*—has promised; *uṭhāila*—has raised; *vacana*—a slogan.

TRANSLATION

"Having taken all my father's money, this rogue claimed that it was taken by some thief. Now he is claiming that my father has promised to give him his daughter in charity.

TEXT 62

তোমরা সকল লোক করহ বিচারে।
'মোর পিতার কন্যা দিতে যোগ্য কি ইহারে ॥' ৬২॥

tomarā sakala loka karaha vicāre
'mora pitāra kanyā dite yogya ki ihāre'

SYNONYMS

tomarā—you; *sakala*—all; *loka*—people; *karaha*—just make; *vicāre*—judgment; *mora*—my; *pitāra*—of the father; *kanyā*—the daughter; *dite*—to give in charity; *yogya*—befitting; *ki*—is it; *ihāre*—to him.

TRANSLATION

"All of you assembled here are gentlemen. Please judge whether it is befitting to offer this poor brāhmaṇa my father's daughter."

TEXT 63

এত শুনি' লোকের মনে হইল সংশয়।
'সম্ভবে,—ধনলোভে লোক ছাড়ে ধর্মভয় ॥' ৬৩ ॥

eta śuni' lokera mane ha-ila saṁśaya
'sambhave,——dhana-lobhe loka chāḍe dharma-bhaya'

SYNONYMS

eta śuni'—hearing all this; *lokera*—of all the people; *mane*—in the minds; *ha-ila*—there was; *saṁśaya*—doubt; *sambhave*—possible; *dhana-lobhe*—by greed for money; *loka*—some man; *chāḍe*—gives up; *dharma-bhaya*—religious principles.

TRANSLATION

Hearing all these statements, all the people gathered there became a little doubtful. They thought that it was quite possible that because of attraction for riches, one might give up his religious principles.

TEXT 64

তবে ছোটবিপ্র কহে,—"শুন, মহাজন।
ন্যায় জিনিবারে কহে অসত্য-বচন ॥ ৬৪ ॥

tabe choṭa-vipra kahe,—"śuna, mahājana
nyāya jinibāre kahe asatya-vacana

SYNONYMS

tabe—at that time; *choṭa-vipra*—the young *brāhmaṇa; kahe*—says; *śuna*—please hear; *mahā-jana*—all gentlemen; *nyāya*—the argument; *jinibāre*—to win; *kahe*—he says; *asatya-vacana*—untruthful statements.

TRANSLATION

At that time, the young brāhmaṇa said: "My dear gentlemen, please hear. Just to gain victory in an argument, this man is lying.

TEXT 65

এই বিপ্র মোর সেবায় তুষ্ট যবে হৈলা ।
'তোরে আমি কন্যা দিব' আপনে কহিলা ॥ ৬৫ ॥

ei vipra mora sevāya tuṣṭa yabe hailā
'tore āmi kanyā diba' āpane kahilā

SYNONYMS

ei vipra—this *brāhmaṇa; mora*—my; *sevāya*—by the service; *tuṣṭa*—fully satisfied; *yabe*—when; *hailā*—he was; *tore*—to you; *āmi*—I; *kanyā*—daughter; *diba*—shall give; *āpane*—of his own accord; *kahilā*—promised.

TRANSLATION

"Being very satisfied with my service, this brāhmaṇa said to me of his own accord, 'I promise to hand over my daughter to you.'

TEXT 66

তবে মুঞি নিষেধিনু,—শুন, দ্বিজবর ।
তোমার কন্যার যোগ্য নহি মুঞি বর ॥ ৬৬ ॥

tabe muñi niṣedhinu,—śuna, dvija-vara
tomāra kanyāra yogya nahi muñi vara

SYNONYMS

tabe—at that time; *muñi*—I; *niṣedhinu*—forbade; *śuna*—hear; *dvija-vara*—O best of the *brāhmaṇas; tomāra*—your; *kanyāra*—for the daughter; *yogya*—suitable; *nahi*—not; *muñi*—I; *vara*—husband.

TRANSLATION

"At that time, I forbade him to do this, telling him, 'O best of the brāhmaṇas, I am not a fit husband for your daughter.

TEXT 67

কাহাঁ তুমি পণ্ডিত, ধনী, পরম কুলীন ।
কাহাঁ মুঞি দরিদ্র, মূর্খ, নীচ, কুলহীন ॥ ৬৭ ॥

kāhāṅ tumi paṇḍita, dhanī, parama kulīna
kāhāṅ muñi daridra, mūrkha, nīca, kula-hīna

SYNONYMS

kāhāṅ—whereas; *tumi*—you; *paṇḍita*—learned scholar; *dhanī*—rich man; *parama*—first-class; *kulīna*—aristocracy; *kāhāṅ*—whereas; *muñi*—I; *daridra*—poor man; *mūrkha*—not educated; *nīca*—fallen; *kula-hīna*—without aristocracy.

TRANSLATION

" 'Whereas you are a learned scholar, a rich man belonging to an aristocratic family, I am a poor man, uneducated and with no claim to aristocracy.'

TEXT 68

তবু এই বিপ্র মোরে কহে বার বার ।
তোরে কন্যা দিলুঁ, তুমি করহ স্বীকার ॥ ৬৮ ॥

tabu ei vipra more kahe bāra bāra
tore kanyā diluṅ, tumi karaha svīkāra

SYNONYMS

tabu—still; *ei*—this; *vipra*—*brāhmaṇa; more*—to me; *kahe*—says; *bāra bāra*—again and again; *tore*—to you; *kanyā*—my daughter; *diluṅ*—I have given in charity; *tumi*—you; *karaha*—make; *svīkāra*—acceptance.

TRANSLATION

"Still, this brāhmaṇa insisted. Again and again he asked me to accept his proposal, saying, 'I have given you my daughter. Please accept her.'

TEXT 69

তবে আমি কহিলাঙ—শুন, মহামতি ।
তোমার স্ত্রী-পুত্র-জ্ঞাতির না হবে সম্মতি ॥ ৬৯ ॥

tabe āmi kahilāṅ——śuna, mahā-mati
tomāra strī-putra-jñātira nā habe sammati

SYNONYMS

tabe—at that time; *āmi*—I; *kahilāṅ*—said; *śuna*—please hear; *mahā-mati*—O intelligent *brāhmaṇa; tomāra*—your; *strī-putra*—wife and children; *jñātira*—kinsmen; *nā habe sammati*—will not agree.

TRANSLATION

"I then said, 'Please hear. You are a learned brāhmaṇa. Your wife, friends and relatives will never agree to this proposal.

TEXT 70

কন্যা দিতে নারিবে, হবে অসত্য-বচন ।
পুনরপি কহে বিপ্র করিয়া যতন ॥ ৭০ ॥

kanyā dite nāribe, habe asatya-vacana
punarapi kahe vipra kariyā yatana

SYNONYMS

kanyā—daughter; *dite*—to give; *nāribe*—you will not be able; *habe*—it will become; *asatya-vacana*—a false statement; *punarapi*—again; *kahe*—he says; *vipra*—the *brāhmaṇa; kariyā yatana*—with great attention.

TRANSLATION

" 'My dear sir, you will not be able to fulfill your promise. Your promise will be broken.' Yet, again and again the brāhmaṇa emphasized his promise.

TEXT 71

কন্যা তোরে দিলুঁ, দ্বিধা না করিহ চিতে ।
আত্মকন্যা দিব, কেবা পারে নিষেধিতে ॥ ৭১ ॥

kanyā tore diluṅ, dvidhā nā kariha cite
ātma-kanyā diba, kebā pāre niṣedhite

SYNONYMS

kanyā—the daughter; *tore*—to you; *diluṅ*—I have given; *dvidhā*—hesitation; *nā*—do not; *kariha*—do; *cite*—within your mind; *ātma-kanyā*—my own daughter; *diba*—I shall give; *kebā*—who; *pāre*—is able; *niṣedhite*—to forbid.

TRANSLATION

" 'I have offered you my daughter. Do not hesitate. She is my daughter, and I shall give her to you. Who can forbid me?'

TEXT 72

তবে আমি কহিলাঙ দৃঢ় করি' মন ।
গোপালের আগে কহ এ-সত্য বচন ॥ ৭২ ॥

tabe āmi kahilāṅ dṛḍha kari' mana
gopālera āge kaha e-satya vacana

SYNONYMS

tabe—at that time; *āmi*—I; *kahilāṅ*—said; *dṛḍha kari' mana*—fixing my mind; *gopālera āge*—in front of the Gopāla Deity; *kaha*—speak; *e-satya vacana*—this truthful statement.

TRANSLATION

"At that time I concentrated my mind and requested the brāhmaṇa to make the promise before the Gopāla Deity.

TEXT 73

তবে ইঁহো গোপালের আগেতে কহিল ।
তুমি জান, এই বিপ্রে কন্যা আমি দিল ॥ ৭৩ ॥

tabe iṅho gopālera āgete kahila
tumi jāna, ei vipre kanyā āmi dila

SYNONYMS

tabe—at that time; *iṅho*—this gentleman; *gopālera*—of the Gopāla Deity; *āgete*—in front; *kahila*—he said; *tumi jāna*—My Lord, please know; *ei vipre*—unto this young *brāhmaṇa; kanyā*—my daughter; *āmi*—I; *dila*—have offered.

TRANSLATION

"Then this gentleman said in front of the Gopāla Deity: 'My dear Lord, please bear witness. I have offered my daughter to this brāhmaṇa in charity.'

TEXT 74

তবে আমি গোপালেরে সাক্ষী করিঞা ।
কহিলাঙ তাঁর পদে মিনতি করিঞা ॥ ৭৪ ॥

tabe āmi gopālere sākṣī kariñā
kahilāṅ tāṅra pade minati kariñā

SYNONYMS

tabe—at that time; *āmi*—I; *gopālere*—to the Gopāla Deity; *sākṣī*—the witness; *kariñā*—making; *kahilāṅ*—said; *tāṅra pade*—at His lotus feet; *minati*—humility; *kariñā*—making.

TRANSLATION

"Accepting the Gopāla Deity as my witness, I then submitted the following at His lotus feet.

TEXT 75

যদি এই বিপ্র মোরে না দিবে কন্যাদান ।
সাক্ষী বোলাইমু তোমায়, হইও সাবধান ॥ ৭৫ ॥

yadi ei vipra more nā dibe kanyā-dāna
sākṣī bolāimu tomāya, ha-io sāvadhāna

SYNONYMS

yadi—if; *ei*—this; *vipra*—*brāhmaṇa;* *more*—to me; *nā*—not; *dibe*—will give; *kanyā-dāna*—his daughter in charity; *sākṣī bolāimu*—I shall call as witness; *tomāya*—You; *ha-io sāvadhāna*—kindly be attentive.

TRANSLATION

" 'If this brāhmaṇa later hesitates to give me his daughter, my dear Lord, I shall call on You as a witness. Please note this with care and attention.'

TEXT 76

এই বাক্যে সাক্ষী মোর আছে মহাজন ।
যাঁর বাক্য সত্য করি মানে ত্রিভুবন ॥" ৭৬ ॥

ei vākye sākṣī mora āche mahājana
yāṅra vākya satya kari māne tribhuvana"

SYNONYMS

ei vākye—in this statement; *sākṣī*—witness; *mora*—my; *āche*—there is; *mahājana*—a great personality; *yāṅra*—whose; *vākya*—words; *satya*—true; *kari*—taking as; *māne*—accepts; *tri-bhuvana*—the whole world.

TRANSLATION

"Thus I have called upon a great personality in this transaction. I have asked the Supreme Godhead to be my witness. The entire world accepts the words of the Supreme Personality of Godhead."

PURPORT

Although the young *brāhmaṇa* described himself as having no claims to aristocracy and being an uneducated common man, still he had one good qualification: he believed that the Supreme Personality of Godhead was the topmost authority, he accepted the words of Lord Kṛṣṇa without hesitation, and he had firm faith in the Lord's consistency. According to Prahlāda Mahārāja, another authority on the Supreme Personality of Godhead, such a staunch and faithful devotee of the Lord must be understood to be a most learned scholar: *tan manye 'dhītam uttamam* (*Śrīmad-Bhāgavatam* 7.5.24). A pure devotee who has firm faith in the words of the Supreme Personality of Godhead is to be considered a most learned scholar, the topmost aristocrat and the richest man in the whole world. All godly qualities automatically exist in such a devotee. In the preaching work of the Kṛṣṇa consciousness movement, we, as the servant of the servant of the servant of the servant of the Supreme Personality of Godhead, fully believe in the words of Kṛṣṇa and His servants, the disciplic succession. In this way we are presenting the words of Kṛṣṇa throughout the world. Even though we are neither a rich man nor a very learned scholar, and even though we do not belong to any aristocracy, this movement is still being welcomed and is very easily spreading all over the world. Although we are very poor and have no professional source of income, Kṛṣṇa supplies money whenever we need it. Whenever we need some men, Kṛṣṇa supplies them. Thus it is stated in *Bhagavad-gītā* (6.22): *yaṁ labdhvā cāparaṁ lābhaṁ manyate nādhikaṁ tataḥ*. Actually, if we can attain the favor of the Supreme Personality of Godhead, Kṛṣṇa, we do not need anything else. We certainly do not need those things which a mundane person considers to be material assets.

TEXTS 77-78

তবে বড়বিপ্র কহে,—"এই সত্য কথা ।
গোপাল যদি সাক্ষী দেন, আপনে আসি' এথা ॥৭৭॥
তবে কন্যা দিব আমি, জানিহ নিশ্চয় ।"
তাঁর পুত্র কহে,—'এই ভাল বাত হয় ॥' ৭৮ ॥

tabe baḍa-vipra kahe,——"ei satya kathā
gopāla yadi sākṣī dena, āpane āsi' ethā

tabe kanyā diba āmi, jāniha niścaya"
tāṅra putra kahe,——'ei bhāla vāta haya'

SYNONYMS

tabe—at that time; *baḍa-vipra*—the elderly *brāhmaṇa; kahe*—says; *ei satya kathā*—this is true; *gopāla*—the Gopāla Deity; *yadi*—if; *sākṣī*—witness; *dena*—gives; *āpane*—personally; *āsi'*—coming; *ethā*—here; *tabe*—at that time; *kanyā*—daughter; *diba*—must give in charity; *āmi*—I; *jāniha*—you all know it; *niścaya*—certainly; *tāṅra*—his; *putra*—son; *kahe*—says; *ei*—this; *bhāla*—nice; *vāta*—statement; *haya*—is.

TRANSLATION

Taking this opportunity, the elderly brāhmaṇa immediately confirmed that this was really true. He said: "If Gopāla personally comes here to serve as a witness, I shall surely give my daughter to the young brāhmaṇa." The elderly brāhmaṇa's son immediately confirmed this, saying, "Yes, this is a very nice settlement."

PURPORT

As the Supersoul within the heart of all living entities, Kṛṣṇa knows everyone's desire, everyone's request and everyone's prayer. Although all these may be contradictory, the Lord has to create a situation in which everyone will be pleased. This is an instance of a marriage negotiation between an elderly *brāhmaṇa* and a youthful one. The elderly *brāhmaṇa* was certainly willing to give his daughter in charity to the young *brāhmaṇa,* but his son and relatives became impediments to this transaction. The elderly *brāhmaṇa* considered how to get out of this situation and still offer his daughter to the young *brāhmaṇa.* His son, an atheist and a very cunning fellow, was thinking of how to stop the marriage. The father and son were thinking in a contradictory way, yet Kṛṣṇa created a situation wherein they both agreed. They both agreed that if the Gopāla Deity would come and serve as a witness, the daughter would be given to the young *brāhmaṇa.*

TEXT 79

বড়বিপ্রের মনে,—'কৃষ্ণ বড় দয়াবান্।
অবশ্য মোর বাক্য তেঁহো করিবে প্রমাণ ॥' ৭৯ ॥

baḍa-viprera mane,——'kṛṣṇa baḍa dayāvān
avaśya mora vākya teṅho karibe pramāṇa'

SYNONYMS

baḍa-viprera mane—within the mind of the elderly *brāhmaṇa; kṛṣṇa*—Lord Kṛṣṇa; *baḍa*—very; *dayāvān*—merciful; *avaśya*—certainly; *mora*—my; *vākya*—words; *teṅho*—He; *karibe*—will make; *pramāṇa*—evidence.

TRANSLATION

The elderly brāhmaṇa thought: "Since Lord Kṛṣṇa is very merciful, He will certainly come to prove my statement."

TEXT 80

পুত্রের মনে,—'প্রতিমা না আসিবে সাক্ষী দিতে'।
এই বুদ্ধ্যে দুইজন হইলা সম্মতে ॥ ৮০ ॥

putrera mane,——'pratimā nā āsibe sākṣī dite'
ei buddhye dui-jana ha-ilā sammate

SYNONYMS

putrera mane—in the mind of the son; *pratimā*—the Deity; *nā*—not; *āsibe*—will come; *sākṣī dite*—to give witness; *ei*—this; *buddhye*—in understanding; *dui-jana*—both the father and the son; *ha-ilā sammate*—agreed.

TRANSLATION

The atheistic son thought: "It is not possible for Gopāla to come and bear witness." Thinking thus, both father and son agreed.

TEXT 81

ছোটবিপ্র বলে,—'পত্র করহ লিখন।
পুনঃ যেন নাহি চলে এসব বচন ॥' ৮১ ॥

choṭa-vipra bale,——'patra karaha likhana
punaḥ yena nāhi cale e-saba vacana'

SYNONYMS

choṭa-vipra—the young *brāhmaṇa; bale*—says; *patra*—paper; *karaha*—do; *likhana*—writing; *punaḥ*—again; *yena*—so that; *nāhi*—not; *cale*—change; *e-saba*—all these; *vacana*—statements.

TRANSLATION

The young brāhmaṇa took this opportunity to speak: "Please write this down on paper in black and white so that you may not again change your word of honor."

TEXT 82

তবে সব লোক মেলি' পত্র ত' লিখিল ।
দুঁহার সম্মতি লঞা মধ্যস্থ রাখিল ॥ ৮২ ॥

tabe saba loka meli' patra ta' likhila
duṅhāra sammati lañā madhyastha rākhila

SYNONYMS

tabe—then; *saba loka*—all the people; *meli'*—gathered together; *patra*—paper; *ta'*—indeed; *likhila*—wrote; *duṅhāra*—of both of them; *sammati*—the agreement; *lañā*—taking; *madhya-stha*—as mediator; *rākhila*—remained.

TRANSLATION

All the assembled people got this statement down in black and white and, taking the signatures of agreement from both of them, served as the mediators.

TEXT 83

তবে ছোটবিপ্র কহে,—শুন, সর্বজন ।
এই বিপ্র—সত্য-বাক্য, ধর্মপরায়ণ ॥ ৮৩ ॥

tabe choṭa-vipra kahe,——śuna, sarva-jana
ei vipra——satya-vākya, dharma-parāyaṇa

SYNONYMS

tabe—at that time; *choṭa-vipra*—the young *brāhmaṇa; kahe*—says; *śuna*—please hear; *sarva-jana*—O all gentlemen present here; *ei vipra*—this elderly *brāhmaṇa; satya-vākya*—always truthful; *dharma-parāyaṇa*—religious.

TRANSLATION

The young brāhmaṇa then said: "Will all you gentlemen present please hear me? This elderly brāhmaṇa is certainly truthful and is following religious principles.

TEXT 84

স্ববাক্য ছাড়িতে ইঁহার নাহি কভু মন ।
স্বজন-মৃত্যু-ভয়ে কহে অসত্য-বচন ॥ ৮৪ ॥

sva-vākya chāḍite iṅhāra nāhi kabhu mana
svajana-mṛtyu-bhaye kahe asatya-vacana

SYNONYMS

sva-vākya—his own promise; *chāḍite*—to give up; *iṅhāra*—of this *brāhmaṇa; nāhi*—not; *kabhu*—at any time; *mana*—the mind; *sva-jana*—of his own kinsmen; *mṛtyu-bhaye*—fearing the suicide; *kahe*—says; *asatya-vacana*—untruthful words.

TRANSLATION

"He had no desire to break his promise, but fearing that his kinsmen would commit suicide, he deviated from the truth.

TEXT 85

ইঁহার পুণ্যে কৃষ্ণে আনি' সাক্ষী বোলাইব ।
তবে এই বিপ্রের সত্য-প্রতিজ্ঞা রাখিব ॥ ৮৫ ॥

iṅhāra puṇye kṛṣṇe āni' sākṣī bolāiba
tabe ei viprera satya-pratijñā rākhiba

SYNONYMS

iṅhāra puṇye—by his piety; *kṛṣṇe*—Lord Kṛṣṇa; *āni'*—bringing; *sākṣī*—witness; *bolāiba*—I shall call; *tabe*—at that time; *ei viprera*—of this *brāhmaṇa; satya*—truthful; *pratijñā*—the promise; *rākhiba*—I shall keep.

TRANSLATION

"By the piety of the elderly brāhmaṇa, I shall call the Supreme Personality of Godhead as a witness. Thus I shall keep his truthful promise intact."

TEXT 86

এত শুনি' নাস্তিক লোক উপহাস করে ।
কেহ বলে, ঈশ্বর—দয়ালু, আসিতেহ পারে ॥ ৮৬ ॥

eta śuni' nāstika loka upahāsa kare
keha bale, īśvara——dayālu, āsiteha pāre

SYNONYMS

eta śuni'—hearing this; *nāstika*—atheistic; *loka*—class of men; *upahāsa*—joking; *kare*—do; *keha bale*—someone says; *īśvara*—God; *dayālu*—merciful; *āsiteha pāre*—He is able to come.

TRANSLATION

Hearing the emphatic statement of the younger brāhmaṇa, some atheists in the meeting began to cut jokes. However, someone else said, "After all, the Lord is merciful, and if He likes, He can come."

TEXT 87

তবে সেই ছোটবিপ্র গেলা বৃন্দাবন ।
দণ্ডবৎ করি' কহে সব বিবরণ ॥ ৮৭ ॥

tabe sei choṭa-vipra gelā vṛndāvana
daṇḍavat kari' kahe saba vivaraṇa

SYNONYMS

tabe—after this; *sei*—that; *choṭa-vipra*—young *brāhmaṇa; gelā*—went; *vṛndāvana*—to Vṛndāvana; *daṇḍavat kari'*—after offering respects; *kahe*—tells; *saba*—all; *vivaraṇa*—the description.

TRANSLATION

After the meeting, the young brāhmaṇa started for Vṛndāvana. Upon arriving there, he first offered his respectful obeisances to the Deity and then narrated everything in full detail.

TEXT 88

"ব্রহ্মণ্যদেব তুমি বড় দয়াময় ।
দুই বিপ্রের ধর্ম রাখ হঞা সদয় ॥ ৮৮ ॥

"brahmaṇya-deva tumi baḍa dayā-maya
dui viprera dharma rākha hañā sadaya

SYNONYMS

brahmaṇya-deva—O Lord of brahminical culture; *tumi*—You; *baḍa*—very; *dayā-maya*—merciful; *dui*—two; *viprera*—of *brāhmaṇas; dharma*—the religious principles; *rākha*—protect; *hañā*—becoming; *sa-daya*—merciful.

TRANSLATION

He said: "My Lord, You are the protector of brahminical culture, and You are also very merciful. Therefore, kindly show Your great mercy by protecting the religious principles of us two brāhmaṇas.

TEXT 89

কন্যা পাব,—মোর মনে ইহা নাহি সুখ ।
ব্রাহ্মণের প্রতিজ্ঞা যায়—এই বড় দুঃখ ॥ ৮৯ ॥

kanyā pāba,——mora mane ihā nāhi sukha
brāhmaṇera pratijñā yāya——ei baḍa duḥkha

SYNONYMS

kanyā pāba—I shall get the daughter; *mora*—my; *mane*—in the mind; *ihā*—this; *nāhi*—is not; *sukha*—happiness; *brāhmaṇera*—of a pure *brāhmaṇa;* *pratijñā*—the promise; *yāya*—becomes lost; *ei*—this; *baḍa*—very much; *duḥkha*—unhappiness.

TRANSLATION

"My dear Lord, I am not thinking to become happy by getting the daughter as a bride. I am simply thinking that the brāhmaṇa has broken his promise, and that is giving me great pain."

PURPORT

It was not at all the intention of the young *brāhmaṇa* to get the daughter of the elderly *brāhmaṇa* in marriage and thus enjoy material happiness and sense gratification. It was not for that reason that the young *brāhmaṇa* went to Vṛndāvana to ask the Supreme Personality of Godhead to act as a witness. His only concern was that the elderly *brāhmaṇa* had promised something, and if Gopāla did not bear witness to that transaction, then the older *brāhmaṇa* would incur a spiritual blemish. Therefore, the young *brāhmaṇa* wanted protection and help from the Deity. The young *brāhmaṇa* was thus a pure Vaiṣṇava, and he had no desire for sense gratification. He wanted only to serve the Supreme Personality of Godhead and the older *brāhmaṇa,* who was also a Vaiṣṇava and very devoted to the Lord.

TEXT 90

এত জানি' তুমি সাক্ষী দেহ, দয়াময় ।
জানি' সাক্ষী নাহি দেয়, তার পাপ হয় ॥ ৯০ ॥

eta jāni' tumi sākṣī deha, dayā-maya
jāni' sākṣī nāhi deya, tāra pāpa haya

SYNONYMS

eta jāni'—knowing this; *tumi*—You; *sākṣī*—witness; *deha*—please give; *dayā-maya*—O most merciful; *jāni'*—knowing; *sākṣī*—witness; *nāhi deya*—does not give; *tāra*—for him; *pāpa*—sin; *haya*—there is.

TRANSLATION

The young brāhmaṇa continued: "My dear sir, You are very merciful and You know everything. Therefore, kindly be a witness in this case. A person who knows things as they are and still does not bear witness becomes involved in sinful activities."

PURPORT

The dealings between a devotee and the Lord are very simple. The young *brāhmaṇa* said to the Lord, "You know everything, but if You do not bear witness, You will be involved in sinful activities." There is no possibility, however, of the Lord's being involved in sinful activities. A pure devotee, even though he knows everything of the Supreme Lord, can speak with the Lord exactly as if He were a common man. Although the dealings between the Lord and His devotee are always very simple and open, there is formality. All these things happen because of the connection between the Lord and the devotee.

TEXT 91

কৃষ্ণ কহে,—বিপ্র, তুমি যাহ স্ব-ভবনে।
সভা করি' মোরে তুমি করিহ স্মরণে ॥ ৯১ ॥

kṛṣṇa kahe,——vipra, tumi yāha sva-bhavane
sabhā kari' more tumi kariha smaraṇe

SYNONYMS

kṛṣṇa kahe—Lord Kṛṣṇa says; *vipra*—My dear *brāhmaṇa; tumi*—you; *yāha*—go back; *sva-bhavane*—to your own home; *sabhā kari'*—calling a meeting of all the men; *more*—of Me; *tumi*—you; *kariha*—just do; *smaraṇe*—remembering.

TRANSLATION

Lord Kṛṣṇa replied: "My dear brāhmaṇa, go back to your home and call a meeting of all the men. In that meeting, just try to remember Me.

TEXT 92

আবির্ভাব হঞা আমি তাহাঁ সাক্ষী দিব ।
তবে দুই বিপ্রের সত্য প্রতিজ্ঞা রাখিব ॥ ৯২ ॥

āvirbhāva hañā āmi tāhāṅ sākṣī diba
tabe dui viprera satya pratijñā rākhiba

SYNONYMS

āvirbhāva—appearance; *hañā*—making; *āmi*—I; *tāhāṅ*—there; *sākṣī*—witness; *diba*—shall give; *tabe*—at that time; *dui*—two; *viprera*—of the *brāhmaṇas; satya*—truthful; *pratijñā*—promise; *rākhiba*—I shall keep.

TRANSLATION

"I shall certainly appear there, and at that time I shall protect the honor of both you brāhmaṇas by bearing witness to the promise."

TEXT 93

বিপ্র বলে,—"যদি হও চতুর্ভুজ-মূর্তি ।
তবু তোমার বাক্যে কারু না হবে প্রতীতি ॥ ৯৩ ॥

vipra bale,——"yadi hao caturbhuja-mūrti
tabu tomāra vākye kāru nā habe pratīti

SYNONYMS

vipra bale—the young *brāhmaṇa* says; *yadi*—if; *hao*—You become; *catuḥ-bhuja*—four-handed; *mūrti*—Deity; *tabu*—still; *tomāra*—Your; *vākye*—in the word; *kāru*—of anyone; *nā*—not; *habe*—there will be; *pratīti*—belief.

TRANSLATION

The young brāhmaṇa replied: "My dear sir, even if You appear there as a four-handed Viṣṇu Deity, still, none of those people will believe in Your words.

TEXT 94

এই মূর্তি গিয়া যদি এই শ্রীবদনে ।
সাক্ষী দেহ যদি- তবে সর্বলোক শুনে ॥ ৯৪ ॥

ei mūrti giyā yadi ei śrī-vadane
sākṣī deha yadi——tabe sarva-loka śune

SYNONYMS

ei—this; *mūrti*—in the form; *giyā*—going; *yadi*—if; *ei*—this; *śrī-vadane*—from Your beautiful face; *sākṣī*—witness; *deha*—You give; *yadi*—if; *tabe*—then; *sarva-loka*—all people; *śune*—will hear.

TRANSLATION

"Only if You go there in this form of Gopāla and speak the words from Your beautiful face will Your testimony be heard by all the people."

TEXT 95

কৃষ্ণ কহে,—"প্রতিমা চলে, কোথাহ না শুনি।"
বিপ্র বলে,—"প্রতিমা হঞা কহ কেনে বাণী ॥ ৯৫ ॥

kṛṣṇa kahe,——"pratimā cale, kothāha nā śuni"
vipra bale,——"pratimā hañā kaha kene vāṇī

SYNONYMS

kṛṣṇa kahe—Lord Kṛṣṇa says; *pratimā cale*—a Deity walks; *kothāha*—anywhere; *nā śuni*—I have not heard; *vipra bale*—the young *brāhmaṇa* replies; *pratimā hañā*—in Your Deity form; *kaha kene vāṇī*—how do You speak words.

TRANSLATION

Lord Kṛṣṇa said: "I've never heard of a Deity's walking from one place to another." The brāhmaṇa replied: "That is true, but how is it that You are speaking to me, although You are a Deity?

TEXT 96

প্রতিমা নহ তুমি,—সাক্ষাৎ ব্রজেন্দ্রনন্দন।
বিপ্র লাগি' কর তুমি অকার্য-করণ ॥" ৯৬ ॥

pratimā naha tumi,——sākṣāt vrajendra-nandana
vipra lāgi' kara tumi akārya-karaṇa"

SYNONYMS

pratimā—a statue; *naha*—are not; *tumi*—You; *sākṣāt*—directly; *vrajendra-nandana*—the son of Nanda Mahārāja; *vipra lāgi'*—for the sake of the *brāhmaṇa; kara tumi*—You can do; *akārya-karaṇa*—an action You have never done before.

TRANSLATION

"My dear Lord, You are not a statue; You are directly the son of Mahārāja Nanda. Now, for the sake of the old brāhmaṇa, You can do something You have never done before."

TEXT 97

হাসিঞা গোপাল কহে,—"শুনহ, ব্রাহ্মণ।
তোমার পাছে পাছে আমি করিব গমন ॥ ৯৭ ॥

hāsiñā gopāla kahe,——"śunaha, brāhmaṇa
tomāra pāche pāche āmi kariba gamana

SYNONYMS

hāsiñā—smiling; *gopāla*—the Lord Gopāla; *kahe*—says; *śunaha*—just hear; *brāhmaṇa*—O my dear *brāhmaṇa; tomāra*—you; *pāche pāche*—behind; *āmi*—I; *kariba*—shall do; *gamana*—walking.

TRANSLATION

Śrī Gopālajī then smiled and said: "My dear brāhmaṇa, just listen to Me. I shall walk behind you, and in this way I shall go with you."

PURPORT

The conversation between Lord Śrī Kṛṣṇa and the *brāhmaṇa* is proof that the Lord in His *arcā-mūrti,* or form made of material elements, is not material, for those elements, although separated from the Lord, are also a part of the Lord's energy, as stated in *Bhagavad-gītā.* Because the elements are the Lord's own energy and because there is no difference between the energy and the energetic, the Lord can appear through any element. Just as the sun can act through the sunshine and thus distribute its heat and light, so Kṛṣṇa, by His inconceivable power, can appear in His original spiritual form in any material element, including stone, wood, paint, gold, silver and jewels, because the material elements are all His energy. The *śāstras* warn, *arcye viṣṇau śilā-dhīḥ:* one should never think of the *arcā-mūrti,* the Deity within the temple, as stone, wood or any other material element. Because of his advanced devotional position, the younger *brāhmaṇa* knew that although the Deity of Gopāla appeared to be stone, He was not stone. He was the son of Nanda Mahārāja, Vrajendra-nandana Himself.

As such, the Deity can act exactly as the Lord did in His original form as Kṛṣṇa. Lord Kṛṣṇa was talking to the young *brāhmaṇa* just to test his knowledge about the *arcā-vigraha.* In other words, those who have understood the science of Kṛṣṇa—Kṛṣṇa's name, form, quality and so forth—can also talk with the Deity. To an ordinary person, however, the Deity will appear to be made of stone, wood or some other material. In the higher sense, since all material elements ultimately emanate from the supreme spiritual entity, nothing is really material. Being omnipotent, omnipresent and omniscient, Kṛṣṇa can deal with His devotees in any form without difficulty. By the mercy of the Lord, the devotee knows perfectly well about the Lord's dealings. Indeed, he can talk face to face with the Lord.

TEXT 98

উলটিয়া আমা তুমি না করিহ দরশনে ।
আমাকে দেখিলে, আমি রহিব সেই স্থানে ॥ ৯৮ ॥

ulaṭiyā āmā tumi nā kariha daraśane
āmāke dekhile, āmi rahiba sei sthāne

SYNONYMS

ulaṭiyā—turning your face; *āmā*—Me; *tumi*—you; *nā*—not; *kariha*—do; *daraśane*—seeing; *āmāke*—Me; *dekhile*—if you see; *āmi*—I; *rahiba*—shall stay; *sei sthāne*—in that very place.

TRANSLATION

The Lord continued: "Do not try to see Me by turning around. As soon as you see Me, I shall remain stationary in that very place.

TEXT 99

নূপুরের ধ্বনিমাত্র আমার শুনিবা ।
সেই শব্দে আমার গমন প্রতীতি করিবা ॥ ৯৯ ॥

nūpurera dhvani-mātra āmāra śunibā
sei śabde āmāra gamana pratīti karibā

SYNONYMS

nūpurera—of the ankle bells; *dhvani-mātra*—the sound only; *āmāra*—My; *śunibā*—you will hear; *sei śabde*—by hearing that sound; *āmāra*—My; *gamana*—coming; *pratīti*—understanding; *karibā*—you will do.

TRANSLATION

"You will know that I am walking behind you by the sound of My ankle bells.

TEXT 100

একসের অন্ন রান্ধি' করিহ সমর্পণ ।
তাহা খাঞা তোমার সঙ্গে করিব গমন ॥ ১০০ ॥

eka-sera anna rāndhi' kariha samarpaṇa
tāhā khāñā tomāra saṅge kariba gamana

SYNONYMS

eka-sera—one kilo; *anna*—of rice; *rāndhi'*—cooking; *kariha*—do; *samarpaṇa*—offering; *tāhā*—that; *khāñā*—eating; *tomāra*—of you; *saṅge*—in the company; *kariba*—I shall do; *gamana*—walking.

TRANSLATION

"Cook one kilo of rice daily and offer it. I shall eat that rice and follow behind you."

TEXT 101

আর দিন আজ্ঞা মাগি' চলিলা ব্রাহ্মণ ।
তার পাছে পাছে গোপাল করিলা গমন ॥ ১০১ ॥

āra dina ājñā māgi' calilā brāhmaṇa
tāra pāche pāche gopāla karilā gamana

SYNONYMS

āra dina—the next day; *ājñā*—permission; *māgi'*—begging; *calilā*—started; *brāhmaṇa*—the young *brāhmaṇa; tāra*—him; *pāche*—behind; *pāche*—behind; *gopāla*—Lord Gopāla; *karilā*—began; *gamana*—following.

TRANSLATION

The next day, the brāhmaṇa begged permission from Gopāla and started for his country. Gopāla followed him, step by step.

TEXT 102

নূপুরের ধ্বনি শুনি' আনন্দিত মন ।
উত্তমান্ন পাক করি' করায় ভোজন ॥ ১০২ ॥

nūpurera dhvani śuni' ānandita mana
uttamānna pāka kari' karāya bhojana

SYNONYMS

nūpurera—of the ankle bells; *dhvani*—the sounds; *śuni'*—hearing; *ānandita*—very much pleased; *mana*—the mind; *uttama-anna*—first-class rice; *pāka*—cooking; *kari'*—doing; *karāya*—causes; *bhojana*—eating.

TRANSLATION

While Gopāla followed the young brāhmaṇa, the tinkling sound of His ankle bells could be heard. The brāhmaṇa became very pleased, and he cooked first-class rice for Gopāla to eat.

TEXT 103

এইমতে চলি' বিপ্র নিজ-দেশে আইলা ।
গ্রামের নিকট আসি' মনেতে চিন্তিলা ॥ ১০৩ ॥

ei-mate cali' vipra nija-deśe āilā
grāmera nikaṭa āsi' manete cintilā

SYNONYMS

ei-mate—in this way; *cali'*—walking; *vipra*—the *brāhmaṇa; nija*—own; *deśe*—to the country; *āilā*—returned; *grāmera*—to the village; *nikaṭa*—near; *āsi'*—coming; *manete*—within his mind; *cintilā*—thought.

TRANSLATION

The young brāhmaṇa walked and walked in this way until he eventually arrived in his own country. When he neared his own village, he began to think as follows.

TEXT 104

এবে মুঞি গ্রামে আইনু, যাইমু ভবন ।
লোকেরে কহিব গিয়া সাক্ষীর আগমন ॥ ১০৪ ॥

ebe muñi grāme āinu, yāimu bhavana
lokere kahiba giyā sākṣīra āgamana

SYNONYMS

ebe—now; *muñi*—I; *grāme*—to the village; *āinu*—have come; *yāimu*—I shall go; *bhavana*—to my home; *lokere*—the people; *kahiba*—I shall tell; *giyā*—going there; *sākṣīra*—of the witness; *āgamana*—about the arrival.

TRANSLATION

"I have now come to my village, and I shall go to my home and tell all the people that the witness has arrived."

TEXT 105

সাক্ষাতে না দেখিলে মনে প্রতীতি না হয়।
ইহাঁ যদি রহেন, তবু নাহি কিছু ভয়॥' ১০৫॥

sākṣāte nā dekhile mane pratīti nā haya
ihāṅ yadi rahena, tabu nāhi kichu bhaya'

SYNONYMS

sākṣāte—directly; *nā*—not; *dekhile*—if seeing; *mane*—in the mind; *pratīti*—assurance; *nā*—not; *haya*—there is; *ihāṅ*—here; *yadi*—if; *rahena*—the Lord stays; *tabu*—still; *nāhi*—there is not; *kichu*—any; *bhaya*—fear.

TRANSLATION

The brāhmaṇa then began to think that if the people didn't directly see the Gopāla Deity, they would not believe that He had arrived. "But even if Gopāla stays here," he thought, "there is still nothing to fear."

TEXT 106

এত ভাবি' সেই বিপ্র ফিরিয়া চাহিল।
হাসিঞা গোপাল-দেব তথায় রহিল॥ ১০৬॥

eta bhāvi' sei vipra phiriyā cāhila
hāsiñā gopāla-deva tathāya rahila

SYNONYMS

eta bhāvi'—thinking like this; *sei*—that; *vipra*—*brāhmaṇa; phiriyā*—turning; *cāhila*—saw; *hāsiñā*—smiling; *gopāla-deva*—Lord Gopāladeva, the Supreme Personality of Godhead; *tathāya*—there; *rahila*—stayed.

TRANSLATION

Thinking this, the brāhmaṇa turned to look back, and He saw that Gopāla, the Supreme Personality of Godhead, was standing there smiling.

TEXT 107

ব্রাহ্মণেরে কহে,—"তুমি যাহ নিজ-ঘর ।
এথায় রহিব আমি, না যাব অতঃপর ॥" ১০৭ ॥

brāhmaṇere kahe,——"tumi yāha nija-ghara
ethāya rahiba āmi, nā yāba ataḥpara"

SYNONYMS

brāhmaṇere kahe—He asked the *brāhmaṇa; tumi*—you; *yāha*—go; *nija-ghara*—to your own home; *ethāya*—here in this place; *rahiba*—shall stay; *āmi*—I; *nā*—not; *yāba*—shall go; *ataḥpara*—hereafter.

TRANSLATION

The Lord told the brāhmaṇa: "Now you can go home. I shall stay here and shall not leave."

TEXT 108

তবে সেই বিপ্র যাই নগরে কহিল ।
শুনিঞা সকল লোক চমৎকার হৈল ॥ ১০৮ ॥

tabe sei vipra yāi nagare kahila
śuniñā sakala loka camatkāra haila

SYNONYMS

tabe—thereafter; *sei*—that; *vipra*—*brāhmaṇa; yāi*—going; *nagare*—to the town; *kahila*—said; *śuniñā*—hearing; *sakala*—all; *loka*—the people; *camatkāra*—struck with wonder; *haila*—were.

TRANSLATION

The young brāhmaṇa then went to the town and informed all the people about Gopāla's arrival. Hearing this, the people were struck with wonder.

TEXT 109

আইল সকল লোক সাক্ষী দেখিবারে ।
গোপাল দেখিঞা লোক দণ্ডবৎ করে ॥ ১০৯ ॥

āila sakala loka sākṣī dekhibāre
gopāla dekhiñā loka daṇḍavat kare

SYNONYMS

āila—came; *sakala*—all; *loka*—the people; *sākṣī*—the witness; *dekhibāre*—to see; *gopāla*—Lord Gopāla; *dekhiñā*—seeing; *loka*—all the people; *daṇḍavat*—offering obeisances; *kare*—do.

TRANSLATION

All the townspeople went to see the witness Gopāla, and when they saw the Lord actually standing there, they all offered their respectful obeisances.

TEXT 110

গোপাল-সৌন্দর্য দেখি' লোকে আনন্দিত।
প্রতিমা চলিঞা আইলা,—শুনিঞা বিস্মিত ॥ ১১০ ॥

gopāla-saundarya dekhi' loke ānandita
pratimā caliñā āilā,——śuniñā vismita

SYNONYMS

gopāla—of Lord Gopāla; *saundarya*—the beauty; *dekhi'*—seeing; *loke*—everyone; *ānandita*—pleased; *pratimā*—the Deity; *caliñā*—walking; *āilā*—came; *śuniñā*—hearing this; *vismita*—surprised.

TRANSLATION

When the people arrived, they were very pleased to see the beauty of Gopāla, and when they heard that He had actually walked there, they were all surprised.

TEXT 111

তবে সেই বড়বিপ্র আনন্দিত হঞা।
গোপালের আগে পড়ে দণ্ডবৎ হঞা ॥ ১১১ ॥

tabe sei baḍa-vipra ānandita hañā
gopālera āge paḍe daṇḍavat hañā

SYNONYMS

tabe—thereafter; *sei*—that; *baḍa-vipra*—elderly *brāhmaṇa; ānandita*—pleased; *hañā*—becoming; *gopālera*—of Lord Gopāla; *āge*—in front; *paḍe*—falls down; *daṇḍavat*—like a stick; *hañā*—becoming.

TRANSLATION

Then the elderly brāhmaṇa, being very pleased, came forward and immediately fell like a stick in front of Gopāla.

TEXT 112

সকল লোকের আগে গোপাল সাক্ষী দিল ।
বড়বিপ্র ছোটবিপ্রে কন্যাদান কৈল ॥ ১১২ ॥

sakala lokera āge gopāla sākṣī dila
baḍa-vipra choṭa-vipre kanyā-dāna kaila

SYNONYMS

sakala—all; *lokera*—of the people; *āge*—in the presence; *gopāla*—Lord Gopāla; *sākṣī*—witness; *dila*—gave; *baḍa-vipra*—the elderly *brāhmaṇa; choṭa-vipre*—unto the young *brāhmaṇa; kanyā-dāna*—giving the daughter in charity; *kaila*—did.

TRANSLATION

Thus in the presence of all the townspeople, Lord Gopāla bore witness that the elderly brāhmaṇa had offered his daughter in charity to the young brāhmaṇa.

TEXT 113

তবে সেই দুই বিপ্রে কহিল ঈশ্বর ।
"তুমি-দুই—জন্মে-জন্মে আমার কিঙ্কর ॥ ১১৩ ॥

tabe sei dui vipre kahila īśvara
"tumi-dui——janme-janme āmāra kiṅkara

SYNONYMS

tabe—thereafter; *sei*—those; *dui*—two; *vipre*—unto the *brāhmaṇas; kahila*—spoke; *īśvara*—the Lord; *tumi-dui*—both of you; *janme-janme*—birth after birth; *āmāra*—My; *kiṅkara*—servants.

TRANSLATION

After the marriage ceremony was performed, the Lord informed both brāhmaṇas: "You two brāhmaṇas are My eternal servants birth after birth."

PURPORT

Like these two *brāhmaṇas* of Vidyānagara, there are many devotees who are eternal servants of the Lord. They are specifically known as *nitya-siddha,* eternally perfect. Although the *nitya-siddhas* appear in the material world and seem to be common members of the world, they never forget the Supreme Personality of Godhead in any condition. This is the symptom of a *nitya-siddha.*

There are two kinds of living entities—*nitya-siddha* and *nitya-baddha.* The *nitya-siddha* never forgets his relationship with the Supreme Personality, whereas the *nitya-baddha* is always conditioned, even before the creation. He always forgets his relationship with the Supreme Personality of Godhead. Here the Lord informs the two *brāhmaṇas* that they are His servants birth after birth. The phrase birth after birth refers to the material world because in the spiritual world there is no birth, death, old age or disease. By the order of the Supreme Personality of Godhead, the *nitya-siddha* remains within this material world like an ordinary man, but the only business of the *nitya-siddha* is to broadcast the glories of the Lord. This incident appears to be an ordinary story about a marriage transaction involving two ordinary people. However, Kṛṣṇa accepted the two *brāhmaṇas* as His eternal servants. Both *brāhmaṇas* took much trouble in these negotiations, just like mundane people, yet they were acting as eternal servants of the Lord. All *nitya-siddhas* within this material world may appear to toil like ordinary men, but they never forget their position as servants of the Lord.

Another point: The elderly *brāhmaṇa* belonged to an aristocratic family and was learned and wealthy. The young *brāhmaṇa* belonged to an ordinary family and was uneducated. But these mundane qualifications do not concern a *nitya-siddha* engaged in the service of the Lord. We have to accept the fact that the *nitya-siddhas* are completely distinct from the *nitya-baddhas,* who are ordinary human beings. Śrīla Narottama dāsa Ṭhākura confirms this statement:

gaurāṅgera saṅgi-gaṇe, nitya-siddha kari' māne,
se yāya vrajendra-suta pāśa
śrī-gauḍa-maṇḍala-bhūmi, yebā jāne cintāmaṇi
tāra haya vraja-bhūme vāsa

One who accepts the associates of Lord Caitanya Mahāprabhu as *nitya-siddhas* is certain to be elevated to the spiritual kingdom to become an associate of the Supreme Lord. One should also know that Gauḍa-maṇḍala-bhūmi—those places in Bengal where Śrī Caitanya Mahāprabhu stayed—are equal to Vrajabhūmi, or Vṛndāvana. There is no difference between the inhabitants of Vṛndāvana and those of Gauḍa-maṇḍala-bhūmi, or Śrīdhāma Māyāpura.

TEXT 114

দুঁহার সত্যে তুষ্ট হইলাঙ, দুঁহে মাগ' বর।"
দুইবিপ্র বর মাগে আনন্দ-অন্তর ॥ ১১৪ ॥

duṅhāra satye tuṣṭa ha-ilāṅ, duṅhe māga' vara"
dui-vipra vara māge ānanda-antara

SYNONYMS

duṅhāra satye—in the truthfulness of both of you; *tuṣṭa ha-ilāṅ*—I have become satisfied; *duṅhe*—both of you; *māga'*—ask; *vara*—some benediction; *dui-vipra*—both the *brāhmaṇas; vara*—a benediction; *māge*—beg; *ānanda*—pleased; *antara*—within.

TRANSLATION

The Lord continued: "I have become very pleased by the truthfulness of you both. Now you can ask for a benediction." Thus with great pleasure the two brāhmaṇas begged for a benediction.

TEXT 115

"যদি বর দিবে, তবে রহ এই স্থানে ।
কিঙ্করেরে দয়া তব সর্বলোকে জানে ॥" ১১৫ ॥

"yadi vara dibe, tabe raha ei sthāne
kiṅkarere dayā tava sarva-loke jāne"

SYNONYMS

yadi—if; *vara*—benediction; *dibe*—You will offer; *tabe*—then; *raha*—stay; *ei sthāne*—in this quarter; *kiṅkarere*—to Your servants; *dayā*—mercy; *tava*—Your; *sarva-loke*—all people; *jāne*—may know.

TRANSLATION

The brāhmaṇas said: "Please remain here so that people all over the world will know how merciful You are to Your servants."

TEXT 116

গোপাল রহিলা, দুঁহে করেন সেবন ।
দেখিতে আইলা সব দেশের লোক-জন ॥ ১১৬ ॥

gopāla rahilā, duṅhe karena sevana
dekhite āilā saba deśera loka-jana

SYNONYMS

gopāla—Lord Gopāla; *rahilā*—stayed; *duṅhe*—both of them; *karena*—do; *sevana*—service; *dekhite*—to see; *āilā*—came; *saba*—all; *deśera*—of the countries; *loka-jana*—the people.

TRANSLATION

Lord Gopāla stayed, and the two brāhmaṇas engaged in His service. After hearing of the incident, many people from different countries began to come to see Gopāla.

TEXT 117

সে দেশের রাজা আইল আশ্চর্য শুনিঞা ।
পরম সন্তোষ পাইল গোপালে দেখিঞা ॥ ১১৭ ॥

se deśera rājā āila āścarya śuniñā
parama santoṣa pāila gopāle dekhiñā

SYNONYMS

se deśera—of that country; *rājā*—the King; *āila*—came; *āścarya*—about the wonder; *śuniñā*—hearing; *parama*—great; *santoṣa*—satisfaction; *pāila*—achieved; *gopāle*—Gopāla; *dekhiñā*—by seeing.

TRANSLATION

Eventually the King of that country heard of this wonderful story, and he also came to see Gopāla and thus became very satisfied.

TEXT 118

মন্দির করিয়া রাজা সেবা চালাইল ।
'সাক্ষিগোপাল' বলি' তাঁর নাম খ্যাতি হৈল ॥১১৮॥

mandira kariyā rājā sevā cālāila
'sākṣi-gopāla' bali' tāṅra nāma khyāti haila

SYNONYMS

mandira—a temple; *kariyā*—constructing; *rājā*—the King; *sevā*—service; *cālāila*—regularly carried on; *sākṣi-gopāla*—by the name Sākṣi-gopāla; *bali'*—known as; *tāṅra*—His; *nāma*—name; *khyāti*—celebrated; *haila*—was.

TRANSLATION

The King constructed a nice temple, and regular service was executed. Gopāla became very famous under the name of Sākṣi-gopāla [the witness Gopāla].

TEXT 119

এই মত বিদ্যানগরে সাক্ষিগোপাল ।
সেবা অঙ্গীকার করি' আছেন চিরকাল ॥ ১১৯ ॥

ei mata vidyānagare sākṣi-gopāla
sevā aṅgīkāra kari' āchena cira-kāla

SYNONYMS

ei mata—in this way; *vidyānagare*—in the town of Vidyānagara; *sākṣi-gopāla*—the witness Gopāla; *sevā*—service; *aṅgīkāra*—acceptance; *kari'*—doing; *āchena*—remains; *cira-kāla*—a long time.

TRANSLATION

Thus Sākṣi-gopāla stayed in Vidyānagara and accepted service for a very long time.

PURPORT

This city of Vidyānagara is situated in Trailaṅga-deśa, South India, on the bank of the River Godāvarī. The place where the Godāvarī flows into the Bay of Bengal is called Koṭadeśa. The Orissa kingdom was very powerful, and this Koṭadeśa was the capital of Orissa. It was then known as Vidyānagara. Formerly this city was situated on the southern side of the River Godāvarī. At that time King Puruṣottama managed to control Orissa and appoint a government. The present city of Vidyānagara is on the southeast side of the river, only twenty to twenty-five miles from Rājamahendrī. During the time of Mahārāja Pratāparudra, Śrī Rāmānanda Rāya was the governor there. Vijaya-nagara is not identical with Vidyānagara.

TEXT 120

উৎকলের রাজা পুরুষোত্তমদেব নাম ।
সেই দেশ জিনি' নিল করিয়া সংগ্রাম ॥ ১২০ ॥

utkalera rājā puruṣottama-deva nāma
sei deśa jini' nila kariyā saṅgrāma

SYNONYMS

utkalera—of Orissa; *rājā*—the King; *puruṣottama-deva*—Puruṣottama; *nāma*—named; *sei deśa*—this country; *jini'*—conquering; *nila*—took; *kariyā*—executing; *saṅgrāma*—fight.

TRANSLATION

Later there was a fight, and this country was conquered by King Puruṣottama of Orissa.

TEXT 121

সেই রাজা জিনি' নিল তাঁর সিংহাসন।
'মাণিক্য-সিংহাসন' নাম অনেক রতন ॥ ১২১ ॥

sei rājā jini' nila tāṅra siṁhāsana
'māṇikya-siṁhāsana' nāma aneka ratana

SYNONYMS

sei rājā—that King (Mahārāja Puruṣottama); *jini'*—conquering; *nila*—took; *tāṅra*—his; *siṁha-āsana*—the throne; *māṇikya-siṁhāsana*—the throne known as Māṇikya-siṁhāsana; *nāma*—named; *aneka*—various; *ratana*—bedecked with jewels.

TRANSLATION

That King was victorious over the King of Vidyānagara, and he took possession of his throne, the Māṇikya-siṁhāsana, which was bedecked with many jewels.

TEXT 122

পুরুষোত্তম-দেব সেই বড় ভক্ত আর্য।
গোপাল-চরণে মাগে,—'চল মোর রাজ্য ॥' ১২২ ॥

puruṣottama-deva sei baḍa bhakta ārya
gopāla-caraṇe māge,—'cala mora rājya

SYNONYMS

puruṣottama-deva—the King; *sei*—that; *baḍa*—very great; *bhakta*—devotee; *ārya*—Āryan; *gopāla-caraṇe*—at the lotus feet of Gopāla; *māge*—begs; *cala*—please come; *mora*—my; *rājya*—to the kingdom.

TRANSLATION

That King became known as Puruṣottama-deva. He was a great devotee and was advanced in the civilization of the Āryans. He begged at the lotus feet of Gopāla: "Please come to my kingdom."

TEXT 123

তাঁর ভক্তিবশে গোপাল তাঁরে আজ্ঞা দিল ।
গোপাল লইয়া সেই কটকে আইল ॥ ১২৩ ॥

tāṅra bhakti-vaśe gopāla tāṅre ājñā dila
gopāla la-iyā sei kaṭake āila

SYNONYMS

tāṅra—his; *bhakti-vaśe*—under the obligation of the devotional service; *gopāla*—Lord Gopāla; *tāṅre*—unto Him; *ājñā dila*—gave the order; *gopāla*—the Gopāla Deity; *la-iyā*—taking; *sei*—that King; *kaṭake*—to the city of Kaṭaka; *āila*—returned.

TRANSLATION

When the King begged Him to come to his kingdom, Gopāla, who was already obliged for his devotional service, accepted his prayer. Thus the King took the Gopāla Deity and went back to Kaṭaka.

TEXT 124

জগন্নাথে আনি' দিল মাণিক্য-সিংহাসন ।
কটকে গোপাল-সেবা করিল স্থাপন ॥ ১২৪ ॥

jagannāthe āni' dila māṇikya-siṁhāsana
kaṭake gopāla-sevā karila sthāpana

SYNONYMS

jagannāthe—unto Jagannātha; *āni'*—bringing; *dila*—presented; *māṇikya-siṁhāsana*—the throne of the name Māṇikya-siṁhāsana; *kaṭake*—at Kaṭaka; *gopāla-sevā*—the service of the Gopāla Deity; *karila sthāpana*—established.

TRANSLATION

After winning the Māṇikya throne, King Puruṣottama took it to Jagannātha Purī and presented it to Lord Jagannātha. In the meantime, he also established regular worship of the Gopāla Deity at Kaṭaka.

TEXT 125

তাঁহার মহিষী আইলা গোপাল-দর্শনে ।
ভক্তি করি' বহু অলঙ্কার কৈল সমর্পণে ॥ ১২৫ ॥

tāṅhāra mahiṣī āilā gopāla-darśane
bhakti kari' bahu alaṅkāra kaila samarpaṇe

SYNONYMS

tāṅhāra mahiṣī—his Queen; *āilā*—came; *gopāla-darśane*—to see the Gopāla Deity; *bhakti kari'*—in great devotion; *bahu*—various; *alaṅkāra*—of ornaments; *kaila*—made; *samarpaṇe*—presentation.

TRANSLATION

When the Gopāla Deity was installed at Kaṭaka, the Queen of Puruṣottamadeva went to see Him and, with great devotion, presented various kinds of ornaments.

TEXT 126

তাঁহার নাসাতে বহুমূল্য মুক্তা হয় ।
তাহা দিতে ইচ্ছা হৈল, মনেতে চিন্তয় ॥ ১২৬ ॥

tāṅhāra nāsāte bahu-mūlya muktā haya
tāhā dite icchā haila, manete cintaya

SYNONYMS

tāṅhāra nāsāte—on the nostril of the Queen; *bahu-mūlya*—very valuable; *muktā*—pearl; *haya*—there was; *tāhā*—that; *dite*—to give; *icchā*—the desire; *haila*—there was; *manete*—in the mind; *cintaya*—thinks.

TRANSLATION

The Queen had a very valuable pearl, which she wore on her nose, and she wished to give it to Gopāla. She then began to think as follows.

TEXT 127

ঠাকুরের নাসাতে যদি ছিদ্র থাকিত ।
তবে এই দাসী মুক্তা নাসায় পরাইত ॥ ১২৭ ॥

ṭhākurera nāsāte yadi chidra thākita
tabe ei dāsī muktā nāsāya parāita

SYNONYMS

ṭhākurera nāsāte—in the nose of the Deity; *yadi*—if; *chidra*—a hole; *thākita*—there were; *tabe*—then; *ei*—this; *dāsī*—maidservant; *muktā*—pearl; *nāsāya*—on the nose; *parāita*—could put on.

TRANSLATION

"If there were a hole in the Deity's nose, I could transfer the pearl to Him."

TEXT 128

এত চিন্তি' নমস্করি' গেলা স্বভবনে ।
রাত্রিশেষে গোপাল তাঁরে কহেন স্বপনে ॥ ১২৮ ॥

eta cinti' namaskari' gelā sva-bhavane
rātri-śeṣe gopāla tāṅre kahena svapane

SYNONYMS

eta cinti'—thinking like that; *namaskari'*—offering obeisances; *gelā*—went; *sva-bhavane*—to the palace of the King; *rātri-śeṣe*—at the end of night; *gopāla*—the Gopāla Deity; *tāṅre*—unto her; *kahena*—says; *svapane*—in a dream.

TRANSLATION

Considering this, the Queen offered her obeisances to Gopāla and returned to her palace. That night she dreamed that Gopāla appeared and began to speak to her as follows.

TEXT 129

"বাল্যকালে মাতা মোর নাসা ছিদ্র করি' ।
মুক্তা পরাঞাছিল বহু যত্ন করি' ॥ ১২৯ ॥

"bālya-kāle mātā mora nāsā chidra kari'
muktā parāñāchila bahu yatna kari'

SYNONYMS

bālya-kāle—in My childhood; *mātā*—mother; *mora*—My; *nāsā*—nose; *chidra kari'*—making a hole; *muktā*—a pearl; *parāñāchila*—was put on it; *bahu*—much; *yatna*—endeavor; *kari'*—taking.

TRANSLATION

"During My childhood My mother made a hole in My nose and with great endeavor set a pearl there.

TEXT 130

সেই ছিদ্র অদ্যাপিহ আছয়ে নাসাতে ।
সেই মুক্তা পরাহ, যাহা চাহিয়াছ দিতে ॥" ১৩০ ॥

sei chidra adyāpiha āchaye nāsāte
sei muktā parāha, yāhā cāhiyācha dite"

SYNONYMS

sei chidra—that hole; *adyāpiha*—still, until now; *āchaye*—is; *nāsāte*—in the nose; *sei*—that; *muktā*—pearl; *parāha*—put on; *yāhā*—which; *cāhiyācha*—you desired; *dite*—to give to Me.

TRANSLATION

"That very hole is still there, and you can use it to set the pearl you desired to give Me."

TEXT 131

স্বপ্নে দেখি' সেই রাণী রাজাকে কহিল ।
রাজাসহ মুক্তা লঞা মন্দিরে আইল ॥ ১৩১ ॥

svapne dekhi' sei rāṇī rājāke kahila
rājā-saha muktā lañā mandire āila

SYNONYMS

svapne dekhi'—seeing the dream; *sei rāṇī*—the Queen; *rājāke*—unto the King; *kahila*—spoke; *rājā-saha*—with the King; *muktā*—the pearl; *lañā*—taking; *mandire*—to the temple; *āila*—they went.

TRANSLATION

After dreaming this, the Queen explained it to her husband, the King. Both the King and the Queen then went to the temple with the pearl.

TEXT 132

পরাইল মুক্তা নাসায় ছিদ্র দেখিঞা ।
মহামহোৎসব কৈল আনন্দিত হঞা ॥ ১৩২ ॥

parāila muktā nāsāya chidra dekhiñā
mahā-mahotsava kaila ānandita hañā

SYNONYMS

parāila—set; *muktā*—the pearl; *nāsāya*—on the nose; *chidra*—the hole; *dekhiñā*—seeing; *mahā-mahotsava*—a great festival; *kaila*—performed; *ānandita*—pleased; *hañā*—being.

TRANSLATION

Seeing the hole in the nose of the Deity, they set the pearl there and, being very pleased, held a great festival.

TEXT 133

সেই হৈতে গোপালের কটকেতে স্থিতি।
এই লাগি 'সাক্ষিগোপাল' নাম হৈল খ্যাতি ॥১৩৩॥

sei haite gopālera kaṭakete sthiti
ei lāgi 'sākṣi-gopāla' nāma haila khyāti

SYNONYMS

sei haite—since that time; *gopālera*—of Gopāla; *kaṭakete*—in the town of Kaṭaka; *sthiti*—the establishment; *ei lāgi*—for this reason; *sākṣi-gopāla*—the witness Gopāla; *nāma*—named; *haila*—became; *khyāti*—celebrated.

TRANSLATION

Since then, Gopāla has been situated in the city of Kaṭaka [Cuttak], and He has been known ever since as Sākṣi-gopāla.

TEXT 134

নিত্যানন্দ-মুখে শুনি' গোপাল-চরিত।
তুষ্ট হৈলা মহাপ্রভু স্বভক্ত-সহিত ॥ ১৩৪ ॥

nityānanda-mukhe śuni' gopāla-carita
tuṣṭa hailā mahāprabhu svabhakta-sahita

SYNONYMS

nityānanda-mukhe—from the mouth of Lord Nityānanda Prabhu; *śuni'*—hearing; *gopāla-carita*—the narration of Gopāla; *tuṣṭa hailā*—became very pleased; *mahāprabhu*—Śrī Caitanya Mahāprabhu; *sva-bhakta-sahita*—with His devotees.

TRANSLATION

Thus Śrī Caitanya Mahāprabhu heard the narration of Gopāla's activities. Both He and His personal devotees became very pleased.

TEXT 135

গোপালের আগে যবে প্রভুর হয় স্থিতি ।
ভক্তগণে দেখে—যেন দুঁহে একমূর্তি ॥ ১৩৫ ॥

gopālera āge yabe prabhura haya sthiti
bhakta-gaṇe dekhe——yena duṅhe eka-mūrti

SYNONYMS

gopālera āge—in front of Gopāla; *yabe*—when; *prabhura*—of Lord Caitanya Mahāprabhu; *haya*—is; *sthiti*—situation; *bhakta-gaṇe*—all the devotees; *dekhe*—see; *yena*—as if; *duṅhe*—both of Them; *eka-mūrti*—one form.

TRANSLATION

When Śrī Caitanya Mahāprabhu was sitting before the Gopāla Deity, all the devotees saw Him and the Deity as being of the same form.

TEXT 136

দুঁহে—এক বর্ণ, দুঁহে—প্রকাণ্ড-শরীর ।
দুঁহে—রক্তাম্বর, দুঁহার স্বভাব—গম্ভীর ॥ ১৩৬ ॥

duṅhe——eka varṇa, duṅhe——prakāṇḍa-śarīra
duṅhe——raktāmbara, duṅhāra svabhāva——gambhīra

SYNONYMS

duṅhe—both of Them; *eka varṇa*—one complexion; *duṅhe*—both of Them; *prakāṇḍa-śarīra*—gigantic bodies; *duṅhe*—both of Them; *rakta-ambara*—red clothes; *duṅhāra*—of both; *svabhāva*—the natures; *gambhīra*—grave.

TRANSLATION

Both of Them were of the same complexion, and both had the same gigantic bodies. Both wore saffron cloth, and both were very grave.

TEXT 137

মহা-তেজোময় দুঁহে কমল-নয়ন ।
দুঁহার ভাবাবেশ, দুঁহে—চন্দ্রবদন ॥ ১৩৭ ॥

mahā-tejo-maya duṅhe kamala-nayana
duṅhāra bhāvāveśa, duṅhe——candra-vadana

SYNONYMS

mahā-tejaḥ-maya—brilliantly effulgent; *duṅhe*—both of Them; *kamala-nayana*—lotus-eyed; *duṅhāra*—of both of Them; *bhāva-āveśa*—absorbed in ecstasy; *duṅhe*—both of Them; *candra-vadana*—moon-faced.

TRANSLATION

The devotees saw that both Lord Caitanya Mahāprabhu and Gopāla were brilliantly effulgent and had eyes like lotuses. They were both absorbed in ecstasy, and Their faces resembled full moons.

TEXT 138

দুঁহা দেখি' নিত্যানন্দপ্রভু মহারঙ্গে ।
ঠারাঠারি করি' হাসে ভক্তগণ-সঙ্গে ॥ ১৩৮ ॥

duṅhā dekhi' nityānanda-prabhu mahā-raṅge
ṭhārāṭhāri kari' hāse bhakta-gaṇa-saṅge

SYNONYMS

duṅhā dekhi'—seeing both of Them; *nityānanda-prabhu*—Lord Nityānanda Prabhu; *mahā-raṅge*—in great jubilation; *ṭhārāṭhāri*—indication; *kari'*—doing; *hāse*—laughs; *bhakta-gaṇa-saṅge*—along with the other devotees.

TRANSLATION

When Nityānanda saw both the Gopāla Deity and Śrī Caitanya Mahāprabhu in that way, He began to exchange remarks with the devotees, all of whom were smiling.

TEXT 139

এইমত মহারঙ্গে সে রাত্রি বঞ্চিয়া ।
প্রভাতে চলিলা মঙ্গল-আরতি দেখিঞা ॥ ১৩৯ ॥

ei-mata mahā-raṅge se rātri vañciyā
prabhāte calilā maṅgala-ārati dekhiñā

SYNONYMS

ei-mata—in this way; *mahā-raṅge*—in great pleasure; *se*—that; *rātri*—night; *vañciyā*—passing; *prabhāte*—in the morning; *calilā*—departed; *maṅgala-ārati*—the *maṅgala-ārati* performance; *dekhiñā*—seeing.

TRANSLATION

Thus with great pleasure Lord Śrī Caitanya Mahāprabhu passed that night in the temple. After seeing the maṅgala-ārati ceremony in the morning, He started on His journey.

TEXT 140

ভুবনেশ্বর-পথে যৈছে কৈল দরশন ।
বিস্তারি' বর্ণিয়াছেন দাস-বৃন্দাবন ॥ ১৪০ ॥

bhuvaneśvara-pathe yaiche kaila daraśana
vistāri' varṇiyāchena dāsa-vṛndāvana

SYNONYMS

bhuvaneśvara-pathe—on the way to Bhuvaneśvara; *yaiche*—as; *kaila*—He did; *daraśana*—visiting; *vistāri'*—vividly; *varṇiyāchena*—has described; *dāsa-vṛndāvana*—Vṛndāvana dāsa Ṭhākura.

TRANSLATION

[In his book Caitanya-bhāgavata] Śrīla Vṛndāvana dāsa Ṭhākura has very vividly described the places visited by the Lord on the way to Bhuvaneśvara.

PURPORT

In his book *Caitanya-bhāgavata, Antya-khaṇḍa,* Śrīla Vṛndāvana dāsa Ṭhākura has very nicely described the Lord's journey en route to Kaṭaka (Cuttak). On that journey, the Lord visited a place known as Bālihastā, or Bālakāṭīcaṭi. He then visited the city of Bhuvaneśvara, where Lord Śiva's temple is located. The temple of Bhuvaneśvara is situated about five to six miles from Bālakāṭīcaṭi. The temple of Lord Śiva is mentioned in the *Skanda Purāṇa* in the narration about the Lord's garden and the one mango tree. A king named Kāśirāja wanted to fight with Lord Kṛṣṇa, and consequently he took shelter of Lord Śiva to acquire the power to fight the Lord. Being pleased with his worship, Lord Śiva helped him fight Kṛṣṇa. Lord Śiva's name is Āśutoṣa, which indicates that he is very easily satisfied when one worships him, regardless of the purpose, and he gives his devotee whatever benediction the devotee wants. Therefore, people are generally very fond of worshiping Lord Śiva. Thus Kāśirāja was helped by Lord Śiva, but in the fight with Lord Kṛṣṇa he was not only defeated but killed. In this way the weapon known as Pāśupata-astra was baffled, and Kṛṣṇa set fire to the city of Kāśī. Later Lord Śiva became conscious of his mistake in helping Kāśirāja, and he begged Lord Kṛṣṇa's forgiveness. As a benediction from Lord Kṛṣṇa, he received a place known as

Ekāmra-kānana. Later, the kings of the Keśarī dynasty established their capital there, and for many hundreds of years they reigned over the state of Orissa.

TEXT 141

কমলপুরে আসি ভার্গীনদী-স্নান কৈল ।
নিত্যানন্দ-হাতে প্রভু দণ্ড ধরিল ॥ ১৪১ ॥

kamalapure āsi bhārgīnadī-snāna kaila
nityānanda-hāte prabhu daṇḍa dharila

SYNONYMS

kamala-pure—to the place known as Kamalapura; *āsi*—coming; *bhārgī-nadī*—in the small river of the name Bhārgīnadī; *snāna kaila*—took bath; *nityānanda-hāte*—in the hands of Lord Nityānanda Prabhu; *prabhu*—Lord Śrī Caitanya Mahāprabhu; *daṇḍa*—the *sannyāsa* staff; *dharila*—left.

TRANSLATION

When Śrī Caitanya Mahāprabhu arrived at Kamalapura, He took His bath in the Bhārgīnadī River and left His sannyāsa staff in the hands of Lord Nityānanda.

PURPORT

In the *Caitanya-bhāgavata* (*Antya-khaṇḍa,* Chapter Two) it is said that when Lord Śrī Caitanya Mahāprabhu arrived at Śrī Bhuvaneśvara, He visited the temple of Lord Śiva known as Gupta-kāśī (the concealed Vārāṇasī). Lord Śiva established this as a place of pilgrimage by bringing water from all holy places and creating the lake known as Bindu-sarovara. Śrī Caitanya Mahāprabhu took His bath in this lake, feeling a great regard for Lord Śiva. From the spiritual point of view, people still go to take a bath in this lake. Actually, by taking a bath there, one becomes very healthy even from the material viewpoint. Taking a bath and drinking the water of this lake can cure any disease of the stomach. Regular bathing certainly cures indigestion. The River Bhārgī or Bhārgīnadī is now known as Daṇḍa-bhāṅgā-nadī. It is situated six miles north of Jagannātha Purī. The reason for the change in names is given as follows.

TEXTS 142-143

কপোতেশ্বর দেখিতে গেলা ভক্তগণ সঙ্গে ।
এথা নিত্যানন্দপ্রভু কৈল দণ্ড-ভঙ্গে ॥ ১৪২ ॥
তিন খণ্ড করি' দণ্ড দিল ভাসাঞা ।
ভক্ত-সঙ্গে আইলা প্রভু মহেশ দেখিঞা ॥ ১৪৩ ॥

kapoteśvara dekhite gelā bhakta-gaṇa saṅge
ethā nityānanda-prabhu kaila daṇḍa-bhaṅge

tina khaṇḍa kari' daṇḍa dila bhāsāñā
bhakta-saṅge āilā prabhu maheśa dekhiñā

SYNONYMS

kapoteśvara—the Śiva temple of the name Kapoteśvara; *dekhite*—to see; *gelā*—went; *bhakta-gaṇa saṅge*—with the devotees; *ethā*—here; *nityānanda-prabhu*—Lord Nityānanda Prabhu; *kaila*—did; *daṇḍa*—of the *sannyāsa* staff; *bhaṅge*—breaking; *tina khaṇḍa*—three parts; *kari'*—making; *daṇḍa*—the staff; *dila*—threw in; *bhāsāñā*—washing away; *bhakta-saṅge*—with the devotees; *āilā*—returned; *prabhu*—Lord Caitanya Mahāprabhu; *maheśa dekhiñā*—having seen the temple of Lord Śiva.

TRANSLATION

When Lord Caitanya Mahāprabhu went to the temple of Lord Śiva known as Kapoteśvara, Nityānanda Prabhu, who was keeping His sannyāsa staff in custody, broke the staff in three parts and threw it into the River Bhārgīnadī. Later this river became known as Daṇḍa-bhāṅgā-nadī.

PURPORT

The mystery of the *sannyāsa-daṇḍa* (staff) of Śrī Caitanya Mahāprabhu has been explained by Śrīla Bhaktisiddhānta Sarasvatī Ṭhākura. Śrī Caitanya Mahāprabhu accepted the order of *sannyāsa* from a Māyāvādī *sannyāsī.* The Māyāvādī *sannyāsīs* generally carry one staff, or *daṇḍa.* Taking advantage of Śrī Caitanya Mahāprabhu's absence, Śrīla Nityānanda Prabhu broke the staff into three parts and threw it into the river now known as the Daṇḍa-bhāṅgā-nadī. In the *sannyāsa* order there are four divisions—*kuṭīcaka, bahūdaka, haṁsa* and *paramahaṁsa.* Only when the *sannyāsī* remains on the *kuṭīcaka* and *bahūdaka* platforms can he carry a staff. However, when one is elevated to the status of *haṁsa* or *paramahaṁsa,* after touring and preaching the *bhakti* cult, he must give up the *sannyāsa* staff.

Śrī Caitanya Mahāprabhu is Śrī Kṛṣṇa, the Supreme Personality of Godhead. It is therefore said, *śrī-kṛṣṇa-caitanya, rādhā-kṛṣṇa nahe anya:* "Two personalities—Śrīmatī Rādhārāṇī and Śrī Kṛṣṇa—are combined in the incarnation of Śrī Caitanya Mahāprabhu." Therefore, considering Śrī Caitanya Mahāprabhu to be an extraordinary person, Lord Nityānanda Prabhu did not wait for the *paramahaṁsa* stage. He reasoned that the Supreme Personality of Godhead is automatically on the *paramahaṁsa* stage; therefore He does not need to carry the *sannyāsa-daṇḍa.*

This is the reason Śrī Nityānanda Prabhu broke the staff into three pieces and threw it into the water.

TEXT 144

জগন্নাথের দেউল দেখি' আবিষ্ট হৈলা ।
দণ্ডবৎ করি প্রেমে নাচিতে লাগিলা ॥ ১৪৪ ॥

jagannāthera deula dekhi' āviṣṭa hailā
daṇḍavat kari preme nācite lāgilā

SYNONYMS

jagannāthera—of Lord Jagannātha; *deula*—the temple; *dekhi'*—seeing; *āviṣṭa*—ecstatic; *hailā*—became; *daṇḍavat kari*—offering obeisances; *preme*—in the ecstasy of love of God; *nācite*—to dance; *lāgilā*—began.

TRANSLATION

After seeing the temple of Jagannātha from a distant place, Śrī Caitanya Mahāprabhu immediately became ecstatic. After offering obeisances to the temple, He began to dance in the ecstasy of love of God.

PURPORT

The word *deula* refers to the temple where the Supreme Personality of Godhead is situated. The present temple of Jagannātha Purī was constructed by King Anaṅga-bhīma. Historians say this temple must have been constructed at least two thousand years ago. During the time of Śrī Caitanya Mahāprabhu, the small buildings surrounding the original temple had not been constructed. Nor was the high platform in front of the temple present during the time of Śrī Caitanya Mahāprabhu.

TEXT 145

ভক্তগণ আবিষ্ট হঞা, সবে নাচে গায় ।
প্রেমাবেশে প্রভু-সঙ্গে রাজমার্গে যায় ॥ ১৪৫ ।

bhakta-gaṇa āviṣṭa hañā, sabe nāce gāya
premāveśe prabhu-saṅge rāja-mārge yāya

SYNONYMS

bhakta-gaṇa—the devotees; *āviṣṭa*—ecstatic; *hañā*—being; *sabe*—all; *nāce*—dance; *gāya*—sing; *prema-āveśe*—absorbed in love of God; *prabhu-saṅge*—with Lord Caitanya; *rāja-mārge*—on the pathway; *yāya*—going.

TRANSLATION

All the devotees became ecstatic in the association of Lord Caitanya, and thus absorbed in love of God, they were dancing and singing while going along the main road.

TEXT 146

হাসে, কান্দে, নাচে প্রভু হুঙ্কার গর্জন ।
তিনক্রোশ পথ হৈল—সহস্র যোজন ॥ ১৪৬ ॥

hāse, kānde, nāce prabhu huṅkāra garjana
tina-krośa patha haila——sahasra yojana

SYNONYMS

hāse—laughs; *kānde*—cries; *nāce*—dances; *prabhu*—Lord Śrī Caitanya Mahāprabhu; *huṅkāra*—ecstatic vibrations; *garjana*—resonations; *tina-krośa*—six miles; *patha*—the way; *haila*—became; *sahasra yojana*—thousands of miles.

TRANSLATION

Śrī Caitanya Mahāprabhu laughed, cried, danced and made many ecstatic vibrations and sounds. Although the temple was only six miles away, to Him the distance seemed thousands of miles.

PURPORT

When Śrī Caitanya Mahāprabhu was in ecstasy, He considered one moment to last as long as twelve years. After seeing the Jagannātha temple from a distant place, the Lord became so ecstatic that He considered the six-mile path many thousands of miles long.

TEXT 147

চলিতে চলিতে প্রভু আইলা 'আঠারনালা' ।
তাহাঁ আসি' প্রভু কিছু বাহ্য প্রকাশিলা ॥ ১৪৭ ॥

calite calite prabhu āilā 'āṭhāranālā'
tāhāṅ āsi' prabhu kichu bāhya prakāśilā

SYNONYMS

calite calite—walking in this way; *prabhu*—the Lord; *āilā*—arrived; *āṭhāra-nālā*—at a place known as Āṭhāranālā; *tāhāṅ*—there; *āsi'*—coming; *prabhu*—the Lord; *kichu*—some; *bāhya*—external consciousness; *prakāśilā*—expressed.

TRANSLATION

Thus walking and walking, the Lord eventually arrived at the place known as Āṭhāranālā. Arriving there, He expressed His external consciousness, speaking to Śrī Nityānanda Prabhu.

PURPORT

There is a bridge situated at the entrance of Jagannātha Purī called Āṭhāranālā which has eighteen arches. *Āṭhāra* means eighteen.

TEXT 148

নিত্যানন্দে কহে প্রভু,—দেহ মোর দণ্ড ।
নিত্যানন্দ বলে,— দণ্ড হৈল তিন খণ্ড ॥ ১৪৮ ॥

nityānande kahe prabhu,——deha mora daṇḍa
nityānanda bale,——daṇḍa haila tina khaṇḍa

SYNONYMS

nityānande—to Lord Nityānanda; *kahe*—asks; *prabhu*—Lord Caitanya; *deha*—give; *mora*—My; *daṇḍa*—*sannyāsa* staff; *nityānanda bale*—Śrī Nityānanda replies; *daṇḍa*—Your *sannyāsa* staff; *haila*—became; *tina khaṇḍa*—divided in three parts.

TRANSLATION

When Lord Caitanya Mahāprabhu had thus regained external consciousness, He asked Lord Nityānanda Prabhu, "Please return My staff." Nityānanda Prabhu then replied, "It has been broken into three parts."

TEXT 149

প্রেমাবেশে পড়িলা তুমি, তোমারে ধরিনু ।
তোমা-সহ সেই দণ্ড-উপরে পড়িনু ॥ ১৪৯ ॥

premāveśe paḍilā tumi, tomāre dharinu
tomā-saha sei daṇḍa-upare paḍinu

SYNONYMS

prema-āveśe—in an ecstatic condition; *paḍilā*—fell down; *tumi*—You; *tomāre*—You; *dharinu*—I caught; *tomā-saha*—with You; *sei*—that; *daṇḍa-upare*—upon that staff; *paḍinu*—I fell down.

TRANSLATION

Nityānanda Prabhu said: "When You fell down in ecstasy, I caught You, but both of Us together fell upon the staff.

TEXT 150

দুইজনার ভরে দণ্ড খণ্ড খণ্ড হৈল ।
সেই খণ্ড কাঁহা পড়িল, কিছু না জানিল ॥ ১৫০ ॥

dui-janāra bhare daṇḍa khaṇḍa khaṇḍa haila
sei khaṇḍa kāṅhā paḍila, kichu nā jānila

SYNONYMS

dui-janāra—of Us two; *bhare*—by the weight; *daṇḍa*—the staff; *khaṇḍa khaṇḍa*—broken to pieces; *haila*—became; *sei*—those; *khaṇḍa*—pieces; *kāṅhā paḍila*—where they fell; *kichu*—anything; *nā jānila*—is not known.

TRANSLATION

"Thus the staff broke under Our weight. Where the pieces have gone, I cannot say.

TEXT 151

মোর অপরাধে তোমার দণ্ড হইল খণ্ড ।
যে উচিত হয়, মোর কর তার দণ্ড ॥ ১৫১ ॥

mora aparādhe tomāra daṇḍa ha-ila khaṇḍa
ye ucita haya, mora kara tāra daṇḍa

SYNONYMS

mora—My; *aparādhe*—by the offense; *tomāra*—Your; *daṇḍa*—*sannyāsa* staff; *ha-ila*—became; *khaṇḍa*—broken; *ye*—whatever; *ucita*—fitting; *haya*—is; *mora*—to Me; *kara*—do; *tāra*—for that; *daṇḍa*—punishment.

TRANSLATION

"It is certainly because of My offense that Your staff has broken. Now You can punish Me on this account as You think proper."

TEXT 152

শুনি' কিছু মহাপ্রভু দুঃখ প্রকাশিলা ।
ঈষৎ ক্রোধ করি' কিছু কহিতে লাগিলা ॥ ১৫২ ॥

śuni' kichu mahāprabhu duḥkha prakāśilā
īṣat krodha kari' kichu kahite lāgilā

SYNONYMS

śuni'—hearing this; *kichu*—some; *mahāprabhu*—Lord Caitanya Mahāprabhu; *duḥkha*—unhappiness; *prakāśilā*—expressed; *īṣat*—little; *krodha*—anger; *kari'*—showing; *kichu*—something; *kahite*—to speak; *lāgilā*—began.

TRANSLATION

After hearing the story about how His staff had been broken, the Lord expressed a little sadness and, displaying a bit of anger, began to speak as follows.

PURPORT

Śrī Nityānanda Prabhu considered Lord Caitanya Mahāprabhu's acceptance of *sannyāsa* to be useless. He therefore relieved the Lord of the trouble of carrying the staff. Śrī Caitanya Mahāprabhu expressed anger because He wanted to teach all other *sannyāsīs* that they should not give up the staff before attaining the platform of *paramahaṁsa.* Seeing that the regulative principles could be slackened by such action, Caitanya Mahāprabhu wanted to carry the staff personally. However, Nityānanda broke it. For this reason Caitanya Mahāprabhu displayed a little anger. It is said in *Bhagavad-gītā, yad yad ācarati śreṣṭhas tat tad evetaro janaḥ:* Whatever great people do, others follow. Śrī Caitanya Mahāprabhu wanted to follow the Vedic principles strictly in order to save inexperienced neophytes who try to imitate *paramahaṁsas.*

TEXT 153

নীলাচলে আনি' মোর সবে হিত কৈলা ।
সবে দণ্ডধন ছিল, তাহা না রাখিলা ॥ ১৫৩ ॥

nīlācale āni' mora sabe hita kailā
sabe daṇḍa-dhana chila, tāhā nā rākhilā

SYNONYMS

nīlācale—to Jagannātha Purī; *āni'*—bringing; *mora*—My; *sabe*—all of you; *hita*—benefit; *kailā*—did; *sabe*—only; *daṇḍa-dhana*—one staff; *chila*—there was; *tāhā*—that also; *nā*—not; *rākhilā*—you kept.

TRANSLATION

Caitanya Mahāprabhu said: "You have all benefited Me by bringing Me to Nīlācala. However, My only possession was that one staff, and you have not kept it.

TEXT 154

তুমি-সব আগে যাহ ঈশ্বর দেখিতে ।
কিবা আমি আগে যাই, না যাব সহিতে ॥ ১৫৪ ॥

tumi-saba āge yāha īśvara dekhite
kibā āmi āge yāi, nā yāba sahite

SYNONYMS

tumi-saba—all of you; *āge*—ahead; *yāha*—go; *īśvara dekhite*—to see Jagannātha; *kibā*—or; *āmi*—I; *āge*—ahead; *yāi*—go; *nā*—not; *yāba*—I shall go; *sahite*—with you.

TRANSLATION

"So all of you should go before or behind Me to see Lord Jagannātha. I shall not go with you."

TEXT 155

মুকুন্দ দত্ত কহে,—প্রভু, তুমি যাহ আগে ।
আমি-সব পাছে যাব, না যাব তোমার সঙ্গে ॥ ১৫৫ ॥

mukunda datta kahe,——prabhu, tumi yāha āge
āmi-saba pāche yāba, nā yāba tomāra saṅge

SYNONYMS

mukunda datta kahe—a devotee named Mukunda Datta said; *prabhu*—my Lord; *tumi*—You; *yāha*—go; *āge*—in front; *āmi-saba*—all of us; *pāche*—behind; *yāba*—shall go; *nā*—not; *yāba*—shall go; *tomāra saṅge*—with You.

TRANSLATION

Mukunda Datta told Śrī Caitanya Mahāprabhu: "My Lord, You should go ahead and allow all the others to follow. We shall not go with You."

TEXT 156

এত শুনি' প্রভু আগে চলিলা শীঘ্রগতি ।
বুঝিতে না পারে কেহ দুই প্রভুর মতি ॥ ১৫৬ ॥

eta śuni' prabhu āge calilā śīghra-gati
bujhite nā pāre keha dui prabhura mati

SYNONYMS

eta śuni'—hearing this; *prabhu*—Lord Śrī Caitanya Mahāprabhu; *āge*—in front of the other devotees; *calilā*—began to go; *śīghra-gati*—very swiftly; *bujhite*—to understand; *nā*—not; *pāre*—able; *keha*—anyone; *dui*—two; *prabhura*—of the Lords; *mati*—intentions.

TRANSLATION

Śrī Caitanya Mahāprabhu then began to walk very swiftly before all the other devotees. No one could understand the real purpose of both the Lords, Caitanya Mahāprabhu and Nityānanda Prabhu.

TEXT 157

ইঁহো কেনে দণ্ড ভাঙ্গে, তেঁহো কেনে ভাঙ্গায় ।
ভাঙ্গাঞা ক্রোধে তেঁহো ইঁহাকে দোষায় ॥ ১৫৭ ॥

iṅho kene daṇḍa bhāṅge, teṅho kene bhāṅgāya
bhāṅgāñā krodhe teṅho iṅhāke doṣāya

SYNONYMS

iṅho—Nityānanda; *kene*—why; *daṇḍa*—the staff; *bhāṅge*—breaks; *teṅho*—Śrī Caitanya Mahāprabhu; *kene*—why; *bhāṅgāya*—allows to break it; *bhāṅgāñā*—after allowing to break it; *krodhe*—in anger; *teṅho*—Śrī Caitanya Mahāprabhu; *iṅhāke*— Lord Nityānanda; *doṣāya*—accuses.

TRANSLATION

The devotees could not understand why Nityānanda Prabhu broke the staff, why Śrī Caitanya Mahāprabhu permitted Him to do so, nor why, after permitting Him, Caitanya Mahāprabhu became angry.

TEXT 158

দণ্ডভঙ্গ-লীলা এই—পরম গম্ভীর ।
সেই বুঝে, দুঁহার পদে যাঁর ভক্তি ধীর ॥ ১৫৮ ॥

daṇḍa-bhaṅga-līlā ei——parama gambhīra
sei bujhe, duṅhāra pade yāṅra bhakti dhīra

SYNONYMS

daṇḍa-bhaṅga-līlā—the pastime of breaking the staff; *ei*—this; *parama*—very; *gambhīra*—grave; *sei bujhe*—one can understand; *duṅhāra*—of both of Them; *pade*—to the lotus feet; *yāṅra*—whose; *bhakti*—devotional service; *dhīra*—fixed.

TRANSLATION

The pastime of the breaking of the staff is very deep. Only one whose devotion is fixed upon the lotus feet of the two Lords can understand it.

PURPORT

One who understands Śrī Caitanya Mahāprabhu and Nityānanda Prabhu in reality can understand Their identity as well as the breaking of the staff. All the previous *ācāryas,* being induced to engage themselves fully in the service of the Lord, gave up attachment for material life and thus accepted the staff, which signifies full engagement of the mind, speech and body in the service of the Lord. Śrī Caitanya Mahāprabhu accepted the regulative principles of the renounced order of life. That is completely clear. However, in the *paramahaṁsa* stage there is no need to accept a *daṇḍa* (staff), and Śrī Caitanya Mahāprabhu was certainly in the *paramahaṁsa* stage. Nonetheless, to indicate that everyone should take *sannyāsa* at the end of life in order to engage fully in the service of the Lord, even *paramahaṁsas* like Śrī Caitanya Mahāprabhu and His confidential devotees follow the regulative principles unfailingly. Indeed, that was His purpose. Nityānanda Prabhu, who was His eternal servitor, believed that there was no need for Śrī Caitanya Mahāprabhu to carry the staff, and to declare to the world that Śrī Caitanya Mahāprabhu was above all regulations, He broke it into three pieces. The pastime known as *daṇḍa-bhaṅga-līlā* is thus explained by Śrīla Bhaktisiddhānta Sarasvatī Ṭhākura.

TEXT 159

ব্রহ্মণ্যদেব-গোপালের মহিমা এই ধন্য ।
নিত্যানন্দ- বক্তা যার, শ্রোতা—শ্রীচৈতন্য ॥ ১৫৯ ॥

brahmaṇya-deva-gopālera mahimā ei dhanya
nityānanda——vaktā yāra, śrotā——śrī-caitanya

SYNONYMS

brahmaṇya-deva—the Supreme Personality of Godhead, who is merciful to the *brāhmaṇas; gopālera*—of Gopāla; *mahimā*—glories; *ei*—these; *dhanya*—glorified; *nityānanda*—Lord Nityānanda Prabhu; *vaktā*—the speaker; *yāra*—of the narration; *śrotā*—the hearer; *śrī-caitanya*—Śrī Caitanya Mahāprabhu.

TRANSLATION

The glories of Lord Gopāla, who is merciful to brāhmaṇas, are very great. The narration of Sākṣi-gopāla was spoken by Nityānanda Prabhu and heard by Śrī Caitanya Mahāprabhu.

PURPORT

There are four points of instruction one should consider in the story of Sākṣi-gopāla. First, the Deity (*arcā-vigraha*) of Śrī Gopāla is eternally *sac-cid-ānanda-vigraha,* the transcendental form of the Lord. Second, the Deity surpasses material regulative principles and extends the reality of transcendental principles. Third, one can be situated in a transcendental position after becoming a *brāhmaṇa,* but as a *brāhmaṇa,* one has to follow the regulative principles very strictly. Lastly, *brahmaṇya-deva* indicates Lord Śrī Kṛṣṇa Himself, who is worshiped thus: *namo brahmaṇya-devāya go-brāhmaṇa-hitāya ca/ jagad-dhitāya kṛṣṇāya govindāya namo namaḥ*. This indicates that a devotee who is under the protection of Kṛṣṇa is automatically situated as a *brāhmaṇa,* and such a *brāhmaṇa* is not illusioned. This is factual.

TEXT 160

শ্রদ্ধাযুক্ত হঞা ইহা শুনে যেই জন ।
অচিরে মিলয়ে তারে গোপাল-চরণ ॥ ১৬০ ॥

śraddhā-yukta hañā ihā śune yei jana
acire milaye tāre gopāla-caraṇa

SYNONYMS

śraddhā-yukta—with faith and love; *hañā*—being; *ihā*—this narration; *śune*—hears; *yei*—which; *jana*—person; *acire*—very soon; *milaye*—gets; *tāre*—he; *gopāla-caraṇa*—the lotus feet of Lord Gopāla.

TRANSLATION

One who hears this narration of Lord Gopāla with faith and love very soon attains the lotus feet of Lord Gopāla.

TEXT 161

শ্রীরূপ-রঘুনাথ-পদে যার আশ ।
চৈতন্যচরিতামৃত কহে কৃষ্ণদাস ॥ ১৬১ ॥

śrī-rūpa-raghunātha-pade yāra āśa
caitanya-caritāmṛta kahe kṛṣṇadāsa

SYNONYMS

śrī-rūpa—Śrīla Rūpa Gosvāmī; *raghunātha*—Śrīla Raghunātha dāsa Gosvāmī; *pade*—at the lotus feet; *yāra*—whose; *āśa*—expectation; *caitanya-caritāmṛta*—

the book named *Caitanya-caritāmṛta; kahe*—describes; *kṛṣṇa-dāsa*—Śrīla Kṛṣṇadāsa Kavirāja Gosvāmī.

TRANSLATION

Praying at the lotus feet of Śrī Rūpa and Śrī Raghunātha, always desiring their mercy, I, Kṛṣṇadāsa, narrate Śrī-Caitanya-caritāmṛta, following in their footsteps.

Thus end the Bhaktivedanta purports to the Śrī Caitanya-caritāmṛta, Madhya-līlā, *Fifth Chapter, describing the activities of Sākṣi-gopāla.*

CHAPTER 6

The Liberation of Sārvabhauma Bhaṭṭācārya

A summary study of the Sixth Chapter is given by Śrīla Bhaktivinoda Ṭhākura in his *Amṛta-pravāha-bhāṣya* as follows: When Śrī Caitanya Mahāprabhu entered the temple of Jagannātha, He immediately fainted. Sārvabhauma Bhaṭṭācārya then took Him to his home. Meanwhile, Gopīnātha Ācārya, the brother-in-law of Sārvabhauma Bhaṭṭācārya, met Mukunda Datta and talked to him about Caitanya Mahāprabhu's acceptance of *sannyāsa* and His journey to Jagannātha Purī. After hearing about Śrī Caitanya Mahāprabhu's fainting and His being carried to the house of Sārvabhauma Bhaṭṭācārya, people crowded there to see the Lord. Śrīla Nityānanda Prabhu and other devotees then visited the Jagannātha temple, and when they came back to the house of Sārvabhauma Bhaṭṭācārya, Śrī Caitanya Mahāprabhu returned to external consciousness. Sārvabhauma Bhaṭṭācārya received everyone and distributed *mahā-prasāda* with great care. Sārvabhauma Bhaṭṭācārya then became acquainted with Śrī Caitanya Mahāprabhu and arranged accommodations at his aunt's house. His brother-in-law, Gopīnātha Ācārya, established that Lord Caitanya Mahāprabhu was Kṛṣṇa Himself, but Sārvabhauma and his many disciples could not accept this. However, Gopīnātha Ācārya convinced Sārvabhauma that no one can understand the Supreme Personality of Godhead without being favored by Him. He proved by śāstric quotation, quotations from the revealed scriptures, that Śrī Caitanya Mahāprabhu was Kṛṣṇa Himself in person. Still, Sārvabhauma did not take these statements very seriously. Hearing all these arguments, Caitanya Mahāprabhu told His devotees that Sārvabhauma was His spiritual master and that whatever he said out of affection was for everyone's benefit.

When Sārvabhauma met Śrī Caitanya Mahāprabhu, he asked Him to hear Vedānta philosophy from him. Śrī Caitanya Mahāprabhu accepted this proposal, and for seven days He continuously heard Sārvabhauma Bhaṭṭācārya explain *Vedānta-sūtra*. However, the Lord remained very silent. Because of His silence, the Bhaṭṭācārya asked Him whether He was understanding the Vedānta philosophy, and the Lord replied, "Sir, I can understand Vedānta philosophy very clearly, but I cannot understand your explanations." There was then a discussion between the Bhaṭṭācārya and Śrī Caitanya Mahāprabhu concerning the authority of the Vedic scriptures, specifically the *Upaniṣads* and *Vedānta-sūtra*. The Bhaṭṭācārya was an impersonalist, but Śrī Caitanya Mahāprabhu proved that the Absolute Truth is the Supreme Personality of Godhead. He proved that the conceptions of the Māyāvādī philosophers concerning the impersonal Absolute Truth are incorrect.

The Absolute Truth is neither impersonal nor without power. The greatest mistake made by Māyāvādī philosophers is in conceiving the Absolute Truth to be impersonal and without energy. In all the *Vedas,* the unlimited energies of the Absolute Truth have been accepted. It is also accepted that the Absolute Truth has His transcendental, blissful, eternal form. According to the *Vedas,* both the Lord and the living entity are equal in quality, but they are different quantitatively. The real philosophy of the Absolute Truth states that the Lord and His creation are inconceivably and simultaneously one and different. The conclusion is that the Māyāvādī philosophers are actually atheists. There was much discussion on this issue between Sārvabhauma and Caitanya Mahāprabhu, but despite all his endeavors, the Bhaṭṭācārya was defeated in the end.

At the request of Sārvabhauma Bhaṭṭācārya, Śrī Caitanya Mahāprabhu then explained the *ātmārāma* verse of *Śrīmad-Bhāgavatam* in eighteen different ways. When the Bhaṭṭācārya came to his senses, Śrī Caitanya Mahāprabhu disclosed His real identity. The Bhaṭṭācārya then recited one hundred verses in praise of Lord Caitanya Mahāprabhu and offered his obeisances. After this, Gopīnātha Ācārya and all the others, having seen the wonderful potencies of Lord Caitanya Mahāprabhu, became very joyful.

One morning after this incident, Śrī Caitanya Mahāprabhu received some *prasāda* from Jagannātha and offered it to Sārvabhauma Bhaṭṭācārya. Without caring for formality, the Bhaṭṭācārya immediately partook of the *mahā-prasāda.* On another day, when the Bhaṭṭācārya asked Śrī Caitanya Mahāprabhu the best way to worship and meditate, the Lord advised him to chant the Hare Kṛṣṇa *mahā-mantra.* On another day, the Bhaṭṭācārya wanted to change the reading of the *tat te 'nukampām* verse because he did not like the word *mukti-pada.* He wanted to substitute the word *bhakti-pada.* Śrī Caitanya Mahāprabhu advised Sarvabhauma not to change the reading of *Śrīmad-Bhāgavatam* because *mukti-pada* indicated the lotus feet of the Supreme Personality of Godhead, Lord Kṛṣṇa. Having become a pure devotee, the Bhaṭṭācārya said, "Because the meaning is hazy, I still prefer *bhakti-pada.*" At this, Śrī Caitanya Mahāprabhu and the other inhabitants of Jagannātha Purī became very pleased. Sārvabhauma Bhaṭṭācārya thus became a pure Vaiṣṇava, and the other learned scholars there followed him.

TEXT 1

নৌমি তং গৌরচন্দ্রং যঃ কুতর্ক-কর্কশাশয়ম্ ।
সার্বভৌমং সর্বভূমা ভক্তিভূমানমাচরৎ ॥ ১ ॥

naumi taṁ gaura-candraṁ yaḥ
kutarka-karkaśāśayam

sārvabhaumaṁ sarva-bhūmā
bhakti-bhūmānam ācarat

SYNONYMS

naumi—I offer my respectful obeisances; *tam*—unto Him; *gaura-candram*—who is known as Lord Gauracandra; *yaḥ*—who; *ku-tarka*—by bad arguments; *karkaśa-āśayam*—whose heart was hard; *sārvabhaumam*—Sārvabhauma Bhaṭṭācārya; *sarva-bhūmā*—the Lord of everything; *bhakti-bhūmānam*—into a great personality of devotion; *ācarat*—converted.

TRANSLATION

I offer my respectful obeisances unto Lord Gauracandra, the Supreme Personality of Godhead, who converted the hardhearted Sārvabhauma Bhaṭṭācārya, the reservoir of all bad logic, into a great devotee.

TEXT 2

জয় জয় গৌরচন্দ্র জয় নিত্যানন্দ ।
জয়াদ্বৈতচন্দ্র জয় গৌরভক্তবৃন্দ ॥ ২ ॥

jaya jaya gauracandra jaya nityānanda
jayādvaitacandra jaya gaura-bhakta-vṛnda

SYNONYMS

jaya jaya gaura-candra—all glories to Lord Gaurahari; *jaya nityānanda*—all glories to Nityānanda Prabhu; *jaya advaita-candra*—all glories to Advaita Ācārya; *jaya gaura-bhakta-vṛnda*—all glories to the devotees of Lord Śrī Caitanya Mahāprabhu.

TRANSLATION

All glories to Lord Caitanya Mahāprabhu! All glories to Lord Nityānanda Prabhu! All glories to Advaita Ācārya! And all glories to the devotees of Lord Caitanya!

TEXT 3

আবেশে চলিলা প্রভু জগন্নাথ-মন্দিরে ।
জগন্নাথ দেখি' প্রেমে হইলা অস্থিরে ॥ ৩ ॥

āveśe calilā prabhu jagannātha-mandire
jagannātha dekhi' preme ha-ilā asthire

SYNONYMS

āveśe—in ecstasy; *calilā*—went; *prabhu*—Lord Śrī Caitanya Mahāprabhu; *jagannātha-mandire*—to the temple of Jagannātha; *jagannātha dekhi'*—seeing the Jagannātha Deity; *preme*—in ecstasy; *ha-ilā*—became; *asthire*—restless.

TRANSLATION

In ecstasy, Śrī Caitanya Mahāprabhu went from Āṭhāranālā to the temple of Jagannātha. After seeing Lord Jagannātha, He became very restless due to love of Godhead.

TEXT 4

জগন্নাথ আলিঙ্গিতে চলিলা ধাঞা ।
মন্দিরে পড়িলা প্রেমে আবিষ্ট হঞা ॥ ৪ ॥

jagannātha āliṅgite calilā dhāñā
mandire paḍilā preme āviṣṭa hañā

SYNONYMS

jagannātha—Lord Jagannātha; *āliṅgite*—to embrace; *calilā*—went; *dhāñā*—very swiftly; *mandire*—in the temple; *paḍilā*—fell down; *preme*—in ecstasy; *āviṣṭa*—overwhelmed; *hañā*—becoming.

TRANSLATION

Lord Śrī Caitanya Mahāprabhu went swiftly to embrace Lord Jagannātha, but when He entered the temple, He was so overwhelmed with love of Godhead that He fainted on the floor.

TEXT 5

দৈবে সার্বভৌম তাঁহাকে করে দরশন ।
পড়িছা মারিতে তেঁহো কৈল নিবারণ ॥ ৫ ॥

daive sārvabhauma tāṅhāke kare daraśana
paḍichā mārite teṅho kaila nivāraṇa

SYNONYMS

daive—by chance; *sārvabhauma*—Sārvabhauma Bhaṭṭācārya; *tāṅhāke*—Him; *kare*—does; *daraśana*—seeing; *paḍichā*—the watchman in the temple; *mārite*—to beat; *teṅho*—he; *kaila*—did; *nivāraṇa*—forbidding.

TRANSLATION

When Śrī Caitanya Mahāprabhu fell down, Sārvabhauma Bhaṭṭācārya happened to see Him. When the watchman threatened to beat the Lord, Sārvabhauma Bhaṭṭācārya immediately forbade him.

TEXT 6

প্রভুর সৌন্দর্য আর প্রেমের বিকার।
দেখি' সার্বভৌম হৈলা বিস্মিত অপার ॥ ৬ ॥

prabhura saundarya āra premera vikāra
dekhi' sārvabhauma hailā vismita apāra

SYNONYMS

prabhura—of Lord Śrī Caitanya Mahāprabhu; *saundarya*—the beauty; *āra*—and; *premera vikāra*—ecstatic transformations; *dekhi'*—seeing; *sārvabhauma*—Sārvabhauma Bhaṭṭācārya; *hailā*—became; *vismita*—surprised; *apāra*—very much.

TRANSLATION

Sārvabhauma Bhaṭṭācārya was very surprised to see the personal beauty of Lord Caitanya Mahāprabhu as well as the transcendental transformations wrought on His body due to love of Godhead.

TEXT 7

বহুক্ষণে চৈতন্য নহে, ভোগের কাল হৈল।
সার্বভৌম মনে তবে উপায় চিন্তিল ॥ ৭ ॥

bahu-kṣaṇe caitanya nahe, bhogera kāla haila
sārvabhauma mane tabe upāya cintila

SYNONYMS

bahu-kṣaṇe—for a long time; *caitanya*—consciousness; *nahe*—there was not; *bhogera*—of offering food; *kāla*—the time; *haila*—it became; *sārvabhauma*—Sārvabhauma Bhaṭṭācārya; *mane*—in the mind; *tabe*—at that time; *upāya*—remedy; *cintila*—thought.

TRANSLATION

Śrī Caitanya Mahāprabhu remained unconscious for a long time. Meanwhile, the time for offering prasāda to Lord Jagannātha came, and the Bhaṭṭācārya tried to think of a remedy.

TEXT 8

শিষ্য পড়িছা-দ্বারা প্রভু নিল বহাঞা।
ঘরে আনি' পবিত্র স্থানে রাখিল শোয়াঞা ॥ ৮ ॥

śiṣya paḍichā-dvārā prabhu nila vahāñā
ghare āni' pavitra sthāne rākhila śoyāñā

SYNONYMS

śiṣya—disciples; *paḍichā*—and watchmen; *dvārā*—by means of; *prabhu*—Lord Śrī Caitanya Mahāprabhu; *nila*—brought; *vahāñā*—carrying; *ghare*—at home; *āni'*—bringing; *pavitra*—purified; *sthāne*—in a place; *rākhila*—kept; *śoyāñā*—lying down.

TRANSLATION

While Lord Caitanya Mahāprabhu was unconscious, Sārvabhauma Bhaṭṭācārya, with the help of the watchmen and some disciples, carried Him to his home and laid Him down in a very sanctified room.

PURPORT

At that time, Sārvabhauma Bhaṭṭācārya lived on the southern side of the Jagannātha Temple. His home was practically on the beach and was known as Mārkaṇḍeya-sarastaṭa. At present it is used as the monastery of Gaṅgāmātā.

TEXT 9

শ্বাস-প্রশ্বাস নাহি উদর-স্পন্দন।
দেখিয়া চিন্তিত হৈল ভট্টাচার্যের মন ॥ ৯ ॥

śvāsa-praśvāsa nāhi udara-spandana
dekhiyā cintita haila bhaṭṭācāryera mana

SYNONYMS

śvāsa-praśvāsa—breathing; *nāhi*—there was not; *udara*—of the abdomen; *spandana*—movement; *dekhiyā*—seeing; *cintita*—full of anxiety; *haila*—became; *bhaṭṭācāryera*—of Sārvabhauma Bhaṭṭācārya; *mana*—the mind.

TRANSLATION

Examining the body of Śrī Caitanya Mahāprabhu, Sārvabhauma saw that His abdomen was not moving and that He was not breathing. Seeing His condition, the Bhaṭṭācārya became very anxious.

TEXT 10

সূক্ষ্ম তুলা আনি' নাসা-অগ্রেতে ধরিল ।
ঈষৎ চলয়ে তুলা দেখি' ধৈর্য হৈল ॥ ১০ ॥

sūkṣma tulā āni' nāsā-agrete dharila
īṣat calaye tulā dekhi' dhairya haila

SYNONYMS

sūkṣma—fine; *tulā*—cotton; *āni'*—bringing; *nāsā*—of the nostril; *agrete*—in front; *dharila*—held; *īṣat*—slightly; *calaye*—moves; *tulā*—the cotton; *dekhi'*—seeing; *dhairya*—patience; *haila*—there was.

TRANSLATION

The Bhaṭṭācārya then took a fine cotton swab and put it before the Lord's nostrils. When he saw the cotton move very slightly, he became hopeful.

TEXT 11

বসি' ভট্টাচার্য মনে করেন বিচার ।
এই কৃষ্ণ-মহাপ্রেমের সাত্ত্বিক বিকার ॥ ১১ ॥

vasi' bhaṭṭācārya mane karena vicāra
ei kṛṣṇa-mahāpremera sāttvika vikāra

SYNONYMS

vasi'—sitting down; *bhaṭṭācārya*—Sārvabhauma Bhaṭṭācārya; *mane*—in his mind; *karena*—does; *vicāra*—consideration; *ei*—this; *kṛṣṇa-mahā-premera*—of ecstatic love for Kṛṣṇa; *sāttvika*—transcendental; *vikāra*—transformation.

TRANSLATION

Sitting beside Śrī Caitanya Mahāprabhu, he thought: "This is a transcendental ecstatic transformation brought about by love of Kṛṣṇa."

TEXT 12

'সূদ্দীপ্ত সাত্ত্বিক' এই নাম যে 'প্রলয়' ।
নিত্যসিদ্ধ ভক্তে সে 'সূদ্দীপ্ত ভাব' হয় ॥ ১২ ॥

'sūddīpta sāttvika' ei nāma ye 'pralaya'
nitya-siddha bhakte se 'sūddīpta bhāva' haya

SYNONYMS

su-uddīpta sāttvika—of the name *sūddīpta-sāttvika; ei*—this; *nāma*—named; *ye*—which; *pralaya*—devastation; *nitya-siddha*—eternally perfected; *bhakte*—in the devotee; *se*—that; *su-uddīpta bhāva*—ecstasy known as *sūddīpta; haya*—becomes manifest.

TRANSLATION

Upon seeing the sign of sūddīpta-sāttvika, Sārvabhauma Bhaṭṭācārya could immediately understand the transcendental ecstatic transformation in the body of Lord Caitanya Mahāprabhu. Such a sign takes place only in the bodies of eternally liberated devotees.

PURPORT

The word *sūddīpta-sāttvika* is explained as follows by Śrīla Bhaktisiddhānta Sarasvatī Ṭhākura: "The *Bhakti-rasāmṛta-sindhu* mentions eight kinds of transcendental transformations in the bodies of advanced devotees. These are sometimes checked by the devotee, and there are two stages of such checking, technically known as *dhūmāyitā* and *jvalitā*. The *dhūmāyitā* (smoking) stage is exhibited when only one or two transformations are slightly present and it is possible to conceal them. When more than two or three transcendental transformations are manifest and it is still possible to conceal them, although with great difficulty, that stage is called *jvalitā* (lighted). When four or five symptoms are exhibited, the *dīpta* (blazing) stage has been reached. When five, six or all eight symptoms are simultaneously manifest, that position is called *uddīpta* (inflamed). And when all eight symptoms are multiplied a thousand times and are all visible at once, the devotee is in the *sūddīpta* (intensely inflamed) stage. *Nitya-siddha-bhakta* indicates the eternally liberated associates of the Lord. Such devotees enjoy the company of the Lord in four relationships—as servant, friend, parent or conjugal lover."

TEXT 13

'অধিরূঢ় ভাব' যাঁর, তাঁর এ বিকার ।
মনুষ্যের দেহে দেখি,—বড় চমৎকার ॥ ১৩ ॥

'adhirūḍha bhāva' yāṅra, tāṅra e vikāra
manuṣyera dehe dekhi,——baḍa camatkāra

SYNONYMS

adhirūḍha bhāva—an ecstasy technically known as *adhirūḍha; yāṅra*—of whom; *tāṅra*—of Him; *e*—this; *vikāra*—transformation; *manuṣyera*—of a human being; *dehe*—in the body; *dekhi*—I see; *baḍa camatkāra*—very wonderful.

TRANSLATION

Sārvabhauma Bhaṭṭācārya considered: "The uncommon ecstatic symptoms of adhirūḍha-bhāva are appearing in the body of Śrī Caitanya Mahāprabhu. This is very wonderful! How are they possible in the body of a human being?"

PURPORT

Adhirūḍha-bhāva, or *adhirūḍha-mahābhāva,* is explained in the *Ujjvala-nīlamaṇi* by Śrīla Rūpa Gosvāmī. Śrīla Bhaktisiddhānta Sarasvatī Ṭhākura quotes Rūpa Gosvāmī as follows: "The loving propensity of the *āśraya* (devotee) toward the *viṣaya* (Lord) becomes so ecstatic that even after enjoying the company of the beloved, the devotee feels that his enjoyment is insufficient. At such a time, the lover sees the beloved in different ways. Such a development of ecstasy is called *anurāga.* When *anurāga* reaches its highest limit and becomes perceivable in the body, it is called *bhāva.* When the bodily symptoms are not very distinct, however, the emotional state is still called *anurāga,* not *bhāva.* When *bhāva* ecstasy is intensified, it is called *mahābhāva.* The symptoms of *mahābhāva* are visible only in the bodies of eternal associates like the *gopīs.*"

TEXT 14

এত চিন্তি' ভট্টাচার্য আছেন বসিয়া ।
নিত্যানন্দাদি সিংহদ্বারে মিলিল আসিয়া ॥ ১৪ ॥

eta cinti' bhaṭṭācārya āchena vasiyā
nityānandādi siṁha-dvāre milila āsiyā

SYNONYMS

eta cinti'—thinking like this; *bhaṭṭācārya*—Sārvabhauma Bhaṭṭācārya; *āchena*—was; *vasiyā*—sitting; *nityānanda-ādi*—all the devotees, headed by Nityānanda Prabhu; *siṁha-dvāre*—at the entrance door of the Jagannātha Temple; *milila*—met; *āsiyā*—coming.

TRANSLATION

While the Bhaṭṭācārya was thinking in this way at his home, all the devotees of Caitanya Mahāprabhu, headed by Nityānanda Prabhu, approached the Siṁha-dvāra [the entrance door of the temple].

TEXT 15

তাঁহা শুনে লোকে কহে অন্যোন্যে বাত্ ।
এক সন্ন্যাসী আসি' দেখি' জগন্নাথ ॥ ১৫ ॥

tāṅhā śune loke kahe anyonye vāt
eka sannyāsī āsi' dekhi' jagannātha

SYNONYMS

tāṅhā—at that place; *śune*—they hear; *loke*—the people in general; *kahe*—talk; *anyonye*—among themselves; *vāt*—topics; *eka*—one; *sannyāsī*—mendicant; *āsi'*—coming there; *dekhi'*—seeing; *jagannātha*—the Deity of Lord Jagannātha.

TRANSLATION

There the devotees heard the people talking about a mendicant who had come to Jagannātha Purī and had seen the Deity of Jagannātha.

TEXT 16

মূর্চ্ছিত হৈল, চেতন না হয় শরীরে ।
সার্বভৌম লঞা গেলা আপনার ঘরে ॥ ১৬ ॥

mūrcchita haila, cetana nā haya śarīre
sārvabhauma lañā gelā āpanāra ghare

SYNONYMS

mūrcchita—unconscious; *haila*—became; *cetana*—consciousness; *nā*—not; *haya*—there is; *śarīre*—in His body; *sārvabhauma*—Sārvabhauma Bhaṭṭācārya; *lañā*—taking Him; *gelā*—went; *āpanāra*—his own; *ghare*—to the home.

TRANSLATION

The people said that the sannyāsī fell unconscious upon seeing the Deity of Lord Jagannātha. Because His consciousness did not return, Sārvabhauma Bhaṭṭācārya took Him to his home.

TEXT 17

শুনি' সবে জানিলা এই মহাপ্রভুর কার্য ।
হেনকালে আইলা তাহাঁ গোপীনাথাচার্য ॥ ১৭ ॥

śuni' sabe jānilā ei mahāprabhura kārya
hena-kāle āilā tāhāṅ gopīnāthācārya

SYNONYMS

śuni'—hearing this; *sabe*—all the devotees; *jānilā*—could understand; *ei*—this; *mahāprabhura*—of Lord Caitanya Mahāprabhu; *kārya*—the activities; *hena-*

kāle—at that time; *āilā*—came; *tāhāṅ*—there; *gopīnātha-ācārya*—of the name Gopīnātha Ācārya.

TRANSLATION

Hearing this, the devotees could understand that they were speaking of Lord Caitanya Mahāprabhu. Just then, Śrī Gopīnātha Ācārya arrived.

TEXT 18

নদীয়া-নিবাসী, বিশারদের জামাতা।
মহাপ্রভুর ভক্ত তেঁহো প্রভুতত্ত্বজ্ঞাতা ॥ ১৮ ॥

nadīyā-nivāsī, viśāradera jāmātā
mahāprabhura bhakta teṅho prabhu-tattva-jñātā

SYNONYMS

nadīyā-nivāsī—an inhabitant of Nadīyā; *viśāradera*—of Viśārada; *jāmātā*—the son-in-law; *mahāprabhura bhakta*—a devotee of Lord Caitanya Mahāprabhu; *teṅho*—he; *prabhu-tattva-jñātā*—a knower of the true identity of Śrī Caitanya Mahāprabhu.

TRANSLATION

Gopīnātha Ācārya was a resident of Nadīyā, the son-in-law of Viśārada and a devotee of Caitanya Mahāprabhu. He knew the true identity of His Lordship.

PURPORT

Maheśvara Viśārada was a classmate of Nīlāmbara Cakravartī's. He lived in the Nadīyā district in a village called Vidyānagara and had two sons named Madhusūdana Vācaspati and Vāsudeva Sārvabhauma. His son-in-law was Gopīnātha Ācārya.

TEXT 19

মুকুন্দ-সহিত পূর্বে আছে পরিচয়।
মুকুন্দ দেখিয়া তাঁর হইল বিস্ময় ॥ ১৯ ॥

mukunda-sahita pūrve āche paricaya
mukunda dekhiyā tāṅra ha-ila vismaya

SYNONYMS

mukunda-sahita—with Mukunda Datta; *pūrve*—previously; *āche*—there was; *paricaya*—acquaintance; *mukunda*—Mukunda Datta; *dekhiyā*—seeing; *tāṅra*—of him (Gopīnātha Ācārya); *ha-ila*—there was; *vismaya*—astonishment.

TRANSLATION

Gopīnātha Ācārya had previously been acquainted with Mukunda Datta, and when he saw him at Jagannātha Purī, he was very astonished.

TEXT 20

মুকুন্দ তাঁহারে দেখি' কৈল নমস্কার।
তেঁহো আলিঙ্গিয়া পুছে প্রভুর সমাচার॥ ২০॥

mukunda tāṅhāre dekhi' kaila namaskāra
teṅho āliṅgiyā puche prabhura samācāra

SYNONYMS

mukunda—Mukunda Datta; *tāṅhāre*—him; *dekhi'*—seeing; *kaila*—offered; *namaskāra*—obeisances; *teṅho*—he; *āliṅgiyā*—embracing; *puche*—inquires; *prabhura*—of Lord Caitanya Mahāprabhu; *samācāra*—news.

TRANSLATION

When Mukunda Datta met Gopīnātha Ācārya, Mukunda Datta offered obeisances unto him. After embracing Mukunda Datta, Gopīnātha Ācārya inquired about news of Śrī Caitanya Mahāprabhu.

TEXT 21

মুকুন্দ কহে,—প্রভুর ইহাঁ হৈল আগমনে।
আমি-সব আসিয়াছি মহাপ্রভুর সনে॥ ২১॥

mukunda kahe,—prabhura ihāṅ haila āgamane
āmi-saba āsiyāchi mahāprabhura sane

SYNONYMS

mukunda kahe—Mukunda replies; *prabhura*—of Lord Caitanya Mahāprabhu; *ihāṅ*—here; *haila*—there was; *āgamane*—coming; *āmi-saba*—all of us; *āsiyāchi*—have come; *mahāprabhura*—Caitanya Mahāprabhu; *sane*—with.

TRANSLATION

Mukunda Datta replied: "The Lord has already arrived here. We have come with Him."

TEXT 22

নিত্যানন্দ-গোসাঞিকে আচার্য কৈল নমস্কার ।
সবে মেলি' পুছে প্রভুর বার্তা বার বার ॥ ২২ ॥

nityānanda-gosāñike ācārya kaila namaskāra
sabe meli' puche prabhura vārtā bāra bāra

SYNONYMS

nityānanda-gosāñike—unto Lord Nityānanda Prabhu; *ācārya*—Gopīnātha Ācārya; *kaila namaskāra*—offered obeisances; *sabe meli'*—meeting them all; *puche*—inquires; *prabhura*—of Lord Caitanya Mahāprabhu; *vārtā*—news; *bāra bāra*—again and again.

TRANSLATION

As soon as Gopīnātha Ācārya saw Nityānanda Prabhu, he offered his obeisances unto Him. In this way, meeting all the devotees, he asked about news of Lord Caitanya Mahāprabhu again and again.

TEXT 23

মুকুন্দ কহে,—'মহাপ্রভু সন্ন্যাস করিয়া ।
নীলাচলে আইলা সঙ্গে আমা-সবা লঞা ॥ ২৩ ॥

mukunda kahe,—'mahāprabhu sannyāsa kariyā
nīlācale āilā saṅge āmā-sabā lañā

SYNONYMS

mukunda kahe—Mukunda Datta replies; *mahāprabhu*—Śrī Caitanya Mahāprabhu; *sannyāsa kariyā*—after accepting the renounced order of life; *nīlācale*—to Jagannātha Purī; *āilā*—has come; *saṅge*—with Him; *āmā-sabā*—all of us; *lañā*—taking.

TRANSLATION

Mukunda Datta continued: "After accepting the sannyāsa order, Lord Caitanya Mahāprabhu has come to Jagannātha Purī and has brought all of us with Him.

TEXT 24

আমা-সবা ছাড়ি' আগে গেলা দরশনে ।
আমি-সব পাছে আইলাও তাঁর অন্বেষণে ॥ ২৪ ॥

āmā-sabā chāḍi' āge gelā daraśane
āmi-saba pāche āilāṅ tāṅra anveṣaṇe

SYNONYMS

āmā-sabā—all of us; *chāḍi'*—leaving; *āge*—ahead; *gelā*—went; *daraśane*—to see Lord Jagannātha; *āmi-saba*—all of us; *pāche*—behind; *āilāṅ*—came; *tāṅra*—of Him; *anveṣaṇe*—in search.

TRANSLATION

"Lord Caitanya Mahāprabhu left our company and walked ahead to see Lord Jagannātha. We have just arrived and are now looking for Him.

TEXT 25

অন্যোন্যে লোকের মুখে যে কথা শুনিল।
সার্বভৌম-গৃহে প্রভু,—অনুমান কৈল ॥ ২৫ ॥

anyonye lokera mukhe ye kathā śunila
sārvabhauma-gṛhe prabhu,——anumāna kaila

SYNONYMS

anyonye—among themselves; *lokera*—of the people in general; *mukhe*—in the mouths; *ye*—that which; *kathā*—talk; *śunila*—was heard; *sārvabhauma-gṛhe*—at the home of Sārvabhauma Bhaṭṭācārya; *prabhu*—the Lord; *anumāna*—a guess; *kaila*—made.

TRANSLATION

"From the talk of the people in general, we have guessed that the Lord is now at the house of Sārvabhauma Bhaṭṭācārya.

TEXT 26

ঈশ্বর-দর্শনে প্রভু প্রেমে অচেতন।
সার্বভৌম লঞা গেলা আপন-ভবন ॥ ২৬ ॥

īśvara-darśane prabhu preme acetana
sārvabhauma lañā gelā āpana-bhavana

SYNONYMS

īśvara-darśane—by seeing Lord Jagannātha; *prabhu*—Lord Śrī Caitanya Mahāprabhu; *preme*—in the ecstasy of love of Godhead; *acetana*—unconscious;

sārvabhauma—Sārvabhauma Bhaṭṭācārya; *lañā gelā*—has taken; *āpana-bhavana*—to his own home.

TRANSLATION

"Upon seeing Lord Jagannātha, Caitanya Mahāprabhu became ecstatic and fell unconscious, and Sārvabhauma Bhaṭṭācārya has taken Him to his home in this condition.

TEXT 27

তোমার মিলনে যবে আমার হৈল মন।
দৈবে সেই ক্ষণে পাইলুঁ তোমার দরশন ॥ ২৭ ॥

tomāra milane yabe āmāra haila mana
daive sei kṣaṇe pāiluṅ tomāra daraśana

SYNONYMS

tomāra—of you; *milane*—in meeting; *yabe*—when; *āmāra*—of me; *haila*—there was; *mana*—the mind; *daive*—by chance; *sei kṣaṇe*—at that very moment; *pāiluṅ*—got; *tomāra*—your; *daraśana*—meeting.

TRANSLATION

"Just as I was thinking of meeting you, by chance we have actually met.

TEXT 28

চল, সবে যাই সার্বভৌমের ভবন।
প্রভু দেখি' পাছে করিব ঈশ্বর দর্শন ॥' ২৮ ॥

cala, sabe yāi sārvabhaumera bhavana
prabhu dekhi' pāche kariba īśvara darśana'

SYNONYMS

cala—let us go; *sabe*—all; *yāi*—we shall go; *sārvabhaumera bhavana*—to the house of Sārvabhauma Bhaṭṭācārya; *prabhu dekhi'*—seeing Lord Śrī Caitanya Mahāprabhu; *pāche*—later; *kariba*—we shall do; *īśvara darśana*—seeing of Lord Jagannātha.

TRANSLATION

"First let us all go to the house of Sārvabhauma Bhaṭṭācārya and see Caitanya Mahāprabhu. Later we shall come to see Lord Jagannātha."

TEXT 29

এত শুনি' গোপীনাথ সবারে লঞা।
সার্বভৌম-ঘরে গেলা হরষিত হঞা ॥ ২৯ ॥

eta śuni' gopīnātha sabāre lañā
sārvabhauma-ghare gelā haraṣita hañā

SYNONYMS

eta śuni'—hearing this; *gopīnātha*—Gopīnātha Ācārya; *sabāre*—all of them; *lañā*—taking with him; *sārvabhauma-ghare*—to the house of Sārvabhauma Bhaṭṭācārya; *gelā*—went; *haraṣita hañā*—becoming very pleased.

TRANSLATION

Hearing this and feeling very pleased, Gopīnātha Ācārya immediately took all the devotees with him and approached the house of Sārvabhauma Bhaṭṭācārya.

TEXT 30

সার্বভৌম-স্থানে গিয়া প্রভুকে দেখিল।
প্রভু দেখি' আচার্যের দুঃখ-হর্ষ হৈল ॥ ৩০ ॥

sārvabhauma-sthāne giyā prabhuke dekhila
prabhu dekhi' ācāryera duḥkha-harṣa haila

SYNONYMS

sārvabhauma-sthāne—to the place of Sārvabhauma Bhaṭṭācārya; *giyā*—going there; *prabhuke*—Lord Śrī Caitanya Mahāprabhu; *dekhila*—all of them saw; *prabhu dekhi'*—seeing the Lord; *ācāryera*—of Gopīnātha Ācārya; *duḥkha*—unhappiness; *harṣa*—happiness; *haila*—there was.

TRANSLATION

Arriving at the home of Sārvabhauma Bhaṭṭācārya, everyone saw the Lord lying unconscious. Seeing Him in this condition, Gopīnātha Ācārya became very unhappy, but at the same time he was happy just to see the Lord.

TEXT 31

সার্বভৌমে জানাঞা সবা নিল অভ্যন্তরে।
নিত্যানন্দ-গোসাঞিরে তেঁহো কৈল নমস্কারে ॥৩১॥

sārvabhaume jānāñā sabā nila abhyantare
nityānanda-gosāñire teṅho kaila namaskāre

SYNONYMS

sārvabhaume—Sārvabhauma Bhaṭṭācārya; *jānāñā*—informing and taking permission; *sabā*—all the devotees; *nila*—took; *abhyantare*—within the house; *nityānanda-gosāñire*—unto Nityānanda Prabhu; *teṅho*—Sārvabhauma Bhaṭṭācārya; *kaila*—offered; *namaskāre*—obeisances.

TRANSLATION

Sārvabhauma Bhaṭṭācārya permitted all the devotees to enter his house, and upon seeing Nityānanda Prabhu, the Bhaṭṭācārya offered Him obeisances.

TEXT 32

সবা সহিত যথাযোগ্য করিল মিলন ।
প্রভু দেখি' সবার হৈল হরষিত মন ॥ ৩২ ॥

sabā sahita yathā-yogya karila milana
prabhu dekhi' sabāra haila haraṣita mana

SYNONYMS

sabā sahita—with all of them; *yathā-yogya*—as it was befitting; *karila*—did; *milana*—meeting; *prabhu dekhi'*—seeing the Lord; *sabāra*—of all; *haila*—became; *haraṣita*—pleased; *mana*—the minds.

TRANSLATION

Sārvabhauma met with all the devotees and offered them a proper welcome. They were all pleased to see Lord Caitanya Mahāprabhu.

TEXT 33

সার্বভৌম পাঠাইল সবা দর্শন করিতে ।
'চন্দনেশ্বর' নিজপুত্র দিল সবার সাথে ॥ ৩৩ ॥

sārvabhauma pāṭhāila sabā darśana karite
'candaneśvara' nija-putra dila sabāra sāthe

SYNONYMS

sārvabhauma—Sārvabhauma Bhaṭṭācārya; *pāṭhāila*—sent them; *sabā*—all; *darśana karite*—to see Lord Jagannātha; *candana-īśvara*—of the name Candaneśvara; *nija-putra*—his son; *dila*—gave; *sabāra sāthe*—with all of them.

TRANSLATION

The Bhaṭṭācārya then sent them all back to see Lord Jagannātha, and he asked his own son Candaneśvara to accompany them as a guide.

TEXT 34

জগন্নাথ দেখি' সবার হইল আনন্দ ।
ভাবেতে আবিষ্ট হৈলা প্রভু নিত্যানন্দ ॥ ৩৪ ॥

jagannātha dekhi' sabāra ha-ila ānanda
bhāvete āviṣṭa hailā prabhu nityānanda

SYNONYMS

jagannātha dekhi'—seeing Lord Jagannātha; *sabāra*—of everyone; *ha-ila*—there was; *ānanda*—pleasure; *bhāvete*—in ecstasy; *āviṣṭa*—overwhelmed; *hailā*—became; *prabhu nityānanda*—Lord Nityānanda.

TRANSLATION

Everyone was then very pleased to see the Deity of Lord Jagannātha. Lord Nityānanda in particular was overwhelmed with ecstasy.

TEXT 35

সবে মেলি' ধরি তাঁরে সুস্থির করিল ।
ঈশ্বর-সেবক মালা-প্রসাদ আনি' দিল ॥ ৩৫ ॥

sabe meli' dhari tāṅre susthira karila
īśvara-sevaka mālā-prasāda āni' dila

SYNONYMS

sabe meli'—meeting all together; *dhari*—caught; *tāṅre*—Him; *su-sthira*—steady; *karila*—made; *īśvara-sevaka*—the priest of the Deity; *mālā*—garland; *prasāda*—offering; *āni'*—bringing; *dila*—gave.

TRANSLATION

When Lord Nityānanda Prabhu nearly fainted, all the devotees caught Him and steadied Him. At that time, the priest of Lord Jagannātha brought a garland that had been offered to the Deity and offered it to Nityānanda Prabhu.

TEXT 36

প্রসাদ পাঞা সবে হৈলা আনন্দিত মনে।
পুনরপি আইলা সবে মহাপ্রভুর স্থানে ॥ ৩৬ ॥

prasāda pāñā sabe hailā ānandita mane
punarapi āilā sabe mahāprabhura sthāne

SYNONYMS

prasāda pāñā—getting this honor of the garland; *sabe*—all of them; *hailā*—became; *ānandita mane*—pleased in the mind; *punarapi*—again; *āilā*—came back; *sabe*—all; *mahāprabhura sthāne*—to the place where Śrī Caitanya Mahāprabhu was staying.

TRANSLATION

Everyone was pleased to receive this garland worn by Lord Jagannātha. Afterwards they all returned to the place where Lord Śrī Caitanya Mahāprabhu was staying.

TEXT 37

উচ্চ করি' করে সবে নাম-সংকীর্তন।
তৃতীয় প্রহরে হৈল প্রভুর চেতন ॥ ৩৭ ॥

ucca kari' kare sabe nāma-saṅkīrtana
tṛtīya prahare haila prabhura cetana

SYNONYMS

ucca—very loudly; *kari'*—doing; *kare*—began; *sabe*—all; *nāma-saṅkīrtana*—chanting of the Hare Kṛṣṇa *mahā-mantra; tṛtīya prahare*—in the forenoon; *haila*—there was; *prabhura*—of Lord Caitanya; *cetana*—consciousness.

TRANSLATION

All of the devotees then began to loudly chant the Hare Kṛṣṇa mantra. Just before noon the Lord regained His consciousness.

TEXT 38

হুঙ্কার করিয়া উঠে 'হরি' 'হরি' বলি'।
আনন্দে সার্বভৌম তাঁর লৈল পদধূলি ॥ ৩৮ ॥

huṅkāra kariyā uṭhe 'hari' 'hari' bali'
ānande sārvabhauma tāṅra laila pada-dhūli

SYNONYMS

huṅkāra kariyā—making a loud sound; *uṭhe*—got up; *hari hari bali'*—chanting Hari, Hari; *ānande*—in pleasure; *sārvabhauma*—Sārvabhauma Bhaṭṭācārya; *tāṅra*—His; *laila*—took; *pada-dhūli*—the dust of the feet.

TRANSLATION

Caitanya Mahāprabhu got up and very loudly chanted, "Hari! Hari!" Sārvabhauma Bhaṭṭācārya was very pleased to see the Lord regain consciousness, and he took the dust of the Lord's lotus feet.

TEXT 39

সার্বভৌম কহে,—শীঘ্র করহ মধ্যাহ্ন ।
মুঞি ভিক্ষা দিমু আজি মহা-প্রসাদান্ন ॥ ৩৯ ॥

sārvabhauma kahe,——śīghra karaha madhyāhna
muñi bhikṣā dimu āji mahā-prasādānna

SYNONYMS

sārvabhauma—Sārvabhuma Bhaṭṭācārya; *kahe*—says; *śīghra*—very soon; *karaha*—do; *madhya-ahna*—midday duties; *muñi*—I; *bhikṣā*—alms; *dimu*—shall offer; *āji*—today; *mahā-prasāda-anna*—remnants of food offered to Lord Jagannātha.

TRANSLATION

The Bhaṭṭācārya informed all of them: "Please take your midday baths immediately. Today I shall offer you mahā-prasāda, the remnants of food offered to Lord Jagannātha."

TEXT 40

সমুদ্রস্নান করি' মহাপ্রভু শীঘ্র আইলা ।
চরণ পাখালি' প্রভু আসনে বসিলা ॥ ৪০ ॥

samudra-snāna kari' mahāprabhu śīghra āilā
caraṇa pākhāli' prabhu āsane vasilā

SYNONYMS

samudra-snāna—a bath in the sea; *kari'*—taking; *mahāprabhu*—Śrī Caitanya Mahāprabhu; *śīghra*—very soon; *āilā*—returned; *caraṇa*—feet; *pākhāli'*—washing; *prabhu*—Lord Caitanya Mahāprabhu; *āsane*—on a seat; *vasilā*—sat.

TRANSLATION

After bathing in the sea, Śrī Caitanya Mahāprabhu and His devotees returned very soon. The Lord then washed His feet and sat down on a carpet to take lunch.

TEXT 41

বহুত প্রসাদ সার্বভৌম আনাইল।
তবে মহাপ্রভু সুখে ভোজন করিল ॥ ৪১ ॥

bahuta prasāda sārvabhauma ānāila
tabe mahāprabhu sukhe bhojana karila

SYNONYMS

bahuta prasāda—varieties of foods offered to Lord Jagannātha; *sārvabhauma*—Sārvabhauma Bhaṭṭācārya; *ānāila*—caused to bring them; *tabe*—at that time; *mahāprabhu*—Śrī Caitanya Mahāprabhu; *sukhe*—in happiness; *bhojana*—lunch; *karila*—accepted.

TRANSLATION

Sārvabhauma Bhaṭṭācārya made arrangements to bring various kinds of mahā-prasāda from the Jagannātha temple. Śrī Caitanya Mahāprabhu then accepted lunch with great happiness.

TEXT 42

সুবর্ণ-থালীর অন্ন উত্তম ব্যঞ্জন।
ভক্তগণ-সঙ্গে প্রভু করেন ভোজন ॥ ৪২ ॥

suvarṇa-thālīra anna uttama vyañjana
bhakta-gaṇa-saṅge prabhu karena bhojana

SYNONYMS

suvarṇa-thālīra—on golden plates; *anna*—rice; *uttama*—first-class; *vyañjana*—vegetables; *bhakta-gaṇa*—the devotees; *saṅge*—with; *prabhu*—Lord Caitanya Mahāprabhu; *karena*—accepts; *bhojana*—lunch.

TRANSLATION

Caitanya Mahāprabhu was offered special rice and first-class vegetables on golden plates. He thus took lunch in the company of His devotees.

TEXT 43

সার্বভৌম পরিবেশন করেন আপনে ।
প্রভু কহে,– মোরে দেহ লাফ্‌রা-ব্যঞ্জনে ॥ ৪৩ ॥

sārvabhauma pariveśana karena āpane
prabhu kahe,——more deha lāphrā-vyañjane

SYNONYMS

sārvabhauma—Sārvabhauma Bhaṭṭācārya; *pariveśana*—distribution; *karena*—does; *āpane*—personally; *prabhu kahe*—Lord Caitanya Mahāprabhu said; *more*—unto Me; *deha*—please give; *lāphrā-vyañjane*—boiled vegetables.

TRANSLATION

While Sārvabhauma Bhaṭṭācarya personally distributed the prasāda, Lord Caitanya Mahāprabhu requested him: "Please give Me only boiled vegetables.

PURPORT

Lāphrā-vyañjana is a preparation in which many vegetables are boiled together, and then a *cheṅkā* is added, consisting of spices like cumin, black pepper and mustard seed.

TEXT 44

পীঠা-পানা দেহ তুমি ইঁহা-সবাকারে ।
তবে ভট্টাচার্য কহে যুড়ি' দুই করে ॥ ৪৪ ॥

pīṭhā-pānā deha tumi iṅhā-sabākāre
tabe bhaṭṭācārya kahe yuḍi' dui kare

SYNONYMS

pīṭhā-pānā—cakes and condensed milk; *deha*—give; *tumi*—you; *iṅhā-sabākāre*—to all these devotees; *tabe*—at that time; *bhaṭṭācārya*—Sārvabhauma Bhaṭṭācārya; *kahe*—said; *yuḍi'*—folding; *dui kare*—two hands.

TRANSLATION

"You can offer the cakes and other preparations made with condensed milk to all the devotees." Hearing this, the Bhaṭṭācārya folded his hands and spoke as follows.

TEXT 45

জগন্নাথ কৈছে করিয়াছেন ভোজন ।
আজি সব মহাপ্রসাদ কর আস্বাদন ॥ ৪৫ ॥

jagannātha kaiche kariyāchena bhojana
āji saba mahāprasāda kara āsvādana

SYNONYMS

jagannātha—Lord Jagannātha; *kaiche*—as; *kariyāchena*—has accepted; *bhojana*—lunch; *āji*—today; *saba*—all of you; *mahā-prasāda*—the remnants of food offered to the Lord; *kara*—do; *āsvādana*—tasting.

TRANSLATION

"Today, all of you please try to taste the lunch just as Lord Jagannātha accepted it."

TEXT 46

এত বলি' পীঠা-পানা সব খাওয়াইলা ।
ভিক্ষা করাঞা আচমন করাইলা ॥ ৪৬ ॥

eta bali' pīṭhā-pānā saba khāoyāilā
bhikṣā karāñā ācamana karāilā

SYNONYMS

eta bali'—saying this; *pīṭhā-pānā*—many kinds of cakes and condensed-milk preparations; *saba*—all; *khāoyāilā*—made to eat; *bhikṣā karāñā*—after offering *prasāda; ācamana karāilā*—made them wash their hands, feet and mouths.

TRANSLATION

After saying this, he made them all eat the various cakes and condensed-milk preparations. After feeding them, he offered them water to wash their hands, feet and mouths.

TEXT 47

আজ্ঞা মাগি' গেলা গোপীনাথ আচার্যকে লঞা ।
প্রভুর নিকট আইলা ভোজন করিঞা ॥ ৪৭ ॥

ājñā māgi' gelā gopīnātha ācāryake lañā
prabhura nikaṭa āilā bhojana kariñā

SYNONYMS

ājñā māgi'—taking permission; *gelā*—went; *gopīnātha ācāryake lañā*—taking Gopīnātha Ācārya; *prabhura*—Lord Caitanya Mahāprabhu; *nikaṭa*—near; *āilā*—went; *bhojana kariñā*—after taking lunch.

TRANSLATION

Begging permission from Lord Caitanya Mahāprabhu and His devotees, Sārvabhauma Bhaṭṭācārya then went with Gopīnātha Ācārya to take lunch. After finishing their lunch, they returned to Lord Caitanya Mahāprabhu.

TEXT 48

'নমো নারায়ণায়' বলি' নমস্কার কৈল ।
'কৃষ্ণে মতিরস্তু' বলি' গোসাঞি কহিল ॥ ৪৮ ॥

'namo nārāyaṇāya' bali' namaskāra kaila
'kṛṣṇe matir astu' bali' gosāñi kahila

SYNONYMS

namaḥ nārāyaṇāya—I offer my respects to Nārāyaṇa; *bali'*—saying; *namaskāra kaila*—offered respects to Lord Caitanya Mahāprabhu; *kṛṣṇe*—unto Lord Kṛṣṇa; *matiḥ astu*—let there be attraction; *bali'*—saying; *gosāñi*—Śrī Caitanya Mahāprabhu; *kahila*—spoke.

TRANSLATION

Offering his obeisances to Caitanya Mahāprabhu, Sārvabhauma Bhaṭṭācārya said, "Namo nārāyaṇāya" [I offer my obeisances to Nārāyaṇa]. In return, Caitanya Mahāprabhu said, "Kṛṣṇe matir astu" [Let your attention be on Kṛṣṇa].

PURPORT

It is the etiquette among *sannyāsīs,* those on the fourth platform of spiritual life, to offer respects by saying, *oṁ namo nārāyaṇāya* ("I offer my respectful obeisances unto Nārāyaṇa"). This greeting is used especially by Māyāvādī *sannyāsīs*. According to the *smṛti* scriptures, a *sannyāsī* should not expect anything from anyone, nor should he consider himself identical with the Supreme Personality of Godhead. Vaiṣṇava *sannyāsīs* never think of themselves as being one with the Lord; they always consider themselves eternal servants of Kṛṣṇa, and they want to see everyone in the world become Kṛṣṇa conscious. For this reason, a Vaiṣṇava *sannyāsī* always offers his blessings to everyone, saying, *kṛṣṇe matir astu* ("May you become Kṛṣṇa conscious").

TEXT 49

শুনি' সার্বভৌম মনে বিচার করিল।
বৈষ্ণব-সন্ন্যাসী ইঁহো, বচনে জানিল ॥ ৪৯ ॥

śuni' sārvabhauma mane vicāra karila
vaiṣṇava-sannyāsī iṅho, vacane jānila

SYNONYMS

śuni'—hearing this; *sārvabhauma*—Sārvabhauma Bhaṭṭācārya; *mane*—within the mind; *vicāra karila*—considered; *vaiṣṇava-sannyāsī*—Vaiṣṇava *sannyāsī*; *iṅho*—this person; *vacane*—by words; *jānila*—understood.

TRANSLATION

Hearing these words, Sārvabhauma understood Lord Caitanya to be a Vaiṣṇava sannyāsī.

TEXT 50

গোপীনাথ আচার্যেরে কহে সার্বভৌম।
গোসাঞির জানিতে চাহি কাহাঁ পূর্বাশ্রম ॥ ৫০

gopīnātha ācāryere kahe sārvabhauma
gosāñira jānite cāhi kāhāṅ pūrvāśrama

SYNONYMS

gopīnātha ācāryere—to Gopīnātha Ācārya; *kahe*—said; *sārvabhauma*—Sārvabhauma Bhaṭṭācārya; *gosāñira*—of Lord Caitanya Mahāprabhu; *jānite*—to know; *cāhi*—I want; *kāhāṅ*—what; *pūrva-āśrama*—previous situation.

TRANSLATION

Sārvabhauma then said to Gopīnātha Ācārya: "I want to know Caitanya Mahāprabhu's previous situation."

PURPORT

The word *pūrvāśrama* refers to one's previous situation in life. Sometimes a person will accept the renounced order from householder life, and sometimes even from student (*brahmacārī*) life. Sārvabhauma Bhaṭṭācārya wanted to know of Śrī Caitanya Mahāprabhu's previous situation as a householder.

TEXT 51

গোপীনাথাচার্য কহে,— নবদ্বীপে ঘর ।
'জগন্নাথ'— নাম, পদবী—'মিশ্র পুরন্দর' ॥ ৫১ ॥

gopīnāthācārya kahe,——navadvīpe ghara
'jagannātha'——nāma, padavī——'miśra purandara'

SYNONYMS

gopīnātha-ācārya kahe—Gopīnātha Ācārya replied; *navadvīpe*—in Navadvīpa; *ghara*—residence; *jagannātha*—of the name Jagannātha; *nāma*—named; *padavī*—the surname; *miśra purandara*—Miśra Purandara.

TRANSLATION

Gopīnātha Ācārya replied: "There was a man named Jagannātha, who was a resident of Navadvīpa, and whose surname was Miśra Purandara.

TEXT 52

'বিশ্বম্ভর'—নাম ইঁহার, তাঁর ইঁহো পুত্র ।
নীলাম্বর চক্রবর্ত্তীর হয়েন দৌহিত্র ॥ ৫২ ॥

'viśvambhara'——nāma iṅhāra, tāṅra iṅho putra
nīlāmbara cakravartīra hayena dauhitra

SYNONYMS

viśvambhara—of the name Viśvambhara; *nāma*—the name; *iṅhāra*—His; *tāṅra*—of Jagannātha Miśra; *iṅho*—He; *putra*—son; *nīlāmbara cakravartīra*—of Nīlāmbara Cakravartī; *hayena*—is; *dauhitra*—grandson (daughter's son).

TRANSLATION

"Lord Caitanya Mahāprabhu is the son of that Jagannātha Miśra, and His former name was Viśvambhara Miśra. He also happens to be the grandson of Nīlāmbara Cakravartī."

TEXT 53

সার্বভৌম কহে,—নীলাম্বর চক্রবর্তী।
বিশারদের সমাধ্যায়ী,—এই তাঁর খ্যাতি ॥ ৫৩ ॥

sārvabhauma kahe,——nīlāmbara cakravartī
viśāradera samādhyāyī,——ei tāṅra khyāti

SYNONYMS

sārvabhauma kahe—Sārvabhauma said; *nīlāmbara cakravartī*—the gentleman named Nīlāmbara Cakravartī; *viśāradera*—of Maheśvara Viśārada (Sārvabhauma's father); *samādhyāyī*—class friend; *ei*—this; *tāṅra*—of him; *khyāti*—acquaintance.

TRANSLATION

The Bhaṭṭācārya said: "Nīlāmbara Cakravartī was a classmate of my father, Maheśvara Viśārada. He knew him as such.

TEXT 54

'মিশ্র পুরন্দর' তাঁর মান্য, হেন জানি।
পিতার সম্বন্ধে দোঁহাকে পূজ্য করি' মানি ॥ ৫৪ ॥

'miśra purandara' tāṅra mānya, hena jāni
pitāra sambandhe doṅhāke pūjya kari' māni

SYNONYMS

miśra purandara—Jagannātha Miśra Purandara; *tāṅra*—his; *mānya*—respectable; *hena*—thus; *jāni*—I know; *pitāra sambandhe*—in relationship to my father; *doṅhāke*—both of them (Nīlāmbara Cakravartī and Jagannātha Miśra); *pūjya*—respectable; *kari'*—thinking; *māni*—I accept.

TRANSLATION

"Jagannātha Miśra Purandara was respected by my father. Thus because of their relationship with my father, I respect both Jagannātha Miśra and Nīlāmbara Cakravartī."

TEXT 55

নদীয়া-সম্বন্ধে সার্বভৌম হৃষ্ট হৈলা।
প্রীত হঞা গোসাঞিরে কহিতে লাগিলা ॥ ৫৫ ॥

nadīyā-sambandhe sārvabhauma hṛṣṭa hailā
prīta hañā gosāñire kahite lāgilā

SYNONYMS

nadīyā-sambandhe—in connection with Nadīyā; *sārvabhauma*—Sārvabhauma Bhaṭṭācārya; *hṛṣṭa*—pleased; *hailā*—became; *prīta hañā*—thus being pleased; *gosāñire*—unto Lord Śrī Caitanya Mahāprabhu; *kahite lāgilā*—began to speak.

TRANSLATION

Hearing that Śrī Caitanya Mahāprabhu belonged to the Nadīyā district, Sārvabhauma Bhaṭṭācārya became very pleased and addressed the Lord as follows.

TEXT 56

'সহজেই পূজ্য তুমি, আরে ত' সন্ন্যাস ।
অতএব হঙ তোমার আমি নিজ-দাস ॥' ৫৬ ॥

'sahajei pūjya tumi, āre ta' sannyāsa
ataeva haṅ tomāra āmi nija-dāsa'

SYNONYMS

sahajei—naturally; *pūjya*—respectable; *tumi*—You; *āre*—over and above this; *ta'*—certainly; *sannyāsa*—the renounced order of life; *ataeva*—therefore; *haṅ*—am; *tomāra*—Your; *āmi*—I; *nija-dāsa*—personal servant.

TRANSLATION

"You are naturally respectable. Besides, You are a sannyāsī; thus I wish to become Your personal servant."

PURPORT

A *sannyāsī* is always to be worshiped and offered all kinds of respect by the *gṛhasthas* (householders). Although Sārvabhauma Bhaṭṭācārya was older than Śrī Caitanya Mahāprabhu, Sārvabhauma respected Him as a *sannyāsī* and as one who had attained the topmost platform of spiritual ecstasy. Thus the Bhaṭṭācārya certainly accepted Him as his master.

TEXT 57

শুনি' মহাপ্রভু কৈল শ্রীবিষ্ণু স্মরণ ।
ভট্টাচার্যে কহে কিছু বিনয় বচন ॥ ৫৭ ॥

śuni' mahāprabhu kaila śrī-viṣṇu smaraṇa
bhaṭṭācārye kahe kichu vinaya vacana

SYNONYMS

śuni'—hearing this; *mahāprabhu*—Lord Caitanya Mahāprabhu; *kaila*—did; *śrī-viṣṇu smaraṇa*—remembering Lord Viṣṇu; *bhaṭṭācārye*—to Sārvabhauma Bhaṭṭācārya; *kahe*—speaks; *kichu*—some; *vinaya vacana*—very humble statements.

TRANSLATION

As soon as Caitanya Mahāprabhu heard this from the Bhaṭṭācārya, He immediately remembered Lord Viṣṇu and began to speak humbly to him as follows.

TEXT 58

"তুমি জগদ্গুরু—সর্বলোক-হিতকর্তা ।
বেদান্ত পড়াও, সন্ন্যাসীর উপকর্তা ॥ ৫৮ ॥

"tumi jagad-guru——sarvaloka-hita-kartā
vedānta paḍāo, sannyāsīra upakartā

SYNONYMS

tumi jagat-guru—you are the master of all people; *sarva-loka*—of all people; *hita-kartā*—the well-wisher; *vedānta paḍāo*—you teach Vedānta philosophy; *sannyāsīra*—of the mendicants in the renounced order of life; *upakartā*—the benefactor.

TRANSLATION

"Because you are a teacher of Vedānta philosophy, you are the master of all the people in the world and their well-wisher as well. You are also the benefactor of all kinds of sannyāsīs.

PURPORT

Because the Māyāvādī *sannyāsīs* teach Vedānta philosophy to their students or disciples, they are customarily called *jagad-guru*. This indicates that they are the benefactors of all people. Although Sārvabhauma Bhaṭṭācārya was not a *sannyāsī* but a householder, he used to invite all the *sannyāsīs* to his home and offer them *prasāda*. Thus he was accepted as the best well-wisher and friend of all the *sannyāsīs*.

TEXT 59

আমি বালক-সন্ন্যাসী—ভান্দ-মন্দ নাহি জানি।
তোমার আশ্রয় নিলুঁ, গুরু করি' মানি ॥ ৫৯ ॥

āmi bālaka-sannyāsī——bhānda-manda nāhi jāni
tomāra āśraya niluṅ, guru kari' māni

SYNONYMS

āmi—I; *bālaka-sannyāsī*—a young *sannyāsī; bhānda-manda*—good and bad; *nāhi*—not; *jāni*—know; *tomāra*—your; *āśraya*—shelter; *niluṅ*—have taken; *guru*—spiritual master; *kari'*—taking as; *māni*—I accept.

TRANSLATION

"I am a young sannyāsī, and I actually have no knowledge of what is good and what is bad. Therefore I am taking shelter of you and accepting you as My spiritual master.

TEXT 60

তোমার সঙ্গ লাগি' মোর ইহাঁ আগমন।
সর্বপ্রকারে করিবে আমায় পালন ॥ ৬০ ॥

tomāra saṅga lāgi' mora ihāṅ āgamana
sarva-prakāre karibe āmāya pālana

SYNONYMS

tomāra—your; *saṅga*—association; *lāgi'*—for the sake of; *mora*—My; *ihāṅ*—here; *āgamana*—arrival; *sarva-prakāre*—in all respects; *karibe*—you will do; *āmāya*—unto Me; *pālana*—maintaining.

TRANSLATION

"I have come here only to associate with you, and I am now taking shelter of you. Will you kindly maintain Me in all respects?

TEXT 61

আজি যে হৈল আমার বড়ই বিপত্তি।
তাহা হৈতে কৈলে তুমি আমার অব্যাহতি ॥" ৬১ ॥

āji ye haila āmāra baḍa-i vipatti
tāhā haite kaile tumi āmāra avyāhati"

SYNONYMS

āji—today; *ye*—that which; *haila*—happened; *āmāra*—My; *baḍa-i*—very great; *vipatti*—obstacle; *tāhā*—that danger; *haite*—from; *kaile*—did; *tumi*—you; *āmāra*—My; *avyāhati*—relief.

TRANSLATION

"The incident that happened today was a great obstacle for Me, but you have kindly relieved Me of it."

TEXT 62

ভট্টাচার্য কহে,—একলে তুমি না যাইহ দর্শনে ।
আমার সঙ্গে যাবে, কিম্বা আমার লোক-সনে ॥ ৬২ ॥

bhaṭṭācārya kahe,——ekale tumi nā yāiha darśane
āmāra saṅge yābe, kimvā āmāra loka-sane

SYNONYMS

bhaṭṭācārya kahe—the Bhaṭṭācārya said; *ekale*—alone; *tumi*—You; *nā*—not; *yāiha*—go; *darśane*—to see the Deity; *āmāra saṅge*—with me; *yābe*—You should go; *kimvā*—or; *āmāra loka-sane*—with my men.

TRANSLATION

The Bhaṭṭācārya replied: "Do not go alone to see the Deity at the Jagannātha Temple. It is better that You go with me or my men."

TEXT 63

প্রভু কহে,—'মন্দির ভিতরে না যাইব ।
গরুড়ের পাশে রহি' দর্শন করিব ॥' ৬৩ ॥

prabhu kahe,——'mandira bhitare nā yāiba
garuḍera pāśe rahi' darśana kariba'

SYNONYMS

prabhu kahe—Śrī Caitanya replied; *mandira*—the temple; *bhitare*—inside; *nā*—never; *yāiba*—I shall go; *garuḍera*—of the column known as the Garuḍa-stambha; *pāśe*—by the side; *rahi'*—staying; *darśana*—seeing; *kariba*—I shall do.

TRANSLATION

The Lord said: "I shall never enter the temple but shall always view the Lord from the side of the Garuḍa-stambha."

TEXT 64

গোপীনাথাচার্যকে কহে সার্বভৌম।
'তুমি গোসাঞিরে লঞা করাইহ দরশন ॥ ৬৪ ॥

gopīnāthācāryake kahe sārvabhauma
'tumi gosāñire lañā karāiha daraśana

SYNONYMS

gopīnātha-ācāryake—to Gopīnātha Ācārya; *kahe*—says; *sārvabhauma*—Sārvabhauma Bhaṭṭācārya; *tumi*—you; *gosāñire*—Lord Caitanya Mahāprabhu; *lañā*—taking; *karāiha*—make Him do; *daraśana*—seeing of Lord Jagannātha.

TRANSLATION

Sārvabhauma Bhaṭṭācārya then told Gopīnātha Ācārya: "Take Gosvāmījī and show Him Lord Jagannātha.

TEXT 65

আমার মাতৃস্বসা-গৃহ—নির্জন স্থান।
তাহাঁ বাসা দেহ, কর সর্ব সমাধান ॥' ৬৫ ॥

āmāra mātṛ-svasā-gṛha——nirjana sthāna
tāhāṅ vāsā deha, kara sarva samādhāna'

SYNONYMS

āmāra—My; *mātṛ-svasā*—of the aunt; *gṛha*—the home; *nirjana sthāna*—very solitary place; *tāhāṅ*—there; *vāsā*—an apartment; *deha*—give; *kara*—make; *sarva*—all; *samādhāna*—arrangements.

TRANSLATION

"Also, the apartment belonging to my maternal aunt is in a very solitary place. Make all arrangements for Him to stay there."

TEXT 66

গোপীনাথ প্রভু লঞা তাহাঁ বাসা দিল।
জল, জলপাত্রাদিক সর্ব সামাধান কৈল ॥ ৬৬ ॥

gopīnātha prabhu lañā tāhāṅ vāsā dila
jala, jala-pātrādika sarva sāmādhāna kaila

SYNONYMS

gopīnātha—Gopīnātha Ācārya; *prabhu*—Lord Caitanya Mahāprabhu; *lañā*—taking; *tāhāṅ*—there; *vāsā*—apartment; *dila*—gave; *jala*—water; *jala-pātra-ādika*—water pots and other vessels; *sarva*—all; *sāmādhāna*—arrangements; *kaila*—made.

TRANSLATION

Thus Gopīnātha Ācārya took Lord Caitanya Mahāprabhu to the residential quarters and showed Him where to find water, tubs and water pots. Indeed, he arranged everything.

TEXT 67

আর দিন গোপীনাথ প্রভু স্থানে গিয়া।
শয্যোত্থান দরশন করাইল লঞা॥ ৬৭ ॥

āra dina gopīnātha prabhu sthāne giyā
śayyotthāna daraśana karāila lañā

SYNONYMS

āra dina—the next day; *gopīnātha*—Gopīnātha Ācārya; *prabhu*—of Lord Caitanya Mahāprabhu; *sthāne*—to the place; *giyā*—going; *śayyā-utthāna*—the rising from bed of Lord Jagannātha; *daraśana*—seeing; *karāila*—caused; *lañā*—taking Him.

TRANSLATION

The next day Gopīnātha Ācārya took Lord Caitanya Mahāprabhu to see the early rising of Lord Jagannātha.

TEXT 68

মুকুন্দদত্ত লঞা আইলা সার্বভৌম স্থানে।
সার্বভৌম কিছু তাঁরে বলিলা বচনে॥ ৬৮ ॥

mukunda-datta lañā āilā sārvabhauma sthāne
sārvabhauma kichu tāṅre balilā vacane

SYNONYMS

mukunda-datta—of the name Mukunda Datta; *lañā*—taking; *āilā*—went; *sārvabhauma*—of Sārvabhauma Bhaṭṭācārya; *sthāne*—to the place; *sārvabhauma*—Sārvabhauma Bhaṭṭācārya; *kichu*—something; *tāṅre*—to Mukunda Datta; *balilā*—said; *vacane*—in words.

TRANSLATION

Gopīnātha Ācārya then took Mukunda Datta with him and went to Sārvabhauma's house. When they arrived, Sārvabhauma addressed Mukunda Datta as follows.

TEXT 69

'প্রকৃতি-বিনীত, সন্ন্যাসী দেখিতে সুন্দর ।
আমার বহুপ্রীতি বাড়ে ইঁহার উপর ॥ ৬৯ ॥

'prakṛti-vinīta, sannyāsī dekhite sundara
āmāra bahu-prīti bāḍe iṅhāra upara

SYNONYMS

prakṛti-vinīta—by nature very humble and meek; *sannyāsī*—renouncer; *dekhite*—to see; *sundara*—very beautiful; *āmāra*—my; *bahu-prīti*—great affection; *bāḍe*—increases; *iṅhāra*—Him; *upara*—upon.

TRANSLATION

"The sannyāsī is very meek and humble by nature, and His person is very beautiful to see. Consequently my affection for Him increases.

PURPORT

Sārvabhauma Bhaṭṭācārya considered Śrī Caitanya Mahāprabhu a very humble and meek person because although Caitanya Mahāprabhu was a *sannyāsī,* He still retained His *brahmacārī* name. The Lord took *sannyāsa* from Keśava Bhāratī in the Bhāratī *sampradāya,* in which the *brahmacārīs* (the assistants of the *sannyāsīs*) are named "Caitanya." Even after accepting *sannyāsa,* Caitanya Mahāprabhu retained the name "Caitanya," meaning a humble servant of a *sannyāsī.* Sārvabhauma Bhaṭṭācārya appreciated this very much.

TEXT 70

কোন্ সম্প্রদায়ে সন্ন্যাস কর্য্যাছেন গ্রহণ ।
কিবা নাম ইঁহার, শুনিতে হয় মন ॥' ৭০ ॥

kon sampradāye sannyāsa karyāchena grahaṇa
kibā nāma iṅhāra, śunite haya mana'

SYNONYMS

kon sampradāye—in which community; *sannyāsa*—the renounced order of life; *karyāchena*—has made; *grahaṇa*—acceptance; *kibā*—what; *nāma*—name; *iṅhāra*—His; *śunite*—to hear; *haya*—it is; *mana*—my mind.

TRANSLATION

"From which sampradāya has He accepted the sannyāsa order, and what is His name?"

TEXT 71

গোপীনাথ কহে,—নাম শ্রীকৃষ্ণচৈতন্য ।
গুরু ইঁহার কেশব-ভারতী মহাধন্য ॥ ৭১ ॥

gopīnātha kahe,——nāma śrī-kṛṣṇa-caitanya
guru iṅhāra keśava-bhāratī mahā-dhanya

SYNONYMS

gopīnātha kahe—Gopīnātha Ācārya replied; *nāma*—His name; *śrī-kṛṣṇa-caitanya*—of the name Śrī Kṛṣṇa Caitanya; *guru—sannyāsa-guru; iṅhāra*—His; *keśava-bhāratī*—of the name Keśava Bhāratī; *mahā-dhanya*—the greatly fortunate personality.

TRANSLATION

Gopīnātha Ācārya replied: "The Lord's name is Śrī Kṛṣṇa Caitanya, and His sannyāsa preceptor is the greatly fortunate Keśava Bhāratī."

TEXT 72

সার্বভৌম কহে,—'ইঁহার নাম সর্বোত্তম ।
ভারতী-সম্প্রদায় ইঁহো—হয়েন মধ্যম ॥' ৭২ ॥

sārvabhauma kahe,——'iṅhāra nāma sarvottama
bhāratī-sampradāya iṅho——hayena madhyama'

SYNONYMS

sārvabhauma kahe—Sārvabhauma Bhaṭṭācārya replied; *iṅhāra*—His; *nāma*—name; *sarva-uttama*—first-class; *bhāratī-sampradāya*—the community of the Bhāratī *sannyāsīs; iṅho*—He; *hayena*—becomes; *madhyama*—middle-class.

TRANSLATION

Sārvabhauma Bhaṭṭācārya said: " 'Śrī Kṛṣṇa' is a very good name, but He belongs to the Bhāratī community. Therefore He is a second-class sannyāsī."

TEXT 73

গোপীনাথ কহে, —ইঁহার নাহি বাহ্যাপেক্ষা ।
অতএব বড় সম্প্রদায়ের নাহিক অপেক্ষা ॥ ৭৩ ॥

gopīnātha kahe,——iṅhāra nāhi bāhyāpekṣā
ataeva baḍa sampradāyera nāhika apekṣā

SYNONYMS

gopīnātha kahe—Gopīnātha Ācārya replied; *iṅhāra*—of the Lord; *nāhi*—there is not; *bāhya-apekṣā*—dependence on any external formality; *ataeva*—therefore; *baḍa*—big; *sampradāyera*—of a community; *nāhika*—there is not; *apekṣā*—necessity.

TRANSLATION

Gopīnātha Ācārya replied: "Śrī Kṛṣṇa Caitanya Mahāprabhu does not rely on any external formality. There is no need for Him to accept the sannyāsa order from a superior sampradāya."

PURPORT

Śrī Caitanya Mahāprabhu accepted *sannyāsa* from the Bhāratī *sampradāya* (community), which belongs to the disciplic succession of Śaṅkarācārya. Śaṅkarācārya introduced names for his *sannyāsa* disciples, and these are ten in number. Out of these, the surnames Tīrtha, Āśrama and Sarasvatī are considered topmost. In the monastery at Śṛṅgerī, the surname Sarasvatī is considered first class, Bhāratī second class and Purī third class. A *sannyāsī* who has very nicely understood the slogan *tat tvam asi* and who takes his bath at the confluence of the rivers Ganges, Yamunā and Sarasvatī is called a Tīrtha. A person who is very eager to accept *sannyāsa,* who is detached from worldly activities, who has no desire for any kind of material facilities and who is thus saved from repeated birth and death is known as Āśrama. When a *sannyāsī* lives in a beautiful, solitary place in the forest and is freed from all material desires, he is called Vana. A *sannyāsī* who always lives in the forest and renounces all connection with the world in order to be elevated to the heavenly planets, where he can live in the *nandana-kānana,* is called Araṇya. One who prefers living in the mountains engaging in the study of *Bhagavad-gītā* and whose intelligence is fixed is called Giri. One who prefers living in great mountains, even among ferocious animals, to attain the summit of philosophical speculation (understanding that the essence of this material world is useless) is called Parvata. A *sannyāsī* who has dipped into the ocean of the Absolute Truth and collected some valuable stones of knowledge from that ocean, who never falls from the regulative principles of a *sannyāsī,* is called Sāgara. One who has learned the classical art of music, who engages in its culture and who has become expert and completely aloof from material attachment is called Sarasvatī. Sarasvatī is the goddess of music and learning, and in one hand she holds a musical instrument called a *vīṇā.* A *sannyāsī* who is always engaged in music for spiritual elevation is called Sarasvatī. One who has become completely educated and is freed from all kinds of ignorance and who is never unhappy, even in a distressed condition, is called Bhāratī. One who has become very expert in absolute knowledge, who is situated in the Absolute Truth and who always discusses the Absolute Truth is called Purī.

All these *sannyāsīs* are assisted by *brahmacārīs,* who are described as follows: One who knows his real identity and is fixed in his particular occupational duty, who is always happy in spiritual understanding, is called Svarūpa-brahmacārī. One who completely knows the Brahman effulgence and is always engaged in the practice of *yoga* is called Prakāśa-brahmacārī. One who has acquired absolute knowledge and who always meditates on the Absolute Truth, knowledge, the unlimited and the Brahman effulgence, thus keeping himself in transcendental bliss, is called Ānanda-brahmacārī. One who is able to distinguish between matter and spirit, who is never disturbed by material transformations and who meditates on the unlimited, inexhaustible, auspicious Brahman effulgence is a first-class, learned *brahmacārī* and is named Caitanya.

When Sārvabhauma Bhaṭṭācārya was talking with Gopīnātha Ācārya about Śrī Caitanya Mahāprabhu's *sannyāsa* community, he appreciated the first name, "Śrī Kṛṣṇa," but did not like the surname "Caitanya," which is the name for a *brahmacārī* belonging to the Bhāratī community. He therefore suggested that the Lord be elevated to the Sarasvatī community. However, Gopīnātha Ācārya pointed out that the Lord does not depend on any external formality. Gopīnātha Ācārya was firmly convinced that Śrī Caitanya Mahāprabhu was Kṛṣṇa Himself and therefore independent of any external ritual or formality. If one wants to engage in pure devotional service, he does not require titular superiority as a Bhāratī or a Sarasvatī.

TEXT 74

ভট্টাচার্য কহে,—'ইঁহার প্রৌঢ় যৌবন ।
কেমতে সন্ন্যাস-ধর্ম হইবে রক্ষণ ॥ ৭৪ ॥

bhaṭṭācārya kahe,——'iṅhāra prauḍha yauvana
kemate sannyāsa-dharma ha-ibe rakṣaṇa

SYNONYMS

bhaṭṭācārya kahe—Sārvabhauma Bhaṭṭācārya replied; *iṅhāra*—His; *prauḍha*—full; *yauvana*—youth; *kemate*—how; *sannyāsa-dharma*—principles of a *sannyāsī; ha-ibe*—there will be; *rakṣaṇa*—protection.

TRANSLATION

The Bhaṭṭācārya inquired: "Śrī Caitanya Mahāprabhu is in His full-fledged youthful life. How can He keep the principles of sannyāsa?

TEXT 75

নিরন্তর ইঁহাকে বেদান্ত শুনাইব ।
বৈরাগ্য-অদ্বৈত-মার্গে প্রবেশ করাইব ॥ ৭৫ ॥

nirantara iṅhāke vedānta śunāiba
vairāgya-advaita-mārge praveśa karāiba

SYNONYMS

nirantara—continuously; *iṅhāke*—to Him; *vedānta*—the Vedānta philosophy; *śunāiba*—I shall recite; *vairāgya*—of renunciation; *advaita*—of monism; *mārge*—on the path; *praveśa*—entrance; *karāiba*—I shall cause Him to make.

TRANSLATION

"I shall continuously recite the Vedānta philosophy before Caitanya Mahāprabhu so that He may remain fixed in His renunciation and thus enter upon the path of monism."

PURPORT

According to Sārvabhauma Bhaṭṭācārya, among *sannyāsīs* the cultivation of Vedānta philosophy helps in becoming detached from sense gratification. Thus a *sannyāsī* can protect the prestige of wearing a loincloth (*kaupīna*). One has to practice sense control as well as mind control and subdue the six forces of speech, mind, anger, tongue, belly and genitals. Then one can become expert in understanding the devotional service of the Lord and thus become a perfect *sannyāsī.* For that purpose one must cultivate knowledge and renunciation regularly. When one is attached to material sense gratification, he cannot protect his *sannyāsa* order. Sārvabhauma Bhaṭṭācārya suggested that by the study of *vairāgya* (renunciation), Śrī Caitanya Mahāprabhu might be saved from the clutches of full-fledged youthful desires.

TEXT 76

কহেন যদি, পুনরপি যোগ-পট্ট দিয়া ।
সংস্কার করিয়ে উত্তম-সম্প্রদায়ে আনিয়া ॥' ৭৬ ॥

kahena yadi, punarapi yoga-paṭṭa diyā
saṁskāra kariye uttama-sampradāye āniyā'

SYNONYMS

kahena—says; *yadi*—if; *punarapi*—again; *yoga-paṭṭa diyā*—offering Him saffron cloth; *saṁskāra*—reformatory process; *kariye*—I perform; *uttama*—first-class; *sampradāye*—to the community; *āniyā*—bringing.

TRANSLATION

Sārvabhauma Bhaṭṭācārya then suggested: "If Śrī Caitanya Mahāprabhu would like, I could bring Him into a first-class sampradāya by offering Him saffron cloth and performing the reformatory process again."

PURPORT

The Bhaṭṭācārya wanted to reinstate Śrī Caitanya Mahāprabhu into the Sarasvatī *sampradāya* because he did not like the Lord's belonging to the Bhāratī *sampradāya* or Purī *sampradāya*. Actually, he did not know the position of Lord Caitanya Mahāprabhu. As the Supreme Personality of Godhead, Caitanya Mahāprabhu did not depend on an inferior or superior *sampradāya*. The Supreme Personality of Godhead remains in the supreme position in all circumstances.

TEXT 77

শুনি' গোপীনাথ-মুকুন্দ দুঁহে দুঃখা হৈলা ।
গোপীনাথাচার্য কিছু কহিতে লাগিলা ॥ ৭৭ ॥

śuni' gopīnātha-mukunda duṅhe duḥkhā hailā
gopīnāthācārya kichu kahite lāgilā

SYNONYMS

śuni'—hearing; *gopīnātha-mukunda*—Gopīnātha Ācārya and Mukunda Datta; *duṅhe*—both; *duḥkhā*—unhappy; *hailā*—became; *gopīnātha-ācārya*—of the name Gopīnātha Ācārya; *kichu*—something; *kahite*—to speak; *lāgilā*—began.

TRANSLATION

Gopīnātha Ācārya and Mukunda Datta became very unhappy when they heard this. Gopīnātha Ācārya therefore addressed Sārvabhauma Bhaṭṭācārya as follows.

TEXT 78

'ভট্টাচার্য' তুমি ইঁহার না জান মহিমা ।
ভগবত্তা-লক্ষণের ইঁহাতেই সীমা ॥ ৭৮ ॥

'bhaṭṭācārya' tumi iṅhāra nā jāna mahimā
bhagavattā-lakṣaṇera iṅhātei sīmā

SYNONYMS

bhaṭṭācārya—my dear Bhaṭṭācārya; *tumi*—you; *iṅhāra*—of Lord Caitanya Mahāprabhu; *nā*—not; *jāna*—know; *mahimā*—the greatness; *bhagavattā*—of being the Supreme Personality of Godhead; *lakṣaṇera*—of symptoms; *iṅhātei*—in Him; *sīmā*—the highest degree.

TRANSLATION

"My dear Bhaṭṭācārya, you do not know the greatness of Lord Caitanya Mahāprabhu. All the symptoms of the Supreme Personality of Godhead are found in Him to the highest degree."

PURPORT

Since the Bhaṭṭācārya was an impersonalist, he had no idea of the Absolute Truth beyond the impersonal effulgence. However, Gopīnātha Ācārya informed him that Caitanya Mahāprabhu was the Supreme Personality of Godhead. Those who know the Absolute Truth know it in three phases, as explained in *Śrīmad-Bhāgavatam:*

vadanti tat tattva-vidas
tattvaṁ yaj jñānam advayam
brahmeti paramātmeti
bhagavān iti śabdyate

"Those who are in knowledge of the nondual Absolute Truth know very clearly what is Brahman, what is Paramātmā and what is the Supreme Personality of Godhead." (*Bhāg.* 1.2.11) The Supreme Personality of Godhead is *ṣaḍ-aiśvarya-pūrṇa,* complete with six opulences. Gopīnatha Ācārya emphasized that all those six opulences were completely existing in Śrī Caitanya Mahāprabhu.

TEXT 79

তাহাতে বিখ্যাত ইঁহো পরম-ঈশ্বর ।
অজ্ঞ-স্থানে কিছু নহে বিজ্ঞের গোচর ॥' ৭৯ ॥

tāhāte vikhyāta iṅho parama-īśvara
ajña-sthāne kichu nahe vijñera gocara'

SYNONYMS

tāhāte—therefore; *vikhyāta*—celebrated; *iṅho*—Lord Caitanya Mahāprabhu; *parama-īśvara*—the Supreme Personality of Godhead; *ajña-sthāne*—before an ignorant person; *kichu*—any; *nahe*—not; *vijñera*—of the person who knows; *gocara*—information.

TRANSLATION

Gopīnātha Ācārya continued: "Lord Caitanya Mahāprabhu is celebrated as the Supreme Personality of Godhead. Those who are ignorant in this connection find the conclusion of knowledgeable men very difficult to understand."

TEXT 80

শিষ্যগণ কহে,—'ঈশ্বর কহ কোন্ প্রমাণে' ।
আচার্য কহে,—'বিজ্ঞমত ঈশ্বর-লক্ষণে' ॥ ৮০ ॥

śiṣya-gaṇa kahe,——'īśvara kaha kon pramāṇe'
ācārya kahe,——'vijña-mata īśvara-lakṣaṇe'

SYNONYMS

śiṣya-gaṇa kahe—the disciples of Sārvabhauma Bhaṭṭācārya said; *īśvara kaha*—you say the Supreme Personality of Godhead; *kon pramāṇe*—by what evidence; *ācārya kahe*—Gopīnātha Ācārya replied; *vijña-mata*—statements of authorized persons; *īśvara-lakṣaṇe*—in understanding the Supreme Personality of Godhead.

TRANSLATION

The disciples of Sārvabhauma Bhaṭṭācārya retaliated: "By what evidence do you conclude that Śrī Caitanya Mahāprabhu is the Supreme Lord?" Gopīnātha Ācārya replied: "The statements of authorized ācāryas who understand the Supreme Personality of Godhead are proof."

PURPORT

Since the appearance of Śrī Caitanya Mahāprabhu, there have been many pseudo incarnations in India who do not present authorized evidence. Five hundred years ago the disciples of Sārvabhauma Bhaṭṭācārya, being very learned scholars, were certainly right in asking Gopīnātha Ācārya for evidence. If a person proposes that he himself is God or that someone else is an incarnation of God or God Himself, he must cite evidence from *śāstra* to prove his claim. Thus the request of the Bhaṭṭācārya's disciples is quite bona fide. Unfortunately, at the present moment it has become fashionable to present an incarnation of God without referring to the *śāstras.* Before an intelligent person accepts someone as an incarnation of God, however, he must ask about the evidence. When the disciples of Sārvabhauma Bhaṭṭācārya challenged Gopīnātha Ācārya, he immediately replied correctly: "We must hear the statements of great personalities in order to understand the Supreme Personality of Godhead." Lord Kṛṣṇa is established as the Supreme Personality of Godhead by statements from authorized persons like

Brahmā, Nārada, Vyāsadeva, Asita, Arjuna and many others. Similarly, Śrī Caitanya Mahāprabhu is also established as the Supreme Personality of Godhead by evidence from the same personalities. This will be explained later.

TEXT 81

শিষ্য কহে,– 'ঈশ্বর-তত্ত্ব সাধি অনুমানে'।
আচার্য কহে,—'অনুমানে নহে ঈশ্বরজ্ঞানে ॥ ৮১ ॥

śiṣya kahe,——'īśvara-tattva sādhi anumāne'
ācārya kahe,——'anumāne nahe īśvara-jñāne

SYNONYMS

śiṣya kahe—the disciples said; *īśvara-tattva*—the truth of the Absolute; *sādhi*—derive; *anumāne*—by hypothesis; *ācārya kahe*—Gopīnātha Ācārya replied; *anumāne*—by hypothesis; *nahe*—there is not; *īśvara-jñāne*—real knowledge of the Supreme Personality of Godhead.

TRANSLATION

The disciples of the Bhaṭṭācārya said: "We derive knowledge of the Absolute Truth by logical hypothesis." Gopīnātha Ācārya replied: "One cannot attain real knowledge of the Supreme Personality of Godhead by such logical hypothesis and argument."

PURPORT

The Māyāvādī philosophers in particular make certain hypotheses about the Absolute Truth. They reason that in the material world we experience that everything is created. If we trace the history of anything, we find a creator. Therefore there must be a creator of this huge cosmic manifestation. By such reasoning they come to the conclusion that a higher power has created this cosmic manifestation. The Māyāvādīs do not accept that great power to be a person. Their brains cannot accommodate the fact that this huge cosmic manifestation can be created by a person. This is because as soon as they think of a person, they think of a person within the material world with limited potency. Sometimes the Māyāvādī philosophers will accept Lord Kṛṣṇa or Lord Rāma as Bhagavān, but they think of the Lord as a person having a material body. The Māyāvādīs do not understand that the Supreme Personality of Godhead, Kṛṣṇa, has a spiritual body. They think of Kṛṣṇa as a great personality, a human being, within whom there is the supreme impersonal power, Brahman. Therefore they finally conclude that the impersonal Brahman is the Supreme, not the personality Kṛṣṇa. This is the basis of Māyāvādī philosophy. However, from the *śāstras* we can understand that the Brahman effulgence is the bodily rays of Kṛṣṇa:

yasya prabhā prabhavato jagad-aṇḍa-koṭi-
koṭiṣv aśeṣa-vasudhādi vibhūti-bhinnam
tad brahma niṣkalam anantam aśeṣa-bhūtaṁ
govindam ādi-puruṣaṁ tam ahaṁ bhajāmi

"I serve the Supreme Personality of Godhead, Govinda, the primeval Lord, the effulgence of whose transcendental body is known as the *brahmajyoti.* That *brahmajyoti,* which is unlimited, unfathomed and all-pervasive, is the cause of the creation of unlimited numbers of planets with varieties of climates and specific conditions of life." (*Brahma-saṁhitā* 5.40)

Māyāvādī philosophers study the Vedic literature, but they do not understand that the Absolute Truth in the last stage of realization is the Supreme Personality of Godhead, Kṛṣṇa. They do accept the fact that there is a creator of this cosmic manifestation, but that is *anumāna* (hypothesis). The Māyāvādī philosopher's logic is something like seeing smoke on a hill. When there is a forest fire on a high hill, smoke is first of all visible. The smoke is created when there is fire. Just as one can conclude that there is fire from smoke, the Māyāvādī philosophers conclude that there must be a creator of the cosmic manifestation.

The disciples of Sārvabhauma Bhaṭṭācārya wanted evidence to show that Śrī Caitanya Mahāprabhu was actually the creator of the cosmic manifestation. Only then would they accept Him as the Supreme Personality of Godhead, the original cause of creation. Gopīnātha Ācārya replied that one could not understand the Supreme Personality of Godhead by guesswork. As Kṛṣṇa says in *Bhagavad-gītā:*

nāhaṁ prakāśaḥ sarvasya
yoga-māyā-samāvṛtaḥ
mūḍho 'yaṁ nābhijānāti
loko mām ajam avyayam

"I am never manifest to the foolish and unintelligent. For them I am covered by My eternal creative potency [*yogamāyā*]; and so the deluded world knows Me not, who am unborn and infallible." (Bg. 7.25) The Supreme Personality of Godhead reserves the right of not being exposed to nondevotees. He can only be understood by bona fide devotees. Lord Kṛṣṇa says elsewhere in *Bhagavad-gītā, bhaktyā mām abhijānāti:* "One can understand Me only by the devotional process." (Bg. 18.55) In the Fourth Chapter of *Bhagavad-gītā* Lord Kṛṣṇa says, *bhakto 'si me sakhā ceti rahasyaṁ hy etad uttamam.* Here Lord Kṛṣṇa informs Arjuna that He is disclosing the secrets of *Bhagavad-gītā* to him because he is His devotee. Arjuna was not a *sannyāsī,* nor was he a Vedāntist or *brāhmaṇa.* He was, however, a devotee of Kṛṣṇa. The conclusion is that we have to understand the Supreme Personality of Godhead from the devotees. Śrī Caitanya Mahāprabhu Himself says, *guru-kṛṣṇa-prasāde pāya bhakti-latā-bīja.* (Cc. *Madhya* 19.151)

More evidence can be cited to show that without the mercy of a devotee or the mercy of Kṛṣṇa, one cannot understand what is Kṛṣṇa and what is the Supreme Personality of Godhead. This is confirmed in the next verse.

TEXT 82

অনুমান প্রমাণ নহে ঈশ্বরতত্ত্বজ্ঞানে ।
কৃপা বিনা ঈশ্বরেরে কেহ নাহি জানে ॥ ৮২ ॥

anumāna pramāṇa nahe īśvara-tattva-jñāne
kṛpā vinā īśvarere keha nāhi jāne

SYNONYMS

anumāna pramāṇa—evidence by hypothesis; *nahe*—there is not; *īśvara-tattva-jñāne*—in understanding the Absolute Truth, the Supreme Personality of Godhead; *kṛpā vinā*—without His mercy; *īśvarere*—the Supreme Personality of Godhead; *keha*—anyone; *nāhi*—not; *jāne*—knows.

TRANSLATION

Gopīnātha Ācārya continued: "One can understand the Supreme Personality of Godhead only by His mercy, not by guesswork or hypothesis."

PURPORT

One cannot understand the Supreme Personality of Godhead simply by exhibiting some mundane magic. Foolish people are enchanted by magical demonstrations, and when they see a few wonderful things done by mystical power, they accept a magician as the Personality of Godhead or an incarnation. This is not the way of realization. Nor should one guess or speculate about an incarnation of God or the Personality of Godhead. One has to learn from the bona fide person or from the Supreme Personality of Godhead Himself, as Arjuna did, by the mercy of Kṛṣṇa. Kṛṣṇa Himself also gives many hints about His potencies as the Supreme Personality of Godhead. One should understand the Supreme Personality of Godhead only through the evidence presented by the *śāstras* and the *mahājanas*. In any case, one must have the mercy of the Lord in order to understand the Supreme Personality of Godhead by devotional service.

TEXT 83

ঈশ্বরের কৃপা-লেশ হয় ত' যাহারে ।
সেই ত' ঈশ্বর-তত্ত্ব জানিবারে পারে ॥ ৮৩ ॥

īśvarera kṛpā-leśa haya ta' yāhāre
sei ta' īśvara-tattva jānibāre pāre

SYNONYMS

īśvarera—of the Personality of Godhead; *kṛpā-leśa*—a little mercy; *haya*—there is; *ta'*—certainly; *yāhāre*—upon whom; *sei ta'*—he certainly; *īśvara-tattva*—the Absolute Truth; *jānibāre*—to know; *pāre*—is able.

TRANSLATION

The Ācārya continued: "If one receives but a tiny bit of the Lord's favor by dint of devotional service, he can understand the nature of the Supreme Personality of Godhead.

TEXT 84

অথাপি তে দেব পদাম্বুজদ্বয়-
প্রসাদ-লেশানুগৃহীত এব হি ।
জানাতি তত্ত্বং ভগবন্মহিম্নো
ন চান্য একোঽপি চিরং বিচিন্বন্ ॥ ৮৪ ॥

athāpi te deva padāmbuja-dvaya-
prasāda-leśānugṛhīta eva hi
jānāti tattvaṁ bhagavan-mahimno
na cānya eko 'pi ciraṁ vicinvan

SYNONYMS

atha—therefore; *api*—indeed; *te*—Your; *deva*—my Lord; *pada-ambuja-dvaya*—of the two lotus feet; *prasāda*—of the mercy; *leśa*—by only a trace; *anugṛhītaḥ*—favored; *eva*—certainly; *hi*—indeed; *jānāti*—one knows; *tattvam*—the truth; *bhagavat*—of the Supreme Personality of Godhead; *mahimnaḥ*—of the greatness; *na*—never; *ca*—and; *anyaḥ*—another; *ekaḥ*—one; *api*—although; *ciram*—for a long period; *vicinvan*—speculating.

TRANSLATION

" 'My Lord, if one is favored by even a slight trace of the mercy of Your lotus feet, he can understand the greatness of Your personality. But those who speculate in order to understand the Supreme Personality of Godhead are unable to know You, even though they continue to study the Vedas for many years.' "

PURPORT

The above verse is from *Śrīmad-Bhāgavatam* (10.14.29). The *Brahma-saṁhitā* states, *vedeṣu durlabham adurlabham ātma-bhaktau* (Bs. 5.33). Although the Supreme Personality of Godhead, Kṛṣṇa, is the ultimate goal of knowledge (*vedaiś ca sarvair aham eva vedyaḥ*), one who is not a pure devotee and who is not engaged in the service of the Lord cannot understand Him. Lord Brahmā therefore confirms this. *Vedeṣu durlabham:* "It is very difficult to understand the Supreme Lord simply through one's studies." *Adurlabham ātma-bhaktau:* "However, it is very easy for the devotees to capture the Lord." The Lord is known as *ajita* (unconquerable). No one can conquer the Supreme Personality of Godhead, but the Lord consents to be conquered by His devotees. That is His nature. As stated in the *Padma Purāṇa:*

ataḥ śrī-kṛṣṇa-nāmādi
na bhaved grahyam indriyaiḥ
sevonmukhe hi jihvādau
svayam eva sphuraty adaḥ

Being pleased by devotional activities, the Lord reveals Himself to His devotees. That is the way to understand Him.

The verse from *Śrīmad-Bhāgavatam* quoted by Gopīnātha Ācārya was originally spoken by Lord Brahmā when he was defeated by Lord Kṛṣṇa. Lord Brahmā had stolen all the calves and cowherd boys in order to test Kṛṣṇa's power. Lord Brahmā admitted that his own extraordinary powers within the universe were not in the least comparable to the unlimited powers of Lord Kṛṣṇa. If Lord Brahmā can make a mistake in understanding Kṛṣṇa, what to speak of ordinary persons, who either misunderstand Kṛṣṇa or falsely present a so-called incarnation of Kṛṣṇa for their own sense gratification.

TEXTS 85-86

যদ্যপি জগদ্‌গুরু তুমি – শাস্ত্র-জ্ঞানবান্ ।
পৃথিবীতে নাহি পণ্ডিত তোমার সমান ॥ ৮৫ ॥
ঈশ্বরের কৃপা-লেশ নাহিক তোমাতে ।
অতএব ঈশ্বরতত্ত্ব না পার জানিতে ॥ ৮৬ ॥

yadyapi jagad-guru tumi——śāstra-jñānavān
pṛthivīte nāhi paṇḍita tomāra samāna

īśvarera kṛpā-leśa nāhika tomāte
ataeva īśvara-tattva nā pāra jānite

SYNONYMS

yadyapi—although; *jagat-guru*—a teacher of many disciples; *tumi*—you; *śāstra-jñānavān*—well versed in Vedic knowledge; *pṛthivīte*—on this earth; *nāhi*—there is not; *paṇḍita*—a learned scholar; *tomāra*—your; *samāna*—equal; *īśvarera*—of the Supreme Personality of Godhead; *kṛpā*—of mercy; *leśa*—a bit; *nāhika*—there is not; *tomāte*—on you; *ataeva*—therefore; *īśvara-tattva*—the Absolute Truth (the Supreme Personality of Godhead); *nā pāra*—are not able; *jānite*—to know.

TRANSLATION

Gopīnātha Ācārya then addressed Sārvabhauma Bhaṭṭācārya: "You are a great scholar and a teacher of many disciples. Indeed, there is no other scholar like you on earth. Nonetheless, because you are bereft of even a pinch of the Lord's mercy, you cannot understand Him, even though He is present in your home.

TEXT 87

তোমার নাহিক দোষ, শাস্ত্রে এই কহে ।
পাণ্ডিত্যাদ্যে ঈশ্বরতত্ত্ব-জ্ঞান কভু নহে ॥' ৮৭ ॥

tomāra nāhika doṣa, śāstre ei kahe
pāṇḍityādye īśvara-tattva-jñāna kabhu nahe'

SYNONYMS

tomāra—your; *nāhika*—there is not; *doṣa*—fault; *śāstre*—the scriptures; *ei*—this; *kahe*—mention; *pāṇḍitya-ādye*—simply by scholarship, etc.; *īśvara-tattva-jñāna*—knowledge of the principles of the Supreme Personality of Godhead; *kabhu*—ever; *nahe*—there is not.

TRANSLATION

"It is not your fault; it is the verdict of the scriptures. You cannot understand the Supreme Personality of Godhead simply by scholarship."

PURPORT

This is a very important verse. Even big scholars cannot understand Kṛṣṇa, yet they dare comment on *Bhagavad-gītā*. Reading *Bhagavad-gītā* means understanding Kṛṣṇa, yet we actually see many scholars making blunders in trying to understand Kṛṣṇa. Gopīnātha Ācārya's statement is confirmed in many places in Vedic literature. In *Kaṭha Upaniṣad* it is stated (*Kaṭha Up.* 1.2.23):

nāyam ātmā pravacanena labhyo
na medhayā na bahunā śrutena
yam evaiṣa vṛṇute tena labhyas
tasyaiṣa ātmā vivṛṇute tanūṁ svām

It is also stated in *Kaṭha Upaniṣad* (1.2.9):

naiṣā tarkeṇa matir āpaneyā
proktānyenaiva sujñānāya preṣṭha
yāṁ tvam āpaḥ satya-dhṛtir vatāsi
tvādṛṅ no bhūyānn aciketaḥ praṣṭā

The fact is that the Supreme Personality of Godhead, the Supersoul, cannot be attained simply by explanations, logic and erudite scholarship. One cannot understand Him simply by one's brain substance. Even by studying all Vedic literature, one cannot understand the Supreme Lord. However, if one is slightly favored by the mercy of the Lord, if the Lord is pleased, one can understand Him. But who are the candidates eligible to receive the mercy of the Lord? Only the devotees. They alone can understand what is the Supreme Personality of Godhead. The Lord reveals Himself to the sincere devotee when He is pleased with his service: *svayam eva sphuraty adaḥ*. One should not try to understand the Lord simply from the statements of the *Vedas,* nor should one uselessly attempt to decry these statements through reasoning and logic.

TEXT 88

সার্বভৌম কহে,— আচার্য, কহ সাবধানে।
তোমাতে ঈশ্বর-কৃপা ইথে কি প্রমাণে ॥ ৮৮ ॥

sārvabhauma kahe,——ācārya, kaha sāvadhāne
tomāte īśvara-kṛpā ithe ki pramāṇe

SYNONYMS

sārvabhauma kahe—Sārvabhauma Bhaṭṭācārya says; *ācārya*—my dear Gopīnātha Ācārya; *kaha*—kindly speak; *sāvadhāne*—very carefully; *tomāte*—unto you; *īśvara-kṛpā*—mercy of the Lord; *ithe*—in this matter; *ki pramāṇe*—by what evidence.

TRANSLATION

Sārvabhauma Bhaṭṭācārya replied: "My dear Gopīnātha Ācārya, please speak with great care. What is the proof that you have received the mercy of the Lord?"

TEXT 89

আচার্য কহে,—"বস্তু-বিষয়ে হয় বস্তু-জ্ঞান।
বস্তুতত্ত্ব-জ্ঞান হয় কৃপাতে প্রমাণ ॥ ৮৯ ॥

ācārya kahe,——"vastu-viṣaye haya vastu-jñāna
vastu-tattva-jñāna haya kṛpāte pramāṇa

SYNONYMS

ācārya kahe—Gopīnātha Ācārya replied; *vastu-viṣaye*—in the matter of the *summum bonum; haya*—there is; *vastu-jñāna*—knowledge of the Supreme; *vastu-tattva*—of the Absolute Truth; *jñāna*—knowledge; *haya*—is; *kṛpāte*—of the mercy; *pramāṇa*—the evidence.

TRANSLATION

Gopīnātha Ācārya replied: "Knowledge of the summum bonum, the Absolute Truth, is evidence of the mercy of the Supreme Lord."

PURPORT

Sārvabhauma Bhaṭṭācārya informed his brother-in-law, Gopīnātha Ācārya, "The Supreme Personality of Godhead may not have shown mercy to me, but what is the proof of His having shown it to you? Kindly let us know about this." In reply to this, Gopīnātha Ācārya said that the *summum bonum,* the Absolute Truth, and His different potencies are identical. Therefore one can understand the substance of the Absolute Truth by the manifestation of His different potencies. The *summum bonum* includes all potencies in one unit. The Absolute Truth combined with different characteristics is the original substance (*vastu*): *parāsya śaktir vividhaiva śrūyate.*

Thus the *Vedas* state that the Absolute Truth has different potencies. When one understands the characteristics of the potencies of the Absolute Truth, one is aware of the Absolute Truth. On the material platform as well, one can understand the substance by the manifestation of its symptoms. For example, when there is heat, it is to be understood that there is fire. The heat of the fire is perceived directly. The fire may not be visible, but one can search out the fire by feeling heat. Similarly, if one can perceive the characteristics of the Absolute Truth, we can know that he has understood the substance of the Absolute Truth by the mercy of the Lord.

In *Bhagavad-gītā* (7.25) it is said, *nāhaṁ prakāśaḥ sarvasya.* The Supreme Personality of Godhead reserves the right of not being exposed to everyone. *Sevonmukhe hi jihvādau svayam eva sphuraty adaḥ:* "The Lord reveals Himself to a devotee when He is completely satisfied by the devotee's service." Thus one cannot understand the Supreme Lord without His mercy. The Absolute Truth cannot be understood by speculation, and this is the conclusion of *Bhagavad-gītā*.

TEXT 90

ইঁহার শরীরে সব ঈশ্বর-লক্ষণ ।
মহা-প্রেমাবেশ তুমি পাঞাছ দর্শন ॥ ৯০ ॥

iṅhāra śarīre saba īśvara-lakṣaṇa
mahā-premāveśa tumi pāñācha darśana

SYNONYMS

iṅhara—His; *śarīre*—in the body; *saba*—all; *īśvara-lakṣaṇa*—characteristics of the Supreme Personality of Godhead; *mahā-prema-āveśa*—absorption in transcendental ecstasy; *tumi*—you; *pāñācha*—have obtained; *darśana*—seeing.

TRANSLATION

Gopīnātha Ācārya continued: "You have seen the symptoms of the Supreme Personality of Godhead in the body of Śrī Caitanya Mahāprabhu during His absorption in an ecstatic mood.

TEXT 91

তবু ত' ঈশ্বর-জ্ঞান না হয় তোমার ।
ঈশ্বরের মায়া এই—বলি ব্যবহার ॥ ৯১ ॥

tabu ta' īśvara-jñāna nā haya tomāra
īśvarera māyā ei——bali vyavahāra

SYNONYMS

tabu ta'—still, however; *īśvara-jñāna*—knowledge of the Supreme Personality of Godhead; *nā*—not; *haya*—there is; *tomāra*—your; *īśvarera*—of the Lord; *māyā*—the illusion; *ei*—this; *bali*—saying; *vyavahāra*—the general term.

TRANSLATION

"Despite directly perceiving the symptoms of the Supreme Lord in the body of Śrī Caitanya Mahāprabhu, you cannot understand Him. This is commonly called illusion.

PURPORT

Gopīnātha Ācārya is pointing out that Sārvabhauma Bhaṭṭācārya had already seen uncommon symptoms of ecstasy in the body of Śrī Caitanya Mahāprabhu.

These uncommon symptoms of ecstatic love indicated the Supreme Person, but despite having seen all these symptoms, the Bhaṭṭācārya could not understand the Lord's transcendental nature. He was considering the Lord's pastimes to be mundane. This was certainly due to illusion.

TEXT 92

দেখিলে না দেখে তারে বহির্মুখ জন।"
শুনি' হাসি' সার্বভৌম বলিল বচন ॥ ৯২ ॥

dekhile nā dekhe tāre bahirmukha jana"
śuni' hāsi' sārvabhauma balila vacana

SYNONYMS

dekhile—even after seeing; *nā*—not; *dekhe*—sees; *tāre*—the Supreme Person; *bahiḥ-mukha jana*—a person influenced by the external energy; *śuni'*—hearing this; *hāsi'*—smiling; *sārvabhauma*—Sārvabhauma Bhaṭṭācārya; *balila*—said; *vacana*—the words.

TRANSLATION

"A person influenced by the external energy is called bahirmukha jana, a mundane person, because despite his perception, he cannot understand the real substance." Hearing Gopīnātha Ācārya say this, Sārvabhauma Bhaṭṭācārya smiled and began to speak as follows.

PURPORT

When one's heart is not cleansed, one cannot awaken the transcendental nature of devotional service. As confirmed in *Bhagavad-gītā:*

yeṣāṁ tv anta-gataṁ pāpaṁ
janānāṁ puṇya-karmaṇām
te dvandva-moha-nirmuktā
bhajante māṁ dṛḍha-vratāḥ

"Persons who have acted piously in previous lives and in this life, whose sinful actions are completely eradicated and who are freed from the duality of delusion engage themselves in My service with determination." (Bg. 7.28)

When one is actually engaged in pure devotional service, it is understood that he has already attained freedom from all reactions to sinful activities. In other words, it is to be understood that devotees are already freed from sin. A sinful person, a miscreant (*duṣkṛti*), cannot engage in devotional service. Nor can one engage in devotional service simply on the basis of scholarly speculation. One has to wait for the mercy of the Lord in order to render pure devotional service.

TEXT 93

ইষ্টগোষ্ঠী বিচার করি, না করিহ রোষ।
শাস্ত্রদৃষ্ট্যে কহি, কিছু না লইহ দোষ ॥ ৯৩ ॥

iṣṭa-goṣṭhī vicāra kari, nā kariha roṣa
śāstra-dṛṣṭye kahi, kichu nā la-iha doṣa

SYNONYMS

iṣṭa-goṣṭhī—discussion among friends; *vicāra*—consideration; *kari*—we do; *nā*—not; *kariha*—make; *roṣa*—anger; *śāstra-dṛṣṭye*—according to the conclusion of scriptures; *kahi*—we speak; *kichu*—any; *nā*—not; *la-iha*—take; *doṣa*—fault.

TRANSLATION

The Bhaṭṭācārya said: "We are just having a discussion among friends and considering the points described in the scriptures. Do not become angry. I am simply speaking on the strength of the śāstras. Please don't take any offense.

TEXT 94

মহা-ভাগবত হয় চৈতন্য-গোসাঞি।
এই কলিকালে বিষ্ণুর অবতার নাই ॥ ৯৪ ॥

mahā-bhāgavata haya caitanya-gosāñi
ei kali-kāle viṣṇura avatāra nāi

SYNONYMS

mahā-bhāgavata—a great devotee; *haya*—is; *caitanya-gosāñi*—Lord Śrī Caitanya Mahāprabhu; *ei*—this; *kali-kāle*—in the age of Kali; *viṣṇura*—of Lord Viṣṇu; *avatāra*—incarnation; *nāi*—there is not.

TRANSLATION

"Śrī Caitanya Mahāprabhu is certainly a great, uncommon devotee, but we cannot accept Him as an incarnation of Lord Viṣṇu because, according to śāstra, there is no incarnation in this age of Kali.

TEXT 95

অতএব 'ত্রিযুগ' করি' কহি বিষ্ণু-নাম ।
কলিযুগে অবতার নাহি,—শাস্ত্রজ্ঞান ॥ ৯৫ ॥

ataeva 'tri-yuga' kari' kahi viṣṇu-nāma
kali-yuge avatāra nāhi,——śāstra-jñāna

SYNONYMS

ataeva—therefore; *tri-yuga*—the Lord, who appears in three *yugas* only; *kari'*—making; *kahi*—we say; *viṣṇu-nāma*—the holy name of Lord Viṣṇu; *kali-yuge*—in the age of Kali; *avatāra*—incarnation; *nāhi*—there is not; *śāstra-jñāna*—the verdict of the scriptures.

TRANSLATION

"Another name for Lord Viṣṇu is Triyuga because there is no incarnation of Lord Viṣṇu in Kali-yuga. Indeed, this is the verdict of revealed scriptures."

PURPORT

The Supreme Personality of Godhead, Lord Viṣṇu, is known as Triyuga, which means that He is manifest in three *yugas*. However, this means that in the age of Kali the Lord appears not directly but in disguise. This is confirmed in *Śrīmad-Bhāgavatam:*

itthaṁ nṛ-tiryag-ṛṣi-deva-jhaṣāvatārair
lokān vibhāvayasi haṁsi jagat-pratīpān
dharmaṁ mahā-puruṣa pāsi yugānuvṛttaṁ
channaḥ kalau yad abhavas tri-yugo 'tha sa tvam

"My Lord, You kill all the enemies of the world in Your multifarious incarnations in the families of men, animals, demigods, *ṛṣis*, aquatics and so on. Thus You illuminate the worlds with transcendental knowledge. In the age of Kali, O Mahāpuruṣa, You sometimes appear in a covered incarnation. Therefore You are known as Triyuga [one who appears in only three *yugas*]." (*Bhag.* 7.9.38)

Śrīla Śrīdhara Svāmī has also verified that Lord Viṣṇu appears in the age of Kali but does not act as He does in other ages. Lord Viṣṇu incarnates for two purposes: *paritrāṇāya sādhūnāṁ vināśāya ca duṣkṛtām*. That is, He comes to engage in pastimes with His devotees and to annihilate the demons. These purposes are visible in the Satya, Tretā and Dvāpara *yugas*, but in Kali-yuga the Lord appears disguised. He does not directly kill demons and give protection to the faithful. Because the Lord is not directly perceived in Kali-yuga but is directly known in the other three *yugas,* His name is Triyuga.

TEXT 96

শুনিয়া আচার্য কহে দুঃখী হঞা মনে।
শাস্ত্রজ্ঞ করিঞা তুমি কর অভিমানে ॥ ৯৬ ॥

śuniyā ācārya kahe duḥkhī hañā mane
śāstra-jña kariñā tumi kara abhimāne

SYNONYMS

śuniyā—hearing this; *ācārya*—Gopīnātha Ācārya; *kahe*—says; *duḥkhī*—unhappy; *hañā*—becoming; *mane*—in the mind; *śāstra-jña*—well versed in Vedic scriptures; *kariñā*—taking as; *tumi*—you; *kara*—do; *abhimāne*—pride.

TRANSLATION

Upon hearing this, Gopīnātha Ācārya became very unhappy. He said to the Bhaṭṭācarya: "You consider yourself the knower of all Vedic scriptures.

TEXT 97

ভাগবত-ভারত দুই শাস্ত্রের প্রধান।
সেই দুইগ্রন্থ-বাক্যে নাহি অবধান ॥ ৯৭ ॥

bhāgavata-bhārata dui śāstrera pradhāna
sei dui-grantha-vākye nāhi avadhāna

SYNONYMS

bhāgavata—*Śrīmad-Bhāgavatam; bhārata*—*Mahābhārata; dui*—two; *śāstrera*—of all Vedic scriptures; *pradhāna*—the most prominent; *sei*—those; *dui-grantha*—of the two scriptures; *vākye*—in the statements; *nāhi*—there is not; *avadhāna*—attention.

TRANSLATION

"Śrīmad-Bhāgavatam and Mahābhārata are the two most important Vedic scriptures, but you have paid no attention to their statements.

TEXT 98

সেই দুই কহে কলিতে সাক্ষাৎ-অবতার।
তুমি কহ,—কলিতে নাহি বিষ্ণুর প্রচার ॥ ৯৮ ॥

sei dui kahe kalite sākṣāt-avatāra
tumi kaha,—kalite nāhi viṣṇura pracāra

SYNONYMS

sei—those; *dui*—two; *kahe*—say; *kalite*—in this age of Kali; *sākṣāt*—direct; *avatāra*—incarnation; *tumi*—you; *kaha*—say; *kalite*—in this age of Kali; *nāhi*—there is not; *viṣṇura*—of Lord Viṣṇu; *pracāra*—manifestation.

TRANSLATION

"In Śrīmad-Bhāgavatam and Mahābhārata it is stated that the Lord appears directly, but you say that in this age there is no manifestation or incarnation of Lord Viṣṇu.

TEXT 99

কলিযুগে লীলাবতার না করে ভগবান্ ।
অতএব 'ত্রিযুগ' করি' কহি তার নাম ॥ ৯৯ ॥

kali-yuge līlāvatāra nā kare bhagavān
ataeva 'tri-yuga' kari' kahi tāra nāma

SYNONYMS

kali-yuge—in this age of Kali; *līlā-avatāra*—a pastime incarnation; *nā*—not; *kare*—does; *bhagavān*—the Supreme Personality of Godhead; *ataeva*—therefore; *tri-yuga*—of the name Triyuga (manifested in three *yugas*); *kari'*—accepting; *kahi*—I say; *tāra nāma*—His holy name.

TRANSLATION

"In this age of Kali there is no līlā-avatāra of the Supreme Personality of Godhead; therefore He is known as Triyuga. That is one of His holy names."

PURPORT

A *līlā-avatāra* is an incarnation of the Lord who performs a variety of activities without making any special endeavor. He always has one pastime after another, all full of transcendental pleasure, and these pastimes are fully controlled by the Supreme Person. The Supreme Person is totally independent of all others in these pastimes. While teaching Sanātana Gosvāmī (Cc. *Madhya* 20.296-298), Śrī Caitanya Mahāprabhu pointed out that one cannot count the number of *līlā-avatāras*:

līlāvatāra kṛṣṇera nā yāya gaṇana
pradhāna kariyā kahi dig-daraśana

"However," the Lord told Sanātana, "I shall explain the chief *līlā-avatāras.*"

matsya, kūrma, raghunātha, nṛsiṁha, vāmana
varāhādi——lekhā yāṅra nā yāya gaṇana

Thus the Lord's incarnations were enumerated, including Matsya, the fish incarnation; Kūrma, the tortoise; Lord Rāmacandra; Nṛsiṁhadeva; Vāmanadeva; and Varāha, the boar incarnation. Thus there are innumerable *līlā-avatāras,* and all of these exhibit wonderful pastimes. Lord Varāha, the boar incarnation, lifted the entire planet earth from the depths of the Garbhodaka Ocean. The tortoise incarnation, Lord Kūrma, became a pivot for the emulsification of the whole sea, and Lord Nṛsiṁhadeva appeared as half-man, half-lion. These are some of the wonderful and uncommon features of *līlā-avatāras.*

In his book *Laghu-bhāgavatāmṛta,* Śrīla Rūpa Gosvāmī has enumerated the following twenty-five *līlā-avatāras:* Catuḥ-sana, Nārada, Varāha, Matsya, Yajña, Nara-Nārāyaṇa, Kapila, Dattātreya, Hayaśīrṣa (Hayagrīva), Haṁsa, Pṛśnigarbha, Ṛṣabha, Pṛthu, Nṛsiṁha, Kūrma, Dhanvantari, Mohinī, Vāmana, Paraśurāma, Rāghavendra, Vyāsa, Balarāma, Kṛṣṇa, Buddha and Kalki.

Śrī Caitanya Mahāprabhu is not mentioned as a *līlā-avatāra* because He is an incarnation in disguise (*channa-avatāra*). In this age of Kali there are no *līlā-avatāras,* but there is an incarnation of the Lord manifested in the body of Śrī Caitanya Mahāprabhu. This has been explained in *Śrīmad-Bhāgavatam.*

TEXT 100

প্রতিযুগে করেন কৃষ্ণ যুগ-অবতার ।
তর্কনিষ্ঠ হৃদয় তোমার নাহিক বিচার ॥ ১০০ ॥

pratiyuge karena kṛṣṇa yuga-avatāra
tarka-niṣṭha hṛdaya tomāra nāhika vicāra

SYNONYMS

prati-yuge—in every age or millennium; *karena*—makes; *kṛṣṇa*—Lord Kṛṣṇa; *yuga-avatāra*—incarnation for the age; *tarka-niṣṭha*—hardened by argument; *hṛdaya*—heart; *tomāra*—your; *nāhika*—there is not; *vicāra*—consideration.

TRANSLATION

Gopīnātha Ācārya continued: "There is certainly an incarnation in every age, and such an incarnation is called the yuga-avatāra. But your heart has become so hardened by logic and argument that you cannot consider all these facts.

TEXT 101

আসন্ বর্ণাস্ত্রয়ো হ্যস্য গৃহ্নতোঽনুযুগং তনূঃ ।
শুক্লো রক্তস্তথা পীত ইদানীং কৃষ্ণতাং গতঃ ॥ ১০১ ॥

āsan varṇās trayo hy asya
gṛhṇato 'nuyugaṁ tanūḥ
śuklo raktas tathā pīta
idānīṁ kṛṣṇatāṁ gataḥ

SYNONYMS

āsan—there were; *varṇāḥ*—colors; *trayaḥ*—three; *hi*—indeed; *asya*—of Him; *gṛhṇataḥ*—accepting; *anuyugam*—according to the age; *tanūḥ*—bodies; *śuklaḥ*—white; *raktaḥ*—red; *tathā*—also; *pītaḥ*—yellow; *idānīm*—at the present moment; *kṛṣṇatām*—blackish; *gataḥ*—has accepted.

TRANSLATION

" 'In the past, your son has had bodies of three different colors, according to the age. These colors were white, red and yellow. In this age [Dvāpara-yuga] He has accepted a blackish body.'

PURPORT

This verse from *Śrīmad-Bhāgavatam* (10.8.13) was spoken by Gargamuni when he was performing the rituals at Lord Kṛṣṇa's name-giving ceremony. He states that the incarnations of the Lord in other ages had been white, red and yellow. This yellow color refers to Śrī Caitanya Mahāprabhu, whose bodily complexion was yellowish. This confirms that in the past Kali-yugas, the Lord also had incarnated in a body that was yellow in hue. It is understood that the Lord incarnates in different colors for the different *yugas* (Satya, Tretā, Dvāpara and Kali). Accepting the color yellow (*pīta*), as well as other characteristics, the Lord incarnated as Śrī Caitanya Mahāprabhu. This is the verdict of all Vedic authorities.

TEXT 102

ইতি দ্বাপর উর্বীশ স্তুবন্তি জগদীশ্বরম্ ।
নানাতন্ত্রবিধানেন কলাবপি তথা শৃণু ॥ ১০২ ॥

iti dvāpara urvīśa
stuvanti jagad-īśvaram
nānā-tantra-vidhānena
kalāv api tathā śṛṇu

SYNONYMS

iti—thus; *dvāpare*—in Dvāpara-yuga; *uru-īśa*—O King; *stuvanti*—offer prayers; *jagat-īśvaram*—unto the Supreme Personality of Godhead; *nānā*—various; *tantra*—of the supplementary Vedic literatures; *vidhānena*—by regulative principles; *kalau*—in the age of Kali; *api*—certainly; *tathā*—so also; *śṛṇu*—hear.

TRANSLATION

" 'In the age of Kali, as well as in Dvāpara-yuga, the people offer prayers to the Supreme Personality of Godhead by various mantras and observe the regulative principles of the supplementary Vedic literatures. Now please hear of this from me.

PURPORT

This is a quotation from *Śrīmad-Bhāgavatam* (11.5.31).

TEXT 103

কৃষ্ণবর্ণং ত্বিষাঽকৃষ্ণং সাঙ্গোপাঙ্গাস্ত্রপার্ষদম্ ।
যজ্ঞৈঃ সংকীর্তনপ্রায়ৈর্যজন্তি হি সুমেধসঃ ॥ ১০৩ ॥

kṛṣṇa-varṇaṁ tviṣākṛṣṇaṁ
sāṅgopāṅgāstra-pārṣadam
yajñaiḥ saṅkīrtana-prāyair
yajanti hi sumedhasaḥ

SYNONYMS

kṛṣṇa-varṇam—chanting the two syllables *"kṛṣ"* and *"ṇa"*; *tviṣā*—by complexion; *akṛṣṇam*—not blackish; *sa-aṅga*—accompanied by personal expansions; *upa-aṅga*—devotees; *astra*—the weapon of chanting the Hare Kṛṣṇa *mantra; pārṣadam*—and associates like Gadādhara, Svarūpa Dāmodara, etc.; *yajñaiḥ*—by sacrifice; *saṅkīrtana*—congregational chanting of the Hare Kṛṣṇa *mantra; prāyaiḥ*—chiefly consisting of; *yajanti*—worship; *hi*—indeed; *su-medhasaḥ*—those who are intelligent.

TRANSLATION

" 'In this age of Kali, those who are intelligent perform the congregational chanting of the Hare Kṛṣṇa mahā-mantra, worshiping the Supreme Personality of Godhead, who appears in this age always describing the glories of Kṛṣṇa. That incarnation is yellowish in hue and is always associated with His plenary

expansions [such as Śrī Nityānanda Prabhu], and personal expansions [such as Gadādhara], as well as devotees and associates [such as Svarūpa Dāmodara].'

PURPORT

This verse from *Śrīmad-Bhāgavatam* (11.5.32) is explained by Śrī Jīva Gosvāmī in his *Krama-sandarbha,* as quoted by Śrīla Bhaktivinoda Ṭhākura in regard to the explanation of *Ādi-līlā,* Third Chapter, verse 51.

TEXT 104

সুবর্ণবর্ণো হেমাঙ্গো বরাঙ্গশ্চন্দনাঙ্গদী ।
সন্ন্যাসকৃচ্ছমঃ শান্তো নিষ্ঠা-শান্তি-পরায়ণঃ ॥ ১০৪ ॥

suvarṇa-varṇo hemāṅgo
varāṅgaś candanāṅgadī
sannyāsa-kṛc chamaḥ śānto
niṣṭhā-śānti-parāyaṇaḥ

SYNONYMS

suvarṇa-varṇaḥ—whose complexion is like gold; *hema-aṅgaḥ*—having a body like molten gold; *vara-aṅgaḥ*—whose body is very beautifully constructed; *candana-aṅgadī*—smeared with the pulp of sandalwood; *sannyāsa-kṛt*—accepting the renounced order of life; *śamaḥ*—self-controlled; *śāntaḥ*—peaceful; *niṣṭhā*—firmly fixed; *śānti*—bringing peace by propagating the Hare Kṛṣṇa *mahā-mantra; parāyaṇaḥ*—always in the ecstatic mood of devotional service.

TRANSLATION

" 'The Lord [in the incarnation of Gaurasundara] has a golden complexion. Indeed, His entire body, which is very nicely constituted, is like molten gold. Sandalwood pulp is smeared all over His body. He will take the fourth order of spiritual life (sannyāsa) and will be very self-controlled. He will be distinguished from Māyāvādī sannyāsīs in that He will be fixed in devotional service and will spread the saṅkīrtana movement.' "

PURPORT

Gopīnātha Ācārya quoted this verse from *Mahābhārata.*

TEXT 105

তোমার আগে এত কথার নাহি প্রয়োজন ।
ঊষর-ভূমিতে যেন বীজের রোপণ ॥ ১০৫ ॥

tomāra āge eta kathāra nāhi prayojana
ūṣara-bhūmite yena bījera ropaṇa

SYNONYMS

tomāra āge—before you; *eta*—so many; *kathāra*—of words; *nāhi*—there is not; *prayojana*—necessity; *ūṣara-bhūmite*—in barren land; *yena*—like; *bījera*—of the seed; *ropaṇa*—sowing.

TRANSLATION

Gopīnātha Ācārya then said: "There is no need to quote so much evidence from the śāstras, for you are a very dry speculator. There is no need to sow seeds in barren land.

TEXT 106

তোমার উপরে তাঁর কৃপা যবে হবে।
এসব সিদ্ধান্ত তবে তুমিহ কহিবে ॥ ১০৬ ॥

tomāra upare tāṅra kṛpā yabe habe
e-saba siddhānta tabe tumiha kahibe

SYNONYMS

tomāra upare—upon you; *tāṅra*—the Lord's; *kṛpā*—mercy; *yabe*—when; *habe*—there will be; *e-saba*—all these; *siddhānta*—conclusions; *tabe*—at that time; *tumiha*—you also; *kahibe*—will quote.

TRANSLATION

"When the Lord will be pleased with you, you will also understand these conclusions and will quote from the śāstras.

TEXT 107

তোমার যে শিষ্য কহে কুতর্ক, নানাবাদ।
ইহার কি দোষ—এই মায়ার প্রসাদ ॥ ১০৭ ॥

tomāra ye śiṣya kahe kutarka, nānā-vāda
ihāra ki doṣa——ei māyāra prasāda

SYNONYMS

tomāra—your; *ye*—which; *śiṣya*—disciples; *kahe*—say; *ku-tarka*—false arguments; *nānā-vāda*—jugglery of philosophy; *ihāra*—their; *ki*—what; *doṣa*—fault; *ei*—this; *māyāra*—of illusion; *prasāda*—benediction.

TRANSLATION

"The false arguments and philosophical word jugglery of your disciples are not faults of theirs. They have simply received the benediction of Māyāvāda philosophy.

TEXT 108

যচ্ছক্তয়ো বদতাং বাদিনাং বৈ, বিবাদ-সংবাদ-ভুবো ভবন্তি।
কুর্বন্তি চৈষাং মুহুরাত্মমোহং,তস্মৈ নমোঽনন্তগুণায় ভূম্নে ॥

yac-chaktayo vadatāṁ vādināṁ vai
vivāda-saṁvāda-bhuvo bhavanti
kurvanti caiṣāṁ muhur ātma-mohaṁ
tasmai namo 'nanta-guṇāya bhūmne

SYNONYMS

yat—whose; *śaktayaḥ*—potencies; *vadatām*—contending; *vādinām*—of the opposing disputants; *vai*—indeed; *vivāda*—of opposition; *saṁvāda*—of agreement; *bhuvaḥ*—objects; *bhavanti*—become; *kurvanti*—do; *ca*—also; *eṣām*—of them; *muhuḥ*—always; *ātma-moham*—illusion of the self; *tasmai*—unto Him; *namaḥ*—obeisances; *ananta*—unlimited; *guṇāya*—who has qualities; *bhūmne*—the Supreme.

TRANSLATION

" 'I offer my respectful obeisances unto the Supreme Personality of Godhead, who is full of unlimited qualities and whose different potencies bring about agreement and disagreement between disputants. Thus the illusory energy again and again covers the self-realization of both disputants.' disputants.'

PURPORT

This is a quotation from *Śrīmad-Bhāgavatam* (6.4.31).

TEXT 109

যুক্তং সন্তি সর্বত্র ভাষন্তে ব্রাহ্মণা যথা।
মায়াং মদীয়ামুদ্গৃহ্য বদতাং কিং নু দুর্ঘটম্ ॥ ১০৯ ॥

yuktaṁ ca santi sarvatra
bhāṣante brāhmaṇā yathā
māyāṁ madīyām udgṛhya
vadatāṁ kiṁ nu durghaṭam

SYNONYMS

yuktam—quite befitting; *cā*—also; *santi*—are; *sarvatra*—everywhere; *bhāṣante*—speak; *brāhmaṇāḥ*—the learned; *yathā*—as much; *māyām*—illusion; *madīyām*—of Me; *udgṛhya*—accepting; *vadatām*—of the speculators; *kim*—what; *nu*—certainly; *durghaṭam*—impossible.

TRANSLATION

" 'In almost all cases, whatever learned brāhmaṇas speak becomes accepted; nothing is impossible for one who takes shelter of My illusory energy and speaks under her influence.' "

PURPORT

In this verse from *Śrīmad-Bhāgavatam* (11.22.4), the Supreme Personality of Godhead explains that His illusory energy can perform the impossible; such is the power of the illusory energy. In many cases philosophical speculators have covered the real truth and have boldly set forth false theories. In ancient times philosophers like Kapila, Gautama, Jaimini, Kaṇāda and similar *brāhmaṇas* propounded useless philosophical theories, and in modern days so-called scientists are setting forth many false theories about the creation, backed up by seemingly logical arguments. This is all due to the influence of the Supreme Lord's illusory energy. The illusory energy, therefore, sometimes appears correct because it is emanating from the Supreme Correct. To avoid the very bewildering illusory influence, one must accept the words of the Supreme Personality of Godhead as they are. Only then can one escape the influence of the illusory energy.

TEXT 110

তবে ভট্টাচার্য কহে, যাহ গোসাঞির স্থানে।
আমার নামে গণ-সহিত কর নিমন্ত্রণে ॥ ১১০ ॥

tabe bhaṭṭācārya kahe, yāha gosāñira sthane
āmāra nāme gaṇa-sahita kara nimantraṇe

SYNONYMS

tabe—thereafter; *bhaṭṭācārya*—Sārvabhauma Bhaṭṭācārya; *kahe*—says; *yāha*—please go; *gosāñira sthane*—to the place of Śrī Caitanya Mahāprabhu; *āmāra nāme*—in my name; *gaṇa-sahita*—with His associates; *kara*—make; *nimantraṇe*—invitation.

TRANSLATION

After hearing this from Gopīnātha Ācārya, Sārvabhauma Bhaṭṭācārya said: "First go to the place where Śrī Caitanya Mahāprabhu is staying and invite Him here with His associates. Ask Him on my account.

TEXT 111

প্রসাদ আনি' তাঁরে করাহ আগে ভিক্ষা।
পশ্চাৎ আসি' আমারে করাইহ শিক্ষা ॥ ১১১ ॥

prasāda āni' tāṅre karāha āge bhikṣā
paścāt āsi' āmāre karāiha śikṣā

SYNONYMS

prasāda āni'—bringing *jagannātha-prasāda; tāṅre*—unto Him; *karāha*—make; *āge*—first; *bhikṣā*—acceptance; *paścāt*—afterwards; *āsi'*—coming here; *āmāre*—unto me; *karāiha*—cause; *śikṣā*—teaching.

TRANSLATION

"Take jagannātha-prasāda and first give it to Caitanya Mahāprabhu and His associates. After that, come back here and teach me well."

TEXT 112

আচার্য—ভগিনীপতি, শ্যালক—ভট্টাচার্য।
নিন্দা-স্তুতি-হাস্যে শিক্ষা করা'ন আচার্য ॥ ১১২ ।

ācārya——bhaginī-pati, śyālaka——bhaṭṭācārya
nindā-stuti-hāsye śikṣā karā'na ācārya

SYNONYMS

ācārya—Gopīnātha Ācārya; *bhaginī-pati*—sister's husband; *śyālaka*—wife's brother; *bhaṭṭācārya*—Sārvabhauma Bhaṭṭācārya; *nindā*—sometimes blaspheming; *stuti*—sometimes by praising; *hāsye*—sometimes by laughing; *śikṣā*—instruction; *karā'na*—causes; *ācārya*—Gopīnātha Ācārya.

TRANSLATION

Gopīnātha Ācārya was the brother-in-law of Sārvabhauma Bhaṭṭācārya; therefore their relationship was very sweet and intimate. Under the circumstances, Gopīnātha Ācārya taught him by sometimes blaspheming him, sometimes praising him and sometimes laughing at him. This had been going on for some time.

TEXT 113

আচার্যের সিদ্ধান্তে মুকুন্দের হৈল সন্তোষ।
ভট্টাচার্যের বাক্যে মনে হৈল দুঃখ-রোষ ॥ ১১৩ ॥

ācāryera siddhānte mukundera haila santoṣa
bhaṭṭācāryera vākya mane haila duḥkha-roṣa

SYNONYMS

ācāryera—of Gopīnātha Ācārya; *siddhānte*—with the conclusions; *mukundera*—of Mukunda Datta; *haila*—there was; *santoṣa*—satisfaction; *bhaṭṭācāryera*—of Sārvabhauma Bhaṭṭācārya; *vākye*—by the words; *mane*—in the mind; *haila*—there was; *duḥkha*—unhappiness; *roṣa*—and anger.

TRANSLATION

Śrīla Mukunda Datta felt very satisfied to hear the conclusive statements of Gopīnātha Ācārya, but he became very unhappy and angry to hear the statements put forward by Sārvabhauma Bhaṭṭācārya.

TEXT 114

গোসাঞিঃর স্থানে আচার্য কৈল আগমন ।
ভট্টাচার্যের নামে তাঁরে কৈল নিমন্ত্রণ ॥ ১১৪ ॥

gosāñira sthāne ācārya kaila āgamana
bhaṭṭācāryera nāme tāṅre kaila nimantraṇa

SYNONYMS

gosāñira sthāne—to the place where Śrī Caitanya Mahāprabhu was staying; *ācārya*—Gopīnātha Ācārya; *kaila*—did; *āgamana*—coming; *bhaṭṭācāryera nāme*—on behalf of Sārvabhauma Bhaṭṭācārya; *tāṅre*—unto Him; *kaila*—made; *nimantraṇa*—invitation.

TRANSLATION

According to the instructions of Sārvabhauma Bhaṭṭācārya, Gopīnātha Ācārya went to Śrī Caitanya Mahāprabhu and invited Him on the Bhaṭṭācārya's behalf.

TEXT 115

মুকুন্দ-সহিত কহে ভট্টাচার্যের কথা ।
ভট্টাচার্যের নিন্দা করে, মনে পাঞা ব্যথা ॥ ১১৫ ॥

mukunda-sahita kahe bhaṭṭācāryera kathā
bhaṭṭācāryera nindā kare, mane pāñā vyathā

SYNONYMS

mukunda-sahita—along with Mukunda; *kahe*—describes; *bhaṭṭācāryera kathā*—all the words of Sārvabhauma Bhaṭṭācārya; *bhaṭṭācāryera*—of Sārvabhauma Bhaṭṭācārya; *nindā*—defamation; *kare*—does; *mane*—in the mind; *pāñā*—getting; *vyathā*—some pain.

TRANSLATION

The Bhaṭṭācārya's statements were discussed before Śrī Caitanya Mahāprabhu. Gopīnātha Ācārya and Mukunda Datta disapproved of the Bhaṭṭācārya's statements because they caused mental pain.

TEXT 116

শুনি মহাপ্রভু কহে ঐছে মৎ কহ ।
আমা প্রতি ভট্টাচার্যের হয় অনুগ্রহ ॥ ১১৬ ॥

śuni mahāprabhu kahe aiche mat kaha
āmā prati bhaṭṭācāryera haya anugraha

SYNONYMS

śuni—hearing them; *mahāprabhu*—Caitanya Mahāprabhu; *kahe*—says; *aiche*—such; *mat kaha*—do not speak; *āmā prati*—toward Me; *bhaṭṭācāryera*—of Sārvabhauma Bhaṭṭācārya; *haya*—there is; *anugraha*—mercy.

TRANSLATION

Hearing this, Śrī Caitanya Mahāprabhu said: "Do not speak like that. Sārvabhauma Bhaṭṭācārya has shown great affection and mercy toward Me.

TEXT 117

আমার সন্ন্যাস-ধর্ম চাহেন রাখিতে ।
বাৎসল্যে করুণা করেন, কি দোষ ইহাতে ॥ ১১৭ ॥

āmāra sannyāsa-dharma cāhena rākhite
vātsalye karuṇā karena, ki doṣa ihāte

SYNONYMS

āmāra—My; *sannyāsa-dharma*—regulative principles of *sannyāsa; cāhena*—he wants; *rākhite*—to keep; *vātsalye*—out of paternal affection; *karuṇā*—mercy; *karena*—does; *ki*—what; *doṣa*—fault; *ihāte*—in this connection.

TRANSLATION

"Out of paternal affection for Me, he wants to protect Me and see that I follow the regulative principles of a sannyāsī. What fault is there in this?"

TEXT 118

আর দিন মহাপ্রভু ভট্টাচার্য-সনে।
আনন্দে করিলা জগন্নাথ দরশনে ॥ ১১৮ ॥

āra dina mahāprabhu bhaṭṭācārya-sane
ānande karilā jagannātha daraśane

SYNONYMS

āra dina—the next day; *mahāprabhu*—Śrī Caitanya Mahāprabhu; *bhaṭṭācārya-sane*—along with Sārvabhauma Bhaṭṭācārya; *ānande*—in great pleasure; *karilā*—did; *jagannātha*—to Lord Jagannātha; *daraśane*—visit.

TRANSLATION

The next morning, Śrī Caitanya Mahāprabhu and Sārvabhauma Bhaṭṭācārya together visited the temple of Lord Jagannātha. Both of them were in a very pleasant mood.

TEXT 119

ভট্টাচার্য-সঙ্গে তাঁর মন্দিরে আইলা।
প্রভুরে আসন দিয়া আপনে বসিলা ॥ ১১৯ ॥

bhaṭṭācārya-saṅge tāṅra mandire āilā
prabhure āsana diyā āpane vasilā

SYNONYMS

bhaṭṭācārya-saṅge—along with Sārvabhauma Bhaṭṭācārya; *tāṅra*—His (Lord Jagannātha's); *mandire*—to the temple; *āilā*—came; *prabhure*—unto Lord Śrī Caitanya Mahāprabhu; *āsana*—sitting place; *diyā*—giving; *āpane*—personally; *vasilā*—sat down.

TRANSLATION

When they entered the temple, Sārvabhauma Bhaṭṭācārya offered Caitanya Mahāprabhu a seat, while he himself sat down on the floor out of due respect for a sannyāsī.

TEXT 120

বেদান্ত পড়াইতে তবে আরম্ভ করিলা ।
স্নেহ-ভক্তি করি' কিছু প্রভুরে কহিলা ॥ ১২০ ॥

vedānta paḍāite tabe ārambha karilā
sneha-bhakti kari' kichu prabhure kahilā

SYNONYMS

vedānta—Vedānta philosophy; *paḍāite*—to instruct; *tabe*—then; *ārambha*—beginning; *karilā*—made; *sneha*—affection; *bhakti*—and devotion; *kari'*—showing; *kichu*—something; *prabhure*—unto the Lord; *kahilā*—said.

TRANSLATION

He then began to instruct Lord Caitanya Mahāprabhu on Vedānta philosophy, and out of affection and devotion, he spoke to the Lord as follows.

PURPORT

The *Vedānta-* or *Brahma-sūtra,* written by Śrīla Vyāsadeva, is a book studied by all advanced spiritual students, especially by the *sannyāsīs* of all religious communities (*sampradāyas*). The *sannyāsīs* must read *Vedānta-sūtra* to establish their final conclusions concerning Vedic knowledge. Here, of course, the *Vedānta* mentioned is the commentary of Śaṅkarācārya, known as *Śārīraka-bhāṣya.* Sārvabhauma Bhaṭṭācārya intended to convert Caitanya Mahāprabhu, who was a Vaiṣṇava *sannyāsī,* into a Māyāvādī *sannyāsī.* He therefore made this arrangement to instruct Him in *Vedānta-sūtra* according to the *Śārīraka* commentary of Śaṅkarācārya. All the *sannyāsīs* of the Śaṅkara-sampradāya enjoy seriously studying the *Vedānta-sūtra* with the *Śārīraka-bhāṣya* commentary. It is said, *vedānta-vākyeṣu sadā ramantaḥ:* "One should always enjoy the studies of the *Vedānta-sūtra.*"

TEXT 121

বেদান্ত-শ্রবণ,—এই সন্ন্যাসীর ধর্ম ।
নিরন্তর কর তুমি বেদান্ত শ্রবণ ॥ ১২১ ॥

vedānta-śravaṇa,—ei sannyāsīra dharma
nirantara kara tumi vedānta śravaṇa

SYNONYMS

vedānta-śravaṇa—hearing of the Vedānta philosophy; *ei*—this; *sannyāsīra*—of a person in the renounced order; *dharma*—factual occupation; *nirantara*—incessantly; *kara*—do; *tumi*—You; *vedānta*—of Vedānta philosophy; *śravaṇa*—hearing.

TRANSLATION

The Bhaṭṭācārya said: "Hearing the Vedānta philosophy is a sannyāsī's main business. Therefore without hesitation You should study Vedānta philosophy, hearing it without cessation from a superior person."

TEXT 122

প্রভু কহে,—'মোরে তুমি কর অনুগ্রহ ।
সেই সে কর্তব্য, তুমি যেই মোরে কহ ॥'১২২ ॥

prabhu kahe,—'more tumi kara anugraha
sei se kartavya, tumi yei more kaha'

SYNONYMS

prabhu kahe—the Lord replied; *more*—unto Me; *tumi*—you; *kara*—show; *anugraha*—mercy; *sei se*—that; *kartavya*—duty; *tumi*—you; *yei*—whatever; *more*—unto Me; *kaha*—say.

TRANSLATION

Lord Caitanya replied: "You are very merciful to Me, and therefore I think it is My duty to obey your order."

TEXT 123

সাত দিন পর্যন্ত ঐছে করেন শ্রবণে ।
ভাল-মন্দ নাহি কহে, বসি' মাত্র শুনে ॥ ১২৩ ॥

sāta dina paryanta aiche karena śravaṇe
bhāla-manda nāhi kahe, vasi' mātra śune

SYNONYMS

sāta dina—seven days; *paryanta*—up to; *aiche*—in this way; *karena*—does; *śravaṇe*—hearing; *bhāla*—right; *manda*—wrong; *nāhi*—not; *kahe*—says; *vasi'*—sitting; *mātra*—only; *śune*—hears.

TRANSLATION

Thus for seven days continuously, Śrī Caitanya Mahāprabhu listened to the Vedānta philosophy expounded by Sārvabhauma Bhaṭṭācārya. However,

Caitanya Mahāprabhu did not say anything and did not indicate whether it was right or wrong. He simply sat there and listened to the Bhaṭṭācārya.

TEXT 124

অষ্টম-দিবসে তাঁরে পুছে সার্বভৌম ।
সাত দিন কর তুমি বেদান্ত শ্রবণ ॥ ১২৪ ॥

aṣṭama-divase tāṅre puche sārvabhauma
sāta dina kara tumi vedānta śravaṇa

SYNONYMS

aṣṭama-divase—on the eighth day; *tāṅre*—unto Him; *puche*—inquires; *sārvabhauma*—Sārvabhauma Bhaṭṭācārya; *sāta dina*—seven days; *kara*—do; *tumi*—You; *vedānta*—the Vedānta philosophy; *śravaṇa*—hearing.

TRANSLATION

On the eighth day, Sārvabhauma Bhaṭṭācārya said to Caitanya Mahāprabhu: "You have been listening to the Vedānta philosophy from me continuously for seven days.

TEXT 125

ভালমন্দ নাহি কহ, রহ মৌন ধরি' ।
বুঝ, কি না বুঝ,—ইহা বুঝিতে না পারি ॥ ১২৫ ॥

bhāla-manda nāhi kaha, raha mauna dhari'
bujha, ki nā bujha,——ihā bujhite nā pāri

SYNONYMS

bhāla-manda—right or wrong; *nāhi kaha*—not speak; *raha*—keep; *mauna*—silence; *dhari'*—holding; *bujha*—understand; *ki*—or; *nā*—not; *bujha*—understand; *ihā*—this; *bujhite*—to understand; *nā*—not; *pāri*—I am able.

TRANSLATION

"You have simply been listening, fixed in Your silence. Since You do not say whether You think it is right or wrong, I cannot know whether You are actually understanding Vedānta philosophy or not."

TEXT 126

প্রভু কহে - "মূর্খ আমি, নাহি অধ্যয়ন।
তোমার আজ্ঞাতে মাত্র করিয়ে শ্রবণ ॥ ১২৬ ॥

prabhu kahe——"mūrkha āmi, nāhi adhyayana
tomāra ājñāte mātra kariye śravaṇa

SYNONYMS

prabhu kahe—the Lord replied; *mūrkha āmi*—I am a fool; *nāhi*—there is not; *adhyayana*—study; *tomāra*—your; *ājñāte*—by the order; *mātra*—only; *kariye*—I do; *śravaṇa*—hearing.

TRANSLATION

Śrī Caitanya Mahāprabhu replied: "I am a fool, and consequently I do not study Vedānta-sūtra. I am just trying to hear it from you because you have ordered Me.

TEXT 127

সন্ন্যাসীর ধর্ম লাগি' শ্রবণ মাত্র করি।
তুমি যেই অর্থ কর, বুঝিতে না পারি॥" ১২৭ ॥

sannyāsīra dharma lāgi' śravaṇa mātra kari
tumi yei artha kara, bujhite nā pāri"

SYNONYMS

sannyāsīra—of one in the renounced order of life; *dharma*—the occupation; *lāgi'*—for the matter of; *śravaṇa*—hearing; *mātra*—only; *kari*—I do; *tumi*—you; *yei*—whatever; *artha*—meaning; *kara*—present; *bujhite*—to understand; *nā*—not; *pāri*—I am able.

TRANSLATION

"Only for the sake of executing the duties of the renounced order of sannyāsa do I listen. Unfortunately, I cannot in the least understand the meaning you are presenting."

PURPORT

Śrī Caitanya Mahāprabhu presented Himself as if He were a *sannyāsī* in name only or, in other words, a number-one fool. Māyāvādī *sannyāsīs* in India are very accustomed to declaring themselves *jagad-gurus,* teachers of the world, although they have no information of the outside world and are limited in their experience to a small town or village, or perhaps to the country of India. Nor do such *sannyāsīs* have sufficient education. Unfortunately, at the present moment there are many foolish *sannyāsīs,* both in India and elsewhere, who simply read and study Vedic literature without understanding the purports. When Caitanya Mahāprabhu was having His discussion with the Chand Kazi, the Mohammedan magistrate of Navadvīpa, He recited a verse from Vedic literature to the effect that the order of *sannyāsa* is prohibited in this age of Kali. Only those who are very serious and who follow the regulative principles and study Vedic literature should accept *sannyāsa.* Śrī Caitanya Mahāprabhu approved of a *sannyāsī's* reading *Vedānta-sūtra,* or *Brahma-sūtra,* but He did not approve the *Śārīraka* commentary of Śaṅkarācārya. Indeed, He said elsewhere, *māyāvādi-bhāṣya śunile haya sarva-nāśa:* "If one hears the *Śārīraka-bhāṣya* of Śaṅkarācārya, he is doomed." Thus a *sannyāsī,* a transcendentalist, must read *Vedānta-sūtra* regularly, but he should not read the *Śārīraka-bhāṣya.* This is the conclusion of Śrī Caitanya Mahāprabhu. The real commentary on *Vedānta-sūtra* is *Śrīmad-Bhāgavatam. Artho 'yaṁ brahma-sūtrānām: Śrīmad-Bhāgavatam* is the original commentary on *Vedānta-sūtra* written by the author himself, Śrīla Vyāsadeva.

TEXT 128

ভট্টাচার্য কহে,—না বুঝি', হেন জ্ঞান যার ।
বুঝিবার লাগি' সেহ পুছে পুনর্বার ॥ ১২৮ ॥

bhaṭṭācārya kahe,——nā bujhi', hena jñāna yāra
bujhibāra lāgi' seha puche punarbāra

SYNONYMS

bhaṭṭācārya kahe—Sārvabhauma Bhaṭṭācārya replied; *nā bujhi'*—not understanding; *hena*—this; *jñāna*—the knowledge; *yāra*—of someone; *bujhibāra lāgi'*—just to understand; *seha*—he also; *puche*—inquires; *punaḥ-bāra*—again.

TRANSLATION

Sārvabhauma Bhaṭṭācārya replied: "I accept that You do not understand, yet even one who does not understand inquires about the subject matter.

TEXT 129

তুমি শুনি' শুনি' রহ মৌন মাত্র ধরি' ।
হৃদয়ে কি আছে তোমার, বুঝিতে না পারি ॥ ১২৯ ॥

tumi śuni' śuni' raha mauna mātra dhari'
hṛdaye ki āche tomāra, bujhite nā pāri

SYNONYMS

tumi—You; *śuni'*—hearing; *śuni'*—hearing; *raha*—keep; *mauna*—silence; *mātra*—only; *dhari'*—holding; *hṛdaye*—in the heart; *ki*—what; *āche*—there is; *tomāra*—Your; *bujhite*—to understand; *nā*—not; *pāri*—am able.

TRANSLATION

"You are hearing again and again, yet You keep silent. I cannot understand what is actually within Your mind."

TEXT 130

প্রভু কহে,—"সূত্রের অর্থ বুঝিয়ে নির্মল।
তোমার ব্যাখ্যা শুনি' মন হয় ত' বিকল ॥ ১৩০ ॥

prabhu kahe,——"sūtrera artha bujhiye nirmala
tomāra vyākhyā śuni' mana haya ta' vikala

SYNONYMS

prabhu kahe—the Lord replied; *sūtrera artha*—the meaning of the *sūtra; bujhiye*—I can understand; *nirmala*—very clearly; *tomāra*—your; *vyākhyā*—explanation; *śuni'*—hearing; *mana*—mind; *haya*—becomes; *ta'*—indeed; *vikala*—disturbed.

TRANSLATION

Śrī Caitanya Mahāprabhu then revealed His mind, saying: "I can understand the meaning of each sūtra very clearly, but your explanations have simply agitated My mind.

PURPORT

The factual meaning of the verses of the *Vedānta-sūtra* is as clear as sunshine. The Māyāvādī philosophers simply try to cover the sunshine with the clouds of interpretations imagined by Śaṅkarācārya and his followers.

TEXT 131

সূত্রের অর্থ ভাষ্য কহে প্রকাশিয়া।
তুমি, ভাষ্য কহ—সূত্রের অর্থ আচ্ছাদিয়া ॥ ১৩১ ॥

sūtrera artha bhāṣya kahe prakāśiyā
tumi, bhāṣya kaha——sūtrera artha ācchādiyā

SYNONYMS

sūtrera artha—meanings of the *sūtras; bhāṣya*—the purport; *kahe*—one speaks; *prakāśiyā*—clearly manifesting; *tumi*—you; *bhāṣya kaha*—make a comment; *sūtrera*—of the verses; *artha*—the meanings; *ācchādiyā*—covering.

TRANSLATION

"The meaning of the verses in the Vedānta-sūtra contain clear purports in themselves, but other purports you presented simply covered the meaning of the sūtra like a cloud.

PURPORT

Please refer to *Ādi-līlā,* Seventh Chapter, verses 106-146, for an explanation of this verse.

TEXT 132

সূত্রের মুখ্য অর্থ না করহ ব্যাখ্যান ।
কল্পনার্থে তুমি তাহা কর আচ্ছাদন ॥ ১৩২ ॥

sūtrera mukhya artha nā karaha vyākhyāna
kalpanārthe tumi tāhā kara ācchādana

SYNONYMS

sūtrera—of the verses; *mukhya*—direct; *artha*—of meanings; *nā*—not; *karaha*—you do; *vyākhyāna*—explanation; *kalpanā-arthe*—because of imaginative meaning; *tumi*—you; *tāhā*—of that; *kara*—do; *ācchādana*—covering.

TRANSLATION

"You do not explain the direct meaning of the Brahma-sūtras. Indeed, it appears that your business is to cover the real meaning."

PURPORT

This is typical of all Māyāvādīs or atheists who interpret the meaning of Vedic literature in their own imaginative way. The real purpose of such foolish people is to impose the impersonalist conclusion on all Vedic literature. The Māyāvādī atheists also interpret *Bhagavad-gītā.* In every verse of *Śrīmad Bhagavad-gītā* it is clearly stated that Kṛṣṇa is the Supreme Personality of Godhead. In every verse,

Vyāsadeva says, *śrī bhagavān uvāca,* "the Supreme Personality of Godhead said," or "the Blessed Lord said." It is clearly stated that the Blessed Lord is the Supreme Person, but Māyāvādī atheists still try to prove that the Absolute Truth is impersonal. In order to present their false, imaginary meanings, they must adopt so much word jugglery and grammatical interpretation that they finally become ludicrous. Therefore Śrī Caitanya Mahāprabhu remarked that no one should hear the Māyāvādī commentaries or purports to any Vedic literature.

TEXT 133

উপনিষদ্-শব্দে যেই মুখ্য অর্থ হয়।
সেই অর্থ মুখ্য,—ব্যাসসূত্রে সব কয়॥ ১৩৩॥

upaniṣad-śabde yei mukhya artha haya
sei artha mukhya,——vyāsa-sūtre saba kaya

SYNONYMS

upaniṣad—of the *Vedas; śabde*—by the words; *yei*—whatever; *mukhya*—direct; *artha*—meaning; *haya*—is; *sei*—that; *artha*—meaning; *mukhya*—chief; *vyāsa-sūtre*—in the *Vedānta-sūtra; saba*—all; *kaya*—describes.

TRANSLATION

Caitanya Mahāprabhu continued: "Vedānta-sūtra is the summary of all the Upaniṣads; therefore whatever direct meaning is there in the Upaniṣads is also recorded in the Vedānta-sūtra or Vyāsa-sūtra.

PURPORT

Śrīla Bhaktisiddhānta Sarasvatī has explained the word *"upaniṣad"* in his *Anubhāṣya.* Please refer to *Ādi-līlā,* Second Chapter, fifth verse, and *Ādi-līlā,* Seventh Chapter, verses 106 and 108, for his explanation.

TEXT 134

মুখ্যার্থ ছাড়িয়া কর গৌণার্থ কল্পনা।
'অভিধা'-বৃত্তি ছাড়ি' কর শব্দের লক্ষণা॥ ১৩৪॥

mukhyārtha chāḍiyā kara gauṇārtha kalpanā
'abhidhā'-vṛtti chāḍi' kara śabdera lakṣaṇā

SYNONYMS

mukhya-artha—direct meaning; *chāḍiyā*—giving up; *kara*—you do; *gauṇa-artha*—indirect meaning; *kalpanā*—imagining; *abhidhā-vṛtti*—the meaning that is understood immediately; *chāḍi'*—giving up; *kara*—you do; *śabdera*—of the words; *lakṣaṇā*—interpretation.

TRANSLATION

"For each verse the direct meaning must be accepted without interpretation. However, you simply abandon the direct meaning and proceed with your imaginative interpretation.

TEXT 135

প্রমাণের মধ্যে শ্রুতি প্রমাণ - প্রধান ।
শ্রুতি যে মুখ্যার্থ কহে, সেই সে প্রমাণ ॥ ১৩৫ ॥

pramāṇera madhye śruti pramāṇa——pradhāna
śruti ye mukhyārtha kahe, sei se pramāṇa

SYNONYMS

pramāṇera—of the evidences; *madhye*—in the midst; *śruti*—the Vedic version; *pramāṇa*—evidence; *pradhāna*—chief; *śruti*—the Vedic version; *ye*—whatever; *mukhya-artha*—chief meaning; *kahe*—says; *sei se*—that indeed; *pramāṇa*—evidence.

TRANSLATION

"Although there is other evidence, the evidence given in the Vedic version must be taken as foremost. Vedic versions understood directly are first-class evidence."

PURPORT

Works that should be consulted are Śrīla Jīva Gosvāmī's *Tattva-sandarbha* (10-11), Śrīla Baladeva Vidyābhūṣaṇa's commentary on that, and the following verses of the *Brahma-sūtra: śāstra-yonitvāt* (Vs. 1.1.3), *tarkāpratiṣṭhānāt* (Vs. 2.1.11) and *śrutes tu śabda-mūlatvāt* (Vs. 2.1.27) as commented upon by Śrī Rāmānujācārya, Śrī Madhvācārya, Śrī Nimbārkācārya and Śrīla Baladeva Vidyābhūṣaṇa. In his book *Sarva-saṁvādinī,* Śrīla Jīva Gosvāmī has noted that although there are ten kinds of evidence—direct perception, the Vedic version, historical reference, hypothesis, and so on—and although they are all generally accepted as evidence, the person presenting a hypothesis, reading the Vedic version, perceiving or interpreting by his experience is certain to be imperfect in four ways. That is, he is subject to commit mistakes, to become illusioned, to cheat and to have imperfect senses. Although the evidence may be correct, the person himself is in danger of being misled due to his material defects. Apart from the direct presentation, there is a chance that an interpretation may not be perfect.

Therefore the conclusion is that only a direct presentation can be considered evidence. An interpretation cannot be accepted as evidence, but may be considered proof of evidence.

In *Bhagavad-gītā,* at the very beginning it is stated:

dhṛtarāṣṭra uvāca
dharma-kṣetre kuru-kṣetre
samavetā yuyutsavaḥ
māmakāḥ pāṇḍavāś caiva
kim akurvata sañjaya

The statements of *Bhagavad-gītā* are themselves proof that there is a place of religious pilgrimage named Kurukṣetra where the Pāṇḍavas and Kurus met to fight. After meeting there, what did they do? This was Dhṛtarāṣṭra's inquiry to Sañjaya. Although these statements are very clear, atheists try to interpret different meanings of the words *dharma-kṣetra* and *kuru-kṣetra.* Therefore Śrīla Jīva Gosvāmī has warned us not to depend on any kind of interpretation. It is better to take the verses as they are, without interpretation.

TEXT 136

জীবের অস্থি-বিষ্ঠা দুই – শঙ্খ-গোময় ।
শ্রুতি-বাক্যে সেই দুই মহা-পবিত্র হয় ॥ ১৩৬ ॥

jīvera asthi-viṣṭhā dui——śaṅkha-gomaya
śruti-vākye sei dui mahā-pavitra haya

SYNONYMS

jīvera—of the living entity; *asthi*—the bone; *viṣṭhā*—stool; *dui*—two; *śaṅkha*—conchshell; *go-maya*—cow dung; *śruti-vākye*—in the words of the Vedic version; *sei*—that; *dui*—two; *mahā*—greatly; *pavitra*—pure; *haya*—are.

TRANSLATION

Caitanya Mahāprabhu continued: "Conchshells and cow dung are nothing but the bones and the stool of some living entities, but according to the Vedic version they are both considered very pure.

PURPORT

According to Vedic principles, bones and dung are generally considered very impure. If one touches a bone or stool, he must take a bath immediately. That is the Vedic injunction. Yet the *Vedas* also enjoin that a conchshell, although the bone of an animal, and cow dung, although the stool of an animal, are very sanctified. Even though such statements appear contradictory, we still accept the fact that conchshells and cow dung are pure and sanctified on the basis of the Vedic version.

TEXT 137

স্বতঃপ্রমাণ বেদ সত্য যেই কয়।
'লক্ষণা' করিলে স্বতঃপ্রামাণ্য-হানি হয়॥ ১৩৭॥

svataḥ-pramāṇa veda satya yei kaya
'lakṣaṇā' karile svataḥ-prāmāṇya-hāni haya

SYNONYMS

svataḥ-pramāṇa—self-evidence; *veda*—Vedic literature; *satya*—truth; *yei*—whatever; *kaya*—say; *lakṣaṇā*—interpretation; *karile*—by making; *svataḥ-prāmāṇya*—self-evidential proof; *hāni*—lost; *haya*—becomes.

TRANSLATION

"The Vedic statements are self-evident. Whatever is stated there must be accepted. If we interpret according to our own imagination, the authority of the Vedas is immediately lost."

PURPORT

Out of four main types of evidence—direct perception, hypothesis, historical reference and the *Vedas*—Vedic evidence is accepted as the foremost. If we want to interpret the Vedic version, we must imagine an interpretation according to what we want to do. First of all, we set forth such an interpretation as a suggestion or hypothesis. As such, it is not actually true, and the self-evident proof is lost.

Śrīla Madhvācārya, commenting on the aphorism *dṛśyate tu* (*Vedānta-sūtra* 2.1.6), quotes the *Bhaviṣya Purāṇa* as follows:

ṛg-yajuḥ-sāmātharvāś ca
bhāratam pañca-rātrakam
mūla-rāmāyaṇaṁ caiva
veda ity eva śabditāḥ

purāṇāni ca yānīha
vaiṣṇavāni vido viduḥ
svataḥ-prāmāṇyam eteṣāṁ
nātra kiñcid vicāryate

The *Ṛg Veda, Yajur Veda, Sāma Veda, Atharva Veda, Mahābhārata, Pañcarātra* and original *Rāmāyaṇa* are all considered Vedic literature. The *Purāṇas* (such as the *Brahma-vaivarta Purāṇa, Nāradīya Purāṇa, Viṣṇu Purāṇa* and *Bhāgavata Purāṇa*) are especially meant for Vaiṣṇavas and are also Vedic literature. As such, whatever is stated within the *Purāṇas,* the *Mahābhārata* and *Rāmāyaṇa* is self-evident. There is no need for interpretation. *Bhagavad-gītā* is also within the *Mahābhārata;* therefore all the statements of *Bhagavad-gītā* are self-evident. There is no need for interpretation, and if we do interpret, the entire authority of Vedic literature is lost.

TEXT 138

ব্যাস-সূত্রের অর্থ—যৈছে সূর্যের কিরণ ।
স্বকল্পিত ভাষ্য-মেঘে করে আচ্ছাদন ॥ ১৩৮ ॥

vyāsa-sūtrera artha——yaiche sūryera kiraṇa
sva-kalpita bhāṣya-meghe kare ācchādana

SYNONYMS

vyāsa-sūtrera—of the *Vedānta-sūtra* by Vyāsadeva; *artha*—the meanings; *yaiche*—just as; *sūryera*—of the sun; *kiraṇa*—shining rays; *sva-kalpita*—imaginative; *bhāṣya*—of the commentary; *meghe*—by the cloud; *kare*—does; *ācchādana*—covering.

TRANSLATION

Śrī Caitanya Mahāprabhu continued: "The Brahma-sūtra, compiled by Śrīla Vyāsadeva, is as radiant as the sun. One who tries to interpret its meaning simply covers that sunshine with a cloud.

TEXT 139

বেদ-পুরাণে কহে ব্রহ্ম-নিরূপণ ।
সেই ব্রহ্ম—বৃহদ্বস্তু, ঈশ্বর-লক্ষণ ॥ ১৩৯ ॥

veda-purāṇe kahe brahma-nirūpaṇa
sei brahma——bṛhad-vastu, īśvara-lakṣaṇa

SYNONYMS

veda-purāṇe—in the *Vedas* and the *Purāṇas; kahe*—it is stated; *brahma-nirūpaṇa*—ascertaining the Supreme; *sei brahma*—that Supreme; *bṛhat-vastu*—the greatest; *īśvara-lakṣaṇa*—means the Supreme Personality.

TRANSLATION

"All Vedic literature and other literature that strictly follows the Vedic principles ascertain that the Supreme Brahman is the Absolute Truth, the greatest of all, and a feature of the Supreme Lord.

PURPORT

The greatest of everything is Śrī Kṛṣṇa. Lord Kṛṣṇa states in *Bhagavad-gītā, vedaiś ca sarvair aham eva vedyaḥ:* "By all the *Vedas,* I am to be known." (Bg. 15.15) In *Śrīmad-Bhāgavatam* it is said that the Absolute Truth is understood in three phases—namely, Brahman, Paramātmā and Bhagavān, the Supreme Personality of Godhead (*brahmeti paramātmeti bhagavān iti śabdyate*). Thus the Supreme Personality of Godhead is the last word in understanding the Absolute Truth, Brahman.

TEXT 140

সর্বৈশ্বর্যপরিপূর্ণ স্বয়ং ভগবান্ ।
তাঁরে নিরাকার করি' করহ ব্যাখ্যান ॥ ১৪০ ॥

sarvaiśvarya-paripūrṇa svayaṁ bhagavān
tāṅre nirākāra kari' karaha vyākhyāna

SYNONYMS

sarva-aiśvarya-paripūrṇa—full with all opulences; *svayam*—personally; *bhagavān*—the Supreme Personality of Godhead; *tāṅre*—Him; *nirākāra*—impersonal; *kari'*—making; *karaha*—you make; *vyākhyāna*—explanation.

TRANSLATION

"Actually, the Supreme Absolute Truth is a person, the Supreme Personality of Godhead, full with all opulences. You are trying to explain Him as impersonal and formless.

PURPORT

Brahman means *bṛhattva,* the greatest of all. The greatest of all is Śrī Kṛṣṇa, the Supreme Personality of Godhead. He possesses all potencies and opulence in full; therefore the Absolute Truth, the greatest of all, is the Supreme Personality of Godhead. Whether one says "Brahman" or "the Supreme Personality of Godhead," the fact is the same, for they are identical. In *Bhagavad-gītā,* Arjuna accepted Kṛṣṇa as *paraṁ brahma paraṁ dhāma.* Although the living entities or material nature are sometimes described as Brahman, Paraṁ Brahma—the Supreme, the greatest of all Brahmans—is still Kṛṣṇa, the Supreme Personality of Godhead. He is full with all opulences, and as such He possesses all riches, all strength, all reputation, all knowledge, all beauty and all renunciation. He is eternally a person and eternally supreme. If one tries to explain the Supreme impersonally, one distorts the real meaning of Brahman.

TEXT 141

'নির্বিশেষ' তাঁরে কহে যেই শ্রুতিগণ ।
'প্রাকৃত' নিষেধি করে 'অপ্রাকৃত' স্থাপন ॥ ১৪১ ॥

'nirviśeṣa' tāṅre kahe yei śruti-gaṇa
'prākṛta' niṣedhi kare 'aprākṛta' sthāpana

SYNONYMS

nirviśeṣa—impersonal; *tāṅre*—Him; *kahe*—say; *yei*—whatever; *śruti-gaṇa*—the *Vedas; prākṛta*—mundane; *niṣedhi*—forbidding; *kare*—does; *aprākṛta*—transcendental; *sthāpana*—confirmation.

TRANSLATION

"Wherever there is an impersonal description in the Vedas, the Vedas mean to establish that everything belonging to the Supreme Personality of Godhead is transcendental and free of mundane characteristics."

PURPORT

There are many impersonal statements about the Supreme Personality of Godhead. As stated in the *Śvetāśvatara Upaniṣad:*

apāṇi-pādo javano grahītā
paśyaty acakṣuḥ sa śṛṇoty akarṇaḥ
sa vetti vedyaṁ na ca tasyāsti vettā
tam āhur agryaṁ puruṣaṁ mahāntam
(*Svet. Up.* 3.19)

Although the Supreme Lord is described as having no hands and legs, He nonetheless accepts all sacrificial offerings. He has no eyes, yet He sees everything. He has no ears, yet He hears everything. When it is stated that the Supreme Lord has no hands and legs, one should not think that He is impersonal. Rather, He has no *mundane* hands or legs like ours. "He has no eyes, yet He sees." This means that He does not have mundane, limited eyes like ours. Rather, He has such eyes that He can see past, present and future, everywhere, in every corner of the universe and in every corner of the heart of every living entity. Thus the impersonal descriptions in the *Vedas* intend to deny mundane characteristics in the Supreme Lord. They do not intend to establish the Supreme Lord as impersonal.

TEXT 142

যা যা শ্রুতির্জল্পতি নির্বিশেষং
সা সাভিধত্তে সবিশেষমেব ।
বিচারযোগে সতি হন্ত তাসাং
প্রায়ো বলীয়ঃ সবিশেষমেব ॥ ১৪২ ॥

yā yā śrutir jalpati nirviśeṣaṁ
sā sābhidhatte saviśeṣam eva
vicāra-yoge sati hanta tāsāṁ
prāyo balīyaḥ saviśeṣam eva

SYNONYMS

yā yā—whatever; *śrutiḥ*—the Vedic hymns; *jalpati*—describe; *nirviśeṣam*—impersonal truth; *sā*—that; *sā*—that; *abhidhatte*—directly describes (like a dictionary meaning); *sa-viśeṣam*—personality; *eva*—certainly; *vicāra-yoge*—when accepted by intelligence; *sati*—being; *hanta*—alas; *tāsām*—of all the Vedic *mantras; prāyaḥ*—mostly; *balīyaḥ*—more powerful; *sa-viśeṣam*—personal variety; *eva*—certainly.

TRANSLATION

Śrī Caitanya Mahāprabhu continued: " 'Whatever Vedic mantras describe the Absolute Truth impersonally only prove in the end that the Absolute Truth is a person. The Supreme Lord is understood in two features—impersonal and personal. If one considers the Supreme Personality of Godhead in both features, he can actually understand the Absolute Truth. He knows that the personal understanding is stronger beause we see that everything is full of variety. No one can see anything that is not full of variety.'

PURPORT

This is a quotation from the *Śrī Caitanya-candrodaya-nāṭaka* (6.67), by Kavi-Karṇapura.

TEXT 143

ব্রহ্ম হৈতে জন্মে বিশ্ব, ব্রহ্মেতে জীবয় ।
সেই ব্রহ্মে পুনরপি হয়ে যায় লয় ॥ ১৪৩ ॥

brahma haite janme viśva, brahmete jīvaya
sei brahme punarapi haye yāya laya

SYNONYMS

brahma haite—from the Supreme Brahman; *janme*—emanates; *viśva*—the whole cosmic manifestation; *brahmete*—in the Absolute Truth; *jīvaya*—exists; *sei*—that; *brahme*—in the Absolute Truth; *punarapi*—again; *haye*—being; *yāya*—goes; *laya*—to annihilation.

TRANSLATION

"Everything in the cosmic manifestation emanates from the Absolute Truth. It remains in the Absolute Truth, and after annihilation it again enters the Absolute Truth.

PURPORT

In the *Taittirīya Upaniṣad,* it is said, *yato vā imāni bhūtāni jāyante:* "The entire material cosmic manifestation is born of the Supreme Brahman." The *Brahma-sūtra* also begins with the verse *janmādy asya yataḥ:* "The Absolute Truth is that from whom everything emanates." (Bs. 1.1.2) That Absolute Truth is Kṛṣṇa. In *Bhagavad-gītā,* Kṛṣṇa says, *ahaṁ sarvasya prabhavo mattaḥ sarvaṁ pravartate:* "I am the source of all spiritual and material worlds. Everything emanates from Me." (Bg. 10.8) Therefore Kṛṣṇa is the original Absolute Truth, the Supreme Personality of Godhead. Again, Kṛṣṇa states in *Bhagavad-gītā, mayā tatam idaṁ sarvaṁ jagad avyakta-mūrtinā:* "By Me, in My unmanifested form, this entire universe is pervaded." (Bg. 9.4) And as confirmed in *Brahma-saṁhitā, goloka eva nivasaty akhilātma-bhūtaḥ:* "Although the Lord always stays in His abode, Goloka Vṛndāvana, He is still all-pervading." (Bs. 5.37) His all-pervasive feature is understood to be impersonal because one does not find the form of the Lord in that all-pervasiveness. Actually, everything is resting on the rays of His bodily effulgence. The *Brahma-saṁhitā* also states:

yasya prabhā prabhavato jagad-aṇḍa-koṭi-
koṭiṣv aśeṣa-vasudhādi-vibhūti-bhinnam

"Due to the rays of the Lord's bodily effulgence, millions of universes are created, just as planets are created from the sun." (Bs. 5.40)

TEXT 144

'অপাদান', 'করণ', 'অধিকরণ'-কারক তিন ।
ভগবানের সবিশেষে এই তিন চিহ্ন ॥ ১৪৪ ॥

'apādāna,' 'karaṇa,' 'adhikaraṇa'-kāraka tina
bhagavānera saviśeṣe ei tina cihna

SYNONYMS

apādāna—ablative; *karaṇa*—instrumental; *adhikaraṇa*—locative; *kāraka*—cases; *tina*—three; *bhagavānera*—of the Supreme Personality of Godhead; *saviśeṣa*—in the personality; *ei*—these; *tina*—three; *cihna*—symptoms.

TRANSLATION

"The personal features of the Supreme Personality of Godhead are categorized in three cases—namely, ablative, instrumental and locative."

PURPORT

Śrīla Bhaktivinoda Ṭhākura states in his *Amṛta-pravāha-bhāṣya* that according to the injunction of the *Upaniṣads* ("the Supreme Absolute Truth is He from whom everything emanates"), it is understood that the whole cosmic manifestation emanated from Brahman, the Supreme Absolute Truth. The creation subsists by the energy of the Supreme Brahman and, after annihilation, merges into the Supreme Brahman. From this we can understand that the Absolute Truth can be categorized in three cases—ablative, instrumental and locative. According to these three cases, the Absolute Truth is positively personified. In this connection, Śrīla Bhaktisiddhānta Sarasvatī quotes the *Aitareya Upaniṣad* (1.1.1):

ātmā vā idam eka evāgra āsīn
nānyat kiñcanam īṣat
sa īkṣata lokān nu sṛjā iti.

Similarly, in the *Śvetāśvatara Upaniṣad* (4.9) it is stated:

chandāṁsi yajñāḥ kratavo vratāni
bhūtaṁ bhavyaṁ yac ca vedā vadanti
yasmān māyī sṛjate viśvam etat
tasmiṁś cānyo māyayā sanniruddhaḥ

And in the *Taittirīya Upaniṣad (3.1.1):*

yato vā imāni bhūtāni jāyante,
yena jātāni jīvanti, yat prayanty abhisaṁviśanti,
tad vijijñāsasva, tad brahma.

This was the answer given by father Varuṇa when questioned by his son Vāruṇī Bhṛgu about the Absolute Truth. In this *mantra,* the word *yataḥ,* the Absolute Truth from which the cosmic manifestation has emanated, is in the ablative case; that Brahman by which this universal creation is maintained is in the instrumental case (*yena*); and that Brahman into which the whole cosmic manifestation merges is in the locative case (*yat* or *yasmin*). It is stated in *Śrīmad-Bhāgavatam:*

idaṁ hi viśvaṁ bhagavān ivetaro
yato jagat-sthāna-nirodha-sambhavāḥ

"The entire universal creation is contained in the gigantic form of the Supreme Personality of Godhead. Everything emanates from Him, everything rests in His energy, and after annihilation everything merges into His person." (*Bhāg.* 1.5.20)

TEXTS 145-146

ভগবান্ বহু হৈতে যবে কৈল মন ।
প্রাকৃত-শক্তিতে তবে কৈল বিলোকন ॥ ১৪৫ ॥
সে কালে নাহি জন্মে 'প্রাকৃত' মনোনয়ন ।
অতএব 'অপ্রাকৃত' ব্রহ্মের নেত্র-মন ॥ ১৪৬ ॥

bhagavān bahu haite yabe kaila mana
prākṛta-śaktite tabe kaila vilokana

se kāle nāhi janme 'prākṛta' mano-nayana
ataeva 'aprākṛta' brahmera netra-mana

SYNONYMS

bhagavān—the Supreme Personality of Godhead; *bahu*—many; *haite*—to become; *yabe*—when; *kaila*—made; *mana*—His mind; *prākṛta*—material; *śaktite*—on the energy; *tabe*—at that time; *kaila*—did; *vilokana*—glancing; *se kāle*—at that time; *nāhi*—not; *janme*—in creation; *prākṛta*—mundane; *manaḥ-nayana*—mind and eyes; *ataeva*—therefore; *aprākṛta*—transcendental; *brahmera*—of the Absolute Truth; *netra-mana*—eyes and mind.

TRANSLATION

Śrī Caitanya Mahāprabhu continued: "When the Supreme Personality of Godhead wished to become many, He glanced over the material energy. Before the creation there were no mundane eyes or mind; therefore the transcendental nature of the Absolute Truth's mind and eyes is confirmed.

PURPORT

In the *Chāndogya Upaniṣad* (6.2.3), it is said, *tad aikṣata bahu syāṁ prajāyeya.* This verse confirms the fact that when the Supreme Personality of Godhead wishes to become many, the cosmic manifestation arises simply by His glancing over material energy. It may be noted that the Supreme Lord glanced over the material nature before the creation of this cosmic manifestation. Before the creation there were no material minds or material eyes; therefore the mind by which the Supreme Personality of Godhead desired to create is transcendental, and the eyes with which He glanced over material nature are also transcendental. Thus the Lord's mind, eyes and other senses are all transcendental.

TEXT 147

ব্রহ্ম-শব্দে কহে পূর্ণ স্বয়ং ভগবান্ ।
স্বয়ং ভগবান্ কৃষ্ণ,—শাস্ত্রের প্রমাণ ॥ ১৪৭ ॥

brahma-śabde kahe pūrṇa svayaṁ bhagavān
svayaṁ bhagavān kṛṣṇa,——śāstrera pramāṇa

SYNONYMS

brahma-śabde—by the word "Brahman"; *kahe*—it is said; *pūrṇa*—complete; *svayam*—personally; *bhagavān*—the Supreme Personality of Godhead; *svayam*—personally; *bhagavān*—the Supreme Personality of Godhead; *kṛṣṇa*—Lord Kṛṣṇa; *śāstrera pramāṇa*—the verdict of all Vedic literature.

TRANSLATION

"The word 'Brahman' indicates the complete Supreme Personality of Godhead, who is Śrī Kṛṣṇa. That is the verdict of all Vedic literature.

PURPORT

This is also confirmed in *Bhagavad-gītā* (15.15), where the Lord says, *vedaiś ca sarvair aham eva vedyaḥ.* The ultimate object in all Vedic literature is Kṛṣṇa. Everyone is searching for Him. This is also confirmed elsewhere in *Bhagavad-gītā:*

bahūnāṁ janmanām ante
jñānavān māṁ prapadyate
vāsudevaḥ sarvam iti
sa mahātmā sudurlabhaḥ

"After many births and deaths, he who is actually in knowledge surrenders unto Me, knowing Me to be the cause of all causes and all that is. Such a great soul is very rare." (Bg. 7.19)

When one has actually become wise through the study of Vedic literature, he surrenders unto Vāsudeva, Bhagavān Śrī Kṛṣṇa. This is also confirmed in *Śrīmad-Bhāgavatam* (1.2.7-8):

vāsudeve bhagavati
bhakti-yogaḥ prayojitaḥ
janayaty āśu vairāgyaṁ
jñānaṁ ca yad ahaitukam

dharmaḥ svanuṣṭhitaḥ puṁsāṁ
viṣvaksena-kathāsu yaḥ
notpādayed yadi ratiṁ
śrama eva hi kevalam

Understanding Vāsudeva is real knowledge. By engaging in the devotional service of Vāsudeva, Kṛṣṇa, one acquires perfect knowledge and Vedic understanding. Thus one becomes detached from the material world. This is the perfection of human life. Although one may perfectly follow religious rituals and ceremonies, he is simply wasting his time (*śrama eva hi kevalam*) if he does not attain this perfection.

Before the creation of the cosmic manifestation, the Supreme Personality of Godhead possessed His totally transcendental mind and eyes. That Supreme Personality of Godhead is Kṛṣṇa. A person may think that there is no direct statement about Kṛṣṇa in the *Upaniṣads,* but the fact is that the Vedic *mantras* cannot be understood by people with mundane senses. As stated in the *Padma Purāṇa, ataḥ śrī kṛṣṇa nāmādi na bhaved grāhyam indriyaiḥ:* a person with mundane senses cannot fully understand the name, qualities, form and pastimes of Śrī Kṛṣṇa. The *Purāṇas* are therefore meant to explain and supplement Vedic knowledge. The great sages present the *Purāṇas* in order to make the Vedic *mantras* understandable for common men (*strī-śūdra-dvija-bandhūnām*). Considering that women, *śūdras* and *dvija-bandhus* (unworthy sons of the twice-born) cannot understand the Vedic hymns directly, Śrīla Vyāsadeva compiled *Mahābhārata.* Actually the Supreme Personality of Godhead is *vedeṣu durlabham* (untraceable in the *Vedas*), but when the *Vedas* are properly understood or when Vedic knowledge is received from devotees, one can understand that all Vedic knowledge leads to Śrī Kṛṣṇa.

The *Brahma-sūtra* (1.1.3) confirms this fact also: *śāstra-yonitvāt.* Commenting upon this *Brahma-sūtra* code (*śāstra-yonitvāt*), Śrī Madhvācārya says: "The *Ṛg Veda, Yajur Veda, Sāma Veda, Atharva Veda, Mahābhārata, Pañcarātra* and the original Vālmīki *Rāmāyaṇa* are all Vedic literature. Any literature following the conclusive statements of this Vedic literature is also to be considered Vedic literature. That literature which does not conform to Vedic literature is simply misleading."

Therefore when reading Vedic literature, we must take the path traversed by great *ācāryas: mahājano yena gataḥ sa panthāḥ*. Unless one follows the path traversed by great *ācāryas,* he cannot understand the real purport of the *Vedas.*

TEXT 148

বেদের নিগূঢ় অর্থ বুঝন না হয় ।
পুরাণ-বাক্যে সেই অর্থ করয় নিশ্চয় ॥ ১৪৮ ॥

vedera nigūḍha artha bujhana nā haya
purāṇa-vākye sei artha karaya niścaya

SYNONYMS

vedera—of the Vedic literature; *nigūḍha*—confidential; *artha*—meaning; *bujhana*—understanding; *nā*—not; *haya*—is; *purāṇa-vākye*—by the words of the *Purāṇas; sei*—that; *artha*—meaning; *karaya*—makes; *niścaya*—certain.

TRANSLATION

"The confidential meaning of the Vedas is not easily understood by common men; therefore that meaning is supplemented by the words of the Purāṇas.

TEXT 149

অহো ভাগ্যমহো ভাগ্যং নন্দগোপব্রজৌকসাম্ ।
যন্মিত্রং পরমানন্দং পূর্ণং ব্রহ্ম সনাতনম্ ॥ ১৪৯ ॥

aho bhāgyam aho bhāgyaṁ
nanda-gopa-vrajaukasām
yan-mitraṁ paramānandaṁ
pūrṇaṁ brahma sanātanam

SYNONYMS

aho—what great; *bhāgyam*—fortune; *aho*—what great; *bhāgyam*—fortune; *nanda*—of Mahārāja Nanda; *gopa*—of other cowherd men; *vraja-okasām*—of the inhabitants of Vrajabhūmi; *yat*—of whom; *mitram*—friend; *parama-ānandam*—the supreme bliss; *pūrṇam*—complete; *brahma*—the Absolute Truth; *sanātanam*—eternal.

TRANSLATION

" 'How greatly fortunate are Nanda Mahārāja, the cowherd men and all the inhabitants of Vrajabhūmi! There is no limit to their fortune because the Ab-

solute Truth, the source of transcendental bliss, the eternal Supreme Brahman, has become their friend.'

PURPORT

This is a quotation from *Śrīmad-Bhāgavatam* (10.14.32) spoken by Lord Brahmā.

TEXT 150

'অপাণি-পাদ'-শ্রুতি বর্জে 'প্রাকৃত' পাণি-চরণ ।
পুনঃ কহে, শীঘ্র চলে, করে সর্ব গ্রহণ ॥ ১৫০ ॥

'apāṇi-pāda'-śruti varje 'prākṛta' pāṇi-caraṇa
punaḥ kahe, śīghra cale, kare sarva grahaṇa

SYNONYMS

apāṇi-pāda-śruti—the *śruti-mantra* beginning *apāni-pādaḥ; varje*—rejects; *prākṛta*—material; *pāṇi-caraṇa*—hands and legs; *punaḥ*—again; *kahe*—says; *śīghra cale*—walks very fast; *kare*—does; *sarva*—of everything; *grahaṇa*—accepting.

TRANSLATION

"The Vedic 'apāṇi-pāda' mantra rejects material hands and legs, yet it states that the Lord goes very fast and accepts everything offered to Him.

TEXT 151

অতএব শ্রুতি কহে, ব্রহ্ম—সবিশেষ ।
'মুখ্য' ছাড়ি' 'লক্ষণা'তে মানে নির্বিশেষ ॥ ১৫১ ॥

ataeva śruti kahe, brahma——saviśeṣa
'mukhya' chāḍi' 'lakṣaṇā'te māne nirviśeṣa

SYNONYMS

ataeva—therefore; *śruti*—Vedic *mantras; kahe*—say; *brahma*—the Absolute Truth; *sa-viśeṣa*—personal; *mukhya*—direct meaning; *chāḍi'*—giving up; *lakṣaṇā'te*—by interpretation; *māne*—accept; *nirviśeṣa*—impersonal.

TRANSLATION

"All these mantras confirm that the Absolute Truth is personal, but the Māyāvādīs, throwing away the direct meaning, interpret the Absolute Truth as impersonal.

PURPORT

According to the *Śvetāśvatara Upaniṣad* (3.19):

apāṇi-pādo javano grahītā
paśyaty acakṣuḥ sa śṛṇoty akarṇaḥ
sa vetti vedyaṁ na ca tasyāsti vettā
tam āhur agryaṁ puruṣaṁ mahāntam

This Vedic *mantra* clearly states, *puruṣaṁ mahāntam.* The word *puruṣa* means "person." That person is confirmed in *Bhagavad-gītā* by Arjuna when he addresses Kṛṣṇa, *puruṣaṁ śāśvatam:* "You are the original person." (Bg. 10.12) This *puruṣaṁ mahāntam* is Śrī Kṛṣṇa. His hands and legs are not mundane, but are completely transcendental. However, when He comes, fools take Him to be an ordinary person (*avajānanti māṁ mūḍhā mānuṣīṁ tanum āśritam*). One who has no Vedic knowledge, who has not studied the *Vedas* from the bona fide spiritual master, does not know Kṛṣṇa. Therefore he is a *mūḍha.* Such fools take Kṛṣṇa to be an ordinary person (*paraṁ bhāvam ajānantaḥ*). They do not actually know what Kṛṣṇa is. *Manuṣyāṇāṁ sahasreṣu kaścid yatati siddhaye.* It is not possible to understand Kṛṣṇa simply by studying the *Vedas* perfectly. One must have the mercy of a devotee (*yat pādam*). Unless one is favored by a devotee, he cannot understand the Supreme Personality of Godhead. Arjuna also confirms this in *Bhagavad-gītā:* "My Lord, it is very difficult to understand Your personality." The less intelligent class of men cannot understand the Supreme Personality of Godhead without being favored by His devotee. Therefore *Bhagavad-gītā* contains another injunction (Bg. 4.34):

tad viddhi praṇipātena
paripraśnena sevayā
upadekṣyanti te jñānaṁ
jñāninas tattva-darśinaḥ

One has to approach a bona fide spiritual master and surrender to him. Only then can one understand the Supreme Personality of Godhead as a person.

TEXT 152

ষড়ৈশ্বর্যপূর্ণানন্দ-বিগ্রহ যাঁহার ।
হেন-ভগবানে তুমি কহ নিরাকার ? ১৫২ ॥

ṣaḍ-aiśvarya-pūrṇānanda-vigraha yāṅhāra
hena-bhagavāne tumi kaha nirākāra?

SYNONYMS

ṣaṭ-aiśvarya-pūrṇa—with six opulences in full; *ānanda*—blissful; *vigraha*—form; *yāṅhāra*—whose; *hena-bhagavāne*—unto that Supreme Personality of Godhead; *tumi*—you; *kaha*—said; *nirākāra*—without any form.

TRANSLATION

"Are you describing as formless that Supreme Personality of Godhead whose transcendental form is complete with six transcendental opulences?

PURPORT

If the Supreme Personality of Godhead is formless, how can He be said to walk very fast and accept everything offered to Him? Rejecting the direct meaning of the Vedic *mantras,* the Māyāvādī philosophers interpret them and try to establish the Absolute Truth as formless. Actually, the Supreme Lord has an eternal, personal form, full of all opulence. The Māyāvādī philosophers try to interpret the Absolute Truth as being without potency. However, in the *Śvetāśvatara Upaniṣad* it is clearly said, *parāsya śaktir vividhaiva śrūyate:* "The Absolute Truth has multi-potencies." (*Śvet. Up.* 6.8)

TEXT 153

স্বাভাবিক তিন শক্তি যেই ব্রহ্মে হয়।
'নিঃশক্তিক' করি' তাঁরে করহ নিশ্চয় ? ১৫৩ ॥

svābhāvika tina śakti yei brahme haya
'niḥśaktika' kari' tāṅre karaha niścaya?

SYNONYMS

svābhāvika—by nature; *tina*—three; *śakti*—potencies; *yei*—which; *brahme*—in the Absolute Truth; *haya*—there are; *niḥśaktika*—without potency; *kari'*—making; *tāṅre*—Him; *karaha*—you do; *niścaya*—ascertainment.

TRANSLATION

"The Supreme Personality of Godhead has three primary potencies. Are you trying to ascertain that He has no potencies?

PURPORT

Śrī Caitanya Mahāprabhu now quotes four verses from the *Viṣṇu Purāṇa* (6.7.61-63 and 1.12.69) to explain the different potencies of the Lord.

TEXT 154

বিষ্ণুশক্তিঃ পরা প্রোক্তা ক্ষেত্রজ্ঞাখ্যা তথাপরা ।
অবিদ্যাকর্মসংজ্ঞান্যা তৃতীয়া শক্তিরিষ্যতে ॥ ১৫৪ ॥

viṣṇu-śaktiḥ parā proktā
kṣetra-jnākhyā tathā parā
avidyā-karma-saṁjñānyā
tṛtīyā śaktir iṣyate

SYNONYMS

viṣṇu-śaktiḥ—the internal potency of Lord Viṣṇu, the Supreme Personality of Godhead; *parā*—spiritual; *proktā*—said; *kṣetra-jña*—the living entities; *ākhyā*—known as; *tathā*—also; *parā*—spiritual; *avidyā*—nescience, or godlessness; *karma*—and fruitive activities; *saṁjñā*—known as; *anyā*—another; *tṛtīyā*—third; *śaktiḥ*—potency; *iṣyate*—is accepted as.

TRANSLATION

" 'The internal potency of the Supreme Lord, Viṣṇu, is spiritual, as verified by the śāstras. There is another spiritual potency, known as kṣetra-jña, or the living entity. The third potency, which is known as nescience, makes the living entity godless and fills him with fruitive activity.

PURPORT

In *Bhagavad-gītā,* in Śrī Kṛṣṇa's discourse on the *kṣetra* and the *kṣetra-jña,* it is clearly stated that the *kṣetra-jña* is the living entity who knows his field of activities. The living entities in the material world are forgetful of their eternal relationship with the Supreme Personality of Godhead. This forgetfulness is called *avidyā,* or nescience. The *avidyā-śakti,* the *avidyā* potency of the material world, provokes fruitive activity. Although this *avidyā-śakti* (material energy, or nescience) is also an energy of the Supreme Personality of Godhead, it is especially intended to keep the living entities in a state of forgetfulness. This is due to their rebellious attitude toward the Lord. Thus although the living entities are constitutionally spiritual, they come under the influence of the potency of nescience. How this happens is described in the following verse.

TEXT 155

যয়া ক্ষেত্রজ্ঞশক্তিঃ সা বেষ্টিতা নৃপ সর্বগা ।
সংসারতাপানখিলানবাপ্নোত্যত্র সন্ততান্ ॥ ১৫৫ ॥

yayā kṣetra-jña-śaktiḥ sā
veṣṭitā nṛpa sarva-gā
saṁsāra-tāpān akhilān
avāpnoty atra santatān

SYNONYMS

yayā—by which; *kṣetra-jña-śaktiḥ*—the living entities, known as the *kṣetra-jña* potency; *sā*—that potency; *veṣṭitā*—covered; *nṛpa*—O King; *sarva-gā*—capable of going anywhere in the spiritual or material worlds; *saṁsāra-tāpān*—miseries due to the cycle of repeated birth and death; *akhilān*—all kinds of; *avāpnoti*—obtains; *atra*—in this material world; *santatān*—arising from suffering or enjoying various kinds of reactions to fruitive activities.

TRANSLATION

" 'O King, the kṣetra-jña-śakti is the living entity. Although he has the facility to live in either the material or spiritual world, he suffers the threefold miseries of material existence because he is influenced by the avidyā [nescience] potency, which covers his constitutional position.

TEXT 156

তয়া তিরোহিতত্বাচ্চ শক্তিঃ ক্ষেত্রজ্ঞসংজ্ঞিতা ।
সর্বভূতেষু ভূপাল তারতম্যেন বর্ততে ॥ ১৫৬ ॥

tayā tirohitatvāc ca
śaktiḥ kṣetra-jña-saṁjñitā
sarva-bhūteṣu bhū-pāla
tāratamyena vartate

SYNONYMS

tayā—by her; *tiraḥ-hitatvāt*—from being freed from the influence; *ca*—also; *śaktiḥ*—the potency; *kṣetra-jña*—*kṣetra-jña; saṁjñitā*—known by the name; *sarva-bhūteṣu*—in different types of bodies; *bhū-pāla*—O King; *tāratamyena*—in different degrees; *vartate*—exists.

TRANSLATION

" 'This living entity, covered by the influence of nescience, exists in different forms in the material condition. O King, he is thus proportionately freed from the influence of material energy, to greater or lesser degrees.'

PURPORT

The material energy acts on the living entity in different degrees, according to how he acquires the association of the three modes of material nature. There are 8,400,000 species of life, some inferior, some superior and some mediocre. The gradations of the bodies are calculated according to the covering of material energy. In the lower categories—including aquatics, trees, plants, insects, birds and so forth—spiritual consciousness is almost nonexistent. In the mediocre category—the human form of life—spiritual consciousness is comparatively awakened. In the superior life forms, spiritual consciousness is fully awakened. Then the living entity understands his real position and tries to escape the influence of material energy by developing Kṛṣṇa consciousness.

TEXT 157

হ্লাদিনী সন্ধিনী সম্বিৎ ত্বয্যেকা সর্বসংশ্রয়ে ।
হ্লাদতাপকরী মিশ্রা ত্বয়ি নো গুণ-বর্জিতে ॥ ১৫৭ ॥

hlādinī sandhinī samvit
tvayy ekā sarva-saṁśraye
hlāda-tāpa-karī miśrā
tvayi no guṇa-varjite

SYNONYMS

hlādinī—the pleasure potency; *sandhinī*—the eternity potency; *samvit*—the knowledge potency; *tvayi*—in You; *ekā*—one spiritual (*cit*) potency; *sarva-saṁśraye*—the shelter of everything; *hlāda*—pleasure; *tāpa-karī*—causing displeasure; *miśrā*—mixed; *tvayi*—in You; *no*—not; *guṇa-varjite*—devoid of all material qualities.

TRANSLATION

" 'The Supreme Personality of Godhead is sac-cid-ānanda-vigraha. This means that He originally has three potencies—the pleasure potency, the potency of eternality and the potency of knowledge. Together these are called the cit potency, and they are present in full in the Supreme Lord. For the living entities, who are part and parcel of the Lord, the pleasure potency in the material world is sometimes displeasing and sometimes mixed. This is not the case with the Supreme Personality of Godhead because He is not under the influence of the material energy or its modes.'

PURPORT

This is a quotation from the *Viṣṇu Purāṇa* (1.12.69).

TEXT 158

সচ্চিদানন্দময় হয় ঈশ্বর-স্বরূপ ।
তিন অংশে চিচ্ছক্তি হয় তিন রূপ ॥ ১৫৮ ॥

sac-cid-ānanda-maya haya īśvara-svarūpa
tina aṁśe cic-chakti haya tina rūpa

SYNONYMS

sat-cit-ānanda-maya—full of eternity, knowledge and bliss; *haya*—is; *īśvara*—of the Supreme Lord; *svarūpa*—the transcendental form; *tina aṁśe*—in three parts; *cit-śakti*—the spiritual potency; *haya*—becomes; *tina*—three; *rūpa*—forms.

TRANSLATION

"The Supreme Personality of Godhead in His original form is full of eternity, knowledge and bliss. The spiritual potency in these three portions [sat, cit and ānanda] assumes three different forms.

PURPORT

According to the verdict of all Vedic literature, the Supreme Personality of Godhead, the living entity and the illusory energy (this material world) constitute the subject matter of knowledge. Everyone should try to understand the relationship between them. First of all, one should try to understand the nature of the Supreme Personality of Godhead. From the *śāstras* we understand that the nature of the Supreme Personality of Godhead is the sum total of eternity, bliss and knowledge. As stated in verse 154 (*viṣṇu-śaktiḥ parā proktā*), the Supreme Personality of Godhead is the reservoir of all potencies, and His potencies are all spiritual.

TEXT 159

আনন্দাংশে 'হ্লাদিনী', সদংশে 'সন্ধিনী' ।
চিদংশে 'সম্বিৎ', যারে জ্ঞান করি মানি ॥ ১৫৯ ॥

ānandāṁśe 'hlādinī,' sad-aṁśe 'sandhinī'
cid-aṁśe 'samvit', yāre jñāna kari māni

SYNONYMS

ānanda-aṁśe—in the part of bliss; *hlādinī*—the pleasure potency; *sat-aṁśe*—in the part of eternity; *sandhinī*—the *sandhinī* potency; *cit-aṁśe*—in the part of knowledge; *samvit*—the *samvit* potency; *yāre*—which; *jñāna*—as knowledge; *kari māni*—we accept.

TRANSLATION

"The three portions of the spiritual potency are called hlādinī [the bliss portion], sandhinī [the eternity portion] and samvit [the knowledge portion]. We accept knowledge of these as full knowledge of the Supreme Personality of Godhead.

PURPORT

To acquire knowledge of the Supreme Personality of Godhead, one must take shelter of the *samvit* potency of the Supreme Lord.

TEXT 160

অন্তরঙ্গা—চিচ্ছক্তি, তটস্থা—জীবশক্তি ।
বহিরঙ্গা—মায়া,—তিনে করে প্রেমভক্তি ॥ ১৬০ ॥

antaraṅgā—cic-chakti, taṭasthā—jīva-śakti
bahiraṅgā—māyā,—tine kare prema-bhakti

SYNONYMS

antaraṅgā—the internal potency; *cit-śakti*—the spiritual potency; *taṭasthā*—the marginal potency; *jīva-śakti*—the living entities; *bahiraṅgā*—the external potency; *māyā*—the illusory energy; *tine*—all three of them; *kare*—do; *prema-bhakti*—devotional service in love.

TRANSLATION

"The spiritual potency of the Supreme Personality of Godhead also appears in three phases—internal, marginal and external. These are all engaged in His devotional service in love.

PURPORT

The spiritual potency of the Lord is manifested in three phases—the internal or spiritual potency, the marginal potency, which is the living entities, and the external potency, known as *māyā-śakti*. We must understand that in each of these three phases the original spiritual potencies of pleasure, eternity and knowledge remain intact. When the potencies of spiritual pleasure and knowledge are both bestowed upon the conditioned souls, the conditioned souls can escape the clutches of the external potency, *māyā*, which acts as a cover obscuring one's spiritual identity. When freed, the living entity awakens to Kṛṣṇa consciousness and engages in devotional service with love and affection.

TEXT 161

ষড়্‌বিধ ঐশ্বর্য—প্রভুর চিচ্ছক্তি-বিলাস ।
হেন শক্তি নাহি মান,—পরম সাহস ॥ ১৬১ ॥

ṣaḍ-vidha aiśvarya——prabhuracic-chakti-vilāsa
hena śakti nāhi māna,——parama sāhasa

SYNONYMS

ṣaṭ-vidha—six kinds; *aiśvarya*—of opulences; *prabhura*—of the Lord; *cit-śakti-vilāsa*—enjoyment in the spiritual potency; *hena śakti*—such sublime potencies; *nāhi*—not; *māna*—you accept; *paramasāhasa*—great impudence.

TRANSLATION

"In His spiritual potency, the Supreme Lord enjoys six kinds of opulence. You do not accept this spiritual potency, and this is due to your great impudence.

PURPORT

The Supreme Personality of Godhead is full with six opulences. All of these potencies are on the transcendental platform. To understand the Supreme Personality of Godhead as impersonal and devoid of potency is to go completely against Vedic information.

TEXT 162

'মায়াধীশ' 'মায়াবশ' —ঈশ্বরে-জীবে ভেদ ।
হেন-জীবে ঈশ্বর-সহ কহ ত' অভেদ ॥ ১৬২ ॥

'māyādhīśa' 'māyā-vaśa'——īśvare-jīve bheda
hena-jīve īśvara-saha kaha ta' abheda

SYNONYMS

māyā-adhīśa—the Lord of energy; *māyā-vaśa*—subjected to the influence of *māyā; īśvare*—in the Supreme Personality of Godhead; *jīve*—in the living entities; *bheda*—the difference; *hena-jīve*—such living entities; *īśvara-saha*—with the Supreme Personality of Godhead; *kaha*—you say; *ta'*—indeed; *abheda*—one and the same.

TRANSLATION

"The Lord is the master of the potencies, and the living entity is the servant of them. That is the difference between the Lord and the living entity. However, you declare that the Lord and the living entities are one and the same.

PURPORT

The Supreme Personality of Godhead is by nature the master of all potencies. By nature, the living entities, being infinitesimal, are always under the influence of the Lord's potencies. According to the *Muṇḍaka Upaniṣad* (3.1.1-2):

dvā suparṇā sayujā sakhāyā
samānaṁ vṛkṣaṁ pariṣa-svajāte
tayor anyaḥ pippalaṁ svādv atty
anaśnann anyo 'bhicākaśīti

samāne vṛkṣe puruṣo nimagno
'nīṣayā śocati muhyamānaḥ
juṣṭaṁ yadā paśyaty anyam īśam
asya mahimānam eti vīta-śokaḥ

The *Muṇḍaka Upaniṣad* completely distinguishes the Lord from the living entities. The living entity is subjected to the reactions of fruitive activity, whereas the Lord simply witnesses such activity and bestows the results. According to the living entity's desires, he is wandering from one body to another and from one planet to another, under the direction of the Supreme Personality of Godhead, Paramātmā. However, when the living entity comes to his senses by the mercy of the Lord, he is awarded devotional service. Thus he is saved from the clutches of *māyā.* At such a time he can see his eternal friend, the Supreme Personality of Godhead, and become free from all lamentation and hankering. This is confirmed in *Bhagavad-gītā* (18.54), where the Lord says, *brahma-bhūtaḥ prasannātmā na śocati na kāṅkṣati:* "One who is thus transcendentally situated at once realizes the Supreme Brahman. He never laments nor desires to have anything." Thus it is definitely proved that the Supreme Personality of Godhead is the master of all potencies and that the living entities are always subjected to these potencies. That is the difference between *māyādhīśa* and *māyā-vaśa.*

TEXT 163

গীতাশাস্ত্রে জীবরূপ 'শক্তি' করি' মানে ।
হেন জীবে 'ভেদ' কর ঈশ্বরের সনে ॥ ১৬৩ ॥

gītā-śāstre jīva-rūpa 'śakti' kari' māne
hena jīve 'bheda' kara īśvarera sane

SYNONYMS

gītā-śāstre—in *Bhagavad-gītā; jīva-rūpa*—the identity of the living entity; *śakti*—potency; *kari'*—making; *māne*—accepts; *hena*—such; *jīve*—living entity; *bheda*—different; *kara*—you make; *īśvarera*—the Supreme Personality of Godhead; *sane*—with.

TRANSLATION

"In Bhagavad-gītā the living entity is established as the marginal potency of the Supreme Personality of Godhead. Yet you say that the living entity is completely different from the Lord.

PURPORT

The *Brahma-sūtra* states that according to the principle of *śakti-śaktimator abhedaḥ,* the living entity is simultaneously one with and different from the Supreme Personality of Godhead. Qualitatively the living entity and the Supreme Lord are one, but in quantity they are different. According to Śrī Caitanya Mahāprabhu's philosophy (*acintya-bhedābheda-tattva*), the living entity and the Supreme Lord are accepted as one and different at the same time.

TEXT 164

ভূমিরাপোঽনলো বায়ুঃ খং মনো বুদ্ধিরেব চ ।
অহঙ্কার ইতীয়ং মে ভিন্না প্রকৃতিরষ্টধা ॥ ১৬৪ ॥

bhūmir āpo 'nalo vāyuḥ
khaṁ mano buddhir eva ca
ahaṅkāra itīyaṁ me
bhinnā prakṛtir aṣṭadhā

SYNONYMS

bhūmiḥ—earth; *āpaḥ*—water; *analaḥ*—fire; *vāyuḥ*—air; *kham*—ether; *manaḥ*—mind; *buddhiḥ*—intelligence; *eva*—certainly; *ca*—and; *ahaṅkāraḥ*—false ego; *iti*—thus; *iyam*—this; *me*—My; *bhinnā*—separated; *prakṛtiḥ*—energy; *aṣṭa-dhā*—eightfold.

TRANSLATION

"'Earth, water, fire, air, ether, mind, intelligence and false ego are My eightfold separated energies.

TEXT 165

অপরেয়মিতস্ত্বন্যাং প্রকৃতিং বিদ্ধি মে পরাম্ ।
জীবভূতাং মহাবাহো যয়েদং ধার্যতে জগৎ ॥ ১৬৫ ॥

apareyam itas tv anyāṁ
prakṛtiṁ viddhi me parām
jīva-bhūtāṁ mahā-bāho
yayedaṁ dhāryate jagat

SYNONYMS

aparā—inferior; *iyam*—this; *itaḥ*—from this; *tu*—but; *anyām*—another; *prakṛtim*—nature; *viddhi*—know; *me*—My; *parām*—transcendental; *jīva-bhūtām*—existing as the living entities; *mahā-bāho*—O mighty-armed one; *yayā*—by which; *idam*—this; *dhāryate*—is sustained; *jagat*—material world.

TRANSLATION

" 'Besides these inferior energies, which are material, there is another energy, a spiritual energy, and this is the living being, O mighty-armed one. The entire material world is sustained by the living entities.'

PURPORT

Verses 164 and 165 are quotations from *Bhagavad-gītā* (7.4-5).

TEXT 166

ঈশ্বরের শ্রীবিগ্রহ সচ্চিদানন্দাকার ।
সে-বিগ্রহে কহ সত্ত্বগুণের বিকার ॥ ১৬৬ ॥

īśvarera śrī-vigraha sac-cid-ānandākāra
se-vigrahe kaha sattva-guṇera vikāra

SYNONYMS

īśvarera—of the Supreme Personality of Godhead; *śrī-vigraha*—the form; *sat-cit-ānanda-ākāra*—complete in eternity, cognizance and bliss; *se-vigrahe*—about that form of the Lord; *kaha*—you say; *sattva-guṇera*—of the quality of material goodness; *vikāra*—transformation.

TRANSLATION

"The transcendental form of the Supreme Personality of Godhead is complete in eternity, cognizance and bliss. However, you describe this transcendental form as a product of material goodness.

TEXT 167

শ্রীবিগ্রহ যে না মানে, সেই ত' পাষণ্ডী ।
অদৃশ্য অস্পৃশ্য, সেই হয় যমদণ্ডী ॥ ১৬৭ ॥

śrī-vigraha ye nā māne, sei ta' pāṣaṇḍī
adṛśya aspṛśya, sei haya yama-daṇḍī

SYNONYMS

śrī-vigraha—the form of the Lord; *ye*—anyone who; *nā*—not; *māne*—accepts; *sei*—he; *ta'*—indeed; *pāṣaṇḍī*—agnostic; *adṛśya*—not to be seen; *aspṛśya*—untouchable; *sei*—he; *haya*—is; *yama-daṇḍī*—subject to be punished by Yamarāja.

TRANSLATION

"One who does not accept the transcendental form of the Lord is certainly an agnostic. Such a person should be neither seen nor touched. Indeed, he is subject to be punished by Yamarāja.

PURPORT

According to the Vedic instructions, the Supreme Personality of Godhead has His eternal, transcendental form, which is always blissful and full of knowledge. Impersonalists think that "material" refers to the forms within our experience and that "spiritual" refers to an absence of form. However, one should know that beyond this material nature is another nature, which is spiritual. Just as there are material forms in this material world, there are spiritual forms in the spiritual world. This is confirmed by all Vedic literature. The spiritual forms in the transcendental world have nothing to do with the negative conception of formlessness. The conclusion is that a person is an agnostic when he does not agree to worship the transcendental form of the Lord.

Actually, at the present moment all systems of religion deny the worship of the form of the Lord due to ignorance of His transcendental form. The first-class materialists (the Māyāvādīs) imagine five specific forms of the Lord, but when they try to equate the worship of such imaginary forms with *bhakti,* they are immediately condemned. Lord Śrī Kṛṣṇa confirms this in *Bhagavad-gītā* (7.15), where He says, *na māṁ duṣkṛtino mūḍhāḥ prapadyante narādhamāḥ.* Bereft of real knowledge due to agnosticism, the Māyāvādī philosophers should not even be seen by the devotees of the Lord, nor touched, because those philosophers are liable to be punished by Yamarāja, the superintendent demigod who judges the activities of sinful men. The Māyāvādī agnostics wander within this universe in different species of life due to their nondevotional activities. Such living entities are subjected to the punishments of Yamarāja. Only the devotees, who are always engaged in the service of the Lord, are exempt from the jurisdiction of Yamarāja.

TEXT 168

বেদ না মানিয়া বৌদ্ধ হয় ত' নাস্তিক।
বেদাশ্রয় নাস্তিক্য-বাদ বৌদ্ধকে অধিক ॥ ১৬৮ ॥

veda nā māniyā bauddha haya ta' nāstika
vedāśraya nāstikya-vāda bauddhake adhika

SYNONYMS

veda—the Vedic literature; *nā*—not; *māniyā*—accepting; *bauddha*—the Buddhists; *haya*—are; *ta'*—indeed; *nāstika*—agnostics; *veda-āśraya*—taking shelter of Vedic civilization; *nāstikya-vāda*—agnosticism; *bauddhake*—even Buddhists; *adhika*—surpassing.

TRANSLATION

"The Buddhists do not recognize the authority of the Vedas; therefore they are considered agnostics. However, those who have taken shelter of the Vedic scriptures yet preach agnosticism in accordance with the Māyāvāda philosophy are certainly more dangerous than the Buddhists.

PURPORT

Although the Buddhists are directly opposed to Vaiṣṇava philosophy, it can easily be understood that the Śaṅkarites are more dangerous because they accept the authority of the *Vedas* yet act contrary to Vedic instruction. *Vedāśraya nāstikya-vāda* means "agnosticism under the shelter of Vedic culture" and refers to the monistic philosophy of the Māyāvādīs. Lord Buddha abandoned the authority of the Vedic literature and therefore rejected the ritualistic ceremonies and sacrifices recommended in the *Vedas*. His *nirvāṇa* philosophy means stopping all material activities. Lord Buddha did not recognize the presence of transcendental forms and spiritual activities beyond the material world. He simply described voidism beyond this material existence. The Māyāvādī philosophers offer lip service to Vedic authority but try to escape the Vedic ritualistic ceremonies. They concoct some idea of a transcendental position and call themselves Nārāyaṇa, or God. However, God's position is completely different from their concoction. Such Māyāvādī philosophers consider themselves above the influence of *karma-kāṇḍa* (fruitive activities and their reactions). For them, the spiritual world is equated with the Buddhist voidism. There is very little difference between impersonalism and voidism. Voidism can be directly understood, but the impersonalism enunciated by Māyāvādī philosophers is not very easily understandable. Of course, Māyāvādī philosophers accept a spiritual existence, but they do not know about the spiritual world and spiritual beings. According to *Śrīmad-Bhāgavatam* (10.2.32):

ye 'nye 'ravindākṣa vimukta-māninas
tvayy asta-bhāvād aviśuddha-buddhayaḥ
āruhya kṛcchreṇa paraṁ padaṁ tataḥ
patanty adho 'nādṛta-yuṣmad-aṅghrayaḥ

The intelligence of the Māyāvādīs is not purified; therefore even though they practice austerities for self-realization, they cannot remain within the impersonal *brahmajyoti.* Consequently, they fall down again into this material world.

The Māyāvādīs' conception of spiritual existence is almost identical to the negation of material existence. The Māyāvādīs believe that there is nothing positive in spiritual life. As a result, they cannot understand devotional service or the worship of the Supreme Person, *sac-cid-ānanda-vigraha.* The Māyāvādī philosophers consider Deity worship in devotional service to be *pratibimba-vāda,* or the worship of a form that is the reflection of a false material form. Thus the Lord's transcendental form, which is eternally blissful and full of knowledge, is unknown to Māyāvādī philosophers. Although the term Bhagavān is explicitly described in *Śrīmad-Bhāgavatam,* they cannot understand it. *Brahmeti paramātmeti bhagavān iti śabdyate:* "The Absolute Truth is called Brahman, Paramātmā and Bhagavān." (*Bhāg.* 1.2.11) The Māyāvādīs try to understand Brahman only, or, at the most, Paramātmā. However, they are unable to understand Bhagavān. Therefore the Supreme Personality of Godhead, Kṛṣṇa, says: *māyayāpahṛta-jñānāḥ.* Because of the Māyāvādī philosophers' temperament, real knowledge is taken from them. Because they cannot receive the mercy of the Lord, they will always be bewildered by His transcendental form. Impersonal philosophy destroys the three phases of knowledge—*jñāna, jñeya* and *jñātā.* As soon as one speaks of knowledge, there must be a person who is the knower, the knowledge itself and the object of knowledge. Māyāvāda philosophy combines these three categories; therefore the Māyāvādīs cannot understand how the spiritual potencies of the Supreme Personality of Godhead act. Because of their poor fund of knowledge, they cannot understand the distinction in the spiritual world between knowledge, the knower and the object of knowledge. Because of this, Śrī Caitanya Mahāprabhu considers the Māyāvādī philosophers more dangerous than the Buddhists.

TEXT 169

জীবের নিস্তার লাগি' সূত্র কৈল ব্যাস ।
মায়াবাদি-ভাষ্য শুনিলে হয় সর্বনাশ ॥ ১৬৯॥

jīvera nistāra lāgi' sūtra kaila vyāsa
māyāvādi-bhāṣya śunile haya sarva-nāśa

SYNONYMS

jīvera—of the living entities; *nistāra*—deliverance; *lāgi'*—for the matter of; *sūtra*—*Vedānta-sūtra; kaila*—made; *vyāsa*—Śrīla Vyāsadeva; *māyāvādi*—of the impersonalists; *bhāṣya*—commentary; *śunile*—if hearing; *haya*—becomes; *sarva-nāśa*—all destruction.

TRANSLATION

"Śrīla Vyāsadeva presented the Vedānta philosophy for the deliverance of conditioned souls, but if one hears the commentary of Śaṅkarācārya, everything is spoiled.

PURPORT

Factually, the devotional service of the Lord is described in *Vedānta-sūtra,* but the Māyāvādī philosophers, the Śaṅkarites, prepared a commentary known as *Śārīraka-bhāṣya,* in which the transcendental form of the Lord is denied. The Māyāvādī philosophers think that the living entity is identical with the Supreme Soul, Brahman. Their commentaries on *Vedānta-sūtra* are completely opposed to the principle of devotional service. Caitanya Mahāprabhu therefore warns us to avoid these commentaries. If one indulges in hearing the Śaṅkarite *Śārīraka-bhāṣya,* he will certainly be bereft of all real knowledge.

The ambitious Māyāvādī philosophers desire to merge into the existence of the Lord, and this may be accepted as *sāyujya-mukti.* However, this form of *mukti* means denying one's individual existence. In other words, it is a kind of spiritual suicide. This is absolutely opposed to the philosophy of *bhakti-yoga. Bhakti-yoga* offers immortality to the individual conditioned soul. If one follows the Māyāvādī philosophy, he misses his opportunity to become immortal after giving up the material body. The immortality of the individual person is the highest perfectional stage a living entity can attain.

TEXT 170

'পরিণাম-বাদ'—ব্যাস-সূত্রের সম্মত ।
অচিন্ত্যশক্তি ঈশ্বর জগদ্রূপে পরিণত ॥ ১৭০ ॥

'pariṇāma-vāda'——vyāsa-sūtrera sammata
acintya-śakti īśvara jagad-rūpe pariṇata

SYNONYMS

pariṇāma-vāda—the theory of transformation; *vyāsa-sūtrera*—of the *Vedānta-sūtra; sammata*—purpose; *acintya-śakti*—inconceivable power; *īśvara*—the

Supreme Personality of Godhead; *jagat-rūpe*—in the form of the cosmic manifestation; *pariṇata*—transformed.

TRANSLATION

"The Vedānta-sūtra aims at establishing that the cosmic manifestation has come into being by the transformation of the inconceivable potency of the Supreme Personality of Godhead.

PURPORT

For a further explanation of *pariṇāma-vāda,* refer to *Ādi-līlā,* Seventh Chapter, verses 121-133.

TEXT 171

মণি যৈছে অবিকৃতে প্রসবে হেমভার ।
জগদ্রূপ হয় ঈশ্বর, তবু অবিকার ॥ ১৭১ ॥

maṇi yaiche avikṛte prasabe hema-bhāra
jagad-rūpa haya īśvara, tabu avikāra

SYNONYMS

maṇi—the touchstone; *yaiche*—just as; *avikṛte*—without being transformed; *prasabe*—produces; *hema-bhāra*—volumes of gold; *jagat-rūpa*—the cosmic manifestation; *haya*—becomes; *īśvara*—the Supreme Personality of Godhead; *tabu*—still; *avikāra*—unchanged.

TRANSLATION

"The touchstone, after touching iron, produces volumes of gold without being changed. Similarly, the Supreme Personality of Godhead manifests Himself as the cosmic manifestation by His inconceivable potency, yet He remains unchanged in His eternal, transcendental form.

PURPORT

According to the commentary of Śrīla Bhaktisiddhānta Sarasvatī Ṭhākura, the purpose of the *janmādy asya* verse in the *Vedānta-sūtra* is to establish that the cosmic manifestation is the result of the transformation of the potencies of the Supreme Personality of Godhead. The Supreme Lord is the master of innumerable eternal energies, which are unlimited. Sometimes these energies are manifested, and sometimes they are not. In any case, all energies are under His control; therefore He is the original energetic, the abode of all energies. A common brain in the conditioned state cannot conceive of how these inconceivable energies abide in the Supreme Personality of Godhead, how He exists in His innumerable forms as the master of both spiritual and material energies, how He is the master of both manifest and potential powers and how contradictory potencies can abide in Him. As long as the living entity is within this material world, in the condition of illusion, he cannot understand the activities of the inconceivable energies of the Lord. Thus the Lord's energies, though factual, are simply beyond the power of the common brain to understand.

When the atheistic philosophers or the Māyāvādīs, being unable to understand the inconceivable energies of the Supreme Personality of Godhead, imagine an impersonal void, their imagination is only the counterpart of materialistic thinking. Within the material world, there is nothing inconceivable. High-thinking philosophers and scientists can tackle the material energy, but not being able to understand the spiritual energy, they can simply imagine an inactive state, such as the impersonal Brahman. This is simply the negative side of material life. By such imperfect knowledge, the Māyāvādī philosophers conclude that the cosmic manifestation is a transformation of the Supreme. Thus they must necessarily also accept the theory of the illusion of the Supreme (*vivarta-vāda*). However, if we accept the inconceivable potencies of the Lord, we can understand how the Supreme Personality of Godhead can appear within this material world without being touched or contaminated by the three modes of material nature.

From the *śāstras* we learn that there is a stone or jewel called a touchstone that can transform iron into gold. Although the touchstone turns iron into gold many times, it remains in its original condition. If such a material stone can maintain its inconceivable energy after producing volumes of gold, certainly the Supreme Personality of Godhead can remain in His original *sac-cid-ānanda* form after creating the cosmic world. As confirmed in *Bhagavad-gītā* (9.10), He acts only through His different energies. *Mayādhyakṣeṇa prakṛtiḥ:* Kṛṣṇa directs the material energy, and that potency works in this material world. This is also confirmed in *Brahma-saṁhitā* (5.44):

sṛṣṭi-sthiti-pralaya-sādhana-śaktir ekā
chāyeva yasya bhuvanāni vibharti durgā
icchānurūpam api yasya ca ceṣṭate sā
govindam ādi-puruṣaṁ tam ahaṁ bhajāmi

The *durgā-śakti* (material energy) acts under the direction of the Supreme Personality of Godhead, and the universal creation, maintenance and destruction are being carried out by the *durgā-śakti*. Kṛṣṇa's direction is in the background. The conclusion is that the Supreme Personality of Godhead remains as He is, even though directing His energy, which makes the diverse cosmic manifestation work so wonderfully.

TEXT 172

ব্যাস—ভ্রান্ত বলি' সেই সূত্রে দোষ দিয়া।
'বিবর্তবাদ' স্থাপিয়াছে কল্পনা করিয়া ॥ ১৭২ ॥

vyāsa——bhrānta bali' sei sūtre doṣa diyā
'vivarta-vāda' sthāpiyāche kalpanā kariyā

SYNONYMS

vyāsa—Śrīla Vyāsadeva; *bhrānta*—mistaken; *bali'*—saying; *sei*—that; *sūtre*—in *Vedānta-sūtra; doṣa*—fault; *diyā*—accusing; *vivarta-vāda*—the theory of illusion; *sthāpiyāche*—has established; *kalpanā*—imagination; *kariyā*—doing.

TRANSLATION

"Śaṅkarācārya's theory states that the Absolute Truth is transformed. By accepting this theory, the Māyāvādī philosophers denigrate Śrīla Vyāsadeva by accusing him of error. They thus find fault in the Vedānta-sūtra and interpret it to try to establish the theory of illusion.

PURPORT

The first verse of the *Brahma-sūtra* is *athāto brahma jijñāsā:* "We must now inquire into the Absolute Truth." The second verse immediately answers, *janmādy asya yataḥ:* "The Absolute Truth is the original source of everything." *Janmādy asya yataḥ* does not suggest that the original person has been transformed. Rather, it clearly indicates that He produces this cosmic manifestation through His inconceivable energy. This is also clearly explained in *Bhagavad-gītā,* where Kṛṣṇa says, *mattaḥ sarvaṁ pravartate:* "From Me, everything emanates." (Bg. 10.8) This is also confirmed in the *Taittirīya Upaniṣad: yato vā imāni bhūtāni jāyante:* "The Supreme Absolute Truth is that from which everything is born." (*Tait. Up.* 3.1.1) Similarly, in the *Muṇḍaka Upaniṣad* (1.1.7), it is stated, *yathorṇa-nābhiḥ sṛjate gṛhṇate ca:* "[The Lord creates and destroys the cosmic manifestation] as a spider creates a web and draws it back within itself." All of these *sūtras* indicate the transformation of the Lord's energy. It is not that the Lord undergoes direct transformation, which is called *pariṇāma-vāda.* However, being very anxious to protect Śrīla Vyāsadeva from criticism, Śaṅkarācārya became a pseudo gentleman and put forward his theory of illusion (*vivarta-vāda*). Śaṅkarācārya concocted this meaning of *pariṇāma-vāda,* and by word jugglery he endeavored very hard to establish *pariṇāma-vāda* as *vivarta-vāda.*

TEXT 173

জীবের দেহে আত্মবুদ্ধি—সেই মিথ্যা হয়।
জগৎ যে মিথ্যা নহে, নশ্বরমাত্র হয় ॥ ১৭৩ ॥

jīvera dehe ātma-buddhi—sei mithyā haya
jagat ye mithyā nahe, naśvara-mātra haya

SYNONYMS

jīvera—of the living entities; *dehe*—in the body; *ātma-buddhi*—considering as the self; *sei*—that; *mithyā*—untruth; *haya*—is; *jagat*—the cosmic manifestation; *ye*—that; *mithyā*—untruth; *nahe*—not; *naśvara-mātra*—only temporary; *haya*—is.

TRANSLATION

"The theory of illusion can be applied only when the living entity identifies himself with the body. As far as the cosmic manifestation is concerned, it cannot be called false, although it is certainly temporary.

PURPORT

The living entity is the eternal servant of Kṛṣṇa. Being part and parcel of the Lord, he is constitutionally pure, but due to his contact with material energy, he identifies himself with either the gross or the subtle material body. Such identification is certainly false and constitutes the genuine platform of the theory of illusion. The living entity is eternal; he can never be subjected to the limits of time, as are his gross and subtle bodies. The cosmic manifestation is never false, but it is subject to change by the influence of the time factor. For a living entity to accept this cosmic manifestation as the field for his sense enjoyment is certainly illusory. This material world is the manifestation of the material energy of the Lord. This is explained by Kṛṣṇa in *Bhagavad-gītā* (7.4):

bhūmir āpo 'nalo vāyuḥ
khaṁ mano buddhir eva ca
ahaṅkāra itīyaṁ me
bhinnā prakṛtir aṣṭadhā

The material world is the inferior energy of the Supreme Personality of Godhead, but it is not a fact that the Supreme Lord has been transformed into this material world. The Māyāvādī philosophers, devoid of true understanding, have confused the theory of illusion and the theory of the cosmic manifestation by word jugglery. The theory of illusion can be applied to a person who identifies himself with the body. The living entity is the superior energy of the Supreme Lord, and the material world is the inferior energy. Both, however, are *prakṛti* (energy). Although the energies are simultaneously one with the Lord and different from Him, the Lord never loses His personal form due to the transformation of His different energies.

TEXT 174

'প্রণব' যে মহাবাক্য—ঈশ্বরের মূর্তি ।
প্রণব হৈতে সর্ববেদ, জগৎ-উৎপত্তি ॥ ১৭৪ ॥

'praṇava' ye mahā-vākya——īśvarera mūrti
praṇava haite sarva-veda, jagat-utpatti

SYNONYMS

praṇava—*oṁkāra; ye*—that which; *mahā-vākya*—transcendental vibration; *īśvarera*—of the Supreme Personality of Godhead; *mūrti*—the form; *praṇava*—*oṁkāra; haite*—from; *sarva-veda*—all Vedic literature; *jagat*—of the material world; *utpatti*—production.

TRANSLATION

"The transcendental vibration oṁkāra is the sound form of the Supreme Personality of Godhead. All Vedic knowledge and this cosmic manifestation are produced from this sound representation of the Supreme Lord.

PURPORT

Oṁkāra is the representation of the Supreme Personality of Godhead in sound. This form of His holy name is accepted as the transcendental vibration (*mahā-vākya*) by virtue of which the temporary material manifestation has come into being. If one takes shelter of the sound representation of the Supreme Personality of Godhead (*oṁkāra*), he can realize his constitutional identity and engage in devotional service even though in conditional life.

TEXT 175

'তত্ত্বমসি'– জীব-হেতু প্রাদেশিক বাক্য ।
প্রণব না মানি' তারে কহে মহাবাক্য ॥ ১৭৫ ॥

'tat tvam asi'——jīva-hetu prādeśika vākya
praṇava nā māni' tāre kahe mahā-vākya

SYNONYMS

tat tvam asi—you are the same; *jīva-hetu*—for the enlightenment of the conditioned soul; *prādeśika*—subsidiary; *vākya*—vibration; *praṇava*—the *oṁkāra* incarnation; *nā*—not; *māni'*—accepting; *tāre*—that; *kahe*—says; *mahā-vākya*—transcendental vibration.

TRANSLATION

"The subsidiary vibration tat tvam asi ["you are the same"] is meant for the understanding of the living entity, but the principal vibration is oṁkāra. Not caring for oṁkāra, Śaṅkarācārya has stressed the vibration tat tvam asi."

PURPORT

Tat tvam asi is accepted as the primary vibration by one who does not accept *praṇava,* the transcendental sound incarnation of the holy name of the Lord, as the chief principle in Vedic literature. By word jugglery, Śaṅkarācārya tried to create an illusory presentation of the Supreme Personality of Godhead in His relationship with the living entities and the cosmic manifestation. *Tat tvam asi* is a warning to the living entity not to mistake the body for the self. Therefore *tat tvam asi* is especially meant for the conditioned soul. The chanting of *oṁkāra* or the Hare Kṛṣṇa *mantra* is meant for the liberated soul. Śrīla Rūpa Gosvāmī has said, *ayi mukta-kulair upāsyamānam* (*Nāmāṣṭaka* 1). Thus the holy name of the Lord is chanted by the liberated souls. Similarly, Parīkṣit Mahārāja says, *nivṛtta-tarṣair upagīyamānāt* (*Bhāg.* 10.1.4). The holy name of the Lord can be chanted by those who have fully satisfied their material desires or who are fully situated on the transcendental platform and devoid of material desire. The name of the Lord can be chanted by one who is completely freed from material contamination (*anyābhilāṣitā-śūnyaṁ jñāna-karmādy-anāvṛtam*). Śaṅkarācārya has indirectly minimized the value of the principal Vedic *mantra* (*oṁkāra*) by accepting a subordinate vibration (*tat tvam asi*) as the most important Vedic *mantra.*

TEXT 176

এইমতে কল্পিত ভাষ্যে শত দোষ দিল ।
ভট্টাচার্য পূর্বপক্ষ অপার করিল ॥ ১৭৬ ॥

ei-mate kalpita bhāṣye śata doṣa dila
bhaṭṭācārya pūrva-pakṣa apāra karila

SYNONYMS

ei-mate—in this way; *kalpita*—imagined; *bhāṣye*—in the commentary; *śata*—hundreds; *doṣa*—of faults; *dila*—gave; *bhaṭṭācārya*—Sārvabhauma Bhaṭṭācārya; *pūrva-pakṣa*—opposing elements; *apāra*—unlimitedly; *karila*—manifested.

TRANSLATION

Thus Śrī Caitanya Mahāprabhu criticized Śaṅkarācārya's Śārīraka-bhāṣya as imaginary, and He pointed out hundreds of faults in it. To defend

Śaṅkarācārya, however, Sārvabhauma Bhaṭṭācārya presented unlimited opposition.

TEXT 177

বিতণ্ডা, ছল, নিগ্রহাদি অনেক উঠাইল ।
সব খণ্ডি' প্রভু নিজ-মত সে স্থাপিল ॥ ১৭৭ ॥

vitaṇḍā, chala, nigrahādi aneka uṭhāila
saba khaṇḍi' prabhu nija-mata se sthāpila

SYNONYMS

vitaṇḍā—counter-arguments; *chala*—imaginary interpretations; *nigraha-ādi*—repulses to the opposite party; *aneka*—various; *uṭhāila*—raised; *saba*—all; *khaṇḍi'*—refuting; *prabhu*—Śrī Caitanya Mahāprabhu; *nija-mata*—His own conviction; *se*—that; *sthāpila*—established.

TRANSLATION

The Bhaṭṭācārya presented various types of false arguments with pseudologic and tried to defeat his opponent in many ways. However, Śrī Caitanya Mahāprabhu refuted all these arguments and established His own conviction.

PURPORT

The word *vitaṇḍā* indicates that a debater, not touching the main point or establishing his own point, simply tries to refute the other person's argument. When one does not touch the direct meaning but tries to divert attention by misinterpretation, he engages in *chala.* The word *nigraha* also means always trying to refute the arguments of the other party.

TEXT 178

ভগবান্—'সম্বন্ধ', ভক্তি—'অভিধেয়' হয় ।
প্রেমা—'প্রয়োজন', বেদে তিনবস্তু কয় ॥ ১৭৮ ॥

bhagavān—'sambandha', bhakti—'abhidheya' haya
premā—'prayojana', vede tina-vastu kaya

SYNONYMS

bhagavān—the Supreme Personality of Godhead; *sambandha*—relationship; *bhakti*—devotional service; *abhidheya*—transcendental activities; *haya*—is; *premā*—love of Godhead; *prayojana*—the ultimate goal of life; *vede*—the *Vedas; tina-vastu*—three subject matters; *kaya*—describe.

TRANSLATION

Śrī Caitanya Mahāprabhu continued: "The Supreme Personality of Godhead is the central point of all relationships, acting in devotional service to Him is one's real occupation, and the attainment of love of Godhead is the ultimate goal of life. These three subject matters are described in Vedic literature.

PURPORT

Bhagavad-gītā also confirms this statement (Bg. 15.15). *Vedaiś ca sarvair aham eva vedyaḥ:* the actual purpose in reading the *Vedas* is to learn how to become a devotee of the Supreme Lord. The Lord Himself advises, *man-manā bhava mad-bhakto mad-yājī māṁ namaskuru* (Bg. 9.34). Therefore, after studying the *Vedas,* one must then execute devotional service by thinking always of the Supreme Lord (*man-manā*), becoming His devotee, worshiping Him and always offering Him obeisances. This is called *viṣṇu-ārādhana,* and it is the supreme occupational duty of all human beings. It is properly discharged in the *varṇāśrama-dharma* system, which divides society into *brahmacarya, gṛhastha, vānaprastha, sannyāsa,* and *brāhmaṇa, kṣatriya, vaiśya* and *śūdra.* This is the whole scheme of Vedic civilization. However, this institution is very difficult to establish in this age; therefore Śrī Caitanya Mahāprabhu advises that we not worry about the Vedic system of *varṇāśrama-dharma.* Rather, we should take directly to the chanting of the Hare Kṛṣṇa *mantra* and simply hear about the Supreme Personality of Godhead from pure devotees. This is the process recommended by Śrī Caitanya Mahāprabhu, and this is the purpose for studying the *Vedas.*

TEXT 179

আর যে যে-কিছু কহে, সকলই কল্পনা।
স্বতঃপ্রমাণ বেদ-বাক্যে কল্পেন লক্ষণা ॥ ১৭৯ ॥

āra ye ye-kichu kahe, sakala-i kalpanā
svataḥ-pramāṇa veda-vākye kalpena lakṣaṇā

SYNONYMS

āra—except this; *ye ye*—whatever; *kichu*—something; *kahe*—says; *sakala-i*—all; *kalpanā*—imagination; *svataḥ-pramāṇa*—self-evident; *veda-vākye*—in the Vedic version; *kalpena*—he imagines; *lakṣaṇā*—an interpretation.

TRANSLATION

"If one tries to explain the Vedic literature in a different way, he is indulging in imagination. Any interpretation of the self-evident Vedic version is simply imaginary.

PURPORT

When a conditioned soul is purified, he is called a devotee. A devotee has his relationship only with the Supreme Personality of Godhead, and his only occupational duty is to execute devotional service to satisfy the Lord. This service is rendered through the Lord's representative, the spiritual master: *yasya deve parā bhaktir yathā deve tathā gurau*. When the devotee executes devotional service properly, he attains the highest perfection of life—love of Godhead: *sa vai puṁsāṁ paro dharmo yato bhaktir adhokṣaje*. The ultimate goal of understanding the *Vedas* is to be elevated to the platform of rendering loving service to the Lord. The Māyāvādī philosophers, however, consider the central point of relationship to be the impersonal Brahman, the function of the living entity to be the acquisition of knowledge of Brahman, resulting in detachment from material activity, and the ultimate goal of life to be liberation, or merging into the existence of the Supreme. All of this, however, is simply due to the imagination of the conditioned soul. It simply opposes him to material activities. One should always remember that all Vedic literatures are self-evident. No one is allowed to interpret the Vedic verses. If one does so, he indulges in imagination, and that has no value.

TEXT 180

আচার্যের দোষ নাহি, ঈশ্বর-আজ্ঞা হৈল ।
অতএব কল্পনা করি' নাস্তিক-শাস্ত্র কৈল ॥ ১৮০ ॥

ācāryera doṣa nāhi, īśvara-ājñā haila
ataeva kalpanā kari' nāstika-śāstra kaila

SYNONYMS

ācāryera—of Śaṅkarācārya; *doṣa*—fault; *nāhi*—there is not; *īśvara-ājñā*—the order of the Supreme Personality of Godhead; *haila*—there was; *ataeva*—therefore; *kalpanā*—imagination; *kari'*—making; *nāstika*—atheistic; *śāstra*—scriptures; *kaila*—prepared.

TRANSLATION

"Actually there is no fault on the part of Śaṅkarācārya. He simply carried out the order of the Supreme Personality of Godhead. He had to imagine some kind of interpretation, and therefore he presented a kind of Vedic literature that is full of atheism.

TEXT 181

স্বাগমৈঃ কল্পিতৈস্ত্বঞ্চ জনান্ মদ্বিমুখান্ কুরু ।
মাঞ্চ গোপয় যেন স্যাৎ সৃষ্টিরেষোত্তরোত্তরা ॥ ১৮১ ॥

svāgamaiḥ kalpitais tvaṁ ca
janān mad-vimukhān kuru
māṁ ca gopaya yena syāt
sṛṣṭir eṣottarottarā

SYNONYMS

sva-āgamaiḥ—with your own theses; *kalpitaiḥ*—imagined; *tvam*—you; *ca*—also; *janān*—the people in general; *mat-vimukhān*—averse to Me and addicted to fruitive activities and speculative knowledge; *kuru*—make; *mām*—Me, the Supreme Personality of Godhead; *ca*—and; *gopaya*—just cover; *yena*—by which; *syāt*—there may be; *sṛṣṭiḥ*—material advancement; *eṣā*—this; *uttarottarā*—more and more.

TRANSLATION

"Addressing Lord Śiva, the Supreme Personality of Godhead said, 'Please make the general populace averse to Me by imagining your own interpretation of the Vedas. Also, cover Me in such a way that people will take more interest in advancing material civilization just to propagate a population bereft of spiritual knowledge.'

PURPORT

This is a quotation from the *Padma Purāṇa, Uttara-khaṇḍa* (62.31).

TEXT 182

মায়াবাদমসচ্ছাস্ত্রং প্রচ্ছন্নং বৌদ্ধমুচ্যতে।
ময়ৈব বিহিতং দেবি কলৌ ব্রাহ্মণমূর্তিনা ॥ ১৮২ ॥

māyāvādam asac-chāstraṁ
pracchannaṁ bauddham ucyate
mayaiva vihitaṁ devi
kalau brāhmaṇa-mūrtinā

SYNONYMS

māyāvādam—the philosophy of Māyāvāda; *asat-śāstram*—false scriptures; *pracchannam*—covered; *bauddham*—Buddhism; *ucyate*—it is said; *mayā*—by me; *eva*—only; *vihitam*—executed; *devi*—O goddess of the material world; *kalau*—in the age of Kali; *brāhmaṇa-mūrtinā*—having the body of a *brāhmaṇa.*

TRANSLATION

"Lord Śiva informed the goddess Durgā, the superintendent of the material world, 'In the age of Kali, I take the form of a brāhmaṇa and explain the Vedas through false scriptures in an atheistic way, similar to Buddhist philosophy.' "

PURPORT

The word *brāhmaṇa-mūrtinā* in this verse refers to the founder of Māyāvāda philosophy, Śaṅkarācārya, who was born in the Mālabara district of southern India. Māyāvāda philosophy states that the Supreme Lord, the living entities and the cosmic manifestation are all transformations of illusory energy. To support this atheistic theory, the Māyāvādīs cite false scriptures, which make people bereft of transcendental knowledge and addicted to fruitive activities and mental speculation.

This verse is a quotation from the *Padma Purāṇa, Uttara-khaṇḍa* (25.7).

TEXT 183

শুনি' ভট্টাচার্য হৈল পরম বিস্মিত ।
মুখে না নিঃসরে বাণী, হইলা স্তম্ভিত ॥ ১৮৩ ॥

śuni' bhaṭṭācārya haila parama vismita
mukhe nā niḥsare vāṇī, ha-ilā stambhita

SYNONYMS

śuni'—hearing; *bhaṭṭācārya*—Sārvabhauma Bhaṭṭācārya; *haila*—became; *parama*—very much; *vismita*—astonished; *mukhe*—in the mouth; *nā*—not; *niḥsare*—vibrates; *vāṇī*—words; *ha-ilā*—became; *stambhita*—stunned.

TRANSLATION

Sārvabhauma Bhaṭṭācārya became very astonished upon hearing this. He became stunned and said nothing.

TEXT 184

প্রভু কহে,—ভট্টাচার্য, না কর বিস্ময় ।
ভগবানে ভক্তি—পরম-পুরুষার্থ হয় ॥ ১৮৪ ॥

prabhu kahe,——bhaṭṭācārya, nā kara vismaya
bhagavāne bhakti——parama-puruṣārtha haya

SYNONYMS

prabhu kahe—the Lord said; *bhaṭṭācārya*—My dear Bhaṭṭācārya; *nā*—not; *kara*—do; *vismaya*—astonishment; *bhagavāne*—unto the Supreme Personality of Godhead; *bhakti*—devotional service; *parama*—the Supreme; *puruṣa-artha*—human interest; *haya*—is.

TRANSLATION

Lord Śrī Caitanya Mahāprabhu then told him: "Do not be astonished. Actually, devotional service unto the Supreme Personality of Godhead is the highest perfection of human activity.

TEXT 185

'আত্মারাম' পর্যন্ত করে ঈশ্বর ভজন ।
ঐছে অচিন্ত্য ভগবানের গুণগণ ॥ ১৮৫ ॥

'ātmārāma' paryanta kare īśvara bhajana
aiche acintya bhagavānera guṇa-gaṇa

SYNONYMS

ātmā-rāma—self-satisfied; *paryanta*—up to; *kare*—do; *īśvara bhajana*—devotional service to the Lord; *aiche*—such; *acintya*—inconceivable; *bhagavānera*—of the Supreme Personality of Godhead; *guṇa-gaṇa*—transcendental qualities.

TRANSLATION

"Even the self-satisfied sages perform devotional service to the Supreme Lord. Such are the transcendental qualities of the Lord. They are full of inconceivable spiritual potency.

TEXT 186

আত্মারামাশ্চ মুনয়ো নির্গ্রন্থা অপ্যুরুক্রমে ।
কুর্বন্ত্যহৈতুকীং ভক্তিমিত্থম্ভূতগুণো হরিঃ ॥ ১৮৬ ॥

ātmārāmāś ca munayo
nirgranthā apy urukrame
kurvanty ahaitukīṁ bhaktim
ittham-bhūta-guṇo hariḥ

SYNONYMS

ātmā-rāmāḥ—persons who take pleasure in being transcendentally situated in the service of the Lord; *ca*—also; *munayaḥ*—great saintly persons who have completely rejected material aspirations, fruitive activities, and so forth; *nirgranthāḥ*—without interest in any material desire; *api*—certainly; *urukrame*—unto the Supreme Personality of Godhead, Kṛṣṇa, whose activities are wonderful; *kurvanti*—do; *ahaitukīm*—causeless, or without material desires; *bhaktim*—devotional service; *ittham-bhūta*—so wonderful as to attract the attention of the self-satisfied; *guṇaḥ*—who has transcendental qualities; *hariḥ*—the Supreme Personality of Godhead.

TRANSLATION

" 'Those who are self-satisfied and unattracted by external material desires are also attracted to the loving service of Śrī Kṛṣṇa, whose qualities are transcendental and whose activities are wonderful. Hari, the Personality of Godhead, is called Kṛṣṇa because He has such transcendentally attractive features.' "

PURPORT

This is the famous *ātmārāma* verse (*Bhāg.* 1.7.10).

TEXT 187

শুনি' ভট্টাচার্য কহে,—'শুন, মহাশয় ।
এই শ্লোকের অর্থ শুনিতে বাঞ্ছা হয় ॥' ১৮৭ ॥

śuni' bhaṭṭācārya kahe,——'śuna, mahāśaya
ei ślokera artha śunite vāñchā haya'

SYNONYMS

śuni'—hearing this; *bhaṭṭācārya kahe*—Sārvabhauma Bhaṭṭācārya said; *śuna*—please hear; *mahā-āśaya*—my dear sir; *ei ślokera*—of this verse; *artha*—the meaning; *śunite*—to hear; *vāñchā*—a desire; *haya*—there is.

TRANSLATION

After hearing the ātmārāma verse, Sārvabhauma Bhaṭṭācārya addressed Śrī Caitanya Mahāprabhu: "My dear sir, please explain this verse. I have a great desire to hear Your explanation of it."

TEXT 188

প্রভু কহে,—'তুমি কি অর্থ কর, তাহা আগে শুনি' ।
পাছে আমি করিব অর্থ, যেবা কিছু জানি ॥' ১৮৮ ॥

prabhu kahe,——'tumi ki artha kara, tāhā āge śuni'
pāche āmi kariba artha, yebā kichu jāni'

SYNONYMS

prabhu kahe—the Lord said; *tumi*—you; *ki*—what; *artha*—meaning; *kara*—do; *tāhā*—that; *āge*—first of all; *śuni'*—hearing; *pāche*—after that; *āmi*—I; *kariba*—shall do; *artha*—meaning; *yebā*—whatever; *kichu*—something; *jāni*—I know.

TRANSLATION

The Lord replied: "First let Me hear your explanation. After that, I shall try to explain what little I know."

TEXT 189

শুনি' ভট্টাচার্য শ্লোক করিল ব্যাখ্যান ।
তর্কশাস্ত্র-মত উঠায় বিবিধ বিধান ॥ ১৮৯ ॥

śuni' bhaṭṭācārya śloka karila vyākhyāna
tarka-śāstra-mata uṭhāya vividha vidhāna

SYNONYMS

śuni'—hearing this; *bhaṭṭācārya*—Sārvabhauma Bhaṭṭācārya; *śloka*—of the verse; *karila*—did; *vyākhyāna*—explanation; *tarka-śāstra*—scriptures dealing with logic; *mata*—according to; *uṭhāya*—raises; *vividha*—various; *vidhāna*—premises.

TRANSLATION

Sārvabhauma Bhaṭṭācārya then began to explain the ātmārāma verse, and, according to the principles of logic, he raised various premises.

TEXT 190

নববিধ অর্থ কৈল শাস্ত্রমত লঞা ।
শুনি' প্রভু কহে কিছু ঈষৎ হাসিয়া ॥ ১৯০ ॥

nava-vidha artha kaila śāstra-mata lañā
śuni' prabhu kahe kichu īṣat hāsiyā

SYNONYMS

nava-vidha—nine kinds; *artha*—meanings; *kaila*—did; *śāstra-mata*—the principles of authorized scriptures; *lañā*—taking; *śuni'*—after hearing that; *prabhu*—Lord Caitanya; *kahe*—began to speak; *kichu*—something; *īṣat*—slightly; *hāsiyā*—smiling.

TRANSLATION

The Bhaṭṭācārya explained the ātmārāma verse in nine different ways on the basis of scripture. After hearing his explanation, Śrī Caitanya Mahāprabhu, smiling a little, began to speak.

PURPORT

The *ātmārāma* verse was discussed at Naimiṣāraṇya at a meeting of many great sages, headed by Śaunaka Ṛṣi. They questioned Śrīla Sūta Gosvāmī, who presided at the meeting, about why Śrīla Śukadeva Gosvāmī, a *paramahaṁsa* already in the transcendental position, was attracted to a discussion of the qualities of Kṛṣṇa. In other words, they wanted to know why Śrī Śukadeva Gosvāmī engaged in the study of *Śrīmad-Bhāgavatam.*

TEXT 191

'ভট্টাচার্য', জানি —তুমি সাক্ষাৎ বৃহস্পতি ।
শাস্ত্রব্যাখ্যা করিতে ঐছে কারো নাহি শক্তি ॥ ১৯১॥

'bhaṭṭācārya', jāni——tumi sākṣāt bṛhaspati
śāstra-vyākhyā karite aiche kāro nāhi śakti

SYNONYMS

bhaṭṭācārya—My dear Bhaṭṭācārya; *jāni*—I know; *tumi*—you; *sākṣāt*—directly; *bṛhaspati*—the learned priest of the demigods named Bṛhaspati; *śāstra-vyākhyā*—explanation of the scriptures; *karite*—to do; *aiche*—such; *kāro*—of anyone else; *nāhi*—there is not; *śakti*—power.

TRANSLATION

Śrī Caitanya Mahāprabhu said: "My dear Bhaṭṭācārya, you are exactly like Bṛhaspati, the priest of the heavenly kingdom. Indeed, no one within this world has the power to explain the scriptures in such a way.

TEXT 192

কিন্তু তুমি অর্থ কৈলে পাণ্ডিত্য-প্রতিভায় ।
ইহা বই শ্লোকের আছে আরো অভিপ্রায় ॥ ১৯২ ॥

kintu tumi artha kaile pāṇḍitya-pratibhāya
ihā va-i ślokera āche āro abhiprāya

SYNONYMS

kintu—but; *tumi*—you; *artha*—meaning; *kaile*—have shown; *pāṇḍitya*—scholarly; *pratibhāya*—with prowess; *ihā va-i*—besides this; *ślokera*—of the verse; *āche*—there is; *āro*—another; *abhiprāya*—purport.

TRANSLATION

"My dear Bhaṭṭācārya, you have certainly explained this verse by the prowess of your vast learning, but you should know that, besides this scholarly explanation, there is another purport to this verse."

TEXT 193

ভট্টাচার্যের প্রার্থনাতে প্রভু ব্যাখ্যা কৈল।
তাঁর নব অর্থ-মধ্যে এক না ছুঁইল ॥ ১৯৩ ॥

bhaṭṭācāryera prārthanāte prabhu vyākhyā kaila
tāṅra nava artha-madhye eka nā chuṅila

SYNONYMS

bhaṭṭācāryera—of Sārvabhauma Bhaṭṭācārya; *prārthanāte*—on the request; *prabhu*—Lord Śrī Caitanya Mahāprabhu; *vyākhyā*—explanation; *kaila*—made; *tāṅra*—his; *nava artha*—of the nine different types of explanations; *madhye*—in the midst; *eka*—one; *nā*—not; *chuṅila*—touched.

TRANSLATION

Upon the request of Sārvabhauma Bhaṭṭācārya, Lord Caitanya Mahāprabhu began to explain the verse, without touching upon the nine explanations given by the Bhaṭṭācārya.

TEXT 194

আত্মারামাশ্চ-শ্লোকে 'একাদশ' পদ হয়।
পৃথক্ পৃথক্ কৈল পদের অর্থ নিশ্চয় ॥ ১৯৪ ॥

ātmārāmāś ca-śloke 'ekādaśa' pada haya
pṛthak pṛthak kaila padera artha niścaya

SYNONYMS

ātmārāmāś ca—known as such; *śloke*—in the verse; *ekādaśa*—eleven; *pada*—words; *haya*—there are; *pṛthak pṛthak*—separately one after another; *kaila*—made; *padera*—of the words; *artha*—the meaning; *niścaya*—certainty.

TRANSLATION

There are eleven words in the ātmārāma verse, and Śrī Caitanya Mahāprabhu explained each word, one after the other.

PURPORT

The words in the *ātmārāma* verse are *ātmārāmāḥ, ca, munayaḥ, nirgranthāḥ, api, urukrame, kurvanti, ahaitukīm, bhaktim, ittham-bhūta-guṇaḥ* and *hariḥ*.

TEXT 195

তত্তৎপদ-প্রাধান্যে 'আত্মারাম' মিলাঞা ।
অষ্টাদশ অর্থ কৈল অভিপ্রায় লঞা ॥ ১৯৫ ॥

tat-tat-pada-prādhānye 'ātmārāma' milāñā
aṣṭādaśa artha kaila abhiprāya lañā

SYNONYMS

tat-tat-pada—all those items; *prādhānye*—principally; *ātmārāma*—the word *ātmārāma; milāñā*—causing to meet; *aṣṭādaśa*—eighteen; *artha*—meanings; *kaila*—did; *abhiprāya*—purpose; *lañā*—accepting.

TRANSLATION

Lord Caitanya Mahāprabhu took each word specifically and combined it with the word "ātmārāma." He thus explained the word "ātmārāma" in eighteen different ways.

TEXT 196

ভগবান্, তাঁর শক্তি, তাঁর গুণগণ ।
অচিন্ত্য প্রভাব তিনের না যায় কথন ॥ ১৯৬ ॥

bhagavān, tāṅra śakti, tāṅra guṇa-gaṇa
acintya prabhāva tinera nā yāya kathana

SYNONYMS

bhagavān—the Supreme Personality of Godhead; *tāṅra śakti*—His potencies; *tāṅra guṇa-gaṇa*—His transcendental qualities; *acintya*—inconceivable; *prabhāva*—the influence; *tinera*—of the three; *nā*—not; *yāya*—possible; *kathana*—to speak.

TRANSLATION

Śrī Caitanya Mahāprabhu said: "The Supreme Personality of Godhead, His different potencies and His transcendental qualities all have inconceivable prowess. It is not possible to explain them fully.

TEXT 197

অন্য যত সাধ্য-সাধন করি' আচ্ছাদন ।
এই তিনে হরে সিদ্ধ-সাধকের মন ॥ ১৯৭ ॥

anya yata sādhya-sādhana kari' ācchādana
ei tine hare siddha-sādhakera mana

SYNONYMS

anya—other; *yata*—all; *sādhya-sādhana*—objectives and transcendental practices; *kari'*—doing; *ācchādana*—covering; *ei tine*—these three; *hare*—take away; *siddha*—successful; *sādhakera*—of the student engaged in spiritual activities; *mana*—the mind.

TRANSLATION

"These three items attract the mind of a perfect student engaged in spiritual activities and overcome all other processes of spiritual activity."

PURPORT

Spiritual activities other than *bhakti-yoga* are divided into three categories—speculative activity conducted by the *jñāna-sampradāya* (learned scholars), fruitive activity conducted by the general populace according to Vedic regulations, and the activities of transcendentalists not engaged in devotional service. There are many different branches of these categories, but the Supreme Personality of Godhead, by His inconceivable potencies and transcendental qualities, attracts the mind of the student engaged in the activities of *karma, jñāna, yoga,* and so forth. The Supreme Lord is full of inconceivable potencies, which are related to His person, His energies and His transcendental qualities. All of these are very attractive to the serious student. Consequently the Lord is known as Kṛṣṇa, the all-attractive one.

TEXT 198

সনকাদি-শুকদেব তাহাতে প্রমাণ ।
এইমত নানা অর্থ করেন ব্যাখ্যান ॥ ১৯৮ ॥

sanakādi-śukadeva tāhāte pramāṇa
ei-mata nānā artha karena vyākhyāna

SYNONYMS

sanaka-ādi—the four *sanas; śukadeva*—and Śukadeva Gosvāmī; *tāhāte*—in that; *pramāṇa*—the evidence; *ei-mata*—in this way; *nānā*—varieties; *artha*—meaning; *karena*—does; *vyākhyāna*—explanation.

TRANSLATION

Śrī Caitanya Mahāprabhu explained the meaning of the verse by giving evidence concerning Śukadeva Gosvāmī and the four ṛṣis Sanaka, Sanat-kumāra, Sanātana and Sanandana. Thus the Lord gave various meanings and explanations.

PURPORT

That Kṛṣṇa is all-attractive is verified by the activities of the four *ṛṣis* and Śukadeva Gosvāmī. All of them were liberated persons, yet they were attracted by the qualities and pastimes of the Lord. It is therefore said: *muktā api līlayā vigrahaṁ kṛtvā bhagavantaṁ bhajante.* (Cc. *Madhya* 24.112) Even liberated persons are attracted by the pastimes of Lord Kṛṣṇa and thus engage in devotional service. From the very beginning of their lives, Śukadeva Gosvāmī and the four Kumāras, known as *catuḥsana,* were liberated and self-realized on the Brahman platform. Nonetheless, they were attracted by the qualities of Kṛṣṇa, and they engaged in His service. The four Kumāras were attracted by the aroma of the flowers offered at the lotus feet of Kṛṣṇa, and in this way they became devotees. Śukadeva Gosvāmī heard *Śrīmad-Bhāgavatam* by the mercy of his father, Vyāsadeva, and he was consequently attracted to Kṛṣṇa and became a great devotee. The conclusion is that the transcendental bliss experienced in the service of the Lord must be superior to *brahmānanda,* the bliss derived from realizing the impersonal Brahman.

TEXT 199

শুনি' ভট্টাচার্যের মনে হৈল চমৎকার ।
প্রভুকে কৃষ্ণ জানি' করে আপনা ধিক্কার ॥ ১৯৯ ॥

śuni' bhaṭṭācāryera mane haila camatkāra
prabhuke kṛṣṇa jāni' kare āpanā dhikkāra

SYNONYMS

śuni'—hearing this; *bhaṭṭācāryera*—of Sārvabhauma Bhaṭṭācārya; *mane*—in the mind; *haila*—there was; *camatkāra*—wonder; *prabhuke*—Lord Śrī Caitanya Mahāprabhu; *kṛṣṇa*—Lord Kṛṣṇa; *jāni'*—accepting as; *kare*—does; *āpanā*—himself; *dhikkāra*—condemnation.

TRANSLATION

Upon hearing Caitanya Mahāprabhu's explanation of the ātmārāma verse, Sārvabhauma Bhaṭṭācārya was struck with wonder. He then understood Lord Śrī Caitanya Mahāprabhu to be Kṛṣṇa in person, and he thus condemned himself in the following words.

TEXT 200

'ইঁহো ত' সাক্ষাৎ কৃষ্ণ,—মুঞি না জানিয়া ।
মহা-অপরাধ কৈনু গর্বিত হইয়া ॥'২০০ ॥

'iṅho ta' sākṣāt kṛṣṇa,——muñi nā jāniyā
mahā-aparādha kainu garvita ha-iyā'

SYNONYMS

iṅho—Śrī Caitanya Mahāprabhu; *ta'*—indeed; *sākṣāt*—directly; *kṛṣṇa*—Lord Kṛṣṇa; *muñi*—I; *nā*—not; *jāniyā*—knowing; *mahā-aparādha*—a great offense; *kainu*—did; *garvita*—proud; *ha-iyā*—being.

TRANSLATION

"Caitanya Mahāprabhu is certainly Lord Kṛṣṇa Himself. Because I could not understand Him and was very proud of my own learning, I have committed many offenses."

TEXT 201

আত্মনিন্দা করি' লৈল প্রভুর শরণ ।
কৃপা করিবারে তবে প্রভুর হৈল মন ॥ ২০১ ॥

ātma-nindā kari' laila prabhura śaraṇa
kṛpā karibāre tabe prabhura haila mana

SYNONYMS

ātma-nindā—self-indictment; *kari'*—doing; *laila*—took; *prabhura*—of the Lord; *śaraṇa*—shelter; *kṛpā*—mercy; *karibāre*—to do; *tabe*—then; *prabhura*—of the Lord; *haila*—it was; *mana*—the mind.

TRANSLATION

When Sārvabhauma Bhaṭṭācārya denounced himself as an offender and took shelter of the Lord, the Lord desired to show him mercy.

TEXT 202

নিজ-রূপ প্রভু তাঁরে করাইল দর্শন ।
চতুর্ভুজ-রূপ প্রভু হইলা তখন ॥ ২০২ ॥

nija-rūpa prabhu tāṅre karāila darśana
catur-bhuja-rūpa prabhu hāilā takhana

SYNONYMS

nija-rūpa—personal form; *prabhu*—the Lord; *tāṅre*—unto him; *karāila*—made; *darśana*—seeing; *catuḥ-bhuja*—four-handed; *rūpa*—form; *prabhu*—the Lord; *hailā*—became; *takhana*—at that time.

TRANSLATION

To show him mercy, Śrī Caitanya Mahāprabhu allowed him to see His Viṣṇu form. Thus He immediately assumed four hands.

TEXT 203

দেখাইল তাঁরে আগে চতুর্ভুজ-রূপ ।
পাছে শ্যাম-বংশীমুখ স্বকীয় স্বরূপ ॥ ২০৩ ॥

dekhāila tāṅre āge catur-bhuja-rūpa
pāche śyāma-vaṁśī-mukha svakīya svarūpa

SYNONYMS

dekhāila—showed; *tāṅre*—unto him; *āge*—at first; *catur-bhuja-rūpa*—the form with four hands; *pāche*—afterwards; *śyāma*—blackish; *vaṁśī-mukha*—with a flute to the mouth; *svakīya*—personal; *svarūpa*—form.

TRANSLATION

Śrī Caitanya Mahāprabhu first showed him the four-handed form and then appeared before him in His original form of Kṛṣṇa, with a blackish complexion and a flute to His lips.

TEXT 204

দেখি' সার্বভৌম দণ্ডবৎ করি' পড়ি' ।
পুনঃ উঠি' স্তুতি করে দুই কর যুড়ি' ॥ ২০৪ ॥

dekhi' sārvabhauma daṇḍavat kari' paḍi'
punaḥ uṭhi' stuti kare dui kara yuḍi'

SYNONYMS

dekhi'—seeing that; *sārvabhauma*—Sārvabhauma Bhaṭṭācārya; *daṇḍavat*—obeisances; *kari'*—doing; *paḍi'*—falling flat; *punaḥ*—again; *uṭhi'*—standing up; *stuti*—prayer; *kare*—does; *dui*—two; *kara*—hands; *yuḍi'*—folding.

TRANSLATION

When Sārvabhauma Bhaṭṭācārya saw the form of Lord Kṛṣṇa manifested in Caitanya Mahāprabhu, he immediately fell down flat to offer Him obeisances. Then he stood up and with folded hands began to offer prayers.

TEXT 205

প্রভুর কৃপায় তাঁর স্ফুরিল সব তত্ত্ব ।
নাম-প্রেমদান-আদি বর্ণেন মহত্ত্ব ॥ ২০৫ ॥

prabhura kṛpāya tāṅra sphurila saba tattva
nāma-prema-dāna-ādi varṇena mahattva

SYNONYMS

prabhura—of the Lord; *kṛpāya*—by the mercy; *tāṅra*—to him; *sphurila*—manifested; *saba*—all; *tattva*—truths; *nāma*—the holy name; *prema-dāna*—distribution of love of Godhead; *ādi*—and so on; *varṇena*—describes; *mahattva*—the importance.

TRANSLATION

By the mercy of the Lord, all truths were revealed to Sārvabhauma Bhaṭṭācārya, and he could understand the importance of chanting the holy name and distributing love of Godhead everywhere.

TEXT 206

শত শ্লোক কৈল এক দণ্ড না যাইতে ।
বৃহস্পতি তৈছে শ্লোক না পারে করিতে ॥ ২০৬ ॥

śata śloka kaila eka daṇḍa nā yāite
bṛhaspati taiche śloka nā pāre karite

SYNONYMS

śata—one hundred; *śloka*—verses; *kaila*—composed; *eka*—one; *daṇḍa*—a duration of twenty-four minutes; *nā*—not; *yāite*—passing; *bṛhaspati*—Bṛhaspati, the priest of the heavenly planets; *taiche*—such; *śloka*—verses; *nā*—not; *pāre*—able; *karite*—to compose.

TRANSLATION

Sārvabhauma Bhaṭṭācārya composed one hundred verses in a very short time. Indeed, not even Bṛhaspati, the priest of the heavenly planets, could compose verses as quickly.

PURPORT

The name of the book of one hundred beautiful verses composed by Sārvabhauma Bhaṭṭācārya is *Suśloka-śataka.*

TEXT 207

শুনি' সুখে প্রভু তাঁরে কৈল আলিঙ্গন ।
ভট্টাচার্য প্রেমাবেশে হৈল অচেতন ॥ ২০৭ ॥

śuni' sukhe prabhu tāṅre kaila āliṅgana
bhaṭṭācārya premāveśe haila acetana

SYNONYMS

śuni'—hearing; *sukhe*—in happiness; *prabhu*—Lord Caitanya Mahāprabhu; *tāṅre*—Sārvabhauma Bhaṭṭācārya; *kaila*—did; *āliṅgana*—embracing; *bhaṭṭācārya*—Sārvabhauma Bhaṭṭācārya; *prema-āveśe*—in the ecstasy of love of God; *haila*—became; *acetana*—unconscious.

TRANSLATION

After hearing the one hundred verses, Śrī Caitanya Mahāprabhu happily embraced Sārvabhauma Bhaṭṭācārya, who was immediately overwhelmed in ecstatic love of Godhead and fell unconscious.

TEXT 208

অশ্রু, স্তম্ভ, পুলক, স্বেদ, কম্প থরহরি ।
নাচে, গায়, কান্দে, পড়ে প্রভু-পদ ধরি' ॥ ২০৮ ॥

aśru, stambha, pulaka, sveda, kampa tharahari
nāce, gāya, kānde, paḍe prabhu-pada dhari'

SYNONYMS

aśru—tears; *stambha*—a stunned condition; *pulaka*—standing of hair; *sveda*—perspiration; *kampa*—trembling; *tharahari*—with great shaking; *nāce*—dances; *gāya*—sings; *kānde*—cries; *paḍe*—falls down; *prabhu-pada*—the lotus feet of the Lord; *dhari'*—catching.

TRANSLATION

Out of ecstatic love of God, the Bhaṭṭācārya shed tears, and his body was stunned. He exhibited an ecstatic mood, and he perspired, shook and trembled. He sometimes danced, sometimes chanted, sometimes cried and sometimes fell down to touch the lotus feet of the Lord.

TEXT 209

দেখি' গোপীনাথাচার্য হরষিত-মন ।
ভট্টাচার্যের নৃত্য দেখি' হাসে প্রভুর গণ ॥ ২০৯ ॥

dekhi' gopīnāthācārya haraṣita-mana
bhaṭṭācāryera nṛtya dekhi' hāse prabhura gaṇa

SYNONYMS

dekhi'—seeing this; *gopīnātha-ācārya*—Gopīnātha Ācārya; *haraṣita-mana*—a pleased mind; *bhaṭṭācāyera*—of Sārvabhauma Bhaṭṭācārya; *nṛtya*—dancing; *dekhi'*—seeing; *hāse*—laughs; *prabhura gaṇa*—the associates of Lord Caitanya Mahāprabhu.

TRANSLATION

While Sārvabhauma Bhaṭṭācārya was in this ecstasy, Gopīnātha Ācārya was very pleased. The associates of Śrī Caitanya Mahāprabhu all laughed to see the Bhaṭṭācārya dance so.

TEXT 210

গোপীনাথাচার্য কহে মহাপ্রভুর প্রতি ।
'সেই ভট্টাচার্যের প্রভু কৈলে এই গতি ॥' ২১০ ॥

gopīnāthācārya kahe mahāprabhura prati
'sei bhaṭṭācāryera prabhu kaile ei gati'

SYNONYMS

gopīnātha-ācārya—of the name Gopīnātha Ācārya; *kahe*—said; *mahāprabhura*—Śrī Caitanya Mahāprabhu; *prati*—to; *sei bhaṭṭācāryera*—of that Bhaṭṭācārya; *prabhu*—my Lord; *kaile*—You have made; *ei gati*—such a situation.

TRANSLATION

Gopīnātha Ācārya told Lord Caitanya Mahāprabhu: "Sir, You have brought all this upon Sārvabhauma Bhaṭṭācārya."

TEXT 211

প্রভু কহে,—'তুমি ভক্ত, তোমার সঙ্গ হৈতে।
জগন্নাথ ইঁহারে কৃপা কৈল ভালমতে ॥' ২১১ ॥

prabhu kahe,—'tumi bhakta, tomāra saṅga haite
jagannātha iṅhāre kṛpā kaila bhāla-mate'

SYNONYMS

prabhu kahe—the Lord said; *tumi bhakta*—you are a devotee; *tomāra saṅga haite*—on account of your association; *jagannātha*—Lord Jagannātha; *iṅhāre*—unto him; *kṛpā*—mercy; *kaila*—showed; *bhāla-mate*—very well.

TRANSLATION

Śrī Caitanya Mahāprabhu replied: "You are a devotee. Because of your association, Lord Jagannātha has shown him mercy."

TEXT 212

তবে ভট্টাচার্যে প্রভু সুস্থির করিল।
স্থির হঞা ভট্টাচার্য বহু স্তুতি কৈল ॥ ২১২ ॥

tabe bhaṭṭācārye prabhu susthira karila
sthira hañā bhaṭṭācārya bahu stuti kaila

SYNONYMS

tabe—then; *bhaṭṭācārye*—unto Sārvabhauma Bhaṭṭācārya; *prabhu*—Lord Śrī Caitanya Mahāprabhu; *su-sthira*—pacification; *karila*—did; *sthira hañā*—being pacified; *bhaṭṭācārya*—Sārvabhauma Bhaṭṭācārya; *bahu*—many; *stuti*—prayers; *kaila*—offered.

TRANSLATION

After this, Śrī Caitanya Mahāprabhu pacified the Bhaṭṭācārya, and when he was quieted, he offered many prayers to the Lord.

TEXT 213

'জগৎ নিস্তারিলে তুমি,—সেহ অল্পকার্য ।
আমা উদ্ধারিলে তুমি,—এ শক্তি আশ্চর্য ॥ ২১৩ ॥

'jagat nistārile tumi,——seha alpa-kārya
āmā uddhārile tumi,——e śakti āścarya

SYNONYMS

jagat—the whole world; *nistārile*—have delivered; *tumi*—You; *seha*—that; *alpa-kārya*—minor activity; *āmā*—me; *uddhārile*—have delivered; *tumi*—You; e—this; *śakti*—power; *āścarya*—wonderful.

TRANSLATION

Sārvabhauma Bhaṭṭācārya said: "My dear Sir, You have delivered the entire world, but that is not a very great task. However, You have also delivered me, and that is certainly the work of very wonderful powers.

TEXT 214

তর্ক-শাস্ত্রে জড় আমি, যৈছে লৌহপিণ্ড ।
আমা দ্রবাইলে তুমি, প্রতাপ প্রচণ্ড' ॥ ২১৪ ॥

tarka-śāstre jaḍa āmi, yaiche lauha-piṇḍa
āmā dravāile tumi, pratāpa pracaṇḍa'

SYNONYMS

tarka-śāstre—due to logical scriptures; *jaḍa*—dull; *āmi*—I; *yaiche*—just like; *lauha-piṇḍa*—an iron bar; *āmā*—me; *dravāile*—melted; *tumi*—You; *pratāpa*—power; *pracaṇḍa*—very great.

TRANSLATION

"I had become dull-headed due to reading too many books on logic. Consequently I had become like an iron bar. Nonetheless, You have melted me, and therefore Your influence is very great."

TEXT 215

স্তুতি শুনি' মহাপ্রভু নিজ বাসা আইলা ।
ভট্টাচার্য আচার্য-দ্বারে ভিক্ষা করাইলা ॥ ২১৫ ॥

stuti śuni' mahāprabhu nija vāsā āilā
bhaṭṭācārya ācārya-dvāre bhikṣā karāilā

SYNONYMS

stuti śuni'—after hearing the prayers; *mahāprabhu*—Śrī Caitanya Mahāprabhu; *nija*—own; *vāsā*—to the residence; *āilā*—returned; *bhaṭṭācārya*—Sārvabhauma Bhaṭṭācārya; *ācārya-dvāre*—through Gopīnātha Ācārya; *bhikṣā*—luncheon; *karāilā*—induced to take.

TRANSLATION

After hearing the prayers offered by Sārvabhauma Bhaṭṭācārya, Śrī Caitanya Mahāprabhu returned to His residence, and the Bhaṭṭācārya, through Gopīnātha Ācārya, induced the Lord to accept lunch there.

TEXT 216

আর দিন প্রভু গেলা জগন্নাথ-দরশনে ।
দর্শন করিলা জগন্নাথ-শয্যোত্থানে ॥ ২১৬ ॥

āra dina prabhu gelā jagannātha-daraśane
darśana karilā jagannātha-śayyotthāne

SYNONYMS

āra dina—the next day; *prabhu*—Lord Caitanya Mahāprabhu; *gelā*—went; *jagannātha-daraśane*—to see Jagannātha in the temple; *darśana karilā*—saw; *jagannātha-śayya-utthāne*—the Lord's rising from bed early in the morning.

TRANSLATION

Early the following morning, Śrī Caitanya Mahāprabhu went to see Lord Jagannātha in the temple, and He saw the Lord rise from His bed.

TEXT 217

পূজারী আনিয়া মালা-প্রসাদান্ন দিলা ।
প্রসাদান্ন-মালা পাঞা প্রভু হর্ষ হৈলা ॥ ২১৭ ॥

pūjārī āniyā mālā-prasādānna dilā
prasādānna-mālā pāñā prabhu harṣa hailā

SYNONYMS

pūjārī—the priest; *āniyā*—bringing; *mālā*—garlands; *prasāda-anna*—remnants of food; *dilā*—offered; *prasāda-anna*—the *prasāda; mālā*—and garlands; *pāñā*—getting; *prabhu*—Lord Caitanya Mahāprabhu; *harṣa*—pleased; *hailā*—became.

TRANSLATION

The priest there presented Him with garlands and prasāda that had been offered to Lord Jagannātha. This pleased Caitanya Mahāprabhu very much.

TEXT 218

সেই প্রসাদান্ন-মালা অঞ্চলে বান্ধিয়া ।
ভট্টাচার্যের ঘরে আইলা ত্বরাযুক্ত হঞা ॥ ২১৮ ॥

sei prasādānna-mālā añcale bāndhiyā
bhaṭṭācāryera ghare āilā tvarāyukta hañā

SYNONYMS

sei prasāda-anna—those remnants of food; *mālā*—and garlands; *añcale*—in the end of His cloth; *bāndhiyā*—binding; *bhaṭṭācāryera*—of Sārvabhauma Bhaṭṭācārya; *ghare*—to the house; *āilā*—went; *tvarā-yukta*—hasty; *hañā*—being.

TRANSLATION

Carefully tying the prasāda and garlands in a cloth, Caitanya Mahāprabhu hastened to the house of Sārvabhauma Bhaṭṭācārya.

TEXT 219

অরুণোদয়-কালে হৈল প্রভুর আগমন ।
সেইকালে ভট্টাচার্যের হৈল জাগরণ ॥ ২১৯ ॥

aruṇodaya-kāle haila prabhura āgamana
sei-kāle bhaṭṭācāryera haila jāgaraṇa

SYNONYMS

aruṇa-udaya—before sunrise; *kāle*—at the time; *haila*—there was; *prabhura*—of Lord Śrī Caitanya Mahāprabhu; *āgamana*—the coming; *sei-kāle*—at that time; *bhaṭṭācāryera*—of Sārvabhauma Bhaṭṭācārya; *haila*—there was; *jāgaraṇa*—arising from bed.

TRANSLATION

He arrived at the Bhaṭṭācārya's house a little before sunrise, just when the Bhaṭṭācārya was arising from bed.

TEXT 220

'কৃষ্ণ' 'কৃষ্ণ' স্ফুট কহি' ভট্টাচার্য জাগিলা ।
কৃষ্ণনাম শুনি' প্রভুর আনন্দ বাড়িলা ॥ ২২০ ॥

'kṛṣṇa' 'kṛṣṇa' sphuṭa kahi' bhaṭṭācārya jāgilā
kṛṣṇa-nāma śuni' prabhura ānanda bāḍilā

SYNONYMS

kṛṣṇa kṛṣṇa—chanting the name of Kṛṣṇa; *sphuṭa*—distinctly; *kahi'*—saying; *bhaṭṭācārya*—Sārvabhauma Bhaṭṭācārya; *jāgilā*—got up from the bed; *kṛṣṇa-nāma*—the holy name of Lord Kṛṣṇa; *śuni'*—hearing; *prabhura*—of Lord Caitanya Mahāprabhu; *ānanda*—pleasure; *bāḍilā*—increased.

TRANSLATION

As Sārvabhauma Bhaṭṭācārya arose from bed, he distinctly chanted, "Kṛṣṇa, Kṛṣṇa." Lord Caitanya was very pleased to hear him chant the holy name of Kṛṣṇa.

TEXT 221

বাহিরে প্রভুর তেঁহো পাইল দরশন ।
আস্তে-ব্যস্তে আসি' কৈল চরণ বন্দন ॥ ২২১ ॥

bāhire prabhura teṅho pāila daraśana
āste-vyaste āsi' kaila caraṇa vandana

SYNONYMS

bāhire—outside the house; *prabhura*—of Lord Śrī Caitanya Mahāprabhu; *teṅho*—he; *pāila*—got; *daraśana*—sight; *āste-vyaste*—with great hurry; *āsi'*—coming there; *kaila*—did; *caraṇa vandana*—worshiping the lotus feet.

TRANSLATION

The Bhaṭṭācārya noticed Śrī Caitanya Mahāprabhu outside, and with great haste he went to Him and offered prayers unto His lotus feet.

TEXT 222

বসিতে আসন দিয়া দুঁহেত বসিলা।
প্রসাদান্ন খুলি' প্রভু তাঁর হাতে দিলা॥ ২২২॥

vasite āsana diyā duṅheta vasilā
prasādānna khuli' prabhu tāṅra hāte dilā

SYNONYMS

vasite—to sit; *āsana*—carpet; *diyā*—offering; *duṅheta*—both of them; *vasilā*—sat down; *prasāda-anna*—the *prasāda; khuli'*—opening; *prabhu*—Śrī Caitanya Mahāprabhu; *tāṅra*—his; *hāte*—in the hand; *dilā*—offered.

TRANSLATION

The Bhaṭṭācārya offered a carpet for the Lord to sit upon, and both of them sat there. Then Śrī Caitanya Mahāprabhu opened the prasāda and placed it in the hands of the Bhaṭṭācārya.

TEXT 223

প্রসাদান্ন পাঞা ভট্টাচার্যের আনন্দ হৈল।
স্নান, সন্ধ্যা, দন্তধাবন যদ্যপি না কৈল॥ ২২৩॥

prasādānna pāñā bhaṭṭācāryera ānanda haila
snāna, sandhyā, danta-dhāvana yadyapi nā kaila

SYNONYMS

prasāda-anna—the remnants of food; *pāñā*—getting; *bhaṭṭācāryera*—of Sārvabhauma Bhaṭṭācārya; *ānanda*—pleasure; *haila*—there was; *snāna*—bathing; *sandhyā*—morning duties; *danta-dhāvana*—washing the teeth; *yadyapi*—although; *nā*—not; *kaila*—finished.

TRANSLATION

At that time, the Bhaṭṭācārya had not even washed his mouth, nor had he taken his bath nor finished his morning duties. Nonetheless, he was very pleased to receive the prasāda of Lord Jagannātha.

TEXT 224

চৈতন্য-প্রসাদে মনের সব জাড্য গেল।
এই শ্লোক পড়ি' অন্ন ভক্ষণ করিল॥ ২২৪॥

caitanya-prasāde manera saba jāḍya gela
ei śloka paḍi' anna bhakṣaṇa karila

SYNONYMS

caitanya-prasāde—by the mercy of Lord Śrī Caitanya Mahāprabhu; *manera*—of the mind; *saba*—all; *jāḍya*—dullness; *gela*—went away; *ei śloka*—these verses; *paḍi'*—reciting; *anna*—remnants of food; *bhakṣaṇa*—eating; *karila*—did.

TRANSLATION

By the mercy of Śrī Caitanya Mahāprabhu, all the dullness in the mind of Sārvabhauma Bhaṭṭācārya was eradicated. After reciting the following two verses, he ate the prasāda offered to him.

TEXT 225

শুষ্কং পর্যুষিতং বাপি নীতং বা দূরদেশতঃ ।
প্রাপ্তিমাত্রেণ ভোক্তব্যং নাত্র কালবিচারণা ॥ ২২৫ ॥

śuṣkaṁ paryuṣitaṁ vāpi
nītaṁ vā dūra-deśataḥ
prāpti-mātreṇa bhoktavyaṁ
nātra kāla-vicāraṇā

SYNONYMS

śuṣkam—dry; *paryuṣitam*—stale; *vā*—or; *api*—although; *nītam*—brought; *vā*—or; *dūra-deśataḥ*—from a distant country; *prāpti-mātreṇa*—only with the receiving; *bhoktavyam*—to be eaten; *na*—not; *atra*—in this; *kāla-vicāraṇā*—consideration of time or place.

TRANSLATION

The Bhaṭṭācārya said: " 'One should eat the mahā-prasāda of the Lord immediately upon receiving it, even though it is dried up, stale or brought from a distant country. One should consider neither time nor place.

TEXT 226

ন দেশনিয়মস্তত্র ন কালনিয়মস্তথা ।
প্রাপ্তমন্নং দ্রুতং শিষ্টৈর্ভোক্তব্যং হরিরব্রবীৎ ॥ ২২৬ ॥

na deśa-niyamas tatra
na kāla-niyamas tathā

prāptam annaṁ drutaṁ śiṣṭair
bhoktavyaṁ harir abravīt

SYNONYMS

na—not; *deśa*—of the country; *niyamaḥ*—regulation; *tatra*—in that; *na*—not; *kāla*—of time; *niyamaḥ*—regulation; *tathā*—so also; *prāptam*—received; *annam*—*prasāda;* *drutam*—hastily; *śiṣṭaiḥ*—by gentlemen; *bhoktavyam*—to be eaten; *hariḥ*—the Lord; *abravīt*—has said.

TRANSLATION

" 'The prasāda of Lord Kṛṣṇa is to be eaten by gentlemen as soon as it is received; there should be no hesitation. There are no regulative principles concerning time and place. This is the order of the Supreme Personality of Godhead.' "

PURPORT

These verses are quoted from the *Padma Purāṇa.*

TEXT 227

দেখি' আনন্দিত হৈল মহাপ্রভুর মন ।
প্রেমাবিষ্ট হঞা প্রভু কৈলা আলিঙ্গন ॥ ২২৭ ॥

dekhi' ānandita haila mahāprabhura mana
premāviṣṭa hañā prabhu kailā āliṅgana

SYNONYMS

dekhi'—seeing this; *ānandita*—very much pleased; *haila*—was; *mahāprabhura*—of Śrī Caitanya Mahāprabhu; *mana*—the mind; *prema-āviṣṭa*—absorbed in the ecstasy of love of God; *hañā*—becoming; *prabhu*—Śrī Caitanya Mahāprabhu; *kailā*—did; *āliṅgana*—embracing.

TRANSLATION

Śrī Caitanya Mahāprabhu was very pleased to see this. He became ecstatic in love of Godhead and embraced Sārvabhauma Bhaṭṭācārya.

TEXT 228

দুইজনে ধরি' দুঁহে করেন নর্তন ।
প্রভু-ভৃত্য দুঁহা স্পর্শে, দোঁহার ফুলে মন ॥ ২২৮ ॥

dui-jane dhari' duṅhe karena nartana
prabhu-bhṛtya duṅhā sparśe, doṅhāra phule mana

SYNONYMS

dui-jane—both of them; *dhari'*—embracing; *duṅhe*—both; *karena*—do; *nartana*—dancing; *prabhu-bhṛtya*—the master and the servant; *duṅhā*—both; *sparśe*—by touching each other; *doṅhāra*—of both of them; *phule*—were excited; *mana*—minds.

TRANSLATION

The Lord and the servant embraced one another and began to dance. Simply by touching each other, they became ecstatic.

TEXT 229

স্বেদ-কম্প-অশ্রু দুঁহে আনন্দে ভাসিলা ।
প্রেমাবিষ্ট হঞা প্রভু কহিতে লাগিলা ॥ ২২৯ ॥

sveda-kampa-aśru duṅhe ānande bhāsilā
premāviṣṭa hañā prabhu kahite lāgilā

SYNONYMS

sveda—perspiration; *kampa*—trembling; *aśru*—tears; *duṅhe*—both of them; *ānande*—in transcendental bliss; *bhāsilā*—floated; *prema-āviṣṭa*—absorbed in ecstatic love of Godhead; *hañā*—being; *prabhu*—the Lord; *kahite*—to speak; *lāgilā*—began.

TRANSLATION

As they danced and embraced, spiritual symptoms manifested in their bodies. They perspired, trembled and shed tears, and the Lord began to speak in His ecstasy.

TEXT 230

"আজি মুঞি অনায়াসে জিনিনু ত্রিভুবন ।
আজি মুঞি করিনু বৈকুণ্ঠ আরোহণ ॥ ২৩০ ॥

"āji muñi anāyāse jininu tribhuvana
āji muñi karinu vaikuṇṭha ārohaṇa

SYNONYMS

āji—today; *muñi*—I; *anāyāse*—very easily; *jininu*—conquered; *tri-bhuvana*—the three worlds; *āji*—today; *muñi*—I; *karinu*—did; *vaikuṇṭha*—to the spiritual world; *ārohaṇa*—ascending.

TRANSLATION

Śrī Caitanya Mahāprabhu said: "Today I have conquered the three worlds very easily. Today I have ascended to the spiritual world."

PURPORT

The goal of human perfection is stated here in brief. One has to surpass all the planetary systems of the material universe, pierce through the covering of the universe and reach the spiritual world known as Vaikuṇṭhaloka. The Vaikuṇṭhalokas are variegated spiritual planets situated in the Lord's impersonal bodily effulgence, known as the *brahmajyoti*. One may aspire to elevate himself to a heavenly planet within the material world, such as the moon, the sun or Venus, but if one is spiritually advanced in Kṛṣṇa consciousness, he does not wish to remain within the material universe, even in a higher planetary system. Rather, he prefers to penetrate the covering of the universe and attain the spiritual world. He can then be situated in one of the Vaikuṇṭha planets there. However, the devotees under the guidance of Śrī Caitanya Mahāprabhu aspire to reach the topmost spiritual planet, known as Goloka Vṛndāvana, the residence of Lord Śrī Kṛṣṇa and His eternal associates.

TEXT 231

আজি মোর পূর্ণ হৈল সর্ব অভিলাষ।
সার্বভৌমের হৈল মহাপ্রসাদে বিশ্বাস ॥ ২৩১ ॥

āji mora pūrṇa haila sarva abhilāṣa
sārvabhaumera haila mahā-prasāde viśvāsa

SYNONYMS

āji—today; *mora*—My; *pūrṇa*—satisfied; *haila*—became; *sarva*—all; *abhilāṣa*—desires; *sārvabhaumera*—of Sārvabhauma Bhaṭṭācārya; *haila*—there was; *mahā-prasāde*—in the remnants of the Lord's food; *viśvāsa*—faith.

TRANSLATION

Caitanya Mahāprabhu continued: "I think that today all My desires have been fulfilled because I see that Sārvabhauma Bhaṭṭācārya has acquired faith in the mahā-prasāda of Lord Jagannātha.

TEXT 232

আজি তুমি নিষ্কপটে হৈলা কৃষ্ণাশ্রয়।
কৃষ্ণ আজি নিষ্কপটে তোমা হৈল সদয়॥ ২৩২॥

āji tumi niṣkapaṭe hailā kṛṣṇāśraya
kṛṣṇa āji niṣkapaṭe tomā haila sadaya

SYNONYMS

āji—today; *tumi*—you; *niṣkapaṭe*—without a doubt; *hailā*—have become; *kṛṣṇa-āśraya*—under the shelter of Lord Kṛṣṇa; *kṛṣṇa*—Lord Kṛṣṇa; *āji*—today; *niṣkapaṭe*—without reservation; *tomā*—unto you; *haila*—has become; *sa-daya*—very merciful.

TRANSLATION

"Indeed, today you have undoubtedly taken shelter of the lotus feet of Kṛṣṇa, and Kṛṣṇa, without reservation, has become very merciful toward you.

TEXT 233

আজি সে খণ্ডিল তোমার দেহাদি-বন্ধন।
আজি তুমি ছিন্ন কৈলে মায়ার বন্ধন॥ ২৩৩॥

āji se khaṇḍila tomāra dehādi-bandhana
āji tumi chinna kaile māyāra bandhana

SYNONYMS

āji—today; *se*—that; *khaṇḍila*—dismantled; *tomāra*—your; *deha-ādi-bandhana*—material bondage due to the bodily concept of life; *āji*—today; *tumi*—you; *chinna*—cut to pieces; *kaile*—did; *māyāra*—of illusory energy; *bandhana*—the shackles.

TRANSLATION

"My dear Bhaṭṭācārya, today you have been released from material bondage in the bodily conception of life; you have cut to pieces the shackles of the illusory energy.

TEXT 234

আজি কৃষ্ণপ্রাপ্তি-যোগ্য হৈল তোমার মন।
বেদ-ধর্ম লঙ্ঘি' কৈলে প্রসাদ ভক্ষণ॥" ২৩৪॥

āji kṛṣṇa-prāpti-yogya haila tomāra mana
veda-dharma laṅghi' kaile prasāda bhakṣaṇa"

SYNONYMS

āji—today; *kṛṣṇa-prāpti*—for attainment of the lotus feet of Kṛṣṇa; *yogya*—fit; *haila*—has become; *tomāra*—your; *mana*—mind; *veda*—of the four *Vedas; dharma*—the principles; *laṅghi'*—surpassing; *kaile*—you have done; *prasāda*—the remnants of food offered to Kṛṣṇa; *bhakṣaṇa*—eating.

TRANSLATION

"Today your mind has become fit to take shelter of the lotus feet of Kṛṣṇa because, surpassing the Vedic regulative principles, you have eaten the remnants of food offered to the Lord.

TEXT 235

যেষাং স এষ ভগবান্ দয়য়েদনন্তঃ
সর্বাত্মনাশ্রিতপদো যদি নির্ব্যলীকম্ ।
তে দুস্তরামতিতরন্তি চ দেবমায়াং
নৈষাং মমাহমিতিধীঃ শ্বশৃগালভক্ষ্যে ॥ ২৩৫ ॥

yeṣāṁ sa eṣa bhagavān dayayed anantaḥ
sarvātmanāśrita-pado yadi nirvyalīkam
te dustarām atitaranti ca deva-māyāṁ
naiṣāṁ mamāham iti dhīḥ śva-śṛgāla-bhakṣye

SYNONYMS

yeṣām—unto those who are fully surrendered souls; *saḥ*—He; *eṣaḥ*—this; *bhagavān*—the Supreme Personality of Godhead; *dayayet*—may show mercy; *anantaḥ*—the unlimited; *sarva-ātmanā*—fully, without reservation; *āśrita-padaḥ*—those who have taken shelter of the Lord; *yadi*—if; *nirvyalīkam*—without duplicity; *te*—such persons; *dustarām*—insurmountable; *atitaranti*—surpass; *ca*—also; *deva-māyām*—the illusory material energy; *na*—not; *eṣām*—this; *mama aham*—"my" and "I"; *iti*—such; *dhīḥ*—intelligence; *śva-śṛgāla-bhakṣye*—in the body, which is to be eaten by dogs and jackals.

TRANSLATION

" 'When a person without reservation takes shelter of the lotus feet of the Supreme Personality of Godhead, the unlimited, merciful Lord bestows His causeless mercy upon him. Thus one can pass over the insurmountable ocean

of nescience. Those whose intelligence is fixed in the bodily conception, who think, "I am this body," are fit food for dogs and jackals. The Supreme Lord never bestows His mercy upon such people.' "

PURPORT

The Supreme Lord never bestows His benediction upon those fixed in the bodily conception. As *Bhagavad-gītā* clearly states:

sarva-dharmān parityajya
mām ekaṁ śaraṇaṁ vraja
ahaṁ tvāṁ sarva-pāpebhyo
mokṣayiṣyāmi mā śucaḥ

"Abandon all varieties of religion and just surrender unto Me. I shall deliver you from all sinful reaction. Do not fear." (Bg. 18.66)

In this verse that Caitanya Mahāprabhu has quoted from *Śrīmad-Bhāgavatam* (2.7.42), the meaning of Śrī Kṛṣṇa's statement is explained. Kṛṣṇa bestowed His causeless mercy upon Arjuna just to get him out of the bodily conception. This was done at the very beginning of the Second Chapter of *Bhagavad-gītā* (Bg. 2.13), where Kṛṣṇa says, *dehino 'smin yathā dehe kaumāraṁ yauvanaṁ jarā.* In this body, there is an owner, and one should not consider the body to be the self. This is the first instruction to be assimilated by a devotee. If one is under the bodily conception, he is unable to realize his true identity and engage in the loving devotional service of the Lord. Unless one comes to the transcendental position, he cannot expect the causeless mercy of the Supreme Lord, nor can he cross over the vast ocean of material nescience. This is also confirmed in *Bhagavad-gītā* (7.14): *mām eva ye prapadyante māyām etāṁ taranti te.* Without surrendering unto the lotus feet of Kṛṣṇa, one cannot expect release from the clutches of *māyā,* the illusory energy. According to *Śrīmad-Bhāgavatam,* Māyāvādī *sannyāsīs* who falsely think of themselves as liberated from the clutches of *māyā* are called *vimukta-māninaḥ.* Actually, they are not liberated, but they think that they have become liberated and have become Nārāyaṇa Himself. Although they have apparently realized that they are not the material body but spirit soul, they nonetheless neglect the duty of the spirit soul, which is to render service to the Supreme Soul. Therefore their intelligence remains unsanctified. Unless one's intelligence is sanctified, he cannot apply it to understanding devotional service. Devotional service begins when the mind, intelligence and ego are completely purified. Māyāvādī *sannyāsīs* do not purify their intelligence, mind and ego, and consequently they cannot engage in the service of the Lord nor expect the causeless mercy of the Lord. Although they rise to a very high position by executing severe austerities and penances, they still hover in the material world without the benediction of the lotus feet of the Lord. Sometimes they rise to the Brahman effulgence, but because their minds are not completely purified, they must return to material existence.

The *karmīs* are fully under the bodily conception of life, and the *jñānīs,* although theoretically understanding that they are not the body, also have no information about the lotus feet of the Lord because they overly stress impersonalism. Consequently both *karmīs* and *jñānīs* are unfit for receiving the mercy of the Lord and becoming devotees. Narottama dāsa Ṭhākura therefore says, *jñāna-kāṇḍa karma-kāṇḍa, kevala viṣera bhāṇḍa:* those who have taken to the process of *karma-kāṇḍa* (fruitive activity) and *jñāna-kāṇḍa* (speculation on the science of transcendence) have simply eaten from poisoned pots. They are condemned to remain in material existence life after life until they take shelter of the lotus feet of Kṛṣṇa. This is confirmed in *Śrīmad Bhagavad-gītā:*

bahūnāṁ janmanām ante
jñānavān māṁ prapadyate
vāsudevaḥ sarvam iti
sa mahātmā sudurlabhaḥ

"After many births and deaths, he who is actually in knowledge surrenders unto Me, knowing Me to be the cause of all causes and all that is. Such a great soul is very rare." (Bg. 7.19)

TEXT 236

এত কহি' মহাপ্রভু আইলা নিজ-স্থানে ।
সেই হৈতে ভট্টাচার্যের খণ্ডিল অভিমানে ॥ ২৩৬ ॥

eta kahi' mahāprabhu āilā nija-sthāne
sei haite bhaṭṭācāryera khaṇḍila abhimāne

SYNONYMS

eta kahi'—speaking in this way; *mahāprabhu*—Śrī Caitanya Mahāprabhu; *āilā*—returned; *nija-sthāne*—to His own residence; *sei haite*—from that time; *bhaṭṭācāryera*—of Sārvabhauma Bhaṭṭācārya; *khaṇḍila*—was dismantled; *abhimāne*—false pride.

TRANSLATION

After speaking to Sārvabhauma Bhaṭṭācārya in this way, Śrī Caitanya Mahāprabhu returned to His residence. From that day on, the Bhaṭṭācārya was free because his false pride had been dismantled.

TEXT 237

চৈতন্য-চরণ বিনে নাহি জানে আন।
ভক্তি বিনু শাস্ত্রের আর না করে ব্যাখ্যান ॥ ২৩৭ ॥

caitanya-caraṇa vine nāhi jāne āna
bhakti vinu śāstrera āra nā kare vyākhyāna

SYNONYMS

caitanya-caraṇa—the lotus feet of Lord Caitanya; *vine*—except; *nāhi*—not; *jāne*—knows; *āna*—other; *bhakti*—devotional service; *vinu*—except; *śāstrera*—of the scripture; *āra*—any other; *nā*—not; *kare*—does; *vyākhyāna*—explanation.

TRANSLATION

From that day on, Sārvabhauma Bhaṭṭācārya did not know anything but the lotus feet of Lord Caitanya Mahāprabhu, and from that day he could explain the revealed scriptures only in accordance with the process of devotional service.

TEXT 238

গোপীনাথাচার্য তাঁর বৈষ্ণবতা দেখিয়া।
'হরি' 'হরি' বলি' নাচে হাতে তালি দিয়া ॥ ২৩৮ ॥

gopīnāthācārya tāṅra vaiṣṇavatā dekhiyā
'hari' 'hari' bali' nāce hāte tāli diyā

SYNONYMS

gopīnātha-ācārya—Gopīnātha Ācārya, the brother-in-law of Sārvabhauma Bhaṭṭācārya; *tāṅra*—of Sārvabhauma Bhaṭṭācārya; *vaiṣṇavatā*—firm faith in Vaiṣṇavism; *dekhiyā*—seeing; *hari hari*—the holy name of the Lord; *bali'*—saying; *nāce*—dances; *hāte tāli diyā*—clapping his two hands.

TRANSLATION

Seeing that Sārvabhauma Bhaṭṭācārya was firmly fixed in the cult of Vaiṣṇavism, Gopīnātha Ācārya, his brother-in-law, began to dance, clap his hands and chant, "Hari! Hari!"

TEXT 239

আর দিন ভট্টাচার্য আইলা দর্শনে।
জগন্নাথ না দেখি' আইলা প্রভুস্থানে ॥ ২৩৯॥

āra dina bhaṭṭācārya āilā darśane
jagannātha nā dekhi' āilā prabhu-sthāne

SYNONYMS

āra dina—the next day; *bhaṭṭācārya*—Sārvabhauma Bhaṭṭācārya; *āilā*—came; *darśane*—to see Lord Jagannātha; *jagannātha*—Lord Jagannātha; *nā dekhi'*—without seeing; *āilā*—came; *prabhu-sthāne*—to the place of Lord Śrī Caitanya Mahāprabhu.

TRANSLATION

The next day, the Bhaṭṭācārya went to visit the temple of Lord Jagannātha, but before he reached the temple, he went to see Caitanya Mahāprabhu.

TEXT 240

দণ্ডবৎ করি' কৈল বহুবিধ স্তুতি ।
দৈন্য করি' কহে নিজ পূর্বদুর্মতি ॥ ২৪০ ॥

daṇḍavat kari' kaila bahu-vidha stuti
dainya kari' kahe nija pūrva-durmati

SYNONYMS

daṇḍavat kari'—after offering obeisances by falling flat on the ground; *kaila*—he did; *bahu-vidha*—various types of; *stuti*—prayers; *dainya kari'*—in great humbleness; *kahe*—describes; *nija*—his personal; *pūrva-durmati*—previous bad disposition.

TRANSLATION

When he met Lord Caitanya Mahāprabhu, the Bhaṭṭācārya fell down flat to offer Him respects. After offering various prayers to Him, he spoke of his previous bad disposition with great humility.

TEXT 241

ভক্তিসাধন-শ্রেষ্ঠ শুনিতে হৈল মন ।
প্রভু উপদেশ কৈল নাম-সংকীর্তন ॥ ২৪১ ॥

bhakti-sādhana-śreṣṭha śunite haila mana
prabhu upadeśa kaila nāma-saṅkīrtana

SYNONYMS

bhakti-sādhana—in the execution of devotional service; *śreṣṭha*—the most important item; *śunite*—to hear; *haila*—it was; *mana*—the mind; *prabhu*—Lord Śrī Caitanya Mahāprabhu; *upadeśa*—advice; *kaila*—gave; *nāma-saṅkīrtana*—chanting of the holy name of the Lord.

TRANSLATION

Then the Bhaṭṭācārya asked Caitanya Mahāprabhu: "Which item is most important in the execution of devotional service?" The Lord replied that the most important item was the chanting of the holy name of the Lord.

PURPORT

There are nine items to be executed in devotional service. These are enumerated in the following verse from *Śrīmad-Bhāgavatam* (7.5.32):

śravaṇaṁ kīrtanaṁ viṣṇoḥ
smaraṇaṁ pāda-sevanam
arcanaṁ vandanaṁ dāsyaṁ
sakhyam ātma-nivedanam

Hearing the glories of the Lord, chanting, remembering, serving the lotus feet of the Lord, offering worship in the temple, offering prayers, becoming a servant of the Lord, becoming the Lord's friend, and *sarvātma-nivedana,* offering oneself fully at the lotus feet of the Lord—these are the nine devotional processes. In *The Nectar of Devotion,* these are expanded into sixty-four items. When Sārvabhauma Bhaṭṭācārya asked the Lord which item was most important, Śrī Caitanya Mahāprabhu immediately answered that the most important item is the chanting of the holy names of the Lord—Hare Kṛṣṇa, Hare Kṛṣṇa, Kṛṣṇa Kṛṣṇa, Hare Hare/ Hare Rāma, Hare Rāma, Rāma Rāma, Hare Hare. He then quoted the following verse from the *Bṛhan-nāradīya Purāṇa* (Thirty-eighth Chapter, verse 126) to confirm His statement.

TEXT 242

হরের্নাম হরের্নাম হরের্নামৈব কেবলম্ ।
কলৌ নাস্ত্যেব নাস্ত্যেব নাস্ত্যেব গতিরন্যথা ॥ ২৪২ ॥

harer nāma harer nāma
harer nāmaiva kevalam
kalau nāsty eva nāsty eva
nāsty eva gatir anyathā

SYNONYMS

hareḥ nāma—the holy name of the Lord Hari; *hareḥ nāma*—the holy name of the Lord Hari; *hareḥ nāma*—the holy name of the Lord; *eva*—certainly; *kevalam*—only; *kalau*—in this age of Kali; *na asti*—there is not; *eva*—certainly; *na asti*—there is not; *eva*—certainly; *na asti*—there is not; *eva*—certainly; *gatiḥ*—means; *anyathā*—other.

TRANSLATION

" 'In this age of quarrel and hypocrisy, the only means of deliverance is the chanting of the holy names of the Lord. There is no other way. There is no other way. There is no other way.' "

PURPORT

Because the people of this age are so fallen, they can simply chant the Hare Kṛṣṇa *mahā-mantra.* In this way they can rid themselves of the bodily conception of life and become eligible to engage in the Lord's devotional service. One cannot engage in the devotional service of the Lord without being purified of all contamination. This is confirmed in *Bhagavad-gītā:*

yeṣāṁ tv anta-gataṁ pāpaṁ
janānāṁ puṇya-karmaṇām
te dvandva-moha-nirmuktā
bhajante māṁ dṛḍha-vratāḥ

"Persons who have acted piously in previous lives and in this life, whose sinful actions are completely eradicated and who are freed from the duality of delusion engage themselves in My service with determination." (Bg. 7.28) Sometimes people are surprised to see young men and women take so seriously to the Kṛṣṇa consciousness movement. By giving up sinful activity—illicit sex, meat eating, intoxication and gambling—and strictly following the injunctions given by the spiritual master, they have become purified of all contamination. They can therefore fully engage in the devotional service of the Lord.

In this age of Kali, *hari-kīrtana* is very, very important. The importance of chanting the holy name of the Lord is stated in the following verses from *Śrīmad-Bhāgavatam:*

kaler doṣa-nidhe rājann
asti hy eko mahān guṇaḥ
kīrtanād eva kṛṣṇasya
mukta-saṅgaḥ paraṁ vrajet

kṛte yad dhyāyato viṣṇuṁ
tretāyāṁ yajato makhaiḥ
dvāpare paricaryāyāṁ
kalau tad dhari-kīrtanāt

"The most important factor in this age of Kali, which is an ocean of faults, is that one can be free from all contamination and become eligible to enter the kingdom of God simply by chanting the Hare Kṛṣṇa *mantra.* The self-realization that was achieved in the Satya millennium by meditation, in the Tretā millennium by the performance of different sacrifices, and in the Dvāpara millennium by worship of Lord Kṛṣṇa can be achieved in the age of Kali simply by chanting the holy names, Hare Kṛṣṇa." (*Bhāg.* 12.3.51-52)

TEXT 243

এই শ্লোকের অর্থ শুনাইল করিয়া বিস্তার ।
শুনি' ভট্টাচার্য-মনে হৈল চমৎকার ॥ ২৪৩ ॥

ei ślokera artha śunāila kariyā vistāra
śuni' bhaṭṭācārya-mane haila camatkāra

SYNONYMS

ei ślokera—of this verse; *artha*—the meaning; *śunāila*—made hear; *kariyā*—doing; *vistāra*—extensive description; *śuni'*—hearing; *bhaṭṭācārya*—of Sārvabhauma Bhaṭṭācārya; *mane*—in the mind; *haila*—there was; *camatkāra*—wonder.

TRANSLATION

Śrī Caitanya Mahāprabhu very elaborately explained the harer nāma verse of the Bṛhan-nāradīya Purāṇa, and Sārvabhauma Bhaṭṭācārya was struck with wonder to hear His explanation.

TEXT 244

গোপীনাথাচার্য বলে,—'আমি পূর্বে যে কহিল ।
শুন, ভট্টাচার্য, তোমার সেই ত' হইল ॥' ২৪৪ ॥

gopīnāthācārya bale,—'āmi pūrve ye kahila
śuna, bhaṭṭācārya, tomāra sei ta' ha-ila'

SYNONYMS

gopīnātha-ācārya—of the name Gopīnātha Ācārya; *bale*—says; *āmi*—I; *pūrve*—previously; *ye*—what; *kahila*—said; *śuna*—hear; *bhaṭṭācārya*—my dear Bhaṭṭācārya; *tomāra*—your; *sei*—that; *ta'*—indeed; *ha-ila*—has happened.

TRANSLATION

Gopīnātha Ācārya reminded Sārvabhauma Bhaṭṭācārya: "My dear Bhaṭṭācārya, what I foretold to you has now taken place."

PURPORT

Previously Gopīnātha Ācārya had informed Sārvabhauma Bhaṭṭācārya that when he would be blessed by the Lord, he would thoroughly understand the transcendental process of devotional service. This prediction was now fulfilled. The Bhaṭṭācārya was fully converted to the cult of Vaiṣṇavism, and he was following the principles automatically, without being pressured. In *Bhagavad-gītā* (2.40) it is therefore said, *svalpam apy asya dharmasya trāyate mahato bhayāt:* simply by performing a little devotional service, one can escape the greatest danger. Sārvabhauma Bhaṭṭācārya had been in the greatest danger because he had adhered to Māyāvāda philosophy. Somehow or other he came into contact with Lord Śrī Caitanya Mahāprabhu and became a perfect devotee. In this way he was saved from the great falldown of impersonalism.

TEXT 245

ভট্টাচার্য কহে তাঁরে করি' নমস্কারে ।
তোমার সম্বন্ধে প্রভু কৃপা কৈল মোরে ॥ ২৪৫ ॥

bhaṭṭācārya kahe tāṅre kari' namaskāre
tomāra sambandhe prabhu kṛpā kaila more

SYNONYMS

bhaṭṭācārya kahe—Sārvabhauma Bhaṭṭācārya replied; *tāṅre*—unto Gopīnātha Ācārya; *kari'*—doing; *namaskāre*—obeisances; *tomāra sambandhe*—on account of your relationship; *prabhu*—Śrī Caitanya Mahāprabhu; *kṛpā*—mercy; *kaila*—showed; *more*—unto me.

TRANSLATION

Offering his obeisances to Gopīnātha Ācārya, the Bhaṭṭācārya said: "Because I am related to you and you are a devotee, by your mercy the Lord has shown mercy to me.

TEXT 246

তুমি—মহাভাগবত, আমি —তর্ক-অন্ধে ।
প্রভু কৃপা কৈল মোরে তোমার সম্বন্ধে ॥ ২৪৬ ॥

tumi——mahābhāgavata, āmi——tarka-andhe
prabhu kṛpā kaila more tomāra sambandhe

SYNONYMS

tumi—you; *mahā-bhāgavata*—a first-class devotee; *āmi*—I; *tarka-andhe*—in the darkness of logical arguments; *prabhu*—the Lord; *kṛpā*—mercy; *kaila*—showed; *more*—unto me; *tomāra*—your; *sambandhe*—by the relationship.

TRANSLATION

"You are a first-class devotee, whereas I am in the darkness of logical arguments. Because of your relationship with the Lord, the Lord has bestowed His benediction upon me."

TEXT 247

বিনয় শুনি' তুষ্ট্যে প্রভু কৈল আলিঙ্গন ।
কহিল,—যাঞা করহ ঈশ্বর দরশন ॥ ২৪৭ ॥

vinaya śuni' tuṣṭye prabhu kaila āliṅgana
kahila,——yāñā karaha īśvara daraśana

SYNONYMS

vinaya śuni'—upon hearing this humbleness of Sārvabhauma Bhaṭṭācārya; *tuṣṭye*—in satisfaction; *prabhu*—the Lord; *kaila*—did; *āliṅgana*—embracing; *kahila*—said; *yāñā*—going; *karaha*—do; *īśvara daraśana*—visiting the temple of Lord Jagannātha.

TRANSLATION

Śrī Caitanya Mahāprabhu was very pleased with this humble statement. After embracing the Bhaṭṭācārya, He said: "Now go see Lord Jagannātha in the temple."

TEXT 248

জগদানন্দ দামোদর,—দুই সঙ্গে লঞা ।
ঘরে আইল ভট্টাচার্য জগন্নাথ দেখিয়া ॥ ২৪৮ ॥

jagadānanda dāmodara,——dui saṅge lañā
ghare āila bhaṭṭācārya jagannātha dekhiyā

SYNONYMS

jagadānanda—of the name Jagadānanda; *dāmodara*—of the name Dāmodara; *dui*—two persons; *saṅge*—with him; *lañā*—taking; *ghare*—to his home; *āila*—returned; *bhaṭṭācārya*—Sārvabhauma Bhaṭṭācārya; *jagannātha*—Lord Jagannātha; *dekhiyā*—seeing in the temple.

TRANSLATION

After visiting the temple of Lord Jagannātha, Sārvabhauma Bhaṭṭācārya returned home with Jagadānanda and Dāmodara.

TEXT 249

উত্তম উত্তম প্রসাদ বহুত আনিলা।
নিজবিপ্র-হাতে দুই জনা সঙ্গে দিলা ॥ ২৪৯ ॥

uttama uttama prasāda bahuta ānilā
nija-vipra-hāte dui janā saṅge dilā

SYNONYMS

uttama uttama—very first-class; *prasāda*—remnants of food offered to Jagannātha; *bahuta*—in great quantity; *ānilā*—brought; *nija-vipra*—of his own *brāhmaṇa* servant; *hāte*—in the hand; *dui*—two; *janā*—persons; *saṅge*—with him; *dilā*—gave.

TRANSLATION

The Bhaṭṭācārya brought large quantities of excellent food remnants blessed by Lord Jagannātha. All this prasāda was given to his own brāhmaṇa servant, along with Jagadānanda and Dāmodara.

TEXT 250

নিজ কৃত দুই শ্লোক লিখিয়া তালপাতে।
'প্রভুকে দিহ' বলি' দিল জগদানন্দ-হাতে ॥ ২৫০ ॥

nija kṛta dui śloka likhiyā tāla-pāte
'prabhuke diha' bali' dila jagadānanda-hāte

SYNONYMS

nija—by him; *kṛta*—composed; *dui*—two; *śloka*—verses; *likhiyā*—writing; *tāla-pāte*—on a leaf of a palm tree; *prabhuke diha*—give to Lord Śrī Caitanya Mahāprabhu; *bali'*—saying this; *dila*—gave it; *jagadānanda-hāte*—in the hands of Jagadānanda.

TRANSLATION

Sārvabhauma Bhaṭṭācārya then composed two verses on the leaf of a palm tree. Giving the palm leaf to Jagadānanda Prabhu, he requested him to deliver it to Śrī Caitanya Mahāprabhu.

TEXT 251

প্রভু-স্থানে আইলা দুঁহে প্রসাদ-পত্রী লঞা ।
মুকুন্দ দত্ত পত্রী নিল তার হাতে পাঞা ॥ ২৫১ ॥

prabhu-sthāne āilā duṅhe prasāda-patrī lañā
mukunda datta patrī nila tāra hāte pāñā

SYNONYMS

prabhu-sthāne—to the place where Śrī Caitanya Mahāprabhu was residing; *āilā*—went back; *duṅhe*—both Jagadānanda and Dāmodara; *prasāda*—the remnants of food; *patrī*—the leaf of a palm tree; *lañā*—taking; *mukunda datta*—of the name Mukunda Datta; *patrī*—the leaf of a palm tree; *nila*—took; *tāra*—of Jagadānanda; *hāte*—in the hand; *pāñā*—receiving.

TRANSLATION

Jagadānanda and Dāmodara then returned to Śrī Caitanya Mahāprabhu, bringing Him both the prasāda and the palm leaf on which the verses were composed. But Mukunda Datta took the palm leaf from the hands of Jagadānanda before he could deliver it to Śrī Caitanya Mahāprabhu.

TEXT 252

দুই শ্লোক বাহির-ভিতে লিখিয়া রাখিল ।
তবে জগদানন্দ পত্রী প্রভুকে লঞা দিল ॥ ২৫২ ॥

dui śloka bāhira-bhite likhiyā rākhila
tabe jagadānanda patrī prabhuke lañā dila

SYNONYMS

dui—two; *śloka*—verses; *bāhira*—outside; *bhite*—on the wall; *likhiyā*—writing; *rākhila*—kept; *tabe*—thereafter; *jagadānanda*—Jagadānanda Prabhu; *patrī*—the palm leaf; *prabhuke*—to the Lord; *lañā*—taking; *dila*—delivered.

TRANSLATION

Mukunda Datta then copied the two verses on the wall outside the room. After this, Jagadānanda took the palm leaf from Mukunda Datta and delivered it to Lord Caitanya Mahāprabhu.

TEXT 253

প্রভু শ্লোক পড়ি' পত্র ছিণ্ডিয়া ফেলিল ।
ভিত্ত্যে দেখি' ভক্ত সব শ্লোক কণ্ঠে কৈল ॥ ২৫৩ ॥

prabhu śloka paḍi' patra chiṇḍiyā phelila
bhittye dekhi' bhakta saba śloka kaṇṭhe kaila

SYNONYMS

prabhu—the Lord; *śloka*—verses; *paḍi'*—reading; *patra*—the palm leaf; *chiṇḍiyā*—tearing to pieces; *phelila*—threw; *bhittye*—on the outside wall; *dekhi'*—seeing; *bhakta*—the devotees; *saba*—all; *śloka*—verses; *kaṇṭhe*—within the neck; *kaila*—kept.

TRANSLATION

As soon as Lord Caitanya Mahāprabhu read the two verses, He immediately tore up the palm leaf. However, all the devotees read these verses on the outside wall, and they all kept them within their hearts. The verses read as follows.

TEXT 254

বৈরাগ্য-বিদ্যা-নিজ-ভক্তিযোগ-শিক্ষার্থমেকঃ পুরুষঃ পুরাণঃ ।
শ্রীকৃষ্ণচৈতন্যশরীরধারী কৃপাম্বুধির্যস্তমহং প্রপদ্যে ॥ ২৫৪ ॥

vairāgya-vidyā-nija-bhakti-yoga-
śikṣārtham ekaḥ puruṣaḥ purāṇaḥ
śrī-kṛṣṇa-caitanya-śarīra-dhārī
kṛpāmbudhir yas tam ahaṁ prapadye

SYNONYMS

vairāgya—detachment from everything that does not help develop Kṛṣṇa consciousness; *vidyā*—knowledge; *nija*—own; *bhakti-yoga*—devotional service; *śikṣā-artham*—just to instruct; *ekaḥ*—the single person; *puruṣaḥ*—the Supreme Person; *purāṇaḥ*—very old, or eternal; *śrī-kṛṣṇa-caitanya*—of Lord Śrī Kṛṣṇa Caitanya Mahāprabhu; *śarīra-dhārī*—accepting the body; *kṛpā-ambudhiḥ*—the ocean of transcendental mercy; *yaḥ*—who; *tam*—unto Him; *aham*—I; *prapadye*—surrender.

TRANSLATION

"Let me take shelter of the Supreme Personality of Godhead, Śrī Kṛṣṇa, who has descended in the form of Lord Caitanya Mahāprabhu to teach us real

knowledge, His devotional service and detachment from whatever does not foster Kṛṣṇa consciousness. He has descended because He is an ocean of transcendental mercy. Let me surrender unto His lotus feet.

PURPORT

This verse and the following verse are included in the *Caitanya-candrodaya-nāṭaka* (6.74), by Śrī Kavi-karṇapura.

TEXT 255

কালান্নষ্টং ভক্তিযোগং নিজং যঃ
প্রাদুষ্কর্তুং কৃষ্ণচৈতন্যনামা ।
আবির্ভূতস্তস্য পাদারবিন্দে
গাঢ়ং গাঢ়ং লীয়তাং চিত্তভৃঙ্গঃ ॥ ২৫৫ ॥

kālān naṣṭaṁ bhakti-yogaṁ nijaṁ yaḥ
prāduṣkartuṁ kṛṣṇa-caitanya-nāmā
āvirbhūtas tasya pādāravinde
gāḍhaṁ gāḍhaṁ līyatāṁ citta-bhṛṅgaḥ

SYNONYMS

kālāt—from misuse of material propensities and attachment to fruitive activities and speculative knowledge over the course of time; *naṣṭam*—destroyed; *bhakti-yogam*—the science of devotional service; *nijam*—which is applicable to Him only; *yaḥ*—one who; *prāduṣkartum*—to revive; *kṛṣṇa-caitanya-nāmā*—named Lord Śrī Kṛṣṇa Caitanya Mahāprabhu; *āvirbhūtaḥ*—who has appeared; *tasya*—His; *pāda-aravinde*—in the lotus feet; *gāḍham gāḍham*—very deeply; *līyatām*—let it be merged; *citta-bhṛṅgaḥ*—my consciousness, like a honeybee.

TRANSLATION

"Let my consciousness, which is like a honeybee, take shelter of the lotus feet of the Supreme Personality of Godhead, who has just now appeared as Śrī Kṛṣṇa Caitanya Mahāprabhu to teach the ancient system of devotional service to Himself. This system had almost been lost due to the influence of time."

PURPORT

As stated in *Bhagavad-gītā:*

yadā yadā hi dharmasya
glānir bhavati bhārata

abhyutthānam adharmasya
tadātmānaṁ sṛjāmy aham

"Whenever and wherever there is a decline in religious practice, O descendant of Bharata, and a predominant rise of irreligion—at that time I descend Myself." (Bg. 4.7)

This is also the case with Caitanya Mahāprabhu's appearance. Śrī Caitanya Mahāprabhu appeared in this world as a disguised incarnation of Kṛṣṇa, but His appearance is confirmed in *Śrīmad-Bhāgavatam, Mahābhārata* and other Vedic scriptures. He appeared to teach the fallen souls in this material world, for in this age of Kali almost everyone has become attached to fruitive and ritualistic activities and mental speculation. Consequently there was a great need to revive the system of devotional service. The Lord Himself personally came down disguised as a devotee so that the fallen populace might take advantage of the Lord's example.

At the conclusion of *Bhagavad-gītā,* Lord Kṛṣṇa advised complete surrender unto Him, promising all protection to His devotee. Unfortunately, people are so fallen that they cannot accept the instructions of Lord Kṛṣṇa; therefore Kṛṣṇa returned with the same mission, but He executed it in a different way. As Lord Śrī Kṛṣṇa, the Supreme Personality of Godhead, He ordered us to surrender unto Himself, but as Lord Śrī Caitanya Mahāprabhu, He taught us *how* to surrender to Kṛṣṇa. Therefore He is praised by the Gosvāmīs: *namo mahā-vadānyāya kṛṣṇa-prema-pradāye te.* Lord Śrī Kṛṣṇa is certainly the Personality of Godhead, but He is not as magnanimous as Śrī Caitanya Mahāprabhu. Lord Kṛṣṇa simply gave orders for one to become His devotee (*man-manā bhava mad-bhaktaḥ*), but Śrī Caitanya Mahāprabhu actually taught the process of Kṛṣṇa consciousness. If one wants to become a devotee of Kṛṣṇa, he must first take shelter of the lotus feet of Śrī Caitanya Mahāprabhu, following in the footsteps of Sārvabhauma Bhaṭṭācārya and other exalted devotees.

TEXT 256

এই দুই শ্লোক—ভক্তকণ্ঠে রত্নহার ।
সার্বভৌমের কীর্তি ঘোষে ঢক্কাবাদ্যাকার ॥ ২৫৬ ॥

ei dui śloka——bhakta-kaṇṭhe ratna-hāra
sārvabhaumera kīrti ghoṣe ḍhakkā-vādyākāra

SYNONYMS

ei dui śloka—these two verses; *bhakta-kaṇṭhe*—on the necks of the devotees; *ratna-hāra*—pearl necklaces; *sārvabhaumera*—of Sārvabhauma Bhaṭṭācārya; *kīrti*—reputation; *ghoṣe*—declare; *ḍhakkā*—of a drum; *vādya*—of the sound; *ākāra*—in the form.

TRANSLATION

These two verses composed by Sārvabhauma Bhaṭṭācārya will always declare his name and fame as loudly as a pounding drum because they have become pearl necklaces around the necks of all devotees.

TEXT 257

সার্বভৌম হৈলা প্রভুর ভক্ত একতান ।
মহাপ্রভুর সেবা-বিনা নাহি জানে আন ॥ ২৫৭ ॥

sārvabhauma hailā prabhura bhakta ekatāna
mahāprabhura sevā-vinā nāhi jāne āna

SYNONYMS

sārvabhauma—Sārvabhauma Bhaṭṭācārya; *hailā*—became; *prabhura*—of the Lord; *bhakta*—a devotee; *ekatāna*—without deviation; *mahā-prabhura*—of Lord Śrī Caitanya Mahāprabhu; *sevā*—service; *vinā*—except; *nāhi*—not; *jāne*—knows; *āna*—anything else.

TRANSLATION

Indeed, Sārvabhauma Bhaṭṭācārya became an unalloyed devotee of Caitanya Mahāprabhu; he did not know anything but the service of the Lord.

TEXT 258

'শ্রীকৃষ্ণচৈতন্য শচীসুত গুণধাম' ।
এই ধ্যান, এই জপ, লয় এই নাম ॥ ২৫৮ ॥

'śrī-kṛṣṇa-caitanya śacī-sūta guṇa-dhāma'
ei dhyāna, ei japa, laya ei nāma

SYNONYMS

śrī-kṛṣṇa-caitanya—Lord Śrī Kṛṣṇa Caitanya Mahāprabhu; *śacī-sūta*—the son of mother Śacī; *guṇa-dhāma*—the reservoir of all good qualities; *ei*—this; *dhyāna*—meditation; *ei*—this; *japa*—chanting; *laya*—he takes; *ei*—this; *nāma*—holy name.

TRANSLATION

The Bhaṭṭācārya always chanted the holy name of Śrī Kṛṣṇa Caitanya, son of mother Śacī and reservoir of all good qualities. Indeed, chanting the holy names became his meditation.

TEXT 259

একদিন সার্বভৌম প্রভু-আগে আইলা ।
নমস্কার করি' শ্লোক পড়িতে লাগিলা ॥ ২৫৯ ॥

eka-dina sārvabhauma prabhu-āge āilā
namaskāra kari' śloka paḍite lāgilā

SYNONYMS

eka-dina—one day; *sārvabhauma*—Sārvabhauma Bhaṭṭācārya; *prabhu-āge*—in front of Lord Śrī Caitanya Mahāprabhu; *āilā*—came; *namaskāra kari'*—after offering obeisances; *śloka*—a verse; *paḍite lāgilā*—began to recite.

TRANSLATION

One day Sārvabhauma Bhaṭṭācārya came before Caitanya Mahāprabhu, and, offering obeisances, began to recite a verse.

TEXT 260

ভাগবতের 'ব্রহ্মস্তবে'র শ্লোক পড়িলা ।
শ্লোক-শেষে দুই অক্ষর-পাঠ ফিরাইলা ॥ ২৬০ ॥

bhāgavatera 'brahma-stave'ra śloka paḍilā
śloka-śeṣe dui akṣara-pāṭha phirāilā

SYNONYMS

bhāgavatera—from *Śrīmad-Bhāgavatam; brahma-stavera*—of the prayers of Lord Brahmā; *śloka*—a verse; *paḍilā*—recited; *śloka-śeṣe*—at the end of the verse; *dui akṣara*—of two syllables; *pāṭha*—the reading; *phirāilā*—changed.

TRANSLATION

He began to quote one of Lord Brahmā's prayers from Śrīmad-Bhāgavatam, but he changed two syllables at the end of the verse.

TEXT 261

তত্তেঽনুকম্পাং সুসমীক্ষমাণো ভুঞ্জান এবাত্মকৃতং বিপাকম্ ।
হৃদ্বাগ্বপুর্ভির্বিদধন্নমস্তে জীবেত যো ভক্তিপদে স দায়ভাক্ ॥

tat te 'nukampāṁ susamīkṣamāṇo
bhuñjāna evātma-kṛtaṁ vipākam
hṛd-vāg-vapurbhir vidadhan namas te
jīveta yo bhakti-pade sa dāya-bhāk

SYNONYMS

tat—therefore; *te*—Your; *anukampām*—compassion; *su-samīkṣamāṇaḥ*—hoping for; *bhuñjānaḥ*—enduring; *eva*—certainly; *ātma-kṛtam*—done by himself; *vipākam*—fruitive results; *hṛt*—with the heart; *vāk*—words; *vapurbhiḥ*—and body; *vidadhan*—offering; *namaḥ*—obeisances; *te*—unto You; *jīveta*—may live; *yaḥ*—anyone who; *bhakti-pade*—in devotional service; *saḥ*—he; *dāya-bhāk*—a bona fide candidate.

TRANSLATION

[The verse read:] "One who seeks Your compassion and thus tolerates all kinds of adverse conditions due to the karma of his past deeds, who engages always in Your devotional service with his mind, words and body, and who always offers obeisances unto You is certainly a bona fide candidate for becoming Your unalloyed devotee."

PURPORT

When reading this verse from *Śrīmad-Bhāgavatam* (10.14.8), Sārvabhauma Bhaṭṭācārya changed the original reading from *mukti-pade* to *bhakti-pade. Mukti* means liberation and merging into the impersonal Brahman effulgence. *Bhakti* means rendering transcendental service unto the Supreme Personality of Godhead. Because of having developed pure devotional service, the Bhaṭṭācārya did not like the word *mukti-pade,* which refers to the impersonal Brahman feature of the Lord. However, he was not authorized to change a word in the *Śrīmad-Bhāgavatam,* as Śrī Caitanya Mahāprabhu will explain. Although the Bhaṭṭācārya changed the word in his devotional ecstasy, Śrī Caitanya Mahāprabhu did not approve of it.

TEXT 262

প্রভু কহে, 'মুক্তিপদে'—ইহা পাঠ হয়।
'ভক্তিপদে' কেনে পড়, কি তোমার আশয় ॥ ২৬২ ॥

prabhu kahe, 'mukti-pade'——ihā pāṭha haya
'bhakti-pade' kene paḍa, ki tomāra āśaya

SYNONYMS

prabhu kahe—the Lord said; *mukti-pade*—the word *"mukti-pade"; ihā*—this; *pāṭha*—the reading; *haya*—is; *bhakti-pade*—*"bhakti-pade"*; *kene*—why; *paḍa*—you read; *ki*—what; *tomāra*—your; *āśaya*—intention.

TRANSLATION

Śrī Caitanya Mahāprabhu immediately pointed out: "In that verse the word is 'mukti-pade,' but you have changed it to 'bhakti-pade.' What is your intention?"

TEXT 263

ভট্টাচার্য কহে,—'ভক্তি'-সম নহে মুক্তি-ফল ।
ভগবদ্ভক্তিবিমুখের হয় দণ্ড কেবল ॥ ২৬৩ ॥

bhaṭṭācārya kahe,——'bhakti'-sama nahe mukti-phala
bhagavad-bhakti-vimukhera haya daṇḍa kevala

SYNONYMS

bhaṭṭācārya—Sārvabhauma Bhaṭṭācārya; *kahe*—said; *bhakti*—devotional service; *sama*—equal to; *nahe*—not; *mukti*—of liberation; *phala*—the result; *bhagavat-bhakti*—to the devotional service of the Supreme Personality of Godhead; *vimukhera*—of one who is averse to; *haya*—it is; *daṇḍa*—the punishment; *kevala*—only.

TRANSLATION

Sārvabhauma Bhaṭṭācārya replied: "The awakening of pure love of Godhead, which is the result of devotional service, far surpasses liberation from material bondage. For those averse to devotional service, merging into the Brahman effulgence is a kind of punishment."

PURPORT

In the *Brahmāṇḍa Purāṇa* it is said:

siddha-lokas tu tamasaḥ
pāre yatra vasanti hi
siddhā brahma-sukhe magnā
daityāś ca hariṇā hatāḥ

"In Siddhaloka [Brahmaloka] there live two kinds of living entities—those who are killed by the Supreme Personality of Godhead due to their having been demons in their previous lives and those who are very fond of enjoying the impersonal effulgence of the Lord." The word *tamasaḥ* means "the coverings of the universe." Layers of material elements cover the universe, and outside these coverings is the impersonal Brahman effulgence. If one is destined to remain in the Lord's impersonal effulgence, he misses the opportunity to render service to the Personality of

Godhead. Therefore devotees consider remaining in the impersonal Brahman effulgence a kind of punishment. Sometimes devotees think of merging into the Brahman effulgence, and consequently they are promoted to Siddhaloka. Because of their impersonal understanding, they are actually punished. Sārvabhauma Bhaṭṭācārya continues to explain the distinction between *mukti-pada* and *bhakti-pada* in the following verses.

TEXTS 264-265

কৃষ্ণের বিগ্রহ যেই সত্য নাহি মানে।
যেই নিন্দা-যুদ্ধাদিক করে তাঁর সনে ॥ ২৬৪ ॥
সেই দুইর দণ্ড হয়—'ব্রহ্মসাযুজ্য-মুক্তি'।
তার মুক্তি ফল নহে, যেই করে ভক্তি ॥ ২৬৫ ॥

kṛṣṇera vigraha yei satya nāhi māne
yei nindā-yuddhādika kare tāṅra sane

sei duira daṇḍa haya—'brahma-sāyujya-mukti'
tāra mukti phala nahe, yei kare bhakti

SYNONYMS

kṛṣṇera—of Lord Śrī Kṛṣṇa; *vigraha*—the transcendental form; *yei*—anyone who; *satya*—as truth; *nāhi*—not; *māne*—accepts; *yei*—anyone who; *nindā*—blaspheming; *yuddha-ādika*—fighting and so forth; *kare*—does; *tāṅra sane*—with Him, Śrī Kṛṣṇa; *sei*—these; *duira*—of the two; *daṇḍa haya*—there is punishment; *brahma-sāyujya-mukti*—merging into the Brahman effulgence; *tāra*—of him; *mukti*—such liberation; *phala*—the result; *nahe*—not; *yei*—who; *kare*—executes; *bhakti*—devotional service.

TRANSLATION

The Bhaṭṭācārya continued: "The impersonalists, who do not accept the transcendental form of Lord Śrī Kṛṣṇa, and the demons, who are always engaged in blaspheming and fighting with Him, are punished by being merged into the Brahman effulgence. But that does not happen to the person engaged in the devotional service of the Lord.

TEXT 266

যদ্যপি সে মুক্তি হয় পঞ্চ-পরকার।
সালোক্য-সামীপ্য-সারূপ্য-সার্ষ্টি-সাযুজ্য আর॥২৬৬॥

yadyapi se mukti haya pañca-parakāra
sālokya-sāmīpya-sārūpya-sārṣṭi-sāyujya āra

SYNONYMS

yadyapi—although; *se*—that; *mukti*—liberation; *haya*—is; *pañca-parakāra*—of five different varieties; *sālokya*—of the name *sālokya; sāmīpya*—of the name *sāmīpya; sārūpya*—of the name *sārūpya; sārṣṭi*—of the name *sārṣṭi; sāyujya*—of the name *sāyujya; āra*—and.

TRANSLATION

"There are five kinds of liberation: sālokya, sāmīpya, sārūpya, sārṣṭi and sāyujya.

PURPORT

Sālokya means that after material liberation one is promoted to the planet where the Supreme Personality of Godhead resides. *Sāmīpya* means remaining an associate of the Supreme Personality of Godhead. *Sārūpya* means attaining a four-handed form exactly like that of the Lord. *Sārṣṭi* means attaining opulences like those of the Supreme Lord, and *sāyujya* means merging into the Brahman effulgence of the Lord. These are the five types of liberation.

TEXT 267

'সালোক্যাদি' চারি যদি হয় সেবা-দ্বার ।
তবু কদাচিৎ ভক্ত করে অঙ্গীকার ॥ ২৬৭ ॥

'sālokyādi' cāri yadi haya sevā-dvāra
tabu kadācit bhakta kare aṅgīkāra

SYNONYMS

sālokya-ādi—beginning with *sālokya; cāri*—four kinds of liberation; *yadi*—if; *haya*—are; *sevā-dvāra*—a means of rendering service to the Lord; *tabu*—still; *kadācit*—occasionally; *bhakta*—a pure devotee; *kare*—makes; *aṅgīkāra*—acceptance.

TRANSLATION

"If there is a chance to serve the Supreme Personality of Godhead, a pure devotee sometimes accepts the sālokya, sārūpya, sāmīpya or sārṣṭi forms of liberation, but never sāyujya.

TEXT 268

'সাযুজ্য' শুনিতে ভক্তের হয় ঘৃণা-ভয়।
নরক বাঞ্ছয়ে, তবু সাযুজ্য না লয় ॥ ২৬৮ ॥

'sāyujya' śunite bhaktera haya ghṛṇā-bhaya
naraka vāñchaye, tabu sāyujya nā laya

SYNONYMS

sāyujya—liberation by merging into the effulgence; *śunite*—even to hear; *bhaktera*—of the devotee; *haya*—there is; *ghṛṇā*—hatred; *bhaya*—fear; *naraka*—a hellish condition of life; *vāñchaye*—he desires; *tabu*—still; *sāyujya*—merging into the effulgence of the Lord; *nā laya*—never accepts.

TRANSLATION

"A pure devotee does not like even to hear about sāyujya-mukti, which inspires him with fear and hatred. Indeed, the pure devotee would rather go to hell than merge into the effulgence of the Lord."

PURPORT

Śrīla Prabodhānanda Sarasvatī has sung: *kaivalyaṁ narakāyate.* The impersonalist's conception of becoming one with the effulgence of the Lord is exactly like hell. Therefore, of the five types of liberation, the first four (*sālokya, sāmīpya, sārūpya* and *sārṣṭi*) are not so undesirable because they can be avenues of service to the Lord. Nonetheless, a pure devotee of Lord Kṛṣṇa rejects even these types of liberation; he only aspires to serve Kṛṣṇa birth after birth. He is not very interested in stopping the repetition of birth, for he simply desires to serve the Lord, even in hellish circumstances. Consequently the pure devotee hates and fears *sāyujya-mukti,* merging into the effulgence of the Lord. This merging is due to an offense committed against the transcendental loving service of the Lord, and therefore it is not at all desirable for a pure devotee.

TEXT 269

ব্রহ্মে, ঈশ্বরে সাযুজ্য দুই ত' প্রকার।
ব্রহ্ম-সাযুজ্য হৈতে ঈশ্বর-সাযুজ্য ধিক্কার ॥ ২৬৯ ॥

brahme, īśvare sāyujya dui ta' prakāra
brahma-sāyujya haite īśvara-sāyujya dhikkāra

SYNONYMS

brahme—in the Brahman effulgence; *īśvare*—in the body of the Lord; *sāyujya*—merging; *dui*—two; *ta'*—indeed; *prakāra*—varieties; *brahma-sāyujya*—merging into the Brahman effulgence; *haite*—than; *īśvara-sāyujya*—merging into the body of the Lord; *dhikkāra*—more abominable.

TRANSLATION

Sārvabhauma Bhaṭṭācārya continued: "There are two kinds of sāyujya-mukti: merging into the Brahman effulgence and merging into the personal body of the Lord. Merging into the Lord's body is even more abominable than merging into His effulgence."

PURPORT

According to the opinion of the Māyāvādī Vedāntists, the living entity's ultimate success is to merge into the impersonal Brahman. The impersonal Brahman, or bodily effulgence of the Supreme Lord, is known as Brahmaloka or Siddhaloka. According to *Brahma-saṁhitā* (5.40), *yasya prabhā prabhavato jagad-aṇḍa-koṭi:* the material universes are generated from the bodily rays of the Supreme Personality of Godhead. *Yogīs* who follow the principles of Patañjali accept the personality of the Absolute Truth, but they want to merge into the transcendental body of the Supreme Lord. That is their desire. Being the greatest authority, the Supreme Lord can easily allow many millions of living entities to merge into His body. The origin of everything is the Supreme Personality of Godhead, Bhagavān, and His bodily effulgence is known as the *brahmajyoti,* Brahmaloka or Siddhaloka. Thus Brahmaloka or Siddhaloka is a place where many sparklike living entities, parts and parcels of the Supreme Lord, are assembled. Because these living entities do not wish to keep their individual existences, they are combined and allowed to remain in Brahmaloka like so many atomic particles of sunshine emanating from the sun.

The word *siddha* is very significant. *Siddha* refers to one who has realized the Brahman effulgence and who has complete knowledge that the living entity is not a material atom but a spiritual spark. This understanding is described in *Bhagavad-gītā* as *brahma-bhūta.* In the conditioned state, the living entity is known as *jīva-bhūta,* or "the living force within matter." *Brahma-bhūta* living entities are allowed to stay in Brahmaloka or Siddhaloka, but unfortunately they sometimes again fall into the material world because they are not engaged in devotional service. This is supported by *Śrīmad-Bhāgavatam* (10.2.32): *ye 'nye 'ravindākṣa.* These semi-liberated souls falsely claim to be liberated, but unless one engages in devotional service to the Lord, he is still materially contaminated. Therefore these living entities have been described as *vimukta-māninaḥ,* meaning that they falsely consider themselves liberated although their intelligence is not yet purified. Although these living entities undergo severe austerities to rise to the platform of Siddhaloka, they cannot remain there perpetually, for they are bereft of *ānanda* (bliss). Even though these living entities attain the *brahma-bhūta* stage and realize the Supreme Personality of Godhead through His bodily effulgence, they nonetheless fall down due to neglecting the Lord's service. They do not properly utilize whatever little knowledge they have of the Supreme Personality of Godhead. Not attaining *ānanda,* or bliss, they come down to the material world to enjoy. This is certainly a falldown for one who is actually liberated. The *bhaktas* consider such a falldown equal to achieving a place in hell.

The followers of the Patañjali *yoga* system actually want to merge into the body of the Supreme Personality of Godhead. This indicates that they do not want to engage in His service despite their knowledge of Him, and thus their position is even more abominable than that of those who want to merge into the Lord's effulgence. These *yogīs* meditate on the four-handed Viṣṇu form of the Lord in order to merge into His body. The Patañjali system describes the form of the Lord as *kleśa-karma-vipākāśayair aparāmṛṣṭaḥ puruṣa-viśeṣa īśvaraḥ:* "The Supreme Personality of Godhead is a person who does not partake of a miserable material life." The *yogīs* accept the eternity of the Supreme Person in their *mantra, sa pūrveṣām api guruḥ kālānavac chedāt:* "Such a person is always supreme and is not influenced by the element of time." The followers of the Patañjali system therefore accept the eternity of the Supreme Personality of Godhead, yet, according to them: *puruṣārtha-śūnyānāṁ pratiprasavaḥ kaivalyaṁ svarūpa-pratiṣṭhā vā citi-śaktir iti.* They believe that in the perfectional stage, the conception of *puruṣa* is vanquished. According to their description: *citi-śaktir iti.* They believe that when one becomes perfect, he cannot remain a person. This *yoga* system is therefore abominable because its final conception is impersonal. In the beginning, these *yogīs* accept the Supreme Personality of Godhead, but they ultimately give up this idea in order to become impersonal. They are most unfortunate because although they have a personal conception of the Absolute Truth, they neglect to render devotional service to the Lord and thus they fall down again into the material world. This is supported by the *Śrīmad-Bhāgavatam* (10.2.32). *Āruhya-kṛcchreṇa paraṁ padaṁ tataḥ patanty adho 'nādṛta-yuṣmad-aṅghrayaḥ:* due to neglecting the lotus feet of the Lord, these *yogīs* again fall down into the material existence (*patanty adhaḥ*). Consequently this path of *yoga* is more abominable than the impersonalists' path. This conclusion is also supported by Lord Kapiladeva in the following verse from *Śrīmad-Bhāgavatam* (3.29.13).

TEXT 270

সালোক্য-সার্ষ্টি-সামীপ্য-সারূপ্যৈকত্বমপ্যুত ।
দীয়মানং ন গৃহ্ণন্তি বিনা মৎ-সেবনং জনাঃ ॥ ২৭০ ॥

sālokya-sārṣṭi-sāmīpya-
sārūpyaikatvam apy uta
dīyamānaṁ na gṛhṇanti
vinā mat-sevanaṁ janāḥ

SYNONYMS

sālokya—the liberation of living in the same planet as the Lord; *sārṣṭi*—to have opulence exactly like that of the Lord; *sāmīpya*—to associate always with the Lord; *sārūpya*—to achieve a body like that of the Lord; *ekatvam*—to merge into the body of the Lord; *api*—although; *uta*—it is said; *dīyamānam*—being offered; *na*—not; *gṛhṇanti*—do accept; *vinā*—without; *mat*—My; *sevanam*—service; *janāḥ*—the pure devotees.

TRANSLATION

Sārvabhauma Bhaṭṭācārya concluded: " 'Even though he is offered all kinds of liberation, the pure devotee does not accept them. He is fully satisfied engaging in the service of the Lord.' "

TEXT 271

প্রভু কহে,—'মুক্তিপদে'র আর অর্থ হয়।
মুক্তিপদ-শব্দে 'সাক্ষাৎ ঈশ্বর' কহয় ॥ ২৭১ ॥

prabhu kahe,——'mukti-pade'ra āra artha haya
mukti-pada-śabde 'sākṣāt īśvara' kahaya

SYNONYMS

prabhu kahe—the Lord said; *mukti-padera*—of the term *"mukti-pade"*; *āra*—another; *artha*—meaning; *haya*—there is; *mukti-pada-śabde*—by the word *"mukti-pada"*; *sākṣāt*—directly; *īśvara*—the Supreme Personality of Godhead; *kahaya*—is said.

TRANSLATION

Lord Śrī Caitanya Mahāprabhu replied: "The word 'mukti-pade' has another meaning. Mukti-pada directly refers to the Supreme Personality of Godhead.

TEXT 272

মুক্তি পদে যাঁর, সেই 'মুক্তিপদ' হয়।
কিম্বা নবম পদার্থ 'মুক্তির' সমাশ্রয় ॥ ২৭২ ॥

mukti pade yāṅra, sei 'mukti-pada' haya
kimvā navama padārtha 'muktira' samāśraya

SYNONYMS

mukti—liberation; *pade*—at the lotus feet; *yāṅra*—of whom; *sei*—such a person; *mukti-pada haya*—is known as *mukti-pada; kimvā*—or; *navama*—ninth; *pada-artha*—subject matter; *muktira*—of liberation; *samāśraya*—shelter.

TRANSLATION

"All kinds of liberation exist under the feet of the Supreme Personality of Godhead; therefore He is known as mukti-pada. According to another meaning, mukti is the ninth subject, and the Supreme Personality of Godhead is the shelter of liberation.

PURPORT

Lord Śrī Kṛṣṇa is also known as Mukunda, or He who gives transcendental bliss by offering all kinds of *mukti. Śrīmad-Bhāgavatam* is divided into twelve cantos, and in the Ninth Canto different kinds of *mukti* are described. But the Tenth Canto is the actual center of all discussions of *mukti* because the Personality of Godhead Śrī Kṛṣṇa, who is the tenth subject discussed in *Śrīmad-Bhāgavatam,* is the exclusive subject of the Tenth Canto. Since all types of *muktis* reside at the lotus feet of Śrī Kṛṣṇa, He may be called *mukti-pada.*

TEXT 273

দুই-অর্থে 'কৃষ্ণ' কহি, কেনে পাঠ ফিরি ।
সার্বভৌম কহে,—ও-পাঠ কহিতে না পারি ॥ ২৭৩ ॥

dui-arthe 'kṛṣṇa' kahi, kene pāṭha phiri
sārvabhauma kahe,——o-pāṭha kahite nā pāri

SYNONYMS

dui-arthe—by two interpretations; *kṛṣṇa*—Lord Śrī Kṛṣṇa; *kahi*—I accept; *kene*—why; *pāṭha*—reading; *phiri*—changing; *sārvabhauma kahe*—Sārvabhauma replied; *o-pāṭha*—such a reading; *kahite*—to say; *nā*—not; *pāri*—am able.

TRANSLATION

"Since I can understand Kṛṣṇa according to these two meanings," Caitanya Mahāprabhu said, "what point is there in changing the verse?" Sārvabhauma Bhaṭṭācārya replied: "I was not able to give that reading to the verse.

TEXT 274

যদ্যপি তোমার অর্থ এই শব্দে কয়।
তথাপি 'আশ্লিষ্য-দোষে' কহন না যায়॥ ২৭৪॥

yadyapi tomāra artha ei śabde kaya
tathāpi 'āśliṣya-doṣe' kahana nā yāya

SYNONYMS

yadyapi—although; *tomāra*—Your; *artha*—meaning; *ei*—this; *śabde*—by the word; *kaya*—is said; *tathāpi*—still; *āśliṣya-doṣe*—by the fault of ambiguity; *kahana*—to say; *nā*—not; *yāya*—possible.

TRANSLATION

"Although Your explanation is correct, it should not be used because there is ambiguity in the word 'mukti-pada.'

TEXT 275

যদ্যপি 'মুক্তি'-শব্দের হয় পঞ্চ বৃত্তি।
রূঢ়িবৃত্ত্যে কহে তবু 'সাযুজ্যে' প্রতীতি॥ ২৭৫॥

yadyapi 'mukti'-śabdera haya pañca vṛtti
rūḍhi-vṛttye kahe tabu 'sāyujye' pratīti

SYNONYMS

yadyapi—although; *mukti*—liberation; *śabdera*—of the word; *haya*—there is; *pañca vṛtti*—five meanings; *rūḍhi-vṛttye*—by the chief or direct meaning; *kahe*—it says; *tabu*—still; *sāyujye*—to become one with the Supreme; *pratīti*—the conception.

TRANSLATION

"The word 'mukti' refers to five kinds of liberation. Usually its direct meaning conveys the idea of becoming one with the Lord.

TEXT 276

মুক্তি-শব্দ কহিতে মনে হয় ঘৃণা-ত্রাস।
ভক্তি-শব্দ কহিতে মনে হয় ত' উল্লাস॥ ২৭৬॥

mukti-śabda kahite mane haya ghṛṇā-trāsa
bhakti-śabda kahite mane haya ta' ullāsa

SYNONYMS

mukti-śabda—the word *mukti; kahite*—by pronouncing; *mane*—in the mind; *haya*—there is; *ghṛṇā*—hatred; *trāsa*—and fear; *bhakti-śabda*—the word *bhakti; kahite*—to speak; *mane*—in the mind; *haya*—there is; *ta'*—indeed; *ullāsa*—transcendental joy.

TRANSLATION

"The very sound of the word 'mukti' immediately induces hate and fear, but when we say the word 'bhakti,' we naturally feel transcendental bliss within the mind."

TEXT 277

শুনিয়া হাসেন প্রভু আনন্দিত-মনে।
ভট্টাচার্যে কৈল প্রভু দৃঢ় আলিঙ্গনে ॥ ২৭৭ ॥

śuniyā hāsena prabhu ānandita-mane
bhaṭṭācārye kaila prabhu dṛḍha āliṅgane

SYNONYMS

śuniyā—hearing this explanation; *hāsena*—laughs; *prabhu*—Śrī Caitanya Mahāprabhu; *ānandita-mane*—with great pleasure in His mind; *bhaṭṭācārye*—unto Sārvabhauma Bhaṭṭācārya; *kaila*—did; *prabhu*—the Lord; *dṛḍha*—firm; *āliṅgane*—embracing.

TRANSLATION

Upon hearing this explanation, the Lord began to laugh and, with great pleasure, immediately embraced Sārvabhauma Bhaṭṭācārya very firmly.

TEXT 278

যেই ভট্টাচার্য পড়ে পড়ায় মায়াবাদে।
তাঁর ঐছে বাক্য স্ফুরে চৈতন্য-প্রসাদে ॥ ২৭৮ ॥

yei bhaṭṭācārya paḍe paḍāya māyāvāde
tāṅra aiche vākya sphure caitanya-prasāde

SYNONYMS

yei—that; *bhaṭṭācārya*—Sārvabhauma Bhaṭṭācārya; *paḍe*—reads; *paḍāya*—teaches; *māyāvāde*—the philosophy of Māyāvāda impersonalism; *tāṅra*—his;

aiche—such; *vākya*—explanation; *sphure*—manifested; *caitanya-prasāde*—by the mercy of Lord Śrī Caitanya Mahāprabhu.

TRANSLATION

Indeed, that very person who was accustomed to reading and teaching Māyāvāda philosophy was now even hating the word "mukti." This was possible only by the mercy of Śrī Caitanya Mahāprabhu.

TEXT 279

লোহাকে যাবৎ স্পর্শি' হেম নাহি করে।
তাবৎ স্পর্শমণি কেহ চিনিতে না পারে ॥ ২৭৯ ॥

lohāke yāvat sparśi' hema nāhi kare
tāvat sparśa-maṇi keha cinite nā pāre

SYNONYMS

lohāke—iron; *yāvat*—as long as; *sparśi'*—touching; *hema*—gold; *nāhi*—not; *kare*—transforms; *tāvat*—until then; *sparśa-maṇi*—the touchstone; *keha*—someone; *cinite*—to recognize; *nā*—not; *pāre*—is able.

TRANSLATION

As long as it does not turn iron into gold by its touch, no one can recognize an unknown stone to be a touchstone.

TEXT 280

ভট্টাচার্যের বৈষ্ণবতা দেখি' সর্বজন।
প্রভুকে জানিল—'সাক্ষাৎ ব্রজেন্দ্রনন্দন' ॥ ২৮০ ॥

bhaṭṭācāryera vaiṣṇavatā dekhi' sarva-jana
prabhuke jānila——'sākṣāt vrajendra-nandana'

SYNONYMS

bhaṭṭācāryera—of Sārvabhauma Bhaṭṭācārya; *vaiṣṇavatā*—clear understanding of Vaiṣṇava philosophy; *dekhi'*—seeing; *sarva-jana*—all persons; *prabhuke*—Lord Śrī Caitanya Mahāprabhu; *jānila*—knew; *sākṣāt*—directly; *vrajendra-nandana*—Kṛṣṇa, the son of Mahārāja Nanda.

TRANSLATION

Upon seeing transcendental Vaiṣṇavism in Sārvabhauma Bhaṭṭācārya, everyone could understand that Lord Caitanya was none other than the son of Nanda Mahārāja, Kṛṣṇa.

TEXT 281

কাশীমিশ্র-আদি যত নীলাচলবাসী ।
শরণ লইল সবে প্রভু-পদে আসি' ॥ ২৮১ ॥

kāśī-miśra-ādi yata nīlācala-vāsī
śaraṇa la-ila sabe prabhu-pade āsi'

SYNONYMS

kāśī-miśra—of the name Kāśī Miśra; *ādi*—heading the list; *yata*—all; *nīlācala-vāsī*—the residents of Jagannātha Purī; *śaraṇa*—shelter; *la-ila*—took; *sabe*—all; *prabhu-pade*—to the lotus feet of the Lord; *āsi'*—coming.

TRANSLATION

After this incident, all the inhabitants of Jagannātha Purī, headed by Kāśī Miśra, came to take shelter of the lotus feet of the Lord.

TEXT 282

সেই সব কথা আগে করিব বর্ণন ।
সার্বভৌম করে যৈছে প্রভুর সেবন ॥ ২৮২ ॥

sei saba kathā āge kariba varṇana
sārvabhauma kare yaiche prabhura sevana

SYNONYMS

sei saba—all these; *kathā*—narrations; *āge*—later; *kariba*—I shall make; *varṇana*—description; *sārvabhauma*—Sārvabhauma Bhaṭṭācārya; *kare*—does; *yaiche*—as; *prabhura*—of the Lord; *sevana*—service.

TRANSLATION

Later I shall describe how Sārvabhauma Bhaṭṭācārya always engaged in the service of the Lord.

TEXT 283

যৈছে পরিপাটী করে ভিক্ষা-নির্বাহন ।
বিস্তারিয়া আগে তাহা করিব বর্ণন ॥ ২৮৩ ॥

yaiche paripāṭī kare bhikṣā-nirvāhana
vistāriyā āge tāhā kariba varṇana

SYNONYMS

yaiche—how; *paripāṭī*—perfectly; *kare*—does; *bhikṣā*—of offering alms; *nirvāhana*—the execution; *vistāriyā*—in full detail; *āge*—later; *tāhā*—that; *kariba varṇana*—I shall describe.

TRANSLATION

I shall also describe in full detail how Sārvabhauma Bhaṭṭācārya perfectly rendered service to Śrī Caitanya Mahāprabhu by offering Him alms.

TEXTS 284-285

এই মহাপ্রভুর লীলা—সার্বভৌম-মিলন ।
ইহা যেই শ্রদ্ধা করি' করয়ে শ্রবণ ॥ ২৮৪ ॥
জ্ঞান-কর্মপাশ হৈতে হয় বিমোচন ।
অচিরে মিলয়ে তাঁরে চৈতন্যচরণ ॥ ২৮৫ ॥

ei mahāprabhura līlā——sārvabhauma-milana
ihā yei śraddhā kari' karaye śravaṇa

jñāna-karma-pāśa haite haya vimocana
acire milaye tāṅre caitanya-caraṇa

SYNONYMS

ei—this; *mahāprabhura*—of Lord Śrī Caitanya Mahāprabhu; *līlā*—pastime; *sārvabhauma-milana*—meeting with Sārvabhauma Bhaṭṭācārya; *ihā*—this; *yei*—anyone who; *śraddhā*—faith; *kari'*—having; *karaye*—does; *śravaṇa*—hearing; *jñāna-karma*—of speculation and fruitive activities; *pāśa*—the net; *haite*—from; *haya*—there is; *vimocana*—liberation; *acire*—very soon; *milaye*—meets; *tāṅre*—such a devotee; *caitanya-caraṇa*—the lotus feet of Lord Caitanya.

TRANSLATION

If one hears with faith and love these pastimes concerning Lord Caitanya Mahāprabhu's meeting with Sārvabhauma Bhaṭṭācārya, he very soon is freed from the net of speculation and fruitive activity and attains the shelter of Śrī Caitanya Mahāprabhu's lotus feet.

TEXT 286

শ্রীরূপ-রঘুনাথ-পদে যার আশ ।
চৈতন্যচরিতামৃত কহে কৃষ্ণদাস ॥ ২৮৬ ॥

śrī-rūpa-raghunātha-pade yāra āśa
caitanya-caritāmṛta kahe kṛṣṇadāsa

SYNONYMS

śrī-rūpa—Śrīla Rūpa Gosvāmī; *raghunātha*—Śrīla Raghunātha dāsa Gosvāmī; *pade*—at the lotus feet; *yāra*—whose; *āśa*—expectation; *caitanya-caritāmṛta*—the book named *Caitanya-caritāmṛta;* *kahe*—describes; *kṛṣṇadāsa*—Śrīla Kṛṣṇadāsa Kavirāja Gosvāmī.

TRANSLATION

Praying at the lotus feet of Śrī Rūpa and Śrī Raghunātha, always desiring their mercy, I, Kṛṣṇadāsa, narrate Śrī Caitanya-caritāmṛta, following in their footsteps.

Thus end the Bhaktivedanta purports to the Śrī Caitanya-caritāmṛta, Madhya-līlā, *Sixth Chapter, describing the liberation of Sārvabhauma Bhaṭṭācārya.*

References

The statements of *Śrī Caitanya-caritāmṛta* are all confirmed by standard Vedic authorities. The following authentic scriptures are quoted in this book on the pages listed. Numerals in bold type refer the reader to *Śrī Caitanya-caritāmṛta's* translations. Numerals in regular type are references to its purports.

Aitareya Upaniṣad, 273

Amṛta-pravāha-bhāṣya (Bhaktivinoda Ṭhākura), 1,191,273

Anubhāṣya (Bhaktisiddhānta Sarasvatī), 264

Bhagavad-gīta, 30, 35, 37, 46, 48, 52, 68, 70, 128, 148, 158, 185, 233, 239, 240, 241, 263-264, 266, 268, 272, 275, 279, 281, 287, 288, 289, 290, 295, 296, 297, 301, 330, 331, 335, 337, 342-343, 351

Bhakti-rasāmṛta-sindhu (Rūpa Gosvāmī), 36, 104, 198

Bhaviṣya Purāṇa, 267

Brahmāṇḍa Purāṇa, 347

Brahma-saṁhitā, 72, 233, 236, 272, 295, 351

Brahma-vaivarta Purāṇa, 268

Bṛhan-nāradīya Purāṇa, 268, **351**

Caitanya-candrodaya-nāṭaka (Kavi-karṇapura), **271, 341-342**

Caitanya-bhāgavata, (Vṛndāvana dāsa Ṭhākura), **3, 5, 178,** 179

Caitanya-caritāmṛta (Kṛṣṇadāsa Kavirāja), 71, 245-246

Chāndogya Upaniṣad, 275

Hari-bhakti-vilāsa (Sanātana Gosvāmī), 26-27

Kaṭha Upaniṣad, 238

Glossary

A

Abhiṣeka—the bathing ceremony of the Deity.
Ācārya—a spiritual master who teaches by his own example.
Acintya-bhedābheda-tattva—Lord Caitanya's "simultaneously one and different" doctrine.
Ajita—the Supreme Lord who is unconquerable.
Amṛta—nectar.
Anna—food grains.
Arcā-mūrti—the form of the Lord made of material elements.
Arcana—Deity worship.
Arcā-vigraha—*See: Arcā-mūrti.*
Āśutoṣa—Lord Śiva who is very easily satisfied when one worships him.
Ātma-nivedana—the devotional process of sacrificing everything for the Lord.
Ātmārāmas—those who are self-satisfied.
Avatāra—an incarnation of the Lord who descends from the spiritual sky.
Avidyā-śakti—material energy, or nescience.

B

Bahirmukha jana—a person influenced by the external energy.
Bhagavān—Kṛṣṇa, who is full in six opulences.
Bhakti-yoga—devotional service to the Lord.
Bhāva—manifestation of ecstatic symptoms in the body of a devotee.
Brahma-bhūta—the state of being freed from material contamination.
Brahmajyoti—the impersonal effulgence emanating from the body of Kṛṣṇa.
Brahman—the all-pervading impersonal aspect of Kṛṣṇa.
Brahmānanda—the bliss derived from realizing the impersonal Brahman.
Brāhmaṇas—the intelligent class of men.
Brahmaṇya-deva—the Supreme Lord of brahminical culture.

C

Channa-avatāra—an incarnation in disguise.

D

Dadhi—yogurt.
Dāna—charity.
Daṇḍa-bhaṅga-līlā—the pastime of Lord Nityānanda breaking the staff of Lord Caitanya.

Daṇḍavats—offering obeisances by falling flat like a stick.
Dāsya—the devotional process of serving the Lord as a friend.
Dhūmāyitā—the stage exhibited by a devotee when only one or two transformations are slightly present and it is possible to conceal them.
Dīkṣā—initiating a disciple with transcendental knowledge.
Dīpta—the stage exhibited by a devotee when four of five ecstatic symptoms are manifest.
Dugdha—milk.
Durgā-śakti—the material energy.
Duṣkṛti—a miscreant.
Dvija-bandhus—unworthy sons of the twice-born.

G

Gauḍa-maṇḍala-bhūmi—the places in Bengal where Lord Caitanya stayed.
Ghṛta—ghee.
Govardhana-dhārī—Kṛṣṇa, the lifter of Govardhana Hill.
Gṛhasthas—householders.

H

Hari-kīrtana—*See: Saṅkīrtana.*
Hlādinī śakti—the bliss portion of the Lord's spiritual potency.
Hṛṣīkeśa—a name of Kṛṣṇa, the master of all senses.

I

Indra—the king of the heavenly planets.

J

Jāḍya—the ecstatic symptom of loss of memory.
Jīva-bhūta—the living force within matter.
Jñāna—knowledge.
Jñāna-kāṇḍa—the division of the *Vedas* dealing with empirical speculation in pursuit of truth.
Jñānī—one who is engaged in the cultivation of knowledge.
Jvalitā—the stage exhibited by a devotee when more than two or three transcendental transformations are manifest and it is possible to conceal them with difficulty.

K

Kali-yuga—the age of quarrel in which we are now living.

Kāma—lust.
Karma—action performed according to scriptural regulations.
Karma-kāṇḍa—the division of the *Vedas* dealing with fruitive activities and their reactions.
Kīrtana—the devotional process of chanting.
Krodha—anger.
Kṛṣṇa-viraha—the feeling of spiritual separation from Kṛṣṇa.
Kṛṣṇe matir astu—greeting of Vaiṣṇava *sannyāsīs* meaning "Let your attention be on Kṛṣṇa."
Kṣīra-corā—Lord Gopīnātha the thief who stole the sweet rice.
Kṣudhā-tṛṣṇa—hunger and thirst.
Kūrma—the tortoise incarnation of the Lord.

L

Līlā-avatāra—an incarnation of the Lord who performs a variety of activities without making any special endeavor.
Lobha—greed.

M

Mahā-mantra—the great chanting for deliverance: Hare Kṛṣṇa, Hare Kṛṣṇa, Kṛṣṇa Kṛṣṇa, Hare Hare/ Hare Rāma, Hare Rāma, Rāma Rāma, Hare Hare.
Mahā-snāna—a vast bath with ghee and water used to bathe the Deity.
Mahā-vākya—transcendental sound vibration.
Mātsarya—enviousness.
Matsya—the fish incarnation of the Lord.
Māyā—illusion; an energy of Kṛṣṇa's which causes the living being to forget Him.
Māyādhīśa—the Lord of all energy.
Māyāvādīs—impersonalists or voidists who believe that ultimately God is formless and without personality.
Māyā-vaśa—subjected to the influence of the illusory energy.
Moha—illusion.
Mūḍha—a fool or rascal.
Mukti—liberation.
Mukti-pada—the Supreme Lord under whose feet exist all kinds of liberation.
Mukunda—the Lord who gives transcendental bliss by offering all kinds of *mukti.*

N

Namo nārāyaṇāya—greeting of Māyāvādī *sannyāsīs* meaning "I offer my obeisances to Nārāyaṇa."
Nirvāṇa—the cessation of all material activities.

Nitya-baddhas—eternally conditioned living beings.
Nitya-siddha-bhaktas—the eternally liberated associates of the Lord.
Nṛsiṁhadeva—the half-man, half-lion incarnation of the Lord.

O

Oṁkāra—the transcendental syllable which represents Kṛṣṇa.

P

Pāda-sevana—the devotional process of serving.
Pañca-gavya—five kinds of products of the cow used to bathe the Deity.
Pañcāmṛta—five kinds of nectar used to bathe the Deity.
Paramahaṁsa—the highest stage of the renounced order of life.
Paramātmā—the Supersoul, the localized aspect of the Supreme Lord within the heart of all living beings.
Paramparā—the disciplic succession through which spiritual knowledge is transmitted.
Pariṇāma-vāda—the theory of transformation in the creation of the universe.
Paṭhana—a *brāhmaṇa's* duty to be conversant with the Vedic scriptures.
Prakṛti—energy or nature.
Praṇava—*See: Oṁkāra.*
Prasāda—spiritualized foods offered to Kṛṣṇa.
Pratibimba-vāda—the worship of a form that is the reflection of a false material form.
Pratigraha—the duty of a *brāhmaṇa* to accept contributions from his followers.
Pūrṇa—complete.
Puruṣa—person or enjoyer.

R

Rāsa-līlā—the group dancing of Kṛṣṇa and His cowherd girlfriends in His Vṛndāvana pastimes.

S

Sac-cid-ānanda-vigraha—the transcendental form of the Lord which is eternal, full of knowledge and blissful.
Ṣaḍ-aiśvarya-pūrṇa—the Supreme Lord who is complete with six opulences.
Sahajiyās—pseudo-devotees with a mundane conception of Kṛṣṇa's pastimes.
Sālokya—the liberation of being promoted to the planet where the Lord resides.
Sāmīpya—the liberation of becoming an associate of the Lord.
Sampradāya—disciplic succession through which spiritual knowledge is transmitted.
Samvit-śakti—the knowledge portion of the Lord's spiritual potency.

Sandhinī śakti—the eternity portion of the Lord's spiritual potency.
Saṅkīrtana—congregational chanting of the glories of the Lord.
Sannyāsa—the fourth order of spiritual life.
Sannyāsa-daṇḍa—the staff carried by a *sannyāsī.*
Sannyāsīs—those in the renounced order of life.
Sārṣṭi—the liberation of attaining opulences like those of the Lord.
Sārūpya—the liberation of attaining a four-handed form exactly like that of the Lord.
Sarvātma-nivedana—*See: Ātma-nivedana.*
Śāstra—revealed scripture.
Sāyujya-mukti—merging into the Brahman effulgence of the Lord.
Sevā-pūjā—Deity worship.
Siddha—one who has realized the Brahman effulgence.
Śiva—the personality in charge of the mode of ignorance.
Śravaṇa—the devotional process of hearing.
Strī—women.
Sūddīpta—the manifestation in a devotee of all eight ecstatic symptoms multiplied a thousand times and all visible at once.
Śūdras—the laborer class of men.
Svādhyāya—the reading of Vedic literature.

T

Tamasaḥ—the coverings of the universe.
Tattva—truth.
Triyuga—a name of Viṣṇu meaning one who appears in only three *yugas.*

U

Uddīpta—the manifestation in a devotee of five, six or all eight ecstatic symptoms simultaneously.

V

Vaikāli-bhoga—food offered to the Deity at the end of the day.
Vaikuṇṭhalokas—variegated spiritual planets situated in the *brahmajyoti.*
Vairāgya—renunciation.
Vaiṣṇava—a devotee of the Supreme Lord Viṣṇu, or Kṛṣṇa.
Vaiśyas—people engaged in agriculture and commerce.
Vanas—forests.
Vandana—the devotional process of praying.
Varāha—the boar incarnation of the Lord.
Vedāśraya nāstikya-vāda—agnosticism under the shelter of Vedic culture.

Vijita-ṣaḍ-guṇa—one who has conquered the six material qualities.
Viṣṇoḥ smaraṇa—the devotional process of remembering.
Vrajendra-nandana—Kṛṣṇa, the son of Nanda Mahārāja.
Vṛndāvana—the site of Kṛṣṇa's pastimes exhibited when He was present on earth 5,000 years ago.

Y

Yājana—the duty of a *brāhmaṇa* to assist others in performing ceremonies.
Yajana—the duty of a *brāhmaṇa* to perform Vedic rituals.
Yamarāja—the demigod who punishes sinful living beings after their deaths.
Yoga—linking the consciousness of the living being with the Supreme Lord.
Yoga-māyā—the eternal creative potency of the Lord.
Yuga-avatāras—the incarnations of the Lord in each millennium who prescribe the process of self-realization for that age.

Bengali Pronunciation Guide

BENGALI DIACRITICAL EQUIVALENTS AND PRONUNCIATION

Vowels

অ a আ ā ই i ঈ ī উ u ঊ ū ঋ ṛ

ৠ ṝ এ e ঐ ai ও o ঔ au

ং ṁ *(anusvāra)* ঁ ṅ *(candra-bindu)* ঃ ḥ *(visarga)*

Consonants

Gutterals:	ক ka	খ kha	গ ga	ঘ gha	ঙ ṅa
Palatals:	চ ca	ছ cha	জ ja	ঝ jha	ঞ ña
Cerebrals:	ট ṭa	ঠ ṭha	ড ḍa	ঢ ḍha	ণ ṇa
Dentals:	ত ta	থ tha	দ da	ধ dha	ন na
Labials:	প pa	ফ pha	ব ba	ভ bha	ম ma
Semivowels:	য ya	র ra	ল la	ব va	
Sibilants:	শ śa	ষ ṣa	স sa	হ ha	

Vowel Symbols

The vowels are written as follows after a consonant:

া ā ি i ী ī ু u ূ ū ৃ ṛ ৄ ṝ ে e ৈ ai ো o ৌ au

For example: কা kā কি ki কী kī কু ku কূ kū কৃ kṛ

কৄ kṝ কে ke কৈ kai কো ko কৌ kau

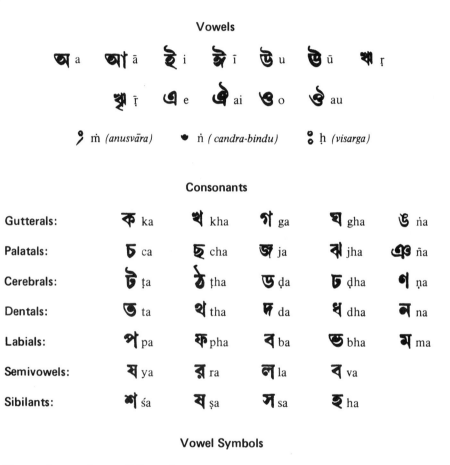

The letter *a* is implied after a consonant with no vowel symbol.

The symbol *virāma* (্) indicates that there is no final vowel. ক্ k

The letters above should be pronounced as follows:

a –like the *o* in h*o*t; sometimes like the *o* in go; final *a* is usually silent.
ā –like the *a* in f*a*r.
i, ī –like the *ee* in m*ee*t.
u, ū –like the *u* in r*u*le.
ṛ –like the *ri* in *ri*m.
ṝ –like the *ree* in *ree*d.
e –like the *ai* in p*ai*n; rarely like *e* in b*e*t.
ai –like the *oi* in b*oi*l.
o –like the *o* in g*o*.
au –like the *ow* in *ow*l.
ṁ –*(anusvāra)* like the *ng* in so*ng*.
ḥ –*(visarga)* a final *h* sound like in Ah.
ṅ –*(candra-bindu)* a nasal *n* sound like in the French word *bon*.
k –like the *k* in *k*ite.
kh –like the *kh* in Ec*kh*art.
g –like the *g* in *g*ot.
gh –like the *gh* in bi*g-h*ouse.
ṅ –like the *n* in ba*n*k.
c –like the *ch* in *ch*alk.
ch –like the *chh* in mu*ch-h*aste.
j –like the *j* in *j*oy.
jh –like the *geh* in colle*ge-h*all.
ñ –like the *n* in bu*n*ch.
ṭ –like the *t* in *t*alk.
ṭh –like the *th* in ho*t-h*ouse.
ḍ –like the *d* in *d*awn.
ḍh –like the *dh* in goo*d-h*ouse.
ṇ –like the *n* in *gn*aw.
t–as in *t*alk but with the tongue against the the teeth.
th–as in ho*t-h*ouse but with the tongue against the teeth.
d–as in *d*awn but with the tongue against the teeth.
dh–as in goo*d-h*ouse but with the tongue against the teeth.
n–as in *n*or but with the tongue against the teeth.
p –like the *p* in *p*ine.
ph –like the *ph* in *ph*ilosopher.
b –like the *b* in *b*ird.
bh –like the *bh* in ru*b-h*ard.
m –like the *m* in *m*other.
y –like the *j* in *j*aw. য
y –like the *y* in *y*ear. য়
r –like the *r* in *r*un.
l –like the *l* in *l*aw.
v –like the *b* in *b*ird or like the *w* in d*w*arf.
ś, ṣ –like the *sh* in *sh*op.
s –like the *s* in *s*un.
h–like the *h* in *h*ome.

This is a general guide to Bengali pronunciation. The Bengali transliterations in this book accurately show the original Bengali spelling of the text. One should note, however, that in Bengali, as in English, spelling is not always a true indication of how a word is pronounced. Tape recordings of His Divine Grace A.C. Bhaktivedanta Swami Prabhupāda chanting the original Bengali verses are available from the International Society for Krishna Consciousness, 3959 Landmark St., Culver City, California 90230.

Index of Bengali and Sanskrit Verses

This index constitutes a complete alphabetical listing of the first and third line of each four-line
rse and both lines of each two-line verse in *Śrī Caitanya-caritāmṛta*. In the first column the trans-
ration is given, and in the second and third columns respectively the chapter-verse references
d page number for each verse are to be found.

C

H

I

L

M

R

S

U

V

Y

General Index

Numerals in bold type indicate references to *Śrī Caitanya-caritāmṛta's* verses. Numerals in regular type are references to its purports.

A

D

H

N

R

W

Y